Lecture Notes in Computer Science   14687

The series Lecture Notes in Computer Science (LNCS), including its subseries Lecture Notes in Artificial Intelligence (LNAI) and Lecture Notes in Bioinformatics (LNBI), has established itself as a medium for the publication of new developments in computer science and information technology research, teaching, and education.

LNCS enjoys close cooperation with the computer science R & D community, the series counts many renowned academics among its volume editors and paper authors, and collaborates with prestigious societies. Its mission is to serve this international community by providing an invaluable service, mainly focused on the publication of conference and workshop proceedings and postproceedings. LNCS commenced publication in 1973.

Masaaki Kurosu · Ayako Hashizume
Editors

Human-Computer Interaction

Thematic Area, HCI 2024
Held as Part of the 26th HCI International Conference, HCII 2024
Washington, DC, USA, June 29 – July 4, 2024
Proceedings, Part IV

Springer

Editors
Masaaki Kurosu
The Open University of Japan
Chiba, Japan

Ayako Hashizume
Hosei University
Tokyo, Japan

ISSN 0302-9743   ISSN 1611-3349 (electronic)
Lecture Notes in Computer Science
ISBN 978-3-031-60440-9   ISBN 978-3-031-60441-6 (eBook)
https://doi.org/10.1007/978-3-031-60441-6

This Springer imprint is published by the registered company Springer Nature Switzerland AG
The registered company address is: Gewerbestrasse 11, 6330 Cham, Switzerland

If disposing of this product, please recycle the paper.

Foreword

This year we celebrate 40 years since the establishment of the HCI International (HCII) Conference, which has been a hub for presenting groundbreaking research and novel ideas and collaboration for people from all over the world.

The HCII conference was founded in 1984 by Prof. Gavriel Salvendy (Purdue University, USA, Tsinghua University, P.R. China, and University of Central Florida, USA) and the first event of the series, "1st USA-Japan Conference on Human-Computer Interaction", was held in Honolulu, Hawaii, USA, 18–20 August. Since then, HCI International is held jointly with several Thematic Areas and Affiliated Conferences, with each one under the auspices of a distinguished international Program Board and under one management and one registration. Twenty-six HCI International Conferences have been organized so far (every two years until 2013, and annually thereafter).

Over the years, this conference has served as a platform for scholars, researchers, industry experts and students to exchange ideas, connect, and address challenges in the ever-evolving HCI field. Throughout these 40 years, the conference has evolved itself, adapting to new technologies and emerging trends, while staying committed to its core mission of advancing knowledge and driving change.

As we celebrate this milestone anniversary, we reflect on the contributions of its founding members and appreciate the commitment of its current and past Affiliated Conference Program Board Chairs and members. We are also thankful to all past conference attendees who have shaped this community into what it is today.

The 26th International Conference on Human-Computer Interaction, HCI International 2024 (HCII 2024), was held as a 'hybrid' event at the Washington Hilton Hotel, Washington, DC, USA, during 29 June – 4 July 2024. It incorporated the 21 thematic areas and affiliated conferences listed below.

A total of 5108 individuals from academia, research institutes, industry, and government agencies from 85 countries submitted contributions, and 1271 papers and 309 posters were included in the volumes of the proceedings that were published just before the start of the conference, these are listed below. The contributions thoroughly cover the entire field of human-computer interaction, addressing major advances in knowledge and effective use of computers in a variety of application areas. These papers provide academics, researchers, engineers, scientists, practitioners and students with state-of-the-art information on the most recent advances in HCI.

The HCI International (HCII) conference also offers the option of presenting 'Late Breaking Work', and this applies both for papers and posters, with corresponding volumes of proceedings that will be published after the conference. Full papers will be included in the 'HCII 2024 - Late Breaking Papers' volumes of the proceedings to be published in the Springer LNCS series, while 'Poster Extended Abstracts' will be included as short research papers in the 'HCII 2024 - Late Breaking Posters' volumes to be published in the Springer CCIS series.

I would like to thank the Program Board Chairs and the members of the Program Boards of all thematic areas and affiliated conferences for their contribution towards the high scientific quality and overall success of the HCI International 2024 conference. Their manifold support in terms of paper reviewing (single-blind review process, with a minimum of two reviews per submission), session organization and their willingness to act as goodwill ambassadors for the conference is most highly appreciated.

This conference would not have been possible without the continuous and unwavering support and advice of Gavriel Salvendy, founder, General Chair Emeritus, and Scientific Advisor. For his outstanding efforts, I would like to express my sincere appreciation to Abbas Moallem, Communications Chair and Editor of HCI International News.

July 2024   Constantine Stephanidis

HCI International 2024 Thematic Areas and Affiliated Conferences

- HCI: Human-Computer Interaction Thematic Area
- HIMI: Human Interface and the Management of Information Thematic Area
- EPCE: 21st International Conference on Engineering Psychology and Cognitive Ergonomics
- AC: 18th International Conference on Augmented Cognition
- UAHCI: 18th International Conference on Universal Access in Human-Computer Interaction
- CCD: 16th International Conference on Cross-Cultural Design
- SCSM: 16th International Conference on Social Computing and Social Media
- VAMR: 16th International Conference on Virtual, Augmented and Mixed Reality
- DHM: 15th International Conference on Digital Human Modeling & Applications in Health, Safety, Ergonomics & Risk Management
- DUXU: 13th International Conference on Design, User Experience and Usability
- C&C: 12th International Conference on Culture and Computing
- DAPI: 12th International Conference on Distributed, Ambient and Pervasive Interactions
- HCIBGO: 11th International Conference on HCI in Business, Government and Organizations
- LCT: 11th International Conference on Learning and Collaboration Technologies
- ITAP: 10th International Conference on Human Aspects of IT for the Aged Population
- AIS: 6th International Conference on Adaptive Instructional Systems
- HCI-CPT: 6th International Conference on HCI for Cybersecurity, Privacy and Trust
- HCI-Games: 6th International Conference on HCI in Games
- MobiTAS: 6th International Conference on HCI in Mobility, Transport and Automotive Systems
- AI-HCI: 5th International Conference on Artificial Intelligence in HCI
- MOBILE: 5th International Conference on Human-Centered Design, Operation and Evaluation of Mobile Communications

List of Conference Proceedings Volumes Appearing Before the Conference

1. LNCS 14684, Human-Computer Interaction: Part I, edited by Masaaki Kurosu and Ayako Hashizume
2. LNCS 14685, Human-Computer Interaction: Part II, edited by Masaaki Kurosu and Ayako Hashizume
3. LNCS 14686, Human-Computer Interaction: Part III, edited by Masaaki Kurosu and Ayako Hashizume
4. LNCS 14687, Human-Computer Interaction: Part IV, edited by Masaaki Kurosu and Ayako Hashizume
5. LNCS 14688, Human-Computer Interaction: Part V, edited by Masaaki Kurosu and Ayako Hashizume
6. LNCS 14689, Human Interface and the Management of Information: Part I, edited by Hirohiko Mori and Yumi Asahi
7. LNCS 14690, Human Interface and the Management of Information: Part II, edited by Hirohiko Mori and Yumi Asahi
8. LNCS 14691, Human Interface and the Management of Information: Part III, edited by Hirohiko Mori and Yumi Asahi
9. LNAI 14692, Engineering Psychology and Cognitive Ergonomics: Part I, edited by Don Harris and Wen-Chin Li
10. LNAI 14693, Engineering Psychology and Cognitive Ergonomics: Part II, edited by Don Harris and Wen-Chin Li
11. LNAI 14694, Augmented Cognition, Part I, edited by Dylan D. Schmorrow and Cali M. Fidopiastis
12. LNAI 14695, Augmented Cognition, Part II, edited by Dylan D. Schmorrow and Cali M. Fidopiastis
13. LNCS 14696, Universal Access in Human-Computer Interaction: Part I, edited by Margherita Antona and Constantine Stephanidis
14. LNCS 14697, Universal Access in Human-Computer Interaction: Part II, edited by Margherita Antona and Constantine Stephanidis
15. LNCS 14698, Universal Access in Human-Computer Interaction: Part III, edited by Margherita Antona and Constantine Stephanidis
16. LNCS 14699, Cross-Cultural Design: Part I, edited by Pei-Luen Patrick Rau
17. LNCS 14700, Cross-Cultural Design: Part II, edited by Pei-Luen Patrick Rau
18. LNCS 14701, Cross-Cultural Design: Part III, edited by Pei-Luen Patrick Rau
19. LNCS 14702, Cross-Cultural Design: Part IV, edited by Pei-Luen Patrick Rau
20. LNCS 14703, Social Computing and Social Media: Part I, edited by Adela Coman and Simona Vasilache
21. LNCS 14704, Social Computing and Social Media: Part II, edited by Adela Coman and Simona Vasilache
22. LNCS 14705, Social Computing and Social Media: Part III, edited by Adela Coman and Simona Vasilache

47. LNCS 14730, HCI in Games: Part I, edited by Xiaowen Fang
48. LNCS 14731, HCI in Games: Part II, edited by Xiaowen Fang
49. LNCS 14732, HCI in Mobility, Transport and Automotive Systems: Part I, edited by Heidi Krömker
50. LNCS 14733, HCI in Mobility, Transport and Automotive Systems: Part II, edited by Heidi Krömker
51. LNAI 14734, Artificial Intelligence in HCI: Part I, edited by Helmut Degen and Stavroula Ntoa
52. LNAI 14735, Artificial Intelligence in HCI: Part II, edited by Helmut Degen and Stavroula Ntoa
53. LNAI 14736, Artificial Intelligence in HCI: Part III, edited by Helmut Degen and Stavroula Ntoa
54. LNCS 14737, Design, Operation and Evaluation of Mobile Communications: Part I, edited by June Wei and George Margetis
55. LNCS 14738, Design, Operation and Evaluation of Mobile Communications: Part II, edited by June Wei and George Margetis
56. CCIS 2114, HCI International 2024 Posters - Part I, edited by Constantine Stephanidis, Margherita Antona, Stavroula Ntoa and Gavriel Salvendy
57. CCIS 2115, HCI International 2024 Posters - Part II, edited by Constantine Stephanidis, Margherita Antona, Stavroula Ntoa and Gavriel Salvendy
58. CCIS 2116, HCI International 2024 Posters - Part III, edited by Constantine Stephanidis, Margherita Antona, Stavroula Ntoa and Gavriel Salvendy
59. CCIS 2117, HCI International 2024 Posters - Part IV, edited by Constantine Stephanidis, Margherita Antona, Stavroula Ntoa and Gavriel Salvendy
60. CCIS 2118, HCI International 2024 Posters - Part V, edited by Constantine Stephanidis, Margherita Antona, Stavroula Ntoa and Gavriel Salvendy
61. CCIS 2119, HCI International 2024 Posters - Part VI, edited by Constantine Stephanidis, Margherita Antona, Stavroula Ntoa and Gavriel Salvendy
62. CCIS 2120, HCI International 2024 Posters - Part VII, edited by Constantine Stephanidis, Margherita Antona, Stavroula Ntoa and Gavriel Salvendy

https://2024.hci.international/proceedings

Preface

Human-Computer Interaction is a Thematic Area of the International Conference on Human-Computer Interaction (HCII). The HCI field is today undergoing a wave of significant innovation and breakthroughs towards radically new future forms of interaction. The HCI Thematic Area constitutes a forum for scientific research and innovation in human-computer interaction, addressing challenging and innovative topics in human-computer interaction theory, methodology, and practice, including, for example, novel theoretical approaches to interaction, novel user interface concepts and technologies, novel interaction devices, UI development methods, environments and tools, multimodal user interfaces, human-robot interaction, emotions in HCI, aesthetic issues, HCI and children, evaluation methods and tools, and many others.

The HCI Thematic Area covers four major dimensions, namely theory and methodology, technology, human beings, and societal impact. The following five volumes of the HCII 2024 proceedings reflect these dimensions:

- Human-Computer Interaction - Part I, addressing topics related to HCI Theory and Design and Evaluation Methods and Tools, and Emotions in HCI;
- Human-Computer Interaction - Part II, addressing topics related to Human-Robot Interaction and Child-Computer Interaction;
- Human-Computer Interaction - Part III, addressing topics related to HCI for Mental Health and Psychological Wellbeing, and HCI in Healthcare;
- Human-Computer Interaction - Part IV, addressing topics related to HCI, Environment and Sustainability, and Design and User Experience Evaluation Case Studies;
- Human-Computer Interaction - Part V, addressing topics related to Multimodality and Natural User Interfaces, and HCI, AI, Creativity, Art and Culture.

The papers in these volumes were accepted for publication after a minimum of two single-blind reviews from the members of the HCI Program Board or, in some cases, from members of the Program Boards of other affiliated conferences. We would like to thank all of them for their invaluable contribution, support, and efforts.

July 2024

Masaaki Kurosu
Ayako Hashizume

Human-Computer Interaction Thematic Area (HCI 2024)

Program Board Chairs: **Masaaki Kurosu,** *The Open University of Japan, Japan* and **Ayako Hashizume,** *Hosei University, Japan*

- Salah Uddin Ahmed, *University of South-Eastern Norway, India*
- Jessica Barfield, *University of Tennessee, USA*
- Valdecir Becker, *Federal University of Paraiba, Brazil*
- Nimish Biloria, *University of Technology Sydney, Australia*
- Zhigang Chen, *Shanghai University, P.R. China*
- Hong Chen, *Daiichi Institute of Technology, Japan*
- Emilia Duarte, *Universidade Europeia, Portugal*
- Yu-Hsiu Hung, *National Cheng Kung University, Taiwan*
- Jun Iio, *Chuo University, Japan*
- Yi Ji, *Guangdong University of Technology, Australia*
- Hiroshi Noborio, *Osaka Electro-Communication University, Japan*
- Katsuhiko Onishi, *Osaka Electro-Communication University, Japan*
- Julio Cesar Reis, *University of Campinas, Brazil*
- Mohammad Shidujaman, *Independent University Bangladesh (IUB), Bangladesh*

The full list with the Program Board Chairs and the members of the Program Boards of all thematic areas and affiliated conferences of HCII 2024 is available online at:

http://www.hci.international/board-members-2024.php

HCI International 2025 Conference

The 27th International Conference on Human-Computer Interaction, HCI International 2025, will be held jointly with the affiliated conferences at the Swedish Exhibition & Congress Centre and Gothia Towers Hotel, Gothenburg, Sweden, June 22–27, 2025. It will cover a broad spectrum of themes related to Human-Computer Interaction, including theoretical issues, methods, tools, processes, and case studies in HCI design, as well as novel interaction techniques, interfaces, and applications. The proceedings will be published by Springer. More information will become available on the conference website: https://2025.hci.international/.

General Chair
Prof. Constantine Stephanidis
University of Crete and ICS-FORTH
Heraklion, Crete, Greece
Email: general_chair@2025.hci.international

https://2025.hci.international/

Contents – Part IV

HCI, Environment and Sustainability

Development of Load Optimization and Anomaly Detection Platform Based on Air Cylinder Consumption Patterns

Ji-hyun Cha[1]([✉]) [iD], Heung-gyun Jeong[1] [iD], Seung-woo Han[1] [iD], Seung-hwa Baek[1] [iD], Hee-Boo Lee[2], Seok-Hee Hwang[3], and Jung-hyun Kim[3]

[1] Cloudnetworks Co., Ltd., 20, Yeongdong-daero 96-gil, Gangnam-gu, Seoul, Korea
{jh.cha,harris.jeong,sw.han,sh.baek}@cloudnetworks.co.kr
[2] Blacksun Co., Ltd., 157, Yangpyeong-ro, Yeongdeungpo-gu, Seoul, Korea
mail@blacksun.co.kr
[3] Linklobe Co., Ltd., 143, Dongtangambaesan-ro, Hwaseong-si, Gyeonggi-do, Korea
{seokhee,jhkim}@linklobe.com

Abstract. In order to drive the pneumatic actuators used in the manufacturing field, a compressed air supply system consisting of an air compressor, a pressure-reducing regulator, a solenoid valve, and an air cylinder is required, and the generated compressed air is consumed in the air cylinder after decompression according to the load rate required by the equipment through the pressure-reducing regulator. The pressure reducing regulator supplies compressed air from the inlet side to the outlet side at the moment when the compressed air is consumed in the actuator and the outlet pressure drops. Overshooting occurs in the process where the pneumatic pressure on the outlet side converges to the pneumatic pressure value set by the organic operation of the diaphragm, pressure regulating spring, and main valve. As a result of checking a large number of equipment used in manufacturing sites, the frequency of occurrence of overshooting pneumatic pressure appears to be dependent on the size of the set pneumatic pressure. If used for a long time in this environment, it can cause wear and damage to the internal sealing ring and packing of the air cylinder. This paper aims to improve the driving reliability and durability of the air cylinder and reduce unnecessary pneumatic consumption by designing a platform that can optimize the strength of compressed air on the outlet side of the pressure regulator to the required load rate. Therefore, by designing a platform to analyze the non-linear characteristics due to the compressibility of air and the friction of air cylinders and the consumption pattern of compressed air consumed by linking multiple facilities, process margins that do not affect productivity and quality can be confirmed. This makes it possible to optimize the outlet air pressure downward.

Keywords: Pneumatic Pattern Analysis · Air Cylinder Consumption Patterns · Energy Savings · Pressure Reducing Regulator · Machine Learning

© The Author(s), under exclusive license to Springer Nature Switzerland AG 2024
M. Kurosu and A. Hashizume (Eds.): HCII 2024, LNCS 14687, pp. 3–14, 2024.
https://doi.org/10.1007/978-3-031-60441-6_1

1 Introduction

Actuators, which constitute the operational units of automation and semi-automation equipment used in manufacturing sites, can be classified based on the input power into electric, pneumatic, and hydraulic types. In particular, pneumatic actuators are widely used in manufacturing facilities due to advantages such as simple maintenance, low device costs, fast response characteristics, high output, and robustness, in addition to operational and economic considerations. To drive these pneumatic actuators, a compressed air supply system is required, consisting of an air compressor, pressure regulator, solenoid valve, and air cylinder. The compressed air generated by the air compressor is regulated according to the load requirements of the equipment through the pressure regulator. It is then consumed during the actuation process of the air cylinder.

When compressed air is consumed by the actuator causing a drop in outlet pressure, the pressure regulator supplies inlet-side compressed air to the outlet side. During the process of converging the outlet pressure to the set pressure determined by the organic operation of the diaphragm, pressure spring, and main valve, overshooting occurs. The overshooting can potentially impact the durability of the air cylinder, so to reduce this, margin testing for the set values is necessary. Additionally, early detection of abnormal patterns in the consumption of compressed air requires the implementation of optimal AI modeling for time-series data".

2 Pneumatic System

2.1 Configuration of Pneumatic Collection Device

At the turntable, two operators manually produce the main trip component of the circuit breaker, the T.C.A. (Trip Coil Assembly). The air cylinder in the Manufacturing Equipment is used in the process where components such as coils, pipes, solder rings, and terminals are stacked. Its purposes can be classified into a pressing jig for securing components during stacking, a solder-fixturing jig for securing components through the cooling stage after the lead melting process, and a jig-up unit for high-frequency induction heating.

To acquire the compressed air consumption data from the air cylinder, pressure sensors have been installed at the inlet and outlet sides of the pressure regulator, as well as at the cap-end port and rod-end port of the air cylinder. To acquire pneumatic data, a data acquisition device for converting the analog signal (voltage) of pressure sensors to digital signals, transmitting them via RS485 for control, and a communication converter device for sending the acquired pressure sensor information to a PC via Wi-Fi are required. Using products from Autonics, these components were configured. The system supports a maximum communication speed of 38,400 bps using the MODBUS RTU protocol via RS485, and the collection cycle for pneumatic values is set at the 25ms level (Fig. 1).

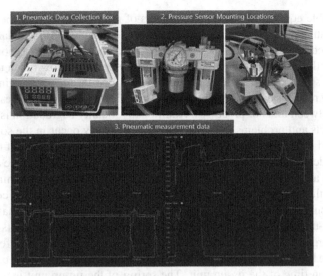

Fig. 1. Pneumatic Data Collection Box & measurement data

2.2   Set Pressure Margin Test

Air Cylinder Operation Test. The system characteristics such as thrust, operating time, load weight, and load ratio based on the diameter and supply pressure of the air cylinder can typically be confirmed through the manufacturer-supplied cylinder specification selection program. For any omitted models, inference can be made through a square root deviation graph. To calculate the thrust, the necessary information includes the cylinder diameter, load diameter, and stroke length. However, what is actually crucial in the thrust calculation of the air cylinder is the effective force, taking into account the moisture resistance of the cylinder's inner packing and the friction resistance of the load metal. Manufacturers typically provide friction coefficients by diameter in a table, and under normal operating conditions, frictional forces are estimated to be in the range of 3–20% of the calculated force. The results of simulating the operation characteristics are as shown in the Fig. 2.

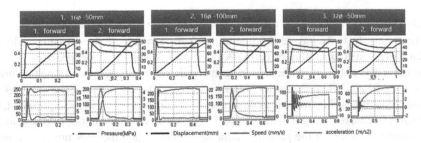

Fig. 2. Air cylinder operating characteristics

For turntable equipment with multiple units of air cylinders, it has been observed that the operating time of the air cylinders is set longer than the standard operating time guaranteed by the manufacturer. Adjusting the operating time to a shorter duration could potentially enhance productivity. However, determining how much the air cylinder operating speed can be increased should be verified through a margin test. Speed margin testing requires balancing adjustments in production input quantities considering throughput between units or processes. Additionally, quality degradation issues such as stacking defects and problems like cold soldering that may occur in the solder melting process should be avoided. For turntable equipment, the rotation speed of the turntable is already predetermined. Within this category, the operational speed of the air cylinders used with jigs and the speed at which operators stack products are determined.

To verify the set pneumatic margin of the turntable, a split test was conducted by reducing the supply pressure of the jig-up unit. The results confirmed that the tension state of the jig-up spring, which reduces the thrust of the air cylinder, affects the required pneumatic margin for each unit. Insufficient input pressure can result in defects such as a decrease in the height of the jig-up unit after one second of operation time or an increase in the operation time of the jig-up unit. The spring of the jig-up unit is a consumable item, and its tension decreases with usage. Therefore, regular replacement is necessary. Interference from foreign substances during the reciprocating motion of the unit and the accumulation of hardened lubricating oil can affect tension. To maintain tension at a certain level and minimize pneumatic margin reduction, it is important to inhibit occurrences such as foreign substance interference and the hardening of accumulated lubricating oil (Table 1 and Fig. 3).

Table 1. Jig-up Unit Pneumatic Margin Test Results

Pneumatic value (kPa)	No1	No2	No3	No4	No5	No6	No7	No8	No9
1. 400	G	G	NG	NG	G	G	NG	NG	G
2. 500	G	G	NG	G	G	G	G	G	G
3. 600	G	G	G	G	G	G	G	G	G

Supply Pressure Pattern Test. To perform a margin test for the proper supply pressure, it is necessary to first analyze the operating characteristics of the pressure reducing regulator. The basic operating principle is as follows. When the outlet pressure exceeds the pressure of the pressure reducing spring, the main valve closes, interrupting the supply of compressed air. When the outlet pressure decreases below the pressure value of the pressure reducing spring due to the consumption of compressed air in the equipment, the main valve opens, restoring it to the set value. The set value on the outlet side is adjusted by adjusting the valve of the pressure reducing spring. When the pressure is increased, the tension of the pressure reducing spring increases, causing the outlet pressure to rise until it reaches the set value. Conversely, when the pressure is decreased, the tension of the pressure reducing spring decreases, causing the outlet pressure to decrease until

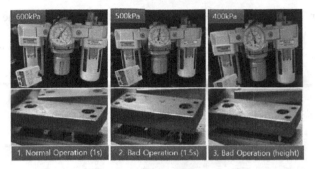

Fig. 3. Jig-Up Operation Test

it reaches the set value. In manufacturing equipment, relief-type pressure regulators are most commonly used. When the pressure in the diaphragm chamber and the outlet pressure reach equilibrium, the main valve closes, maintaining the set value. However, if the outlet pressure rises above the set value, the main valve, diaphragm, and pressure reducing spring work together organically to exhaust air to the atmosphere (Fig. 4).

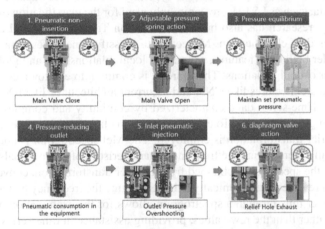

Fig. 4. The operating principle of a pressure regulator. Source of Information: SMC Website

The important point to note here is that when the outlet-side equipment consumes air, causing the pressure to drop below the set value, there is a momentary supply of high pressure from the inlet side to the outlet side. This results in a momentary occurrence of pressure exceeding the set value. The pressure overshooting generated at the outlet side increases the pressure in the diaphragm chamber, opening the diaphragm valve. Subsequently, the excess pressure is discharged through the relief hole. However, in such an environment, if the air cylinder operates for an extended period, it may lead to wear and damage of internal sealing rings and packings. To address these issues, a margin test was conducted on the supply pressure of the turntable equipment. As a result, by reducing the outlet pressure from the existing 600 kPa to around 400 kPa, the size of the overshooting air pressure decreased, confirming an improvement in the durability of the air cylinder. To achieve this, it is essential to manage the tension of the jig-up spring at a certain level to ensure trouble-free operation (Fig. 5).

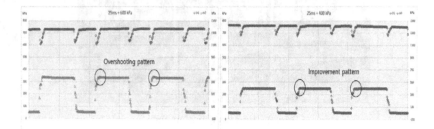

Fig. 5. Jig-Up Operation Test

2.3 Air Cylinder Modeling

Time Series Data Anomaly Detection. Typically, architectures capable of handling time-series data, such as LSTM, are commonly used for the classification of time-series data. Recently, research has also been conducted on Transformer-based architectures for time-series data classification. Moreover, to classify time-series data, it is necessary to consider both local features, examining local relationships, and global features, accounting for overall variations. Therefore, it is common to employ a combination of window-based architectures like CNN and recurrent architectures like RNN to address these aspects. Time-series data, characterized by continuity and complex periodicity, is often challenging to classify. To enhance clarity in classification, a Mel-spectrogram based on Fourier transformation is employed. The Mel spectrogram is commonly utilized for visually representing the frequency characteristics of audio signals. It involves preprocessing the spectrogram obtained from Fourier transformation, converting it into a Mel scale represented logarithmically to better capture the frequency patterns. Analyzing changes over time through a spectrogram allows for the examination of frequency components rather than the raw values, providing assistance in time-series processing. In the context of general time-series data, the characteristics of detection sensors often reveal that distinct changes at lower frequencies contain more informative patterns than abrupt changes at higher frequencies. Therefore, using Mel spectrograms is appropriate for capturing such lower-frequency variations in time-series data (Fig. 6).

Model Design. The architecture structure of the yield prediction model involves preprocessing the input time-series data into Mel spectrograms. Subsequently, a CNN model is employed to analyze local relationships. During this process, it is necessary to significantly increase and then reduce the number of channels. This approach is widely utilized in models such as V2Sa. Local features analyzed by CNN are recurrently combined for the analysis of global variations using Bidirectional LSTM. This can be regarded as a Serial Association Model. Ultimately, the hidden features reflecting both local and global characteristics are passed through a Dense network to create a classifier that categorizes as 0 (normal) or 1 (abnormal) (Fig. 7).

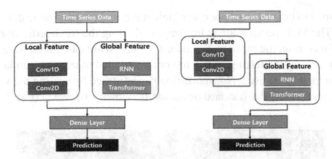

Fig. 6. Time-series data considering both local relationships and global variations

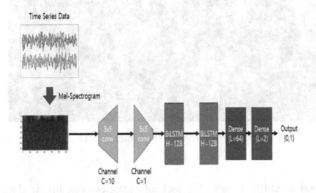

Fig. 7. The structure of the pneumatic data defect prediction model

The input and output data are both numerical, and the values are collected at different frequencies depending on the sensor's sampling interval. In the turntable facility, where multiple semi-finished products are processed simultaneously, additional preprocessing is required to trace which product's manufacturing process is utilizing the real-time pneumatic values. With an imaging collection device inspecting the surface condition of the finished product, it is possible to accurately distinguish the rotation cycles of the turntable. Providing this information as timestamps allows for the separation of pneumatic data into time-based intervals. By tracking the production process, it becomes possible to define unit processes where pneumatic systems are employed. Predefining when each production process occurs in terms of cycles before the completion of the finished product allows for the preprocessing of pneumatic data based on the specific usage patterns for each product. Product-specific pneumatic data is input into the pneumatic-based yield prediction model, and the output values range from 0 to 1. This range represents the probability of defects occurring for individual products. Taking the average of the defect probability over time allows for the prediction of the yield.

Model Implementation. The model is broadly divided into three layers: short_term_layer, long_term_layer, and cls_layer. Each layer incorporates the previously mentioned CNN, BiLSTM, and Dense network. The detailed structures of each layer are planned to be improved once a sufficient amount of pneumatic data is collected in the future. The Mel spectrogram is implemented using the torchaudio library. During the training data phase, the mean and standard deviation are calculated for each channel (lines 26–29). During the testing phase, the pre-computed mean and standard deviation from the training data are used. Normalization is performed by scaling the values so that the mean becomes 0 and the standard deviation becomes 1 (line 32) (Fig. 8).

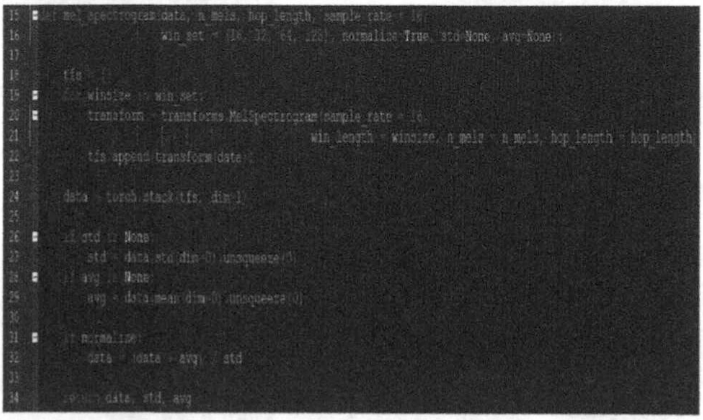

Fig. 8. Mel spectrogram implementation function

Experiment and Results. Due to the lack of sufficient pneumatic data, the model's anomaly detection performance was evaluated using the well-known open dataset called the FordA dataset. The FordA dataset, released by Ford in 2008, consists of data related to automotive engine noise. It is designed for detecting defects in specific internal components of a car. The dataset consists of a total of 500 numerical entries. Although the sample rate is unspecified, it is mentioned that the data is analog engine noise measured at regular intervals. The first column of the dataset represents labels, taking on values of -1 or 1. The subsequent 500 columns provide data related to engine noise. The model is composed of approximately 1 million parameters and processed data consisting of

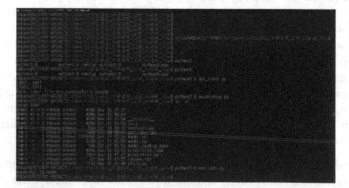

Fig. 9. Match rate between prediction result and label value

500 frames at a rate of over 100 frames per second. The measured accuracy is 93.1%. Considering that the pneumatic data collected in the field exhibits time-series patterns similar to those used in the model, it is expected to demonstrate sufficient classification performance (Fig. 9).

3 Platform Configuration

3.1 Edge Device Management System

In addition to pneumatic data collection devices, it is necessary to manage Edge Devices that can easily connect to and collect data from various protocol sensor devices. Therefore, a management service structure for Edge Devices, focusing on status inquiry and control for multiple Edge Devices, has been designed. The pneumatic data collection management service performed in the Cloud primarily aims to verify and control the status of each installed Edge Device in the field. To initiate the development of the initial AI model, there may be a substantial volume of data loading. Concerned about the potential high costs associated with uploading all this data to Cloud storage, a design decision was made to introduce Network Attached Storage (NAS).

The communication protocol between the Edge Devices and the services within the Cloud is based on WebSocket. To establish the Control Flow from the Cloud to Edge Devices within a Private Network, it was determined that PubSub and WebSocket should be utilized. Among PubSub and WebSocket, WebSocket was chosen because PubSub does not have a bidirectional communication structure, which is essential for this use case.

Edge Device Start – Event. After the Air-Pressure service is launched on the Edge Device, it attempts to establish a WebSocket connection with the configured Cloud URL. In case of connection failure, it retries the connection at intervals defined internally (every 10 s). Upon successful connection, the Cloud validates the device and adds it to the list of connected devices. To obtain the latest information about the device from the Cloud, the "INFO" command is sent from the Cloud to the Edge Device. Subsequently, the Edge Device relays device configuration, disk capacity, network information, and other relevant details back to the Cloud.

Collector Start and Collector Stop – Event. To initiate or stop data collection on the Edge Device, the commands "COLLECTOR_START" and "COLLECTOR_STOP" are respectively sent. Upon receiving these commands, the Edge Device performs the defined actions associated with each command.

Collector State – Event. If the responsible person needs to check the real-time status of data collection, they can make a request for that information (Fig. 10).

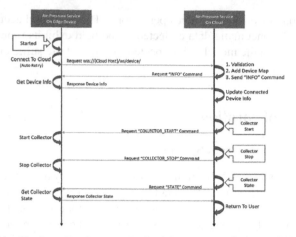

Fig. 10. Edge Device - Service communication sequence diagram within the cloud

3.2 Implementing the Power and Pneumatic Data Collection Protocols

For power and pneumatic data collection, communication between the pneumatic data collection device and the Edge Device uses the MODBUS protocol, which defines policies and specifications for serial data and implements data collection functions. The Collector Manager (for data collection configuration) and the Data Collector (for executing data collection) are separate areas, defining the data collection (Collector) items. Each Collector has a separate connection to the MODBUS Client. The execution of the Modbus Client occurs when the Start is called through the API. It takes the configurations defined in the Collector Manager area and the execution options received at the Start, such as the duration of the collection, for execution (Fig. 11).

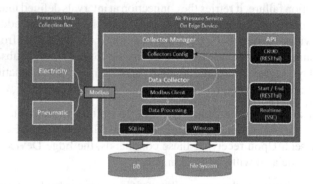

Fig. 11. The architecture of the pneumatic data collection system

3.3 Pneumatic Monitoring Platform

To facilitate real-time monitoring of collected power and pneumatic data, a React-based web service has been implemented. Through the 'File Manager' menu, users can inspect pneumatic serial data stored in JSON format within daily folders under MODBUS protocol. The implemented SSE (Server-Sent Events) API in the pneumatic data collection system allows receiving and outputting events, enabling the observation of real-time data changes. Users can track trends in data changes through event reception and output facilitated by SSE API (Fig. 12).

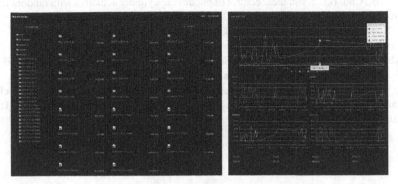

Fig. 12. Pneumatic Monitoring Platform

4 Conclusion

The frequency and magnitude of overshooting pressure occurring at the outlet of the pressure regulator tend to increase with higher outlet pressure settings. Prolonged operation of the cylinder under such conditions can lead to wear and damage to internal sealing rings and packings. To address this issue, there is a need to design a pneumatic monitoring platform and an AI model. This AI model would analyze the pressure values inputted at the inlet and outlet of the pressure regulator, as well as at the ports of the cylinder. By ensuring process margins that do not impact productivity, quality deterioration, or equipment operating conditions, it is possible to secure a decrease in outlet pressure without compromising productivity or quality. Reducing outlet pressure not only enhances the operational reliability and durability of the air cylinder but also has the potential to decrease unnecessary pneumatic consumption.

Additionally, after constructing the CNN model, the accuracy of the pneumatic yield prediction model was measured using the FordA dataset, which exhibits the most similar patterns in terms of continuity and periodicity. The results confirmed an accuracy level of over 90%. Future plans involve acquiring pneumatic data linked to process margins in manufacturing facilities to further enhance the model's accuracy.

Acknowledgements. This work was supported by project for Smart Manufacturing Innovation R&D funded Korea Ministry of SMEs and Startups in 2022. (RS-2022-00141143).

References

1. Oh, H.-i., Kim, I.-s., Kim, G.-b.: Model Reference Adaptive Control of the Pneumatic System with Load Variation: Mechanical System Engineering, Kumoh National Institute of Technology. (Received 2 March 2015; received in revised form 15 March 2015; accepted 18 May 2015)
2. Shin, C.B., Cho, H.C.: Nonlinear control of pneumatic cylinder actuators with random friction nature. J. Korean Soc. Mech. Technol. **17**(2), 273–280 (2015)
3. Cho, N.-K., Chung, Y.-G., Nam, J.-W., Cho, I.-H.: Pressure drop characteristics and control method of pneumatic regulator for gas supply. J. Korean Soc. Propul. Eng. **11**, 347–352 (2009)
4. Shayto, R., Porter, B., Chandia, R., Papa, M., Shenoi, S.: Assessing the integrity of field devices in Modbus networks. IFIP Adv. Inf. Commun. Technol. 115–128 (2007)
5. Zhao, L., Shaocheng, Q., Zeng, J., Zhao, Q.: Energy-saving and management of telecom operators' remote computer rooms using IoT technology. IEEE Access **8**, 166197–166211 (2020)

MORE THAN ONE MILAN: Urban Interactive Experience: An Olfactory Map Project

Liyuan Dong[✉] [ID], Pinjia Lai [ID], and Tianqi Zhao [ID]

Politecnico di Milano, Piazza Leonardo da Vinci, 32, 20133 Milan, Italy
{liyuan.dong,laipin,tianqi.zhao}@mail.polimi.it

Abstract. In recent times, designers have started to acknowledge the importance of smell across diverse design domains. Within the context of Human-Computer Interaction (HCI), designers are venturing into the systematic incorporation of smell within the design process, moving beyond employing smell solely as a sensory enhancer. Memory and emotions are greatly influenced by smell, prompting interaction designers to leverage these aspects.

Map nowadays predominantly prioritize visual and auditory elements, overlooking the importance of incorporating smell into urban exploration. More Than One Milan: The Olfactory Map project employ smell as the core element in the design endeavors, stimulate individuals' sensory perceptions using smells, nurtures their imagination and curiosity and amplifies their motivation to venture into their chosen destinations. Another objective is to establish olfactory memory cues for places, thus crafting a multi-sensory strategy for memory improvement.

This paper will begin by introduction that examine the current state of olfactory design and map design. It will then establish the foundation of the project's design methodology, followed by an explanation of the conceptualization, research, testing, and iterative process undertaken in the project.

Keywords: Olfactory map · Multisensory experience · HCI · Urban exploration · Interaction design · Synesthetic design

1 Introduction

As the design community has come to realise the potential of smell in human-computer interaction, designers have begun to explore how to integrate the sense of smell into all aspects of design [1]. Beyond the boundaries of the traditional perfume industry, the sense of smell has been given a new meaning, not just as a simple sensory stimulus, but also as a bridge between emotion and memory [2,3]. Although olfactory memory is inherently transient, the close connection between smell and the rest of the human sensory system can inspire a richer experience [4].

© The Author(s), under exclusive license to Springer Nature Switzerland AG 2024
M. Kurosu and A. Hashizume (Eds.): HCII 2024, LNCS 14687, pp. 15–29, 2024.
https://doi.org/10.1007/978-3-031-60441-6_2

In HCI, this design trend has inspired designers to use olfactory elements to enhance sensory interactions and emotional connections for users [1,2].

From sensory-dependent city location [5,7] to digital maps with predominantly audio-visual elements, city maps have evolved with a gradual dilution of olfactory elements [8,9]. Today, there is an urgent need to reconsider how maps can be used to enhance people's multi-sensory perception of the city, so that they are not only a guide for direction but also a medium for experience when navigating [6].

Through an interactive olfactory installation, we offer a new way of exploring the area, aiming to construct a narrative urban experience for the user through the power of olfactory association, that transcends the limitations of vision and text. We investigated the association between smell and memory, and how matching different smells to different places in the city creates a new connection [10]. We then designed interactive prototypes to validate the design concept through field testing and user experience, ensuring that these prototypes are not only easy to use but also provide an enjoyable sensory experience. Ultimately, we have analysed how olfactory-based HCI design can enrich the urban exploration experience, and explored the prospects and challenges of applying this approach to future urban experience design.

2   Background and Significance

2.1   The Importance of Olfactory in Human-Computer Interaction (HCI)

Smell is a crucial aspect of human senses, impacting our experiences and emotions [1]. Smell is a message that can convey emotions and memories [3]. Initially, smell was primarily valued in the perfume industry [11]. However, designers have recently begun recognizing the significance of smell in various design disciplines. In the realm of Human-Computer Interaction (HCI), designers are exploring the systematic integration of smell with design, going beyond using smell as a mere sensory enhancer. Emotions and memory are greatly influenced by smell, prompting interaction designers to leverage these aspects [1,2]. For instance, MIT's BioEssence project alleviates anxiety through smell, while Amy Radcliffe's odor camera captures scents to preserve memories that can be invoked by releasing the scent once again [12,13].

2.2   The Evolution of Map Navigation Experience

Evolution of Map Usage: Perception: Initially, people relied on perception to determine the location of cities, such as visually using churches as landmarks and using the smell of leather goods shops and restaurants to identify locations. Paper Maps: With the development of printing technology, people started using paper maps for navigation. Digital Maps: With the advancement of computer technology, digital maps on mobile phones emerged. People could not only navigate but also search for relevant information and mark locations [13,14]. However, during the process of map development, the significance of smell in urban exploration gradually declined. People began to overlook the existence of smell, and more city map information became visually oriented. Therefore, it is worth contemplating how to enhance people's multi-sensory experience in maps and enrich their navigation experience in the city [6].

2.3   The Relationship Between City Roaming and Smell

Smell is closely associated with memory. It can evoke not only people's recollections of past events but also create impressions of new things based on the sensory experience of smell [2,3]. Utilizing this notion, we combine smell with city maps to augment people's memory of different places in the city and enrich their experiential senses from multiple dimensions. On one hand, we aim to stimulate people's sensory perceptions through smell, encouraging speculation and fantasy about unknown areas, thereby increasing users' motivation to explore their destination. On the other hand, we intend to establish olfactory memory points for regions and cities, creating a multi-sensory approach to memory.

2.4   Cross-sensory Associations

Smell features are matched or related to other sensory features [6]. As illustrated in the figure below, sensory features associated with smell include vision, hearing, temperature, and material. Smell can also influence our perception of the body, including body silhouettes and gender. On a subjective level, familiarity with and liking of smells are two dimensions for evaluating them. In the following text, we will use this criterion to research and analyze users' impressions of various smells and analyze the store environment, and then pair them together (Fig. 1).

3   Project Concept

The Olfactory Map project introduces a comprehensive and interactive system designed to enhance the exploration of the Brera district in Milan through a multi-sensory experience, combining both digital and physical elements. This system features two primary components: a map installation of the Brera area, which incorporates visual cues representing 6 distinct scents across 26 abstract models of various locations; and a portable scent-dispensing olfactory device. There are also scent cards that are designed to activate the device and the installation. Each card, containing scent information, represents a location. Users use the card to activate the portable device and map installation, encouraging exploration of the Brera area through experiencing scents.

The system naturally guides users to explore Brera area through the sense of olfactory. Initially, users receive a portable device and 3 random scent cards.

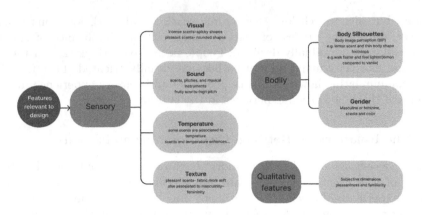

Fig. 1. Research on the Scents

Each card triggers the device to emit a corresponding scent. By experiencing these scents, users can choose to visit locations of interest, and then obtain new scent cards at these locations. In this interactive manner, users gradually explore the Brera area's representative locations while collecting scent cards. During this process, they have the opportunity to visit or encounter some main locations with the map installation which shows the entire scent map of the Brera area. By using all the collected cards to trigger the map installation's console, users will see a comprehensive map that display their experience path (Figs. 2, 3 and 4).

4   Research on the Place, Smell and Visual

4.1   Research and Consideration

Our aim is to create a scent map for the Brera district in Milan, establishing a distinctive olfactory identity for this area. This endeavor requires an in-depth exploration of cross-sensory dynamics, particularly how individuals perceive and interpret fundamental scents in conjunction with other human senses: sight, touch and hearing. Hence we will include the elements of color, texture, temperature and sound as our main research goals. These factors are integral as they profoundly shape the experience and intensity of scents. Notably, visual elements play a pivotal role, given the well-documented cross modal correspondences between colors and scents. These correlations are not just of academic interest but are also increasingly relevant to designers seeking to encapsulate the olfactory qualities of their designs through color schemes.

Fig. 2. Portable Device Prototype

Fig. 3. Design of the NFC Cards for 26 Venues (Stores)

Fig. 4. MAP Installation Prototype

Research Methodology. For deciding the map area, aiming to provide people with a better and continuous urban exploration experience, we chose three representative and moderately sized areas in Milan: "Duomo," "Navigli," and "Brera." We visited these three areas, analysed the diversity, uniqueness, density, and historical significance of the stores in each area. We focus on diversity to ensure a representative mix of retail, cultural, and historical sites, along with popular landmarks. Geographic spread throughout the district is crucial to cover various neighbourhoods, and special attention should be given to locations with unique sensory characteristics.

We conducted preliminary research by on-site explorations, involving initial walkthroughs to observe and identify potential areas fitting the selection criteria. During these explorations, sensory observations are key in noting places with distinct smells, sounds, or visual elements. We also enrich the selection process by engaging interviews and digital ethnography research methods to investigate people's perceptions of the locations. This allows local residents, business owners, and visitors offer perspectives on quintessential Brera locations. By using adjectives to describe the objective sensory experiences of the locations in terms of visuals, sounds, temperature, and textures, and by summarizing the subjective descriptions of the locations based on Google Maps reviews, we compiled and summarized the results.

The final selection process involves shortlisting potential locations, ensuring a balanced representation of different space types. The selected locations were plotted on a map to visualize their distribution and confirm comprehensive coverage.

Design Process of the Locations. Upon selecting the 26 locations, we organized them into 6 distinct categories, each represented by a unique scent, served as main stops where the map devices were placed. These locations are iconic landmarks within the area and serve as stopping points during the exploring experience, offering sufficient public space for people to interact with the map installation. The remaining 20 locations are sub stops where participants can collect cards. These locations include various types of stores that are open regularly, as well as periodic markets or art exhibitions.

In parallel, we harnessed our in-depth understanding of each site's ambiance and characteristics to craft abstract visual patterns. These patterns capture the essence of each venue, serving as visual complements that resonate with both the scents and the broader aesthetic experience. The design process for these visuals was rooted in comprehensive data encompassing smells, sounds, colors, textures, and temperatures, with photographs, audio recordings, and detailed notes from our site visits providing essential reference materials.

For each venue, we pinpointed the most prominent scent and sensory elements and compiled concise sensory profiles. Following this, brainstorming sessions were conducted to ideate abstract interpretations of each site's odour and sensory profile. The outcome was a set of patterns that not only reflect but also enhance the overarching identity of Brera.

4.2   Selection and Matching Process

In general, the category of basic scents includes 10 different smells, some of which might be perceived as less pleasant. However, given our goal to create an overall pleasant experience, we opted to select aromas from the category of perfume scents. To ensure a comprehensive and inclusive representation of smell types, we chose the following eight scents for our project: grapefruit, myrrh, cedar wood, black pepper, spearmint, vanilla, lavender, and eucalyptus.

To effectively match the selected scents with the locations, we prepared corresponding fragrance essential oils for the selected scents and developed questionnaires for participant feedback. This step was crucial for objectively completing the matching process, utilizing a dataset for reliable conclusions. The questionnaire was designed to explore the varied perceptions people have of these scents, enhancing the accuracy of our scent-location alignment.

The questionnaire was divided into two primary sections: open-ended and closed-ended questions. The open-ended section focused on the sensations and associative memories each scent evoked, sought to capture the depth and nuance of personal scent experiences. While the closed-ended questions concentrated on more quantifiable aspects of the scents, such as their intensity, the emotions they stirred, their perceived shape, and their temperature associations. This approach was designed not only to gather rich, subjective insights but also to quantitatively validate our previous research. The ultimate objective was to ensure that the scents chosen were a true reflection of the ambiance and character of each Brera location, thereby creating a more authentic and immersive sensory experience (Fig. 5).

4.3   Result and Discussion

Through the questionnaire, we collected responses from 23 participants regarding their perceptions of the 8 smells. Drawing inspiration from the scent description template called "EssCards" described in "Sniff Before You Act: Exploration of

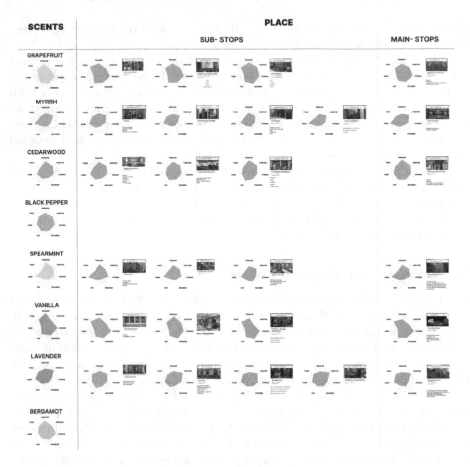

Fig. 5. Matching Results

Scent-Feature Associations for Designing Future Interactions," [10] we organized the data and information from the questionnaire into charts. After comparing and analysing the results, we found similarities between eucalyptus and grapefruit, as well as between black pepper and vanilla. Therefore, we decided to remove eucalyptus and black pepper, resulting in a final selection of 6 scents. These scents will serve as the foundation for the subsequent olfactory map design.

The feedback-driven matching process resulted in each selected scent being uniquely paired with a specific location in Brera. Intriguingly, this process also revealed some unexpected results and inconsistencies in how scents were perceived and preferred. These revelations compelled us to reevaluate and, in some instances, revise our initial pairings, ensuring they resonated more accurately with public sentiment and perception, thereby refining the overall sensory map.

Additionally, the exercise provided valuable insights into the dynamic role scents play in shaping the experience of a place. We discovered that specific scents could significantly enhance or transform the ambiance of a location, fostering deeper engagement or offering fresh perspectives on the space. This aspect of the project highlighted the potent influence of olfactory elements in the context of spatial experience and interaction.

5 Design of the Portable Device (Olfactory Display)

The core design principle of the device was to achieve portability while maintaining the functionality of odor recognition. During the design process, we utilized sketches, paper models, and 3D models for refinement, iterating based on feedback collected through basic user testing.

5.1 Product Design

Considering the need for users to conveniently carry the device while exploring the city and interact with it at any time, we initially explored various designs through sketches, eventually settling on a form similar to a cross-body bag. The functional components of the operating device were housed within this "bag". Building upon the sketches, we created a lo-fi prototype using cardboard as the primary material. This simple model, paired with an introduction to the interaction process, was tested by 6 users. Test results showed that users quickly grasped the interaction method but desired more explicit feedback. Based on this, we reduced the device size and optimized the 3 small indicator lights on the surface into 1 larger light indicator (Fig. 6).

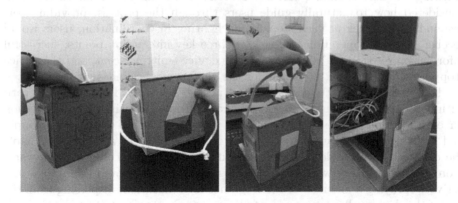

Fig. 6. Low Fidelity Prototype of the Portable Device

Next, we used 3D software SketchUp to assist in creating 3D models, we fully considered the design aesthetics and consistency of the product style. Orange and white semi-transparent acrylic panels were used as the main material for the device body. This choice not only facilitated light transmission but also contributed to a modern and avant-garde feel. Additionally, we added visual elements like logos, icons, and LED indicators on the device surface to increase legibility. These additions provided users with clear feed forward cues, enhancing the overall user experience. The combination of functionality and visual appeal aimed to create a pleasant, immersive experience for users interacting with the olfactory map system (Fig. 7).

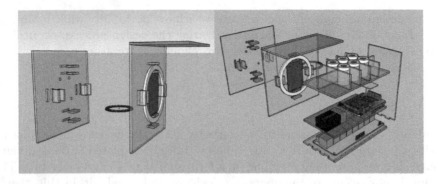

Fig. 7. 3D Modelling

5.2   Interaction Design

As envisioned in the project concept, the user-device interaction process involved the user triggering the device's odor recognition function, followed by the device emitting the corresponding scent. We broke down this entire interaction and considered how to naturally guide users through the process, providing corresponding feedback at each step. Using lighting in coordination, users would receive successful operation feedback at three key interaction points: successful information recognition by the device, the device emitting scent, and the device stopping scent emission, preparing for the next scent recognition.

To create an interactive scent device prototype, an RFID reader and card with NFC technology were used for scent recognition and switching. Information for each location on the Brera scent map was encoded into cards; users simply had to bring the card close to the NFC reader surface to activate. To enable the compact portable device to emit 6 different scents, we used 6 grove water atomizers, coordinated with an 8-channel relay. The designated atomizer would activate spraying a fine mist of the fragrance for a duration, dispersing from the top of the device, allowing users to fully experience the scent (Fig. 8).

6   Design of the Map Installation

6.1   Product Design

The map installation, designed for public spaces, visually displays a scent map and tracks user collections, featuring a two-part design with a vertical display

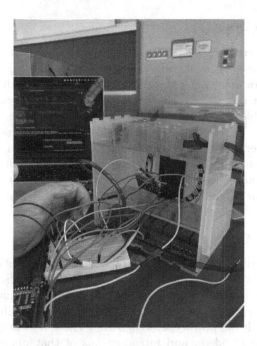

Fig. 8. Inner Structure of the Device

for the map and a horizontal console for interactions. After prototyping and user testing, we simplified the console based on feedback. In refining Brera's scent map, we represented 6 scents with unique colors and shapes on a grid, complemented by 26 3D printed models for specific locations. This approach unified the olfactory device system, enhancing user engagement with the scent map's visual and tactile elements (Fig. 9).

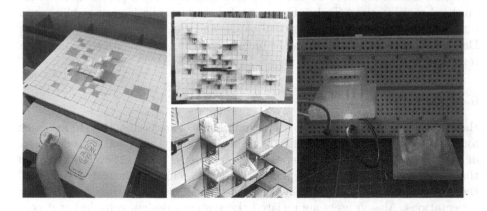

Fig. 9. Iteration Process of the Map Installation Prototype

6.2   Interaction Design

The purpose of map interaction is to allow users to intuitively understand the scent information they have already collected and encourage them to continue exploring the entire area. After iteration, each time a user brings a new card close to the card-reading area, the corresponding location on the map lights up. Like the portable device, the high-fidelity prototype of the map installation used Arduino Uno, driven by RFID. This allows users to use the same set of RFID cards to operate both the device and the installation, ensuring system consistency. Each small location model has an LED bulb underneath, with a lit yellow light representing feedback to the user. The placement of the wiring and Arduino boards was carefully considered during the fabrication process.

6.3   User Testing

The prototype used for user testing was a high-fidelity iteration, consisting of a portable scent device, a map installation, and 6 scent cards. All three proto-types were 1:1 models with Arduino-enabled interaction. To simulate a real-world environment, all tests were conducted outdoors, with test subjects encouraged to walk around with the prototype. When they chose a location to explore, we showed them photos, videos, and introductions of that place to simulate the experience of visiting the site.

The test aimed to A) ascertain if users could understand and successfully complete the interaction process, B) evaluate if the scent experience met users' expectations and motivated further interaction, and C) assess users' understanding and feelings towards the information conveyed by the scent map. 6 participants were invited for testing. We focused on their interaction with the system, noting moments of hesitation or inquiry. After testing, each user completed UX and usability questionnaires, providing feedback and impressions. Task 1: Interact with the portable scent device using 3 scent cards, choose a preferred scent, and walk around the city with the device, learning about and providing feedback on the chosen locations. Task 2: Encounter the map installation in a public space, interact with it using the collected 6 cards, and check the locations collected. Describe their understanding and feelings about the scent map installation content verbally (Fig. 10).

6.4   User Feedbacks

Based on the user testing results, users completed the tasks smoothly. In feedback for Task 1, 2 users mentioned some differences between the actual characteristics of their chosen locations and their scent perceptions. However, everyone agreed that exploring an unfamiliar city using scent as a clue significantly heightened their curiosity and enjoyment, even if the results slightly diverged from their expectations. Also, 5 users appreciated the system's design, considering it cool to carry such a "bag" while traversing the city. For Task 2, participants found the interaction easy to understand and operate, effectively motivating them to

Fig. 10. User Testing

collect more cards. Although interpretations of the colorful patterns on the scent map varied, through the interaction process, they all understood the information conveyed by the map.

However, some feedback and observations indicated areas for improvement. 3 users suggested considering more inclusive dimensions for the map installation's height and placement, catering to a broader range of users. Additionally, we noted that the intensity of the interactive feedback lights might be affected by natural outdoor lighting, potentially impacting the map installation's interaction process. Lastly, observing participants during Task 1, we noticed they opened map apps for navigation after choosing their desired locations. To optimize the interaction process and facilitate users' arrival at chosen locations, we considered incorporating a mobile app synchronized with the scent recognition device, featuring navigation capabilities.

7   Conclusion and Future Work

After several iterations and user testing, our interactive system has matured in functionality and user experience quality. Looking ahead, we aim to integrate a navigation app to enhance user experience fluidity, merging our olfactory interaction project with commonly used digital mediums like smartphones in a "phygital" approach. This integration is intended to accommodate social computing needs and boost user acceptance. The comprehensive study of the Brera scent system and interactive product design encourages us to contemplate and document our process, aspiring to extend our olfactory-centered sensory map research and interactive urban exploration devices to other cities or regions. We plan to incorporate unique local features into personalized designs, aiming to establish a new standard for urban exploration and connection.

Overall, in recent years, designers have begun to recognize the importance of olfactory in various design fields. In the field of Human-Computer Interaction (HCI), designers are starting to systematically integrate olfactory into the design process, rather than merely using it as a sensory enhancer. Memory and emotion are greatly influenced by smell, prompting interaction designers to fully utilize these aspects. Therefore, adding olfactory elements to visual and auditory memories to make them a more meaningful sensory dimension is a logical step. Our design concept, starting with a scent map, adds an olfactory experience to the visually and auditorily dominated urban maps, making it the core of a multi-sensory urban exploration experience. Based on our research of the scent map of shops and venues in Brera, a famous district in the center of Milan, we designed an olfactory recognition system. This system cultivates users' imagination and curiosity about unfamiliar places through olfactory stimulation, encouraging them to actively visit these destinations. Meanwhile, the process from experiencing a scent to exploring the corresponding location builds people's memories of the city through olfactory clues. Scent, closely linked with other senses, serves as a breakthrough in enhancing urban sensory experiences. Utilizing scents to evoke emotions and memories is a method to recreate the spirit of urban places. This application in the HCI field aligns with SDG 11.4's goal to protect and safeguard global cultural and natural heritage, offering people an opportunity to immerse themselves in urban culture beyond just visual and auditory means. Additionally, considering the unique olfactory culture of each city forms a part of future considerations for reproducing urban scents.

References

1. Maggioni, E., et al.: SMELL SPACE: mapping out the olfactory design space for novel interactions. ACM Trans. Comput.-Hum. Interac. (TOCHI) **27**(5), 1–26 (2020)
2. Obrist, M., Tuch, A.N., Hornbaek, K.: Opportunities for odor: experiences with smell and implications for technology. In: Proceedings of the SIGCHI Conference on Human Factors in Computing Systems (2014)
3. Kaye, J.N.: Symbolic olfactory display. Diss. Massachusetts Institute of Technology (2001)
4. Leret, S.C., Visch, V.: From smells to stories: the design and evaluation of the smell memory kit. Int. J. Des. **11**(1), 65–77 (2017)
5. Vasilikou, C.: Sensory Navigation in the City Centre. Perceptual paths, sense walks and interactive atmospheres. Ambiances, tomorrow. In: Proceedings of 3rd International Congress on Ambiances. September 2016, Volos, Greece, vol. 1. International Network Ambiances; University of Thessaly (2016)
6. Fischler-Ruiz, W., et al.: Olfactory landmarks and path integration converge to form a cognitive spatial map. Neuron **109**(24), 4036–4049 (2021)
7. Spence, C.: Senses of place: architectural design for the multisensory mind. Cognitive Res. Principles Implications **5**(1), 46 (2020)
8. Ritzer, I., Tomaselli, K.G.: Media cities: mapping urbanity and audio-visual configurations. J. African Cinemas **10**(1–2), 3–7 (2018)
9. Driver, F.: On geography as a visual discipline. Antipode **35**(2), 227–231 (2003)

10. Brianza, G., Cornelio, P., Maggioni, E., Obrist, M.: Sniff before you act: exploration of scent-feature associations for designing future interactions. In: Ardito, C., Lanzilotti, R., Malizia, A., Petrie, H., Piccinno, A., Desolda, G., Inkpen, K. (eds.) INTERACT 2021. LNCS, vol. 12933, pp. 281–301. Springer, Cham (2021). https://doi.org/10.1007/978-3-030-85616-8_17
11. Reinarz, J.: Past Scents: Historical Perspectives on Smell. University of Illinois Press (2014)
12. Amores, J., et al.: Bioessence: a wearable olfactory display that monitors cardiorespiratory information to support mental wellbeing. In: 2018 40th Annual International Conference of the IEEE Engineering in Medicine and Biology Society (EMBC). IEEE (2018)
13. Bagrow, L.: History of cartography. Routledge (2017)
14. MacEachren, A.M.: How Maps Work: Representation, Visualization, and Design. Guilford Press (2004)

Designing a Smart Cooling Vest to Reduce Heat Stress for Construction Workers

Farhad Hossain[1] (ID), Mengru Xue[1](✉) (ID), Safin Rahman[1], Tariquzzaman Azad[1], and Mohammad Shidujaman[2] (ID)

[1] Ningbo Innovation Center, Zhejiang University, Ningbo, China
{22151447,mengruxue,22251411,22251396}@zju.edu.cn
[2] RIoT Research Centre, Department of Computer Science and Engineering, Independent University, Dhaka, Bangladesh
Shidujaman@iub.edu.bd

Abstract. In the realm of construction work, laborers frequently contend with adverse weather conditions and the resultant heat stress, which detrimentally impacts their general well-being and job performance. The adoption of smart cooling vests has emerged as a viable solution to confront these challenges. This research endeavors to delve into the fundamental attributes and advantages associated with cooling vests, particularly focusing on active cooling mechanisms and ergonomic design, with the ultimate aim of optimizing thermal regulation and enhancing the overall well-being and occupational safety of construction workers in high-temperature environments. The key objective of this study revolves around evaluating the effectiveness of an intelligent cooling vest in regulating body temperature, ensuring optimal comfort, and mitigating the inherent hazards of heat-related ailments. To achieve this, a user study involving 15 participants was conducted. The findings indicate positive feedback from the majority of participants, emphasizing the potential of the smart cooling vest. Additionally, participants provided valuable suggestions that can contribute to further advancements in the design and functionality of the cooling vest, making it an even more effective solution for addressing heat-related challenges in occupational settings. The study includes a comparative analysis of the results obtained from the intelligent cooling vest against established cooling methods. This analysis aims to identify distinct benefits and assess the potential for widespread implementation across various sectors.

Keywords: Smart Cooling Vest · Peltier Effect · Thermostat Integration · Occupational Heat Stress

1 Introduction

Construction workers often encounter challenging working conditions, including high temperatures and physically demanding tasks, significantly elevating their risk of heat-related illnesses [4]. Heat stress poses a serious threat to their health and productivity, potentially leading to conditions such as heat exhaustion and heat stroke if not adequately

© The Author(s), under exclusive license to Springer Nature Switzerland AG 2024
M. Kurosu and A. Hashizume (Eds.): HCII 2024, LNCS 14687, pp. 30–43, 2024.
https://doi.org/10.1007/978-3-031-60441-6_3

controlled [7, 8]. Recently, wearable technology, particularly cooling vests, has emerged as a potential solution to mitigate the adverse effects of heat stress on workers [1]. However, existing cooling vests lack built-in heat stress detection functions, requiring workers to rely on subjective symptoms or alternative monitoring techniques [2]. These vests may also prove insufficient for individuals engaged in heavy lifting or working in heated conditions due to limited cooling durations, bulkiness, and compatibility issues with personal protective equipment (PPE) [3].

An extensive analysis of current cooling vests reveals inherent limitations, such as restricted cooling durations and mobility obstacles [12]. In response, the study proposes an innovative approach based on the Peltier effect, incorporating advanced components like Peltier plates, heat sinks, DC fans, Arduino Uno control, a temperature sensor, and a solar panel into the design of a technologically advanced cooling vest. This comprehensive solution aims to provide consistent and customized cooling for construction workers during their demanding work schedules.

The research methodology employs a dynamic thermal model to analyze heat and mass transmission within the cooling vest, based on the Peltier effect. A detailed field study is underway, involving a heterogeneous group of 15 individuals from the construction industry. The study incorporates fatigue questionnaires, interviews, and live demonstrations of cooling vest prototypes to gain insights into daily routines, emotions, and the effectiveness of the proposed solution.

Anticipating positive outcomes, the study envisions the innovative cooling vest as a means to effectively regulate central body temperature. The integration of technologies like Arduino Uno, a temperature sensor, and a solar panel ensures sustainable power sources for dynamic cooling mechanisms. Positioned as a holistic solution, the proposed cooling vest addresses existing constraints, offering a forward-thinking approach to combating heat stress and related health hazards. While acknowledging potential cost implications, the study emphasizes the potential benefits of enhanced heat stress management, improved workplace safety, and increased productivity.

Recognizing the affordability challenge for workers with limited resources or smaller enterprises, the research aims to contribute to the field by detailing the design process, presenting findings, and discussing opportunities and implications for creating a smart cooling vest tailored to the needs of construction workers in the hot summer season. Ultimately, the smart cooling vest is envisioned as a tool to help construction workers work more effortlessly and efficiently.

2 Related Work

2.1 Cooling Wearables for Construction Workers

In the context of wearable cooling devices designed for construction workers, the escalating risk of heat-related illnesses during elevated summer temperatures constitutes a significant research concern [13]. Incidents of documented heat strokes and associated health issues among workers underscore the gravity of this problem. Health problems, such as heat exhaustion, heat stroke, and cramps, become more prevalent under conditions of heat stress [23]. Although minimizing heat exposure and augmenting the body's natural cooling mechanisms are imperative, the acknowledged efficacy of cooling clothing in establishing a protective microclimate is a pivotal aspect [12]. Nevertheless, challenges arise in integrating cooling garments into a work environment, considering factors such as ergonomics (weight, mobility, and convenience), safety, and thermal comfort. Given the prevalence of extreme heat in construction work, there is a compelling need for comprehensive investigations into diverse cooling strategies, including the utilization of cooling vests [11, 12]. The primary objective is to mitigate heat stress and enhance worker comfort. The treatment of heat stroke, with a focus on reducing the body's core temperature and optimizing organ system function, constitutes a critical consideration [26, 27].

Smart cooling vests incorporate various techniques, such as water cooling, phase change materials (PCM), and evaporative cooling, to extract surplus heat from the skin and improve thermal comfort [1, 7]. However, a notable drawback observed in many smart cooling vests is the absence of adjustable parameters, restricting users' ability to customize their cooling levels. This limitation compromises individuals' capacity to maintain a consistently comfortable body temperature, potentially leading to fluctuations. In light of these challenges, our current cooling vest distinguishes itself by addressing the limitations of existing technologies. One noteworthy innovation is the incorporation of adjustable parameters, enabling users to tailor the vest's temperature to their comfort. This feature aims to eliminate the risk of extreme fluctuations and, consequently, reduce the likelihood of fatigue and exhaustion due to overheating for construction workers, ultimately contributing to enhanced overall performance.

2.2 Cooling Design for Construction Workers

The escalating challenges attributed to global warming and prolonged summer seasons necessitate innovative technological interventions, and one noteworthy solution under consideration is the incorporation of Peltier plates [20, 21]. Despite its potential, the Peltier plate faces inherent limitations, notably inefficient cooling of large areas due to heat dissipation, hindering its widespread application for cooling rooms or expansive spaces. Previous research has delved into specific applications, such as eco-friendly refrigerators and portable food warmers and coolers, leveraging the Peltier effect and showcasing its efficacy in certain contexts [15–17].

In exploring alternatives to address these challenges, researchers have investigated cooling methods like smart clothing employing phase change materials (PCMs), gel, water, or ice-cooling garments, analyzing their impact on thermal comfort. Although cost-effective, PCM cooling vests exhibit limitations, including finite cooling capacity and reduced effectiveness over time [5, 9, 10]. Similarly, ice-cooling garments, advantageous for maintaining thermal comfort during surgery, confront issues related to a delayed cooling process [2, 10, 24]. Shortcomings observed in commercial paraffin cooling vests, such as limited cooling capability and the need for constant melting or recharging, underscore the imperative for advancements in cooling technology.

This research introduces a novel smart cooling vest designed to address these drawbacks through the implementation of a dynamic thermal model, eliminating the necessity for constant melting or recharging. The vest's innovative design ensures prolonged and steady cooling without compromising efficiency, positioning it as an ideal solution for individuals working in sweltering conditions. Emphasizing the shortcomings of existing cooling technologies, this study positions the smart cooling vest as a pioneering and effective alternative for enduring high temperatures and adverse weather conditions in occupational settings.

2.3 Cooling Design for Construction Workers

Heat stroke, a severe and potentially fatal condition, highlights the critical significance of precise temperature sensing for early detection [13, 19]. Identifiable indicators encompass altered awareness, a core body temperature surpassing 40 °C, and an array of physiological symptoms such as rapid pulse, heightened breathing rate, and skin alterations [25, 29]. Heat stroke poses substantial risks to the central nervous system, resulting in confusion, seizures, and dysfunction in respiratory, cardiovascular, hepatic, renal, and blood coagulation systems [14].

Despite the development of cooling vests intended to actively regulate body temperature and mitigate heat-related risks, persistent challenges hinder their efficacy in addressing heat stroke [15]. The inadequacies of current cooling technologies are evident in their inability to fully alleviate strain on physiological systems, notably the cardiovascular system [18]. Prolonged exposure to elevated temperatures and physical exertion may exacerbate this strain, adversely affecting cognitive and physical functioning [22].

While traditional treatment methods, such as immersion in cool water, have demonstrated effectiveness, their universal applicability remains uncertain [5]. Cooling vests present a potential solution by maintaining body temperature within a comfortable range, thereby reducing the risk of heat-related injuries and enhancing overall performance. However, the discussion acknowledges existing gaps in cooling vest technology, emphasizing the imperative for further advancements to comprehensively address the multifaceted challenges posed by heat stress in occupational settings.

The advocacy for improved workplace safety through the mandatory use of cooling vests aligns with broader objectives to mitigate heat-related diseases and cardiovascular issues, marking a crucial step toward enhancing worker well-being. This research underscores the importance of ongoing innovation and development in cooling vest technology to ensure its effectiveness in diverse occupational contexts and its potential to contribute significantly to overall worker health and safety.

3 Realization of Prototype

We conducted extensive research on heat stress management in the construction industry and developed an innovative cooling vest to address existing challenges. The vest aims to effectively control body temperature, enhance comfort, and reduce heat-related risks at construction sites. It incorporates advanced materials and technology, including a temperature sensor, rechargeable battery, solar panel, and Peltier fan.

Field testing ensures durability and practicality in harsh environments. The vest's key component, the temperature sensor, continuously monitors body temperature, allowing the system to adjust cooling levels using a thermostat. The rechargeable battery, coupled with a solar panel, ensures prolonged use without frequent recharging. The

Peltier fan, managed by an Arduino microcontroller, provides targeted cooling, promoting air circulation and preventing overcooling. The vest's adaptability and customization options make it versatile for various conditions. Real-time monitoring enhances user comfort and safety by dynamically responding to body temperature variations, preventing overheating. The vest's smart features, including customized cooling and real-time data collection, represent a significant advancement in worker safety and well-being in high-temperature environments.

3.1 Design Overview

In our pursuit of addressing the challenges posed by heat stress in the construction industry, we've meticulously crafted the design and implementation of our innovative smart cooling vest. The primary goal was to not only mitigate existing issues but also pioneer a highly advanced cooling solution that surpasses conventional vests in terms of efficacy and user comfort. It incorporates advanced materials and technology such as-

Lightweight and Ergonomic Design. The smart cooling vest boasts a thoughtful design, prioritizing lightweight and ergonomic considerations. This ensures that the vest is not a hindrance to the wearer, facilitating ease of movement and comfort during extended periods of use in challenging work environments.

Advanced Cooling Capabilities. To achieve superior cooling performance, we've employed revolutionary materials and technology. The heart of the cooling system lies in the implementation of a Peltier fan, leveraging the Peltier effect to efficiently transfer heat between materials. This groundbreaking fan allows for precise temperature control, effectively reducing the risks associated with heat stress.

Sustainability through Solar Power. Recognizing the need for sustainability, our design incorporates a rechargeable battery powered by a solar panel. This dual-feature not only provides a consistent power source for prolonged usage but also aligns with eco-friendly practices by harnessing renewable solar energy.

Comprehensive System Integration. Our all-inclusive system comprises essential components such as a temperature sensor, rechargeable battery, wiring adapter, relay channel, DC adapter, adjusting Peltier fan, Arduino micro-controller, thermostat, and solar panel. Each component plays a crucial role in optimizing the vest's functionality, ensuring a seamless and effective cooling experience.

Real-Time Temperature Control. At the core of our innovation is the highly sensitive temperature sensor, continuously monitoring the wearer's body temperature. This real-time data is processed by the Arduino micro-controller, acting as the central processing unit. The closed-loop control system enables precise adjustments to the cooling settings, preventing overcooling or undercooling and ensuring optimal thermal comfort.

Customization and Adaptability. The Arduino micro-controller introduces a layer of adaptability and customization, empowering users to create personalized cooling profiles. This flexibility accommodates individual preferences, environmental factors, and specific work conditions, enhancing the versatility of the smart cooling vest.

Practicality Tested in Field Conditions. To validate the practicality and durability of our design, extensive field testing has been conducted across multiple construction sites. This rigorous testing ensures that the vest is not only technologically advanced but also practical for long-term use in the demanding environments encountered by construction workers.

3.2 Design Implementation

Within the realm of mitigating heat stress within the construction industry, our research endeavors have systematically tackled existing limitations while presenting a viable solution to augment cooling vest technology. The primary aim of our investigation is to assess the effectiveness of an advanced cooling vest in regulating body temperature, ensuring user comfort, and mitigating heat-related risks within construction settings.

In pursuit of this objective, we have developed a comprehensive system that incorporates key components such as a temperature sensor, rechargeable battery, wiring adapter, relay channel, DC adapter, adjusting Peltier fan, Arduino micro-controller, and a solar panel (refer to Fig. 1 for visual representation). These integrated components synergistically optimize the functionality of the cooling vest. A pivotal component is the highly sensitive temperature sensor, continuously monitoring the wearer's body temperature, enabling precise cooling regulation to ensure comfort and prevent overheating [2].

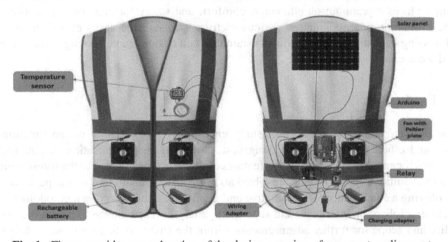

Fig. 1. Figure provides an exploration of the design overview of our smart cooling vest.

The inclusion of the well-established Peltier plate cooling technology, alongside modern components such as the Arduino Uno, temperature sensor, and solar panel, represents a pioneering approach in the domain of heat stress management (Fig. 2).

By leveraging the strengths of each component, we have not only enhanced the efficacy of the cooling system but also empowered users with real-time temperature data and prolonged usability through solar-powered recharging. This integrated innovation underscores our commitment to addressing real-world challenges with a holistic and

Fig. 2. The figure shows our smart cooling vest prototype.

user-centric solution, emphasizing sustainability through the incorporation of renewable energy sources. The thermostat embedded in the smart cooling vest offers dynamic temperature control by continuously monitoring the wearer's body temperature, effectively preventing overheating or excessive cooling. This precision and customization make our innovation a superior choice for individuals working in high-temperature environments.

The incorporation of cutting-edge components in our smart cooling vest, including a temperature sensor, rechargeable battery, Peltier fan, Arduino micro-controller, and solar panel, places a premium on efficiency, comfort, and safety for construction workers. The evaluation process employs various metrics to ensure the vest's effectiveness in addressing heat stress and providing sustainable and customizable cooling solutions in real work conditions.

4 Evaluation

The primary objectives of the user study encompass an evaluation of the functionality and efficacy of the smart cooling vest, alongside the identification of potential avenues for enhancing the design and features of the smart cooling vest in the foreseeable future. Additionally, our research involved an in-depth examination of user experiences, employing a combination of quantitative and qualitative data collection methodologies, including follow-up interviews and subsequent analysis. The aim was to assess the viability and scope for further advancements within the smart cooling vest and highlight the challenges outcome.

4.1 Participant

We visited our nearest construction site, where we encountered a total of 15 participants, all of whom were employed as construction workers and willingly took part in our user study. Each participant provided written informed consent to be part of our research.

The active involvement of these construction workers in evaluating the prototype of the smart cooling vest became a crucial foundation for advancing our research on mitigating occupational heat stress. Their invaluable insights and feedback played a pivotal role in refining and optimizing the design and functionality of the vest.

This collaborative engagement not only contributes to the development of a tailored solution for construction workers but also enriches the broader landscape of wearable technology and worker safety. The constructive feedback provided by each participant constitutes an essential component of our research findings, shedding light on the practical implications and real-world effectiveness of the smart cooling vest.

We extend our sincere gratitude to the participants for dedicating their time, offering valuable feedback, and demonstrating a commitment to the success of this innovative project. Their collective effort contributes to creating a more comfortable and safer work environment in high-temperature settings, showcasing the positive impact of this collaborative endeavor.

4.2 Procedure

To gain a comprehensive insight into the challenges faced by construction workers regarding the hot summer season in their everyday lives and to substantiate the potential utility of our smart cooling vest, our research methodology involved engaging with these individuals. To achieve a more profound comprehension of the daily struggles encountered by construction workers, we employed an exploratory-structured interview approach (Fig. 3).

Fig. 3. During the user study, users wear our smart cooling vest.

In the course of the user study, participants were provided with the cooling vest and instructed to wear it for a duration of 20 min. Subsequently, a series of structured questionnaires was administered to solicit participant observations and insights. The aim of this methodology was to systematically collect and analyze user feedback on the cooling vest's effectiveness and user experience, thereby contributing valuable data to our research investigation. Questionnaires are given below:

- How would you describe your overall experience wearing the smart cooling vest in a construction work environment?
- Can you elaborate on any specific instances where you felt the smart cooling vest positively impacted your comfort and well-being during extended periods of use?

- Were there any challenges or drawbacks you encountered while using the smart cooling vest, and if so, could you provide details on those aspects?
- In what ways do you think the smart cooling vest contributed to or hindered your productivity and performance on construction sites?
- How did the adjustable features, such as real-time temperature control and personalized settings, affect your satisfaction and usability of the smart cooling vest?

Additionally, in this research study, a comprehensive Likert-scale survey was employed as the primary data collection method to systematically ascertain quantitative information regarding parental satisfaction with their currently utilized of our smart cooling vest. This survey instrument was systematically designed to gather data on various aspects related to the performance of the smart cooling vest. The Likert-scale, with its structured response format, allowed for the systematic measurement of participants' perceptions and experiences, facilitating a detailed analysis of the vest's effectiveness. This research design aimed to provide a robust foundation for objectively evaluating the performance of the smart cooling vest through a quantitative lens.

4.3 Measurement

Quantitative Data. We carried out an extensive Likert-scale survey [30] to systematically collect numerical data regarding parental contentment with their current reminders and our groundbreaking proposed reminder application. Following this, the obtained information was transferred to a dedicated Excel spreadsheet for further scrutiny. The computations were executed using the Likert scale scoring system in accordance with the provided analysis guidelines, as detailed in reference [30].

Qualitative Data. During the user study, careful attention was given to documenting significant observations, aiming to integrate these notes into the subsequent compilation of qualitative data.

To thoroughly explore and extract insights from the responses to the questionnaire, the data from the questionnaire underwent a systematic analysis technique known as thematic analysis [31].

5 Result

5.1 Quantitative Result

An examination of the Likert scale responses was conducted to discern the prevailing sentiment among participants, yielding predominantly positive feedback. This favorable reception underscores the potential success of our smart cooling vest concept. The constructive responses garnered from the survey participants serve as a strong indication of the viability and acceptance of our proposed technology.

This optimistic feedback sets a positive tone for the progression of our project into the subsequent phases of development. Detailed quantitative user feedback, as presented in Table 1, further elucidates the specific aspects of our smart cooling vest that have resonated positively with respondents, as captured through the administered questionnaire.

Table 1. The overall average on the Likert scale for the questions in the online survey.

Question No	Online survey Questionnaire	Average Likert scale
1	How would you rate the overall comfort level of the smart cooling vest during extended periods of use in a hot environment?	4.01
2	How satisfied are you with the customization options of the smart cooling vest, such as adjustable cooling levels and personalized settings?	4.07
3	In your opinion, how effective is the vest in preventing heat-related illnesses, such as heat exhaustion or heat stroke?	4.11
4	How would you rate the durability and reliability of the smart cooling vest prototype in terms of its cooling performance over extended periods of use?	4.17
5	How satisfied are you with the real-time temperature regulation provided by the thermostat in the smart cooling vest?	4.09

The Likert scale's average percentage of user feedback, serves as a critical metric for the comprehensive analysis of overall user feedback.

This metric provides valuable insights into the collective sentiment and perceptions of the surveyed user population, facilitating a deeper understanding of the feedback's implications and significance.

5.2 Qualitative Result

In addition to the quantitative data gathered through scaled responses, qualitative insights were collected through open-ended comments from participants. The qualitative results provide a more nuanced understanding of users' experiences with the smart cooling vest prototype.

Overall Comfort Level. The majority of participants expressed a heightened sense of comfort during extended use in hot environments. Comments frequently highlighted the vest's lightweight design, improved breathability, and the absence of discomfort typically associated with traditional cooling methods. P3 stated that *"the vest was pleasantly comfortable, allowing me to move freely and making me feel better overall."*

Customization Options. Users appreciated the customization options, particularly the adjustable cooling levels and personalized settings. The ability to tailor the vest's performance to individual preferences was well-received, offering a level of adaptability not commonly found in existing cooling solutions. Participant 6 said that *"I can regulate my desired level of coolness according to the intensity of the heat, I really enjoyed having that power."*

Effectiveness in Preventing Heat-Related Illnesses. Participants generally perceived the vest as effective in preventing heat-related illnesses. The real-time temperature regulation, combined with the vest's ability to maintain a comfortable temperature range, garnered positive feedback. Users noted feeling more protected against potential health risks associated with heat exposure. P3 command that *"I felt safer wearing this vest, it kept me cool."*

Durability and Reliability. The durability and reliability of the smart cooling vest prototype received positive remarks. Users acknowledged the vest's ability to consistently deliver cooling performance over extended periods. Comments highlighted its robust construction, suggesting potential for long-term use in demanding work environments. P12 said that *"I would want to utilize this during my working hours because it held up nicely."*

Real-Time Temperature Regulation. The real-time temperature regulation provided by the thermostat was well-received. Users appreciated the continuous monitoring and adjustments, ensuring a consistently comfortable experience. The thermostat's role in preventing both overheating and excessive cooling was emphasized. Participant 15 expressed that *"I never felt too hot or too cold thanks to the thermostat, which made a substantial difference and impressive piece of technology."*

These qualitative insights complement the quantitative findings, offering a richer understanding of users' perspectives on the smart cooling vest prototype. The combination of positive scaled responses and favorable comments underscores the potential of this innovation in addressing the challenges of heat stress in the construction industry.

In our feedback collection, several participants emphasized the importance of integrating safety guidelines and educational content within the smart cooling vest system. These valuable insights underline the participants' recognition of the vest not just as a cooling solution but as a comprehensive tool for promoting user well-being and safety in high-temperature work environments. However, a subset of participants also raised concerns about potential over-reliance on the smart cooling vest. They noted that users might depend heavily on the vest features, which could pose challenges if the vest malfunctions or is temporarily unavailable. Striking a balance between providing advanced features and ensuring users maintain a level of self-reliance may present design considerations for future iterations of the smart cooling vest.

5.3 User Suggestions

Customizable Cooling Profiles. Users suggested incorporating customizable cooling profiles, allowing individuals to tailor the vest's settings based on their specific comfort preferences and work conditions.

Integration with Health Monitoring Devices. Participants highlighted the potential for integrating health monitoring devices, such as heart rate monitors, to provide additional insights into the wearer's physiological responses and enhance the vest's overall functionality.

Performance Tracking for Optimal Usage. Some users recommended a feature for tracking the vest's performance over time, providing insights into its effectiveness during various work scenarios and environmental conditions.

Emergency Assistance Integration. Participants emphasized the importance of an emergency assistance feature, allowing wearers to quickly access help or notify supervisors in case of extreme conditions or emergencies, adding an additional layer of safety to the vest.

Smart Connectivity for Seamless Operation. Suggestions were made to explore smart connectivity options, enabling the vest to integrate with other wearable devices or construction site management systems for more seamless and coordinated operation.

These user insights underscore the need for a versatile and user-centric approach in the development of smart cooling vests. The diverse requirements, from customization to safety features, emphasize the importance of creating a holistic solution that addresses the specific needs of individuals working in high-temperature environments.

6 Discussion

It becomes evident that the integration of the thermostat into the smart cooling vest represents a significant leap forward in addressing the challenges associated with occupational heat stress [26]. In our research findings positive feedback received from the majority of the construction workers underscores the potential of this innovation to enhance user comfort and safety. The real-time temperature control facilitated by the thermostat emerges as a crucial feature, allowing for precise regulation of the cooling mechanism. This dynamic capability, as observed in user experiences, plays a pivotal role in maintaining optimal body temperature, preventing both overheating and excessive cooling.

The thermostat's continuous monitoring and adjustments align with users' daily routines and provide a level of customization that has been lacking in traditional cooling vests [2, 5, 8]. However, it is essential to acknowledge the nuanced nature of user feedback. Some workers expressed concerns and provided negative feedback, emphasizing the importance of addressing specific drawbacks. These concerns primarily revolved around issues such as bulkiness, limited battery life, and challenges in adapting to the new technology. While the majority of users found the vest comfortable, these critical voices highlight areas for improvement. To address these challenges and further refine the smart cooling vest, future work should focus on enhancing the design for improved ergonomics and user adaptability.

Incorporating lightweight and durable materials, optimizing battery efficiency, and providing comprehensive user training can mitigate the identified drawbacks. In conclusion, the thermostat-enhanced smart cooling vest demonstrates substantial promise in reshaping the landscape of occupational heat stress management. The positive responses from users highlight its potential benefits, while constructive criticism points the way forward for refinement and future iterations. The ongoing pursuit of innovation in wearable technology holds the key to developing even more effective solutions for the well-being and productivity of workers facing extreme heat conditions.

7 Future Work and Conclusion

In the subsequent phase of our research, we intend to enhance the functionality and design of our smart cooling vest in accordance with valuable user feedback. This research paper introduces an innovative methodology grounded in the utilization of the Peltier effect. The proposed design integrates sophisticated components such as Peltier plates, heat sinks, DC fans, Arduino Uno control unit, a temperature sensor, and a solar panel. These elements collectively contribute to the development of a technologically advanced cooling vest.

The primary objective of this holistic solution is to furnish consistent and personalized cooling solutions tailored specifically for construction workers engaged in strenuous work schedules. Ultimately, the envisioned smart cooling vest stands as a prospective instrument aimed at facilitating enhanced ease and efficiency for construction workers in the execution of their tasks.

References

1. Inoue, D., et al.: Partial cooling of the upper body with a water-cooled vest in an environment exceeding body temperature. J. Occup. Health 65(1) (2023)
2. Byrne, J.E., et al.: Cooling vest improves surgeons' thermal comfort without affecting cognitive performance: a randomised cross-over trial. Occup. Environ. Med. 80(6), 339–345 (2023)
3. Ciuha, U., Valenčič, T., Ioannou, L.G., Mekjavic, I.B.: Efficacy of cooling vests based on different heat-extraction concepts: the HEAT-SHIELD project. J. Thermal Biol. 112 (2023)
4. Roelofsen, P., Jansen, K.: Comfort and performance improvement through the use of cooling vests for construction workers. Int. J. Cloth. Sci. Technol. 35(1), 152–161 (2023)
5. Ciuha, U., Valenčič, T., Mekjavic, I.B.: Cooling efficiency of vests with different cooling concepts over 8-hour trials. Ergonomics 64(5), 625–639 (2021)
6. Chan, A.P., Yang, Y., Song, W.F.: Evaluating the usability of a commercial cooling vest in the Hong Kong industry. Int. J. Occup. Saf. Ergon. 24(1), 73–81 (2018)
7. Hamdan, H., Ghaddar, N., Ouahrani, D., Ghali, K., Itani, M.: PCM cooling vest for improving thermal comfort in hot environments. Int. J. Therm. Sci. 102, 154–167 (2016)
8. Gao, C., Kuklane, K., Holmér, I.: Cooling vests with phase-change material packs: the effects of temperature gradient, mass, and covering area. Ergonomics53(5), 716–723 (2010)
9. Gao, C., Kuklane, K., Holmér, I.: Thermoregulatory manikins are desirable for evaluations of intelligent clothing and smart textiles. In: Proceedings of the 8th International Meeting on Thermal Manikin and Modeling (8I3M), pp. 1–5 (2010)
10. Zhao, Y., Yi, W., Chan, A.P., Wong, F.K., Yam, M.C.: Evaluating the physiological and perceptual responses to wearing a newly designed cooling vest for construction workers. Annal. Work Expos. Health 61(7), 883–901 (2017)
11. Mokhtari Yazdi, M., Sheikhzadeh, M.: Personal cooling garments: a review. J. Textile Inst. 105(12), 1231–1250 (2014)
12. Chan, A.P., Zhang, Y., Wang, F., Wong, F.F., Chan, D.: A field study of the effectiveness and practicality of a novel hybrid personal cooling vest worn during rest in the Hong Kong construction industry. J. Thermal Biol. 70, 21–27 (2017)
13. Gaudio, F.G., Grissom, C.K.: Cooling methods in heat stroke. J. Emerg. Med. 50(4), 607–616 (2016)

14. Sheridan, S.C., Lee, C.C.: Temporal trends in absolute and relative extreme temperature events across. J. Geophys. Res.: Atmos. **123**(21), 11–889 (2018). North America
15. Akram, M.N., Nirmani, H.R., Jayasundere, N.D.: A study on the thermal and electrical characteristics of the thermoelectric cooler TEC1-127 series in the 2016. In: 7th International Conference on Intelligent Systems, Modeling, and Simulation (ISMS) pp. 430–434 (2016)
16. Rokde, K., Patle, M., Kalamdar, T., Gulhane, R., Hiware, R.: Peltier-based, eco-friendly smart refrigerators for rural areas. Int. J. **7**(5) (2017)
17. Attavane, P., Arjun, G.B., Radhakrishna, R., Jadav, S.R.: Solar-powered portable food warmer and cooler based on the Peltier effect in 2017. In: The 2nd IEEE International Conference on Recent Trends in Electronics, Information, and Communication Technology (RTEICT), pp. 1975–1978 (2017)
18. Fleischer, N.L., et al.: The public health impact of heat-related illness among migrant farmworkers. Am. J. Prev. Med. **44**(3), 199–206 (2013)
19. Hifumi, T., Kondo, Y., Shimizu, K., Miyake, Y.: Heat stroke. J. Intens. Care **6**(1), 1–8 (2018)
20. O'Hara, R., Eveland, E., Fortuna, S., Reilly, P., Pohlman, R.: Current and future cooling technologies used in preventing heat illness and improving work capacity for battlefield soldiers: a review of the literature. Military Med. **173**(7), 653–657 (2008)
21. Rowlinson, S., Jia, Y.A.: Application of the predicted heat strain model in the development of localized, threshold-based heat stress management guidelines for the construction industry. Annal. Occup. Hygiene **58**(3), 326–339 (2014)
22. LaDou, J., Harrison, R. (eds.): Current Occupational and Environmental Medicine, p. 864 (2007)
23. Keim, S.M., Guisto, J.A., Sullivan, J.B.: Environmental thermal stress. Annal. Agricult. Environ. Med. **9**(1) (2002)
24. Wexler, R.K.: Evaluation and treatment of heat-related illnesses. Am. Fam. Physician **65**(11), 2307 (2002)
25. Health, Division of Standards, Development, and Technology Transfer Occupational Exposure to Hot Environments: Revised Criteria 1986 US Department of Health and Human Services, Public Health Service, Centers for Disease Control, National Institute for Occupational Safety and Health, Division of Standards Development and Technology Transfer, pp. 86–113 (1986)
26. Wendt, D., Van Loon, L.J., Marken Lichtenbelt, W.D.: Thermoregulation during exercise in the heat: strategies for maintaining health and performance. Sports Med. **37**, 669–682 (2007)
27. Parsons, K.: Human Thermal Environments: The Effects of Hot, Moderate, and Cold Environments on Human Health, Comfort, and Performance. CRC Press (2014)
28. Miller, V.S., Bates, G.P.: The thermal work limit is a simple, reliable heat index for the protection of workers in thermally stressful environments. Ann. Occup. Hyg. **51**(6), 553–561 (2007)
29. Parsons, K.C.: International standards for the assessment of the risk of thermal strain on clothed workers in hot environments. Ann. Occup. Hyg. **43**(5), 297–308 (1999)
30. Joshi, A., Kale, S., Chandel, S., Pal, D.K.: Likert scale: explored and explained. Br. J. Appl. Sci. Technol. **7**(4) (2015)
31. Herzog, C., Handke, C., Hitters, E.: Analyzing Talk and Text II: Thematic Analysis, pp. 385–401. Springer (2019)

Designing Meaning: The Construct of Sustainability in Brand Identities

Liene Jākobsone[1,2]([✉]) [iD] and Jana Ločmele[1]

[1] Art Academy of Latvia, Kalpaka bulvāris 13, Riga 1050, Latvia
[2] Institute of Contemporary Art, Design and Architecture (LMDA)
of the Art Academy of Latvia, Riga, Latvia
liene.jakobsone@lma.lv
https://lmda.lma.lv/en/

Abstract. The proliferation of environmental claims, including cases of greenwashing, has become the subject of the most recent developments in policy-making that seeks to empower consumers for EU's green transition. But how much protection can such efforts actually provide? Hypothesising the important role visuality plays in implicit communication of societal values, the aim of this on-going research is to uncover and analyse the design of layered meanings that contributes to the construction of perceived sustainability. A distinction between the conceptual and constructive properties of the notion of sustainability is made, first, by arguing a concept of sustainability which encompasses the broader socio-economic context, while the construct is presented as a product of said context: a complex narrative structure built from various semiotic resources within a dominant social paradigm. In an attempt to uncover the elements shaping the construct of sustainability, a case-study method is applied, analysing the images posted over a period of one year on Instagram accounts of Latvia's top five Greenest Brands of 2023, as established by the most recent findings of the annual Brand Capital study. The results are a series of narrative patterns observed in brand communication that are put forward for further discussion on perceived greenness.

Keywords: Sustainability · Greenwashing · Ontological design · Visual studies · Social semiotics

1 Introduction

Driven by feelings of profound confusion in the face of an abundance of green promises and an avid curiosity to explore their intricate nature in hopes of gaining deeper understanding and criticality, the aim of this research is to uncover and analyse the design of layered meanings that contribute to an arguable language or, better yet, construct of sustainability. The study hypothesises the significant role of visuality in sustainability communication and seeks to explore its semiotic and narrative prevalence in brand identities. It is situated in a context where wicked problems, first formulated in the 1970s (Rittel and Webber 1973) amidst rising climate concerns (Hardin 1968; Meadows et al. 1972), further developed in light of new environmental policy (WCED 1987; Daly 1997) and in the advent of the ontological turn in the 1990s (Buchanan 1992), and placed in the Anthropocene at the beginning of the new millennium (Crutzen and Stoermer 2000; Crutzen 2024), have arguably created similarly wicked solutions: problem-solving efforts so entangled in the complexities of our time, that their effectiveness becomes difficult to measure. One such solution is the European Union's response to greenwashing known as the Green Claims Directive (OEIL 2023). Put forward by EU's top policy makers, it acknowledges the "wealth of claims on the "green" nature of products" (EPRS 2023) and aims to protect consumers from unsubstantiated environmental claims such as "environmentally friendly," "natural," "biodegradable," "climate neutral" or "eco" (European Parliament 2023). But in an age of image-centricity and increasing visuality (Bachmann-Medick 2016; Mitchell 1995; Stöckl et al. 2020), how much consumer protection can such an attempt actually provide? As this ongoing research seeks to show, there is plenty of wickedness in our problem-solving as well.

To address the complexities brought upon by the entangled meanings that shape the notion of sustainability, this research puts forward a distinction between its conceptual and constructive properties, first, arguing a concept of sustainability, then—the construct. Sustainability as a concept is seen as the broader socio-economic context shaping this research. It is established in an overview of supranational policy-making, the ontologies of the dominant social paradigm governing and influencing environmentally conscious human (inter)action, as well as design perspectives on scenarios for future coexistence and well-being. Meanwhile, the construct is argued as a product of the concept: a complex narrative structure where the resources provided by the overarching concept, contribute to and build localised greenness. It is further analysed in the example of brand identities, focusing on the visual narratives that contribute to perceived greenness.

2   The Construct of Sustainability: A Contextual Discourse Overview

2.1   Design, Environmental Policy, and the Ontologies of the DSP

Design has always been influenced by the larger political, historical, geographical, environmental, socio-economic, and cultural contexts. In a sense, policy-making is itself a design that encompasses almost all of these factors in an action-oriented way. Although the notion of sustainability has been argued and theorised for much longer than that (Robin et al., 2013), the aforementioned key developments in environmental policy-thinking during the past half century have lead to a broader recognition of design's almost inevitable relationality with the emergent concept of sustainability, and in doing so have underscored its attitudes towards nature as well, which in a broader sense can be seen as the human-nature relationship. However, this relationship is a complex construct as, first and foremost, it exists within a dominant social paradigm or DSP which "can be seen as the presiding, unwritten set of rules and ideas that together dictate how members of that society should live their lives" (Bogert et al. 2022). As recent scholarly work shows, human-nature relationship types "identified by their respective characteristics and core values" can be organised according to a "gradient of anthropocentrism to ecocentrism," positioning the industrialised DSP—the DSP of industrialised, "often Western societies"—as an anthropocentric notion that does little to go beyond "acknowledging" and "caring for nature" (Bogert et al. 2022). In this context, "even the sustainability and green efforts of the industrialized DSP often cannot reach beyond instrumental value and economic worth," suggesting well argued limitations to environmental policies developed within the industrialised DSP.

Such fields of study as sustainable consumption research and practice also hold a view on the twofold nature of an environmentally conscious Western society. As part of a broader network of arguably anti-consumerist sociopolitical ideologies that are influencing some of the policies being put forward today, the work carried out in this academic discipline combining economics and management science (Gumbert 2019a; Gumbert 2019b; Isenhour et al. 2019; Fuchs et al. 2021; Kalfagianni et al. 2019) provides a realist socio-economic take on the issue of green consumerism in the face of the climate crisis. On the one hand, consumers are nudged to make more sustainable choices, on the other—those choices, however educated, are still mostly bound to be made within the industrialised DSP. In this sense, perspectives put forward for sustainable consumption can be seen as one of the milder approaches to the overuse of available resources: painfully aware of the ideological power of the market economy, it doesn't call for large-scale (re)design to facilitate systemic changes or shifts (Bogert et al. 2022) that often border green or techno-utopian imaginaries or, on the contrary, come into being as "watered-down governmental agreements" (Escobar 2018, 202), and instead argues focusing on policy-making efforts that challenge the system from within. Furthermore, this acknowledgment has lead scholars to examine the phenomenological and agentic properties of the (nonhuman) market economy and, by proxy, of the designed world, raising awareness of the loopy, ontological effect many environmental problem-solution policies operating within the industrialised DSP are in fact experiencing.

Arguably, the largest part of design proposals exist within the so-called industrialised DSP where their best chance at survival, as articulated by Klaus Krippendorff in some of his last reflections on the nature of design and its discourse, is "to anticipate and allow all relevant stakeholders to interpret and act upon such proposals in their own discourses" (Krippendorff 2021, 338). This observation speaks to several key aspects of designing for/from the consumer culture. For one, it affirms the necessity for design to primarily establish a relationship with its human audience or stakeholders, therefore highlighting its inherent anthropocentricity. A design that seeks to be even moderately successful in the market economy needs to be approachable and "legible": its users have to be able to discern its meaning or attribute one of their own. Such designs are for the consumer. At the same time, by "reading" a design and interpreting it according to their needs, desires and values, the user also contributes to the broader design context and discourse, inadvertently affirming that "designers can no longer claim exclusive authority over what their designed artifacts come to mean to others and how these meanings may be enacted" (Krippendorff 2021, 338). These user contributions can be seen as examples of meaning-making and as such they point to two other aspects important to this research, the social and the ontological, both of which consider how design is from the consumer or rather how any design created is already impacted by the existent designed world.

Putting these arguments into context with current developments in environmental policy-making, this research further hypothesises that the impact of such solutions can only reach part of the problem they are designed to solve. In the case of the present study, the design problem is the proliferation of unsubstantiated environmental claims often made at the expense of eco-conscious European consumers: a result of an increasing interest in consuming more responsibly and a growing demand for sustainable products and services in the first place. Its subsequent solution proposed by policymakers is EU's Green Claims Directive designed for empowering consumers to make more educated, environmentally-friendly choices (EU Council 2023; European Parliament, 2023; OEIL 2023). These efforts, however, mostly extend to claims made through the (unfounded) use of certificates and labels, as well as other mostly textual information employed in brand communication strategies, but as this research seeks to show, the various messages of sustainability that can be observed in brand identity design are much more verbally and visually implicit than the scope of current attempts made to keep them in check with EU's green transition. From a design research and practice perspective, this observation exposes the challenges and limits of designing policies for systemic change within the industrialised DSP, by hinting at a lack of futuring and transition design literacy and the ontological nature of such processes, including those aimed at protecting consumers from false greenness.

2.2 Critical Perspectives on Sustainability in Design

The shifts in environmental policy-thinking experienced by the West during the past half-century coincided with the development of new critical movements in design practice and theory as well. First articulated during the late 1960s and the 1970s in works put forward, notably, by Richard Buckminster-Fuller (1969) and Victor Papanek (1973), their critiques exhibited a new and acute awareness of the conflict between consumer culture and the Earth's finite capacities to sustain it, and paved the way for new critical perspectives that since the late 1980s and 1990s have continued to contribute to the design discourse as pathways for analysing and interpreting the human-nature relationships encoded in the designed world. These ideas on designing for a planet in crisis still play an important role in the understanding of the concept (and construct) of (un)sustainability, and much like some of the advancements in other academic disciplines like economics and governance mentioned above, they seem to be acutely aware of the ideological powers governing societal structures.

Some of the most significant developments in critical perspectives on sustainability have emerged in the field of philosophy of design, particularly in the works of Tony Fry where the concept of defuturing has been developed over the best part of the past three decades (Fry 1999; 2009; 2020). In essence, defuturing—also referred to as "future-destroying" by Arturo Escobar (Escobar 2018, 205)—sees designing as an action that carries the capacity to cancel various future scenarios, as "[in] our endeavour to sustain ourselves in the short term we collectively act in destructive ways towards the very things we and all other beings fundamentally depend upon" (Fry 2009, 22), and calls for a "[redirection] toward Sustainment" (Fry 2009, 46). In Fry's early philosophy, "Sustainment" is a term put forward in place of "sustainable development," defined by the Brundtland Report in 1987 as a process that "seeks to meet the needs and aspirations of the present without compromising the ability to meet those of the future" (WCED 1987, 40). Fry vehemently critiqued the report for seeing sustainable development as attainable only through economic and technological growth—innovation—and blind to the "incommensurate" nature of capitalism and environmentalism (Fry 2009, 44), as well as for the lack of "a conceptually sound or practically workable definition of 'sustainability'" (Fry 2009, 43). He sought out to provide a sounder one through his ideas on Sustainment, calling it "the arrival of a moment of continual material and cultural change to keep what sustains in dominance" (Fry 2009, 45), or in other words, a fundamentally paradigmatic shift in Western thinking. In this sense, the changes Fry called for surpassed even the calls for systemic shifts. Furthermore, Fry's acknowledgment of "directorial consequence of the 'thinging' (the ongoing effects and environmental impacts) of some 'thing' designed" (Fry 1999, 40), references another theoretical concept influenced by Heideggerian thought—ontological design.

Throughout his work, allusions to an ontological shift are made, wether in considerations on the nature of the role of actors for change or "redirection" (Fry 2009, 11) or when admitting that any "new philosophy of design" has to manifest through "an ontological shift that transforms how design is viewed, heard, felt, thought, understood, explained and done" (Fry 2020, 5). These are contextualisations of a concept first put forward by Terry Winograd and Fernando Flores (Winograd and Flores 1986), which has since, "with a few exceptions [. . .], remained little developed" (Escobar 2018, 202). Most notably, it has been advanced in the works of Anne-Marie Willis, who proposes to view the human-nature relationship from an ontological perspective which sees it as a "double movement—we design our world, while our world acts back on us and designs us" (Willis 2006, 80). What Willis calls ontological design (Willis 2018), speaks to the agentic nature of design: "design designs" (Willis 2006, 95). This view aims at highlighting the loopy effect design is often bound to experience, and that designing outside a DSP can be a nearly impossible task demanding levels of utmost, if even attainable criticality.

The expansion of the design discourse has also lead to a proliferation of "design thinking" advocacy, where a "design-led approach to (business) innovation has gained great popularity outside the design professions [...], precisely due to the perception of design's real or potential contribution in addressing "wicked" (intractable) problems and of design as an agent of change" (Escobar 2018, 203). Herein lies an acknowledgment of the seemingly different paths design discourse has taken over the last fifty years: on the one hand, it has developed into, what Escobar calls, a discipline of "critical design studies" (Escobar 2018, 202), and such concepts as defuturing and ontological design exemplify its theoretical aspects; on the other, it exhibits a tendency already put into context in the early 1990s (Buchanan 1992) to overuse design as an appealing way to signal a solution-prone attitude, often without harbouring any real potential to solicit substantial change. In a sense, bridging the gap between theory and practice lies the emergent concept of transition design, a transdisciplinary approach that demonstrates the capacity to acknowledge the limitations of design philosophies and paradigmatic characteristics of Western, industrialised societies by "[proposing a] design-led societal transition toward more sustainable futures" (Irwin et al. 2024, 1). Its key proponents are Terry Irwin, Gideon Kossoff and Cameron Tonkinwise who have developed a visionary framework for achieving the much sought out systemic change in hopes of addressing the "wicked" problems (Irwin et al. 2024, 1-7). In this spirit, Escobar suggests "that life-changing transitions—transitions toward entirely new ways of being-in-the-world-are possible however unthinkable they might seem in particular current situations" (Escobar 2018, 202). He continues by admitting that these transitions can occur through a "simple observation: that in designing tools (objects, structures, policies, expert systems, discourses, even narratives) we are creating ways of being" (Escobar 2018, 202), an idea that essentially puts "thinging" into the context of designs for pluriversal transitions, and a fitting summary for design theory and practice as a tool that carries the power to shape or counteract paradigms and ideologies, and the policies they influence.

3 The Construct of Sustainability: The Case of Brand Identities

3.1 Arguing the Emergence of 'Green' Communication

The Role of Visuality. This research has hypothesised the importance of visuality in communicating sustainability, and it is in large part based on theories put forward by semioticians and visual culture scholars over the past decades. Coinciding with other theoretical advancements in the humanities and social sciences during the 1990s like the developments in materialist thought and the rise of interest in ontologies, W.J.T. Mitchell announced a "pictorial turn" (Mitchell 1995), a turn that "has led to a new epistemological awareness of images in the study of culture" (Bachmann-Medick 2016, 245), and signalled a new era in iconology and the development of a new image science. Its later influence on visual studies, for example, has lead to a better understanding of the "visual construction of the social field" (Mitchell 2005, 345). What started as a response to the dominance of the linguistic turn, a "critique of knowledge and language" seeking to draw attention to the lack of "visual literacy" in Western societies (Bachmann-Medick 2016, 245), within a decade developed into "a postlinguistic, postsemiotic rediscovery of the picture as a complex interplay between visuality, apparatus, institutions, discourse, bodies and figurality" (Mitchell 1995, 16). This "visual construction of the social field" could be seen as "contextualised and connected to technologised and mediatised perceptual influences, as well as to economic and cultural power relations" (Bachmann-Medick 2016, 257), situating images as important meaning-makers in the broader cultural and socio-economic context that, through various technology and media, carry the power to create meaningful perceptions, including those of perceived brand greenness.

To this point, the role of visuality has been argued in other fields of study as well, including economics and branches of political science studying governance and policy, environmental and organization studies, as well as communication and media studies and design practice and research, all relevant to the subject of the present paper. Furthermore, this interdisciplinary interest in the power of the visual also allows to contextualise images in different social settings, including those formed by "economic and cultural power relations." For example, when considering the constituent elements of greenwashing from an economics perspective, it is argued that such action "encompasses a variety of modes of misleading communication intended to positively influence stakeholders," one of these modes being "the use of visual imagery" (Lyon and Montgomery 2015, 224–225). This has allowed for similar studies to be carried out in organization science and environmental sustainability studies, highlighting the role of imagery and visuality in corporate attempts at greenwashing (Kassinis and Panayiotou 2018). Similarly, considering contemporary design discourse, Krippendorff admits that designers have the capacity to "visually or verbally encourage stakeholders to interpret and act" (Krippendorff 2021, 338-339), putting the interactive aspect of designed artefacts once again front and centre: the "visual encouragement" attributed to any design is only a part of the meaning-making process, as it always plays out in a broader social context where it is to be read and interpreted.

Meaning-Making and Social Semiotics. The implicitness of green messages can in part be explained by the nature of sustainability communication which is an intrinsically social phenomenon itself: the values agreed upon as good for our common future, are shaped through social agreements (Godemann and Michelsen 2011, 6). As such, it does not have to be explicit to communicate said values in a specific social context. Here, the possible existence of a more implicit language of sustainability used within the Western paradigm to communicate the agreed upon need for collective action for future sustainment, can be further analysed within the framework of social semiotics where the interpersonal function of the resources used in meaning-making plays a significant role. Furthermore, a social semiotic approach is deterministic, stressing the importance of outside factors: it considers (visual) language as produced by social actors in a social context (Kress and van Leeuwen 2021, 14). The importance of both physical and social contexts is also emphasised by Krippendorff. He argues that designing "requires exploration of both, the diversity of contexts in which these [design] artifacts might find themselves" and the meaning-making power design carries in any social context as seen in "the multiplicity of interpretations that diverse stakeholders' discourse communities encourage in order to interactively create their worlds" (Krippendorff 2021, 339). In this case, these interpretations can be seen as contributions to a collectively recognisable construct of, for example, sustainability, created in interactions within the designed world. Following the formula provided by Kress and van Leeuwen further and applying it to the case of brand identities, a language of sustainability is used by designers as social actors in a social context with a growing need for communicating the sustainability of products and services in a market economy influenced by various environmental policies.

3.2   The Case of Brand Identities

Case Study Methodology. Developing the social aspect important to this research even further, our attention is focused on brand communication on social media. The method used by this research is a case study of brand identities, and it focuses on the analysis of semiotic resources and narrative elements observed in their visual communication. The scope of the research is narrowed to the images posted over a period of one year on Instagram accounts of Latvia's top five Greenest Brands of 2023 (Baltic Brand 2023). These images are arguably involved in communicating sustainability, thus having the potential to reveal the characteristics of a language that contributes to the design of meanings that construct perceived "greenness." In other words, this sample is seen as an example of an existing vocabulary that is currently used in brand identity design and, hypothetically, carries the potential to influence the emergent construct of sustainability; as such, it is of great interest to the present study.

The brands in question, ranked from first to fifth, are Latvijas valsts meži, Silvanols, Madara, Seal and Stenders accordingly (Baltic Brand 2023). In total, a sample of 1014 images was selected for analysis from all five corresponding official brand Instagram accounts: @*latvijasvalstsmezi* (Latvijas valsts meži 2023), @*silvanols.lv* (Silvanols 2023), @*madaracosmetics* (MÁDARA Organic Skincare 2023), @*sealspodriba* (Seal 2024) and @*stenderscosmetics* (STENDERS 2023). Four different sectors of industry are represented by these brands: Latvijas valsts meži (LVM), translated as Latvian State Forests, is a state-owned joint stock forestry company which manages the forest lands of Latvia's State; Silvanols is a pharmaceutical company; Seal is "is the largest manufacturer of household chemicals, body care, plant fertilisers and disinfection agents in Latvia" (Seal); and Madara and Stenders are both cosmetics companies.

These rankings are part of a broader market research methodology developed by Brand Capital and carried out annually for almost 20 years. It is the largest "brand and lifestyle study" in the region, gathering data on more than 600 brands through more than 300 survey questions (Baltic Brand 2023). Through their research, Brand Capital seeks to determine consumer attitudes in all the Baltic countries, Estonia, Latvia and Lithuania, in five value attribution categories: the rankings include data on the Most Loved, Greenest, Most Humane, Most Searched and Bravest brands across all three Baltic countries. The latest rankings based on data collected by the market research company Norstat through online surveys of "more than 3028 economically active citizens of the Baltic states aged from 15 to 74 during June and July 2023," were revealed during the Baltic Brand Forum held on 22 September 2023 in Tallinn, Estonia, marking 19 consecutive years of Brand Capital research in the region (Baltic Brand 2023).

The geographical limitations of the Brand Capital study allow to situate the present case study in a specific cultural and socio-economic context. Although part of the European Union and largely adherent to Western paradigms, the countries share a complex relationship with East/West attributes, highlighted by the urge to often self-identify with constructs like Northeastern or North-Eastern Europe that convey the dualism of paradigmatic contexts experienced by the countries over the last century. This situational context is important to the social semiotic arguments advanced in this study, but it can also be seen as a meaningful contribution to the broader design discourse. Drawing on the importance of localised design fictions in "fostering appreciation for diverse worldviews and a pluriversal imagination," this case study too speaks to the significance "diversity in knowledge, worldviews and perception in various geographical regions" can bring to problem-solving and criticality in design (Jākobsone 2023). Although mostly "locally inspired" and at least partly determined by local aspects of cultural, historical, socio-economic, political and even geographical contexts unique to the region, this perspective allows to view the present case study of Latvia's greenest brands as at the same time limited and limitless. On the one hand, it speaks to the context of a particular region, but on the other, it is precisely this specificity that carries the potential to contribute to the design discourse in ways that only local stories can. Furthermore, insights from the peripheries of dominant paradigms might provide ways for breaking out of the loops of green thinking, green politics, green consumerism and ultimate unsustainability.

So far, some of the limitations of the scope of this research discussed include the modality in focus—images posted on brand Instagram accounts—, some of its quantitative features and aspects pertinent to the locality of this study. Other narrowing factors are target audience reach, the chronological limits and the degree to which each brand has quantitatively contributed to the sample put forward for further analysis. It has to be acknowledged that brand communication on Instagram is curated for a relatively niche audience and does not in any way provide an all-encompassing view of the brands' verbal and visual identities and overall communication strategy. It does, however, constitute a highly image-centric and socially interactive example in content used for connecting with at least segments of their audiences. The degree of importance of Instagram presence in these strategies also varies from brand to brand. This can be observed in the total amount of images posted by each brand over the period of one year, from 1 October 2022 to 30 September 2023, roughly the period of time between the announcement of one years' brand ranking to the next. Latvijas valsts meži had posted 265 images from a total of 170 posts, Silvanols had 67 out of 42, Madara had the strongest Instagram presence with a total of 411 images from a record 237 entries, Seal counted 113 from 49, and Stenders—158 images from 152 posts during the time period in question.

Arguing how the case study methodology is relevant to the aim of this paper—uncovering narrative designs that contribute to the emergent construct of sustainability—, it seems important to clarify that this research does not aim to explore or discuss how sustainable these brands actually are, nor does it aim to expose possible greenwashing: such is the interest of the Green Claims Directive. The goal here is not to investigate if Latvia's top greenest brands meet the "minimum requirements on the substantiation and communication of voluntary environmental claims and environmental labelling" (EPRS 2023) envisioned for protecting consumers from greenwashing in the EU and empowering them for the green transition. Instead, the focus here is on an analysis or, better yet, a close reading of the corpus of images through a (social) semiotic perspective, which allows for interpreting social media content as deliberately constructed imagery (rather than a record of reality) that follows some kind of a grammar of the visual (Kress and van Leeuwen 2021). Moreover, the attribution of greenness through a consumer survey is argued here as a case of mirrored socio-economic values available for further research into the visuality and semiotic properties of the sustainability construct, and the images posted on brand Instagram accounts—a case for exploring the constituent elements that contribute to the emergent construct of sustainability. Linguistic metaphors used by social semioticians Kress and van Leeuwen are then developed further with particular interest in narrative patterns that can be observed in the sample of images selected for this case study. However implicit or explicit the messages of sustainability encoded in the imagery, the deterministic social semiotic approach provides means for viewing this content as an example of visual language produced by several social actors in a complex social context, and to use it for further analysis in hopes of deepening the understanding of arguable sustainability communication and its semiotic and narrative prevalence in brand identities.

Perceived Brand Greenness: Narrative Patterns of Sustainability. As previously argued, the social semiotic nature of content posted on brand Instagram accounts allows for further interpretation of these images as narrative elements in an attempt to determine what are the patterns that contribute to the design and (social) construct of sustainability. By analogy to the anthropocentrism-ecocentrism relationship gradient put forward by scholars (Bogert et al. 2022), the images in the sample have been interpreted according to a human-nature divide or scale, and in the context of this paper, several narrative patterns constructing sustainability through extensions of the human-nature relationship have been put forward for further analysis.

Human and Nature. These images range from depictions of seemingly undisrupted, humanless landscapes depicting various habitats, including forests and meadows—core imagery for Latvijas valsts meži or Latvian State Forests and Madara, whose brand name is Latvian for *Galium album* or white bedstraw, a common flowering plant found in meadows—, as well as riverbeds, lakes, even reeds, and the seaside, to more complex juxtapositions where some footprint of human presence can be observed. Then the range expands from images introducing man-made elements into the landscape without the actual depiction of a human figure to portrait photography in nature. Some design artefacts introduced are, for example, a woven basket full of foraged mushrooms lying in the moss, or a wooden staircase on a trail in a natural park; maybe it's an empty dirt road that leads through a forest covered in serene winter snow, but soon enough a silhouette of someone carrying a sleigh appears, and in another image a hand picks up the basket; another hand is shown draping a rainbow flag over a meadow full of cow parsley, and two palms hold up the cherry tomato harvest. Then the nature trails and empty landscapes become full of satisfied visitors, foraging and frolicking, relaxed and happy to have "successfully left behind" (Lürzer's Archive, 2011) their problems in forests, meadows and shores alike, sometimes even venturing into the city and distantly gazing at the urban landscape.

Product and Nature. Developing the human presence even further, another important story shaping the strong narrative of a healthy human-nature relationship is that of product and nature. Here, the product becomes the central design artefact, in various juxtapositions with elements from the natural environment. This broadly represented category includes an array of examples in various composition techniques, both in visible studio settings, as well as on set designs staged *en plein air*. A background of freshly picked garden cucumbers with a bottle of fertiliser or the staging of a new "eco line" of household chemicals sitting on a piece of bright green astroturf in a white studio; fragile flowers and twigs wrapped around a bottle of toilet cleaner or face cream packaging, a bottle of C vitamin concentrate sitting proudly on an overgrown chanterelle mushroom in the middle of the forest, a jar of supplements enrobed in illustrations of plants or set against a backdrop of lingering shadows of flowers and leaves on pastel green or blue backgrounds; bath bombs in pastel neons placed on seashore-like sand with bits of dried algae and barely visible fragments of seashells, or soothing moisturisers for stressed and irritated skin sitting on a block of pink-hued marble. These images, for one, signal the impact design can have on nature to bend it to arguably human priorities; at the same time, the gardening motif also alludes to generally positive attitudes linked to home gardening, and the persistent view that home-grown and, by extension, local is better, cleaner, ecological and organic and therefore, on most occasions, also wrongfully synonymous with official logos used to label organically grown produce from certified farms. Here, the visual representations of traditions of growing produce at home are used as a storytelling tool that helps advance the brand's relationship with another aspect of nature, the cultivated kind. Another strategy is putting natural ingredients and the power of nature front and centre, signalling the human capacity to capture it along the way; and in some cases elements of the natural environment serve as an exaggeration of the product-nature relationship: a bath bomb could dissolve if the sea washed over it, the pink marble stone, polished and smooth, mimics the texture of a redness-prone skin that no longer flakes.

Product/Service and Human. This final narrative category returns to the use of the human image in a highly anthropogenic way: here, for the most part, end users are depicted in various settings using the products or services offered by the five brands in question. In many cases, this means a more implicit allusion to, for example, the product through a close-up of the human face and traces of the product (or in rare examples, of other organic matter like pollen or drops of water), seen as examples of the importance of textural qualities depicted through images, but also as markers of the "natural" in natural beauty. For cosmetics, this signifies the concept of nude in skincare and make-up. However, most images are almost exclusively anthropogenic —with the exception of Latvijas valsts meži where nature is the service—, depicting not only products in use by their human audiences, but also in the context of man-made environments, like studio sets or interiors of bathrooms, family rooms or cabins. Furthermore, elements of the natural environment are introduced rarely and scarcely, while in some cases they appear at least partly substituted by the introduction of the aforementioned textures.

4   Conclusion

The case-study exploration of the imagery used in brand communication through the use of a human-nature relationship perspective has allowed to identify three main categories of narrative patterns in the construction of perceived brand greenness: images that depict human and nature, those that focus on product and nature, and visual representations of product/service and human. These categories, much like value systems analysed in the anthropocentrism-ecocentrism gradient (Bogert et al., 2022), employ visual resources depicting or evoking nature on different scales, some representing seemingly unscathed landscapes where the only marker of human presence is the digital photography itself, others creating almost exclusively anthropogenic scenes where the direct allusion to the natural environment, in these examples shown from an anthropocentric perspective, as well as at times further stereotyped or romanticised for its derived societal values (Bogert et al., 2022), is the product itself. However, in most cases, the narrative interplay between these three distinct categories of storytelling allows for an overall balanced, if not slightly nature-dense visual Instagram presence.

To the point of the contextual and structural elements that are forming the notion of sustainability, the social context of a given environment seems to influence the construct, and therefore it is arguably more localised than the concept.

This can be observed through imagery depicting local natural resources and nature iconography, as well as evoking traditions like foraging or other social practices, rituals and festive events characteristic of the target audience. The images reveal themselves as designed to interact with users in ways that facilitate desired legibility in the given, mostly local context: while still allowing audience interpretations (Krippendorff 2021, 338) and often without direct signalling to an environmentally friendly agenda or discourse, through the employment of various narrative patterns brands are able to establish and communicate the importance of the nature-human relationship in their brand identity. Whereas in regard to the concept, it is important to note the transdisciplinarity observed and required to holistically approach the "wicked" problems of the 21st century put in perspective by theoretical and practical advancements in economics, governance and policy, environmental, organisation, communication and media studies, as well as design. In the case of the present study, the intersection of these disciplines has allowed this research to reveal that even the greenest of brands are operating within the industrialised DSP—a difficult cycle to break as seen from an ontological design perspective—, signalling that there are few signs of systemic changes and shifts that so many voices in academia and policy-making have been calling for the best part of the past half century.

Furthermore, the results of this ongoing research show that, even though the brands are perceived as environmentally friendly (perceived greenness), the images used by even the greenest brands often do not employ explicit signs of greenness, targeted by current policies put forward to facilitate EU's green transition such as the consumer protection efforts in the form of the newly formulated Green Claims Directive (EU Council 2023; European Parliament, 2023; OEIL 2023). This discovery not only affirms the significance of broader, overarching constructs in visual communication and meaning-making governed by the prevalence of the industrialised DSP (Bogert et al., 2022), but also leads us to regard the language and construct of sustainability as phenomena in an active process of formation: designers construct brand identities through verbal and visual means of expression, adding a layer of meanings for the consumer market to interpret. Consumers, in turn, learn to read text and imagery used by green brands as signs of sustainability, thus assigning new meanings to them and furthering the entangled nature of sustainability communication and revealing the ontological nature of our designed world.

Disclosure of Interests. The authors have no competing interests to declare that are relevant to the content of this article.

References

Bachmann-Medick, D.: Cultural Turns: New Orientations in the Study of Culture. De Gruyter, Boston (2016)
Baltic Brand: Baltic Brands 2023. https://balticbrands.eu/en/. Website. Accessed 8 Oct 2023

Bogert, J.M., et al.: Reviewing the relationship between neoliberal societies and nature: implications of the industrialized dominant social paradigm for a sustainable future. Ecology Soc. **27**(2) (2022)

Buchanan, R.: Wicked problems in design thinking. Design Issues **8**(2) (1992)

Council of the EU: Council and Parliament reach provisional agreement to empower consumers for the green transition. https://www.consilium.europa.eu/en/press/press-releases/2023/09/19/council-and-parliament-reach-provisional-agreement-to-empower-consumers-for-the-green-transition/. Press release. Accessed 8 Oct 2023

Crutzen, P.J.: Geology of mankind. Nature **415**(23) (2002)

Crutzen, P.J., Stoermer, E.F.: The "Anthropocene". Global Change Newsletter (41) (2000)

Daly, H.E.: Beyond Growth: The Economics of Sustainable Development. Beacon Press, Boston (1997)

Escobar, A.: Stirring the anthropological imagination: ontological design in spaces of transition. In: Clarke, A.J. (ed.) Design Anthropology: Object Cultures in Transition. Bloomsbury Academic, London (2018)

European Parliament: Parliament backs new rules for sustainable, durable products and no greenwashing (2023). https://www.europarl.europa.eu/news/en/press-room/20230505IPR85011/parliament-backs-new-rules-for-sustainable-durable-products-and-no-greenwashing/. Press release. Accessed 8 Oct 2023

European Parliament Legislative Observatory (OEIL): Substantiation and communication of explicit environmental claims (Green Claims Directive) (2023). https://oeil.secure.europarl.europa.eu/oeil/popups/summary.do?id=1738310&t=e&l=en. Legislative proposal. Accessed 8 Oct 2023

European Parliamentary Research Service (EPRS): "Green claims" directive (2023). https://www.europarl.europa.eu/RegData/etudes/BRIE/2023/753958/EPRS_BRI(2023)753958_EN.pdf. Briefing. Accessed 6 Nov 2023

Fry, T.: A New Design Philosophy: An Introduction to Defuturing. University of New South Wales Press, Sidney (1999)

Fry, T.: Design Futuring: Sustainability. Ethics and New Practice. Berg, Oxford (2009)

Fry, T.: Defuturing: A New Design Philosophy. Bloomsbury Publishing, London (2020)

Fuchs, D., et al.: Consumption Corridors. Routledge, London (2021)

Fuller, R.B.: Operating Manual for Spaceship Earth. Southern Illinois University Press, Carbondale (1969)

Godemann, J., Michelsen, G.: Sustainability Communication - An Introduction. In: Godemann, J., Michelsen, G. (eds.) Sustainability Communication. Springer, Dordrecht (2011)

Gumbert, T.: Freedom, autonomy, and sustainable behaviours: the politics of designing consumer choice. In: Isenhour, C., et al. (eds.) Power and Politics in Sustainable Consumption Research and Practice. Routledge, New York (2019)

Gumbert, T.: Materiality and nonhuman agency. In: Kalfagianni, A., et al. (eds.) Routledge Handbook of Global Sustainability Governance. Routledge, New York (2019)

Hardin, G.: The tragedy of the commons. Science **162**(3859) (1968)

Irwin, T., et al.: Transition design 2015. https://design.cmu.edu/sites/default/files/Transition_Design_Monograph_final.pdf. Monograph. Accessed 25 Jan 2024

Isenhour, C., et al. (eds.): Power and Politics in Sustainable Consumption Research and Practice. Routledge, Abington, New York (2019)

Jäkobsone, L.: Design fiction localised. In: Vaes, K., Verlinden, J.C. (eds.) Connectivity and Creativity in Times of Conflict. Academia Press, Ghent (2023)

Kalfagianni, A., et al. (eds.): Routledge Handbook of Global Sustainability Governance. Routledge, New York (2019)

Kassinis, G., Panayiotou, A.: Visuality as greenwashing: the case of BP and deepwater horizon. Organiz. Environ. **31**(1) (2018)

Kress, G., van Leeuwen, T.: Reading Images: The Grammar of Visual Design, 3rd edn. Routledge, New York (2021)

Krippendorff, K.: Design Discourse. In: Schwer, T., Vöckler, K. (eds.) Der Offenbacher Ansatz: Zur Theorie der Produktsprache. transcript Verlag, Bielefeld (2021)

Latvijas valsts meži: Instagram timeline posts (1 Oct 2022 - 30 Sept 2023). https://www.instagram.com/latvijasvalstsmezi/. Accessed 6 Oct 2023

Lyon, T.P., Montgomery, A.W.: The means and end of greenwash. Organiz. Environ. **28**(2) (2015)

Lürzer's Archive: "Latvian State Forests, !MOOZ, Riga." Tourism campaign for the Latvian State Forests (2011). https://www.luerzersarchive.com/work/?search=mooz&media_type=print. Accessed 31 Jan 2024

Meadows, D.H., et al.: The Limits to Growth: A Report for the Club of Rome's Project on the Predicament of Mankind. Universe Books, New York (1972)

Mitchell, W.J.T.: The Pictorial Turn. In: Picture Theory: Essays on Verbal and Visual Representation. The University of Chicago Press, Chicago (1995)

Mitchell, W.J.T.: What Do Pictures Want? The Lives and Loves of Images. The University of Chicago Press, Chicago (2005)

MÁDARA Organic Skincare: Instagram timeline posts (1 Oct 2022 - 30 Sept 2023). https://www.instagram.com/madaracosmetics/. Accessed 6 Oct 2023

Papanek, V.: Design for the Real World: Human Ecology and Social Change. Bantam Books, Toronto (1973)

Rittel, H.W.J., Webber, M.M.: Dilemmas in a general theory of planning. Policy Sci. **4**(2) (1973)

Robin, L., et al. (eds.): The Future of Nature: Documents of Global Change. Yale University Press, New Haven (2013)

Seal: About us. https://www.seal.lv/en/about-us. Website (2024). Accessed 26 Jan 2024

Seal: Instagram timeline posts (1 Oct 2022 - 30 Sept 2023). https://www.instagram.com/seal_spodriba/. Accessed 6 Oct 2023

Silvanols: Instagram timeline posts (1 Oct 2022 - 30 Sept 2023). https://www.instagram.com/silvanols.lv/. Accessed 6 Oct 2023

STENDERS: Instagram timeline posts (1 Oct 2022 - 30 Sept 2023). https://www.instagram.com/stenderscosmetics/. Accessed 6 Oct 2023

Stöckl, H., et al.: Shifts towards image-centricity in contemporary multimodal practices: an introduction. In: Stöckl, H., et al. (eds.) Shifts towards Image-Centricity in Contemporary Multimodal Practices. Routledge, New York (2020)

Willis, A.M.: Ontological Design, Criticality and What Comes After Design? https://vimeo.com/277288664. Video lecture (2018). Accessed 8 Oct 2023

Willis, A.M.: Ontological designing. Design Philosophy Papers **4**(2) (2006)

Winograd, T., Flores, F.: Understanding Computers and Cognition: A New Foundation for Design. Addison-Wesley Publishing Company, Reading (1986)

World Commission on Environment and Development (WCED): Our Common Future. Oxford University Press, New York (1987)

Generative AI for Sustainable Design: A Case Study in Design Education Practices

Meng Li[1](✉) iD, Yaning Li[2,7] iD, Chenyang He[2,7] iD, Houxiang Wang[2,7] iD,
Jiaqian Zhong[1] iD, Shengxin Jiang[2,7] iD, Mingtao He[2,7] iD, Zhining Qiao[2,7] iD,
Jiawang Chen[2,7] iD, Yuan Yin[3] iD, Ray Lc[4] iD, Ji Han[5] iD, Zengyao Yang[1],
and Mohammad Shidujaman[6] iD

[1] School of Mechanical Engineering, Xi'an Jiaotong University, Xianning Road 28,
710049 Xi'an, People's Republic of China
limeng.81@mail.xjtu.edu.cn
[2] Joint School of Design and Innovation, Xi'an Jiaotong University, Xianning Road 28,
710049 Xi'an, People's Republic of China
[3] Dyson School of Design Engineering, Imperial College London, London SW7 2AZ, UK
[4] School of Creative Media, City University of Hong Kong, Level 7,
18 Tat Hong Avenue, Hong Kong SAR, People's Republic of China
[5] Business School, University of Exeter, Exeter EX4 4QJ, UK
[6] RIoT Research CenterDepartment of Computer Science and Engineering,
Independent University Bangladesh (IUB), 16 Aftab Uddin Ahmed Road, Dhaka 1229,
Bangladesh
[7] XJTU-POLIMI Joint School of Design and Innovation, Politecnico di Milano,
Piazza Leonardo da Vinci, 32-20133 Milan, Italy

Abstract. The Sustainable Development Goals are currently the universal missions for all fields of engineering and design. However, many design problems in sustainable development are profoundly complex and nearly reach the limits of human capacity. This design challenge often involves a vast volume of data in social, economic, technological, and environmental factors. In response to this challenge, industrial and academic communities have devoted a large amount of effort in developing new technologies like artificial intelligence and applying them as new design tools. Generative AI is the latest advancement among these tools which can empower human designers with its capability to process massive data from diverse sources and recast them in a comprehensible form.

Despite the heated discussion on the relationship between creative innovation and frontier technologies, little attention was focused on empowering the next generation of designers with the new skills in the AI era. This study hence conducted a two-week design workshop to explore the interactions between generative AI tools and novice designers.

Keywords: Generative AI · Design Thinking · Sustainable Development Goals · Design Education

© The Author(s), under exclusive license to Springer Nature Switzerland AG 2024
M. Kurosu and A. Hashizume (Eds.): HCII 2024, LNCS 14687, pp. 59–78, 2024.
https://doi.org/10.1007/978-3-031-60441-6_5

1 Introduction

Design for a sustainable future is a universal goal of the design communities worldwide in the next decades. Many designers and design organizations have devoted their effort in promoting design for sustainability. However, the process of generating a sustainable design often entangles with complex social, economical, and technological factors. Moreover, designers need to envision a systematic solution instead of a single of product or service to tackle the problems with sustainability. A bottleneck in this design challenge is collecting and comprehending a vast amount of data efficiently and accurately, as well as exploring diverse concepts and solutions in fast iterations to create the final design. Many problems that designers and engineers are dealing with are very, very complex and beginning to reach the limits of human capacity, as stated by the vice president of research at Autodesk [1]. To address the challenges in design for sustainability, many researchers and designers put efforts into exploring emerging technologies like artificial intelligence (AI) as design tools in different design fields [2].

Generative AI (GAI) is the latest development among emerging technologies, which is able to empower humans by performing very complex problems and recasting them [1]. Despite the long-lasting discussion about the integration of artistic creation and frontier technologies, there was little attention on cultivating the next generation of designers with AI skills until recently [3]. Under the fast-pacing advancement of AI technologies, understanding how future designers can interact with the generative AI to augment their design abilities is of paramount importance. Thus, the aim of this study is to explore the interactions between generative AI tools and novice designers in developing sustainable product-service systems.

2 Related Work

2.1 Generative AI Can Play a Multi-faceted Role in Design for Sustainability

Sustainable Development Goals (SDGs) proposed by the United Nations in 2015 represent the general challenges that the design community need to handle to create a sustainable future for human society in the next decades [4]. The SDGs cover seventeen topics from eradication of poverty to clean water, below-water lives, and affordable clean energy, which often involve complex social, economic, and technological issues. Design for the SDGs thus is bound with collecting, analyzing and understanding a large amount of information then coming up with innovative solutions. Studies also demonstrated the art and technology cross-disciplinary approaches helps students manifest the abstract notions of sustainability [31].

Artificial intelligence can process massive ecological culture and other data, to extract effective information, so that designers can enhance design value and functional significance. Machines can replace a large number of tedious and inefficient "manual labor" repetitive work, which can effectively shorten the design cycle, greatly improve work efficiency, save human, physical and financial resources, and release the creativity of designers. This new human-machine adaptation relationship is the most effective driving force for improving the efficiency of sustainable design [5].

By using more efficient algorithms and model structures, generative AI can reduce the need for large amounts of computing resources, thereby improving sustainability. As efforts towards AI for sustainability are growing rapidly, the concept sustainable AI is emerging, indicating the changes in the entire lifecycle of AI products for promoting social value and environmentally friendly architecture [6].

2.2 Design Thinking with AI

In the 1960s and 1970s, the relevant theoretical research on artificial intelligence and interactive art began, and many new art concepts have been proposed, such as "artificial life art", "network art", and "natural intelligence" [7]. For the first time, the artists and designers interact their works and arts with the forefront of scientific research and emerging technologies. It discussed a deep relationship between artistic creations and frontier technologies, such as artificial intelligence and robotics, and then led to new possibilities of creations in the design fields. It profoundly predicts that during the new era of AI explosion, human intelligence will merge deeply with machine intelligence, greatly enriching the human brain with faster, more accurate, larger storage and more efficient, precise data sharing capabilities.

Digital design has provided a vision of future design expression since the 1980s, raising questions about human-machine-environment interaction, artificial intelligence and social behaviorism through the analysis of artists' digital artworks [8]. In 2015, digital design expanded the practice into the fields of virtual reality, augmented reality, and interactive public installations. Ever since, artificial and technological systems have been merging and impacting future intelligence on innovative creation.

Compared with traditional design thinking, the new design thinking supported by artificial intelligence will grant designers great convenience when they want to create unique things with high efficiency. French artist Kimbell proposed that designers who focus on specific conventions find themselves rethinking design in a useful way, and new design thinking with AI support can achieve it [9]. Through summarizing the conventions AI provides, designers can better understand the target feature, design process and produce many innovative designs and ideas, which have the characteristics of visualization and creativity.

Design combined with AI can generate a vast amount of visual content with incredible speed and creativity, providing artists, designers, and creators with unprecedented inspiration and materials [10]. Design thinking supported by AI can stimulate creativity, enhance idea generation and optimize design results. This new way of thinking has opened up many unexpected innovations and opportunities. Designers can easily produce a variety of visual representations, whether images, videos or entire works of art. With the support of AI, design thinking can also solve practical problems for specific populations by coming up with meaningful ideas. It can help people of all professional backgrounds to solve problems with novel solutions [11]. At the same time, it can help us to define the problem, stimulate our inspiration and creativity, and promote our thinking. It can also help us to test the design output and iterate the design thinking. In short, with the help of AI, the whole design thinking has been greatly improved.

2.3 Generative AI as Design Tools

The large language models (LLMs) are the first wave of Generative AI (GAI), also known as AI-generated content (AIGC). By the end of 2023, the commercially available LLMs have evolved to 1800B data volumes [12]. AI chatbots, like ChatGPT, can help with multiplied and difficult tasks, and results can be published faster, freeing academics up to focus on new innovative designs. This could significantly accelerate innovation and potentially lead to breakthroughs across many disciplines. Such a large language model has enormous potential in many creative fields. For the design fields with generative AI tools, it is of great significance to know how to use the technology judiciously for specific research practices and extraction of large information.

The text-to-image generative AI models are the second frontiers in AIGC which has evolved over a quite long period with many representative works. AlignDRAW is a pioneering work that generates images from natural languages, but suffers from unrealistic results [13]. After that, Text-conditional Generative Adversarial Network (GAN) is the first end-to-end differential architecture from the character level to pixel level [14]. Typical GAN-based methods are mainly in the small-scale data regime [15–17], while autoregressive methods exploit large-scale data for text-to-image generation [18–21]. Representative autoregressive methods include DALL·E from OpenAl and Parti from Google [18, 21]. However, the autoregressive nature makes these methods suffer from high computation costs and sequential error accumulation.

More recently, there has been an emerging trend of diffusion models (DM) as the new state-of-the-art model in text-to-image generation. Diffusion-based text-to-image synthesis has attracted massive attention and already come out in the market in 2022, such as Midjourney (MJ). Like Imagen and Latent Diffusion models (LDM), these generative models have reached a new level in text-to-image generation [22]. A mainstream LDM model is Stable Diffusion (SD), generating images based on text prompts. With this AI tool, images can be generated with the prompts that have never appeared in the previous training, demonstrating the high generalization ability of the diffusion model. In general, the application of GAI can greatly promote innovation and development in the design field, like improving design efficiency and quality, and enabling designers to better cope with complex design challenges [23].

With AI technology, design processes need to be re-balanced with new skills under this AIGC era. On the one hand, AI could optimize academic training - for example, by providing feedback to improve designers' creative and innovative skills. On the other hand, it might reduce the need for certain skills, such as the ability to perform a literature search or the ability to make fine sketching. In the meantime, it might introduce new skills, such as prompt engineering (the process of designing and crafting the text that is used to prompt AI chatbots), or applying the re-tuning adaption like Low-Rank Adaptation (LoRA) [24]. The loss of certain skills might not necessarily be problematic, instead understanding how the next generation of designers will develop new competencies of interacting with GAI tools for sustainable design becomes of critical significance. This study therefore aims to explore the research question:

"How generative AI tools can assist novice designers in a design thinking process for sustainability?"

It includes four sub-questions (SQs) as shown below:

- **SQ1:** What is the usability of GAI chatbots in discovering design problems regarding the SDGs?
- **SQ2:** What is the usability of GAI image tools in defining concepts for a sustainable design?
- **SQ3:** What is the usability of GAI image tools in developing sustainable product-service systems?
- **SQ4:** What is the usability of GAI image tools in delivering the final design of these systems?

3 Methodology

3.1 Participants

To answer the research question and sub-questions, a study involving 34 students (11 females, between ages 17 and 20, Mean (M) = 18.36, Standard Deviation (SD) = 0.924; 23 males, between ages 18 and 22, M = 18.61, SD = 0.973) was conducted. The participants were recruited from Xi'an Jiaotong University and were divided into 12 teams. Among all the teams, 10 teams contained 3 students, while 2 teams only had 2 members. In terms of the knowledge background, 23 participants majored in Industrial Design, 8 of them majored in Architecture, and 3 participants from other engineering majors such as Energy and Dynamics. All participants voluntarily joined the workshop and provided informed consent. As most participants were first- and second-year students with little experience in design practices, therefore they are considered novice designers.

3.2 Procedure

The study was conducted in a three-week GAI-aided design workshop in Xi'an Jiaotong University from November to December 2023. The workshop was divided into four sessions and conceived following the Double Diamond Model [25] to investigate how GAI tools can assist novice designers' design thinking process in a design task for sustainability. The design of the workshop follows the Human-AI Co-Creation Model developed by Wu's team [34].

In this study, the researchers selected three typical GAI tools - ChatGPT (based on GPT3.5), Midjourney (chatbot via Discord), and Stable Diffusion (via WebUI) with LoRA considering both their advanced functionalities and prevalence among the design community [2]. The combination of these tools composes a basic production pipeline of generative design with a high freedom of content manipulation [1]. This study also developed a protocol via the miro[1] online collaborative board, which guided the teams throughout the workshop. After each session, the participants needed to fill in a designated questionnaire about their attitudes towards the interactions with the GAI tools. The procedures of the workshop are shown in Fig. 1 and introduced in detail as follows.

Session 1. At the beginning of session 1 (15 min), a pre-record introduction demonstrated to the participants how to interact with ChatGPT. In the second part (15 min), the participants were guided to create an initial overview of the SDGs and then each team

---

[1] https://miro.com/app/board/uXjVNKkikiM=/.

Session 1 (60 mins)	Session 2 (120 mins)	Session 3 (180 mins)	Session 4 (180 mins)
Discover SDGs and Select a topic	Define the topic and brainstorming	Develop a concept	Deliver the detailed design
ChatGPT	ChatGPT, MJ	ChatGPT, SD	MJ, SD
Video Demo	Tutorial	Tutorial	Tutorial
SDG selection	Sample image	Concept generation	Redraw the concept
Keywords generation	Mood board generation	3 design iterations	Detailed design generation
Questionnaire I	Questionnaire II	Questionnaire III	Questionnaire IV

Fig. 1. The Workshop procedure on the miro online white board

filtered out a sub-topic of SDGs via the dialogues with ChatGPT. In the last part (30 min), the participants were asked to explore their major intersects with the chosen topic to further their design inspiration, and then generate keywords related to the selected topic.

Session 2. In the first part of session 2 (15 min), the participants were taught to use ChatGPT to translate the selected sustainable topic and its corresponding keywords into the prompts that can be recognized by Midjourney (MJ). The second part (15 min) first demonstrated the interface and interaction of the Midjourney then allowed a free hands-on for each team to create a sample image with their prompts. In the third part (90 min), each team created a mood board via Midjourney. The teams utilized ChatGPT and Midjourney to generate and select 16 images systematically which satisfyingly represented the selected topic, keywords, and their personal preferences. This stage serves as a catalyst for brainstorming to provide a means for the control and optimization of subsequent design concepts.

Session 3. In the first part of session 3 (30 min), a tutorial on Stable Diffusion (SD) was provided to the team to help them get familiar with the WebUI interface and various parameters, including but not limited to affirmative keywords, negative keywords, iteration steps, model selection, and sampling techniques. The second part (30 min) allowed the teams to operate SD to generate their sample concept with modified prompts. The last part (120 min) encouraged the teams to modify the prompts to manipulate their design precisely and then generate two or three most satisfied conceptual images as the initial visualization of the design.

Session 4. At the beginning of the last session (30 min), the team were taught to acquire the advanced techniques of fine adaptation (e.g., LoRA model) and localized redrawing with Stable Diffusion (SD). In the second part (30 min), the teams were asked to redraw their concepts with LoRA models and manipulate the relevant control parameters by combining the existing prompts. In the last part (120 min), the researchers introduced resources like websites and forums where the teams can find different fine-tuned SD models and LoRA models and encouraged them to employ the redrawing approach on their concepts to progressively advance towards a final design with details.

3.3 Measurements

To measure and investigate the perceived usability of GAI tools, four questionnaires were designed according to the four sessions. They all shared a similar structure: the questionnaires start with the participant's familiarity with each GAI tool, then move to a self-developed 5-point Likert scale regarding the usability when interacting with the tool, and end up with open question(s) to reflect the general evaluation [35].

Questionnaire I: ChatGPT-Aided Discovery. Questionnaire I focused on the usability of ChatGPT and was delivered after session 1. Among the 17 questions of this questionnaire, the first and last ones were open questions about the selected SDG and the most useful keywords provided by ChatGPT. Q2-Q16 were on a 5-point Likert scale regarding the accuracy, richness, and readability of ChatGPT, as well as its capacity to get satisfying outcomes. On this scale, 1 refers to "Strongly disagree" and 5 refers to "Strongly agree". The detailed information is listed in Table 1.

Table 1. The sample questions about the usability of ChatGPT-aided design phases.

Items	Question
Q4	The information provided by ChatGPT is strongly related to the topic I chose
Q5	The ChatGPT produces a relatively rich content
Q7	The text generated by ChatGPT is clearly, smoothly and easy to understand
Q8	In order to get a satisfactory answer to a question, my team and I went through many iterations of prompt words
Q9	The prompt word has a great impact on the quality of the ChatGPT generation results
Q10	My team and I could get satisfactory results by modifying the prompt words
Q11	I trust the information given by ChatGPT
Q12	The information generated by ChatGPT meets the needs of me and the team
Q13	My team and I were able to apply the content generated by ChatGPT to the team cooperation to support the goals of the task
Q14	The information generated by ChatGPT provides a new perspective or thinking direction for me and my team
Q15	The information generated by ChatGPT limits the thinking and decisions of me and the team
Q16	ChatGPT has played an integral role in this mission

Questionnaire II: Midjourney-Aided Brainstorming in Developing. Questionnaire II focused on the usability of Midjourney to generate a mood board as the inspiration for the concepts and was delivered after session 2. Like Questionnaire I, it ended also with an open question about the general experience of using Midjourney. Among its 18 questions, Q1-Q17 were designed according to 5-point Likert scale, focusing on the accuracy of prompt-image pairing, the relevance with the design topic, the alignment of expected styles, and the controllability of the outcomes alike. The detailed information of Questionnaire II is listed in Table 2.

Table 2. The sample questions list about the usability of Midjourney-aided design phases.

Items	Questions
Q3	I had a positive attitude towards Midjourney performance before starting the Midjourney practice
Q4	The pictures generated by Midjourney are matched with the keywords
Q5	The pictures generated by Midjourney are strongly related with the design theme
Q6	The content and concept of the pictures generated by Midjourney met my expectations
Q7	The pictures created by Midjourney were generated in style as I expected
Q8	The pictures generated by Midjourney are rich enough
Q9	For me, the task of generating satisfactory pictures with Midjourney is difficult
Q10	In order to obtain satisfactory pictures, my team and I carried out several iterations such as prompt words and parameters
Q11	My team and I were able to get satisfactory pictures by modifying the parameters and prompt words
Q12	I think the process of Midjourney and text diagram is controllable
Q13	I think the process of Midjourney text drawing is not clear and transparent enough
Q14	The mood board generated by Midjourney can accurately reflect design concepts and emotions
Q15	The mood board that combines pictures generated by Midjourney is a great way to inspire and direct our design
Q16	I think Midjourney has exceeded my expectations
Q17	Overall, I think Midjourney has made an outstanding contribution to the completion of the mood board

Questionnaire III: Stable Diffusion-Aided Product-Service Design in Developing. Questionnaire III focused on the usability of Stable Diffusion (SD) in creating the initial design of a sustainable product-service system and was delivered after session 3. It included 20 questions and 18 of them utilized the same 5-point Likert scale, like the questionnaire I and II. It focused on the creative flexibility, image styles, and image-concept alignment of SD, then ended with two open questions about the problems and difficulties, as well as the general experience of using SD. The detailed information is listed in Table 3.

Table 3. The sample questions list about the usability of Stable Diffusion (SD)-aided product-service system design.

Items	Questions
Q3	I was positive about SD performance before starting the SD practice
Q4	I think the pictures generated by SD matches the corresponding keywords
Q5	I think the pictures generated by SD can accurately reflect the SDGs
Q6	I think the pictures generated by SD are consistent with the design concept
Q7	I think the content and concept of the pictures generated by SD are creative
Q8	I think the conceptual design of SD generation is feasible
Q9	SD generated pictures in a style that I and my team expected
Q10	SD improves my degree of freedom to generate pictures
Q11	The rich choice of parameters of SD puzzles me
Q12	My team and I were able to generate satisfactory pictures by adjusting the parameters of the SD
Q13	I can try to compare the prompt words and parameters to the corresponding picture effect
Q14	I think the process of SD text diagram is controllable
Q15	I think the process of using text to generate picture of SD is not clear and transparent enough
Q16	I think the SD has exceeded my expectations
Q17	The product pictures obtained with SD agree with the team and I on the design concept
Q18	The pictures generated by SD can bring new inspiration to me and the idea of the product

Questionnaire IV: Stable Diffusion-Aided Design Finalization in Delivering. Questionnaire IV focused on the usability of SD to refine the product-service design to generate the final version and was delivered after session 4. 17 of the 18 questions in this questionnaire were 5-Likert scale, regarding the regulation of image consistency, learnability, control, and the alignment of aesthetic preferences. Like the Questionnaire III, it ended also with an open question about the further experience about interacting with SD. The detailed information is listed in Table 4.

Table 4. The sample questions list about the usability of Stable Diffusion (SD)-aided final design delivery.

Items	Question
Q2	The redrawn picture generated by SD can correspond to the corresponding prompt words
Q3	The redrawn picture generated by SD shows the precision of the design concept in detail
Q4	The redrawn pictures generated by SD are consistent in content and concept
Q5	The redrawn pictures generated by SD remained consistent in style
Q6	SD repainted the aesthetic and expectations of me and my team
Q7	The process of redrawing of SD is controllable
Q8	The operation of controlling SD local redrawing is simple and easy to learn
Q9	The process of redrawing of SD is not clear and transparent enough
Q10	My team and I can flexibly adjust the content of the picture
Q11	My team and I were able to adjust the style and atmosphere of the pictures flexibly
Q12	The redrawing of SD has a high degree of freedom
Q13	The freedom of redrawing of SD meets the needs of my team and me to create personalized pictures
Q14	Redrawn pictures generated by SD are unique and creative
Q15	Redrawing of SD provides many possibilities for me and my team to conceive of product pictures
Q16	Redrawing of SD meets my vision and requirements for pictures of product
Q17	Redrawing of SD meets my expectations for it to achieve functionality and effects

4 Results

The participants rated the usability of AIGC according to the interactions during the workshop, and these activities were assessed using the above-mentioned questionnaires. These scales assessed the efficiency of the GAI tools in facilitating design learning and demonstrated the impact of different interaction elements on design outcomes throughout the four stages in a design thinking process (Fig. 2).

4.1 SQ1 Usability of ChatGPT in Discovery and Definition

According to Questionnaire I (Fig. 3), the participants recognized the indispensable role of ChatGPT during the Discover and Definition phases and strongly agreed on the general usability of this tool ($M = 4.16$, $SD = 0.801$). There is a unanimous agreement in acknowledging the significant impact of prompts ($M = 4.16$, $SD = 0.801$), as well as the capacity to get pleasing outcomes through modification ($M = 4.38$, $SD = 0.554$). A strong association ($p < 0.05$, Pearson) exists between the accuracy, richness, and

Fig. 2. The AIGC-aided design activities involved in the workshop. a) discover SDGs and select a topic then generate keywords with ChatGPT; b) generate a sample image then define mood board via Midjourney; c) develop a concept of a sustainable product-service system and iterate it via Stable Diffusion; d) deliver detailed design of the system via Stable Diffusion.

readability of the information generated by ChatGPT and its capacity to provide new perspectives and directions regarding the need fulfillment. The strongest significant connections among these factors are richness (r = 0.708, p < 0.01), inspiration (r = 0.696, p < 0.01), and readability (r = 0.626, p < 0.01). Moreover, there exists a notable correlation (r = 0.380, p < 0.05) between the proficiency in using ChatGPT and fine prompts modification.

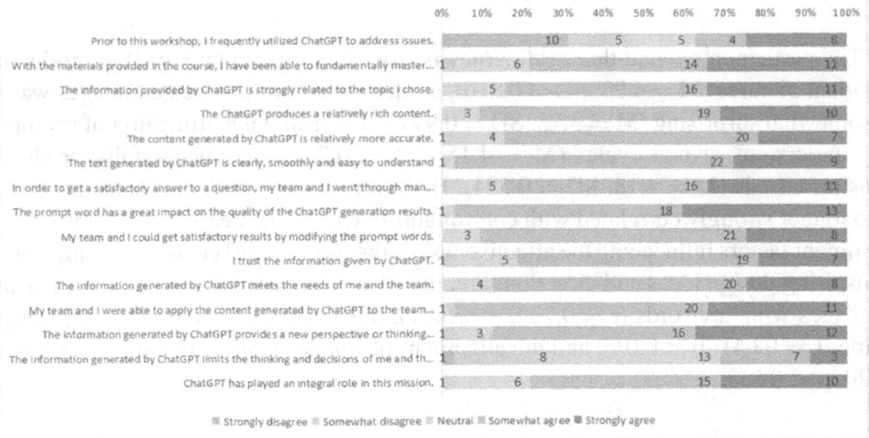

Fig. 3. Participant's attitudes toward the usability of ChatGPT in the Discovery phases.

4.2 SQ2 Usability of Midjourney in Developing Conceptual Designs

Figure 2 shows the participants perceived that Midjourney had a beneficial impact on the brainstorming activities by making the mood board for conceptualization (M = 4.18, SD = 0.727).

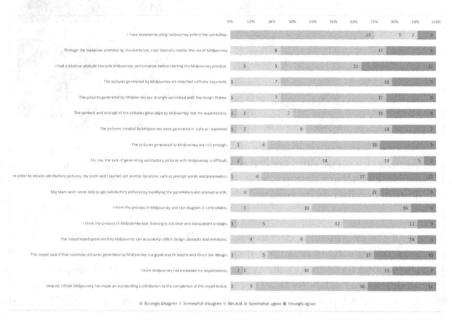

Fig. 4. Participant's attitudes toward the usability of Midjourney in developing conceptual designs.

The participants found that Midjourney performed exceptionally well in producing abundant pictures (M = 4.03, SD = 0.810), while the style of the created images was to be somewhat surprising (M = 3.73, SD = 0.977). Regarding the utilization of prompts, they underwent several cycles (M = 4.15, SD = 0.755) and successfully produced pleasing visuals (M = 4.18, SD = 0.584). However, the knowledge of basic processes is no longer strongly correlated with controllability (p > 0.05, Pearson). The three most prominent factors influencing the effectiveness of the mood board created by Midjourney in inspiring design ideas and directions are, in order of importance, the accurate pairing of images with keywords (r = 0.720, p < 0.01), the strong correlation with the design theme (r = 0.641, p < 0.01), and the alignment of image styles with expectations (r = 0.620, p < 0.01).

4.3 SQ3 Usability of Stable Diffusion in Developing Sustainable Product-Service Systems

Figure 3 indicates that the participants experienced a significant increase in design inspirations through Stable Diffusion (M = 4.13, SD = 0.554). They also recognized the substantial level of creative flexibility in generating images due to the abundance of parameters (M = 3.97, SD = 0.782). The assessment of the produced images reveals that the image style is comparatively less satisfactory (M = 3.41, SD = 1.012). The three most strongly correlated factors with the statement "Product image matches the concept" are: the image accurately reflects the theme (r = 0.751, p < 0.01), the image style adheres to expectations (r = 0.643, p < 0.01), and the image aligns with key words (r = 0.635, p < 0.01) (Fig. 5).

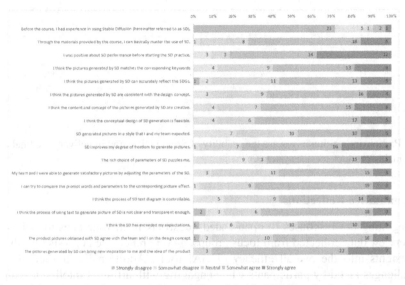

Fig. 5. Participant's attitudes toward the usability of Stable Diffusion in developing sustainable product service systems.

4.4 SQ4 Usability of Stable Diffusion in Delivering the Final Design of a Sustainable Systems

When it came to improving concepts by redrawing (Fig. 4), Stable Diffusion showed comparatively lower effectiveness in terms of being able to regulate and maintain consistency (M = 3.59, SD = 1.103). Participants found redraw operations relatively difficult to learn (M = 3.34, SD = 1.208) and control (M = 3.41, SD = 1.012). There is a strong link between successfully mastering redraw operations and achieving the conceptual and demand-related criteria for product images (r = 0.47, p < 0.01). Furthermore, the three most strongly associated aspects with achieving the criteria for product photographs in terms of idea and demand are the ability to easily modify the image style (r = 0.815, p < 0.01), satisfying creative requirements by offering greater flexibility (r = 0.736, p < 0.01), and ensuring the image aligns with aesthetic preferences (r = 0.725, p < 0.01) (Fig. 6).

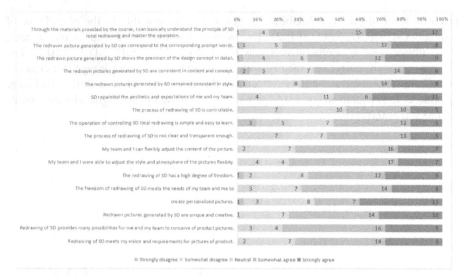

Fig. 6. Participant's attitudes toward the usability of Stable Diffusion in delivery the final design of sustainable product service systems.

4.5 Qualitative Reflections

By integrating the responses to open-ended questions from four questionnaires with the interview data collected from focus groups, a comprehensive analysis reveals valuable insights into the overall efficacy of GAI tools. Additionally, it sheds light on the challenges faced by participants while engaging with artificial intelligence and the corresponding solutions.

AIGC Tasks Performance. When evaluating GAI-aided design tasks, the text-based information offered by ChatGPT in human-AI dialogue to format text-to-image prompts was rated highly effective. It demonstrates the capacity of GAI to handle substantial amounts of information and possesses a notable level of semantic comprehension. Image generation activities benefit from the efficiency advantage, since they can produce a significant quantity of images that depict basic concepts, thereby reducing the need for manual sketching. During the whole design process, AIGC tools demonstrate exceptional efficiency in managing data and producing content.

ChatGPT Prompt Strategy. The researchers collected the prompts that the students thought were most helpful. Certain prompts, such as "atmospheric" and "landscape", were phrases relating to specific fields, like "SDGs", "sustainable agriculture scenarios", and "environmentally friendly design"; while others directly addressed the themes or concepts related to the topics. Some, such as "Create a visual narrative showcasing the development of wind farms" or "Design an infographic highlighting the utilization of biomass" explained certain tasks or needs. Students also brought up a few technical requirements, such as "VR", "underwater adventure game", "recyclable and degradable", and so forth. Some concentrated on certain design characteristics, such as "community art," "minimalist design," and so on.

Differences Between Midjourney and Stable Diffusion. The images produced by Stable Diffusion exhibit substantial deviations from the anticipated results, as indicated on 8 occasions. Participants attribute this issue to inadequate training and inappropriate selection of large model types. Its performance was sub-optimal when it came to editing concept images and adjusting details, since it lacked the ability to properly comprehend human thoughts, thus falling short of manual alterations. Midjourney demonstrated proficiency in producing artistic creations, however it lacked adaptability, encountering difficulties in maintaining control and frequently yielding conventional compositions.

Challenges in Text-Image Generation. The participants discovered that AI-generated creativity in image generation is more geared towards merged thoughts, as opposed to people's autonomous mental processes. The process of fine-tuning and enhancing semantic comprehension poses major challenges. In addition, there is a perceived lack of flexibility and control when mapping prompt words. The key problem is the lack of a clear relationship between cues and visuals, as well as an insufficient level of logical consistency and refinement in the images produced. Resolving the issue needs repeated testing for much time, professional coaching, and select groups using other AIGC tools as supplemental resources.

User Expectation. Participants are of the opinion that the AIGC tool has the potential to improve internal support and tutorials, hence reducing the amount of time spent searching for external resources. Several recommendations were made to enhance Stable Diffusion. These suggestions encompassed incorporating design styles and models, expanding the range of possibilities for precise adjustment and modification, and improving comprehension of the relationship between natural language and instructions. These points were repeatedly highlighted as areas for development.

5   Discussion

Generative AI has made headlines with intriguing tools like ChatGPT or DALL·E, suggesting a new era of AI is coming [18, 26]. These tools have found utility in diverse creative tasks, like education, gaming, media, advertising, film, music, painting, programming, mobile software, and functionality [18]. Similar to the observation in this study, the versatility and effectiveness of Generative AI tools have made them increasingly prevalent and indispensable in various aspects of design ability [36]. The following sections will discuss the utilities of AIGC tools in the four design stages.

5.1   Generative AI in Discovery

The Role of Generative AI in Discovering New Insights. The utilization of ChatGPT, along with other natural language processing (NLP) tools like Ernie Bot, holds significant promise in facilitating substantial advancements in comprehension of complex topics, like climate change dynamics and sustainable development [27]. The formidable capacity of ChatGPT in exploring and analyzing board information about the topic, generating comprehensive design scenarios, and evaluating the efficacy of concepts presents an opportunity for designers and developers [28]. Leveraging these technologies can provide crucial insights into the potential design opportunities in a specific SDG. By employing AI-driven methodologies, novice designers can make informed decisions and develop robust strategies to adapt to the sustainability, like with the climate change issues [29].

The Impact on Research and Innovation. Generative AI accelerates the discovery process by automating the analysis of large data sets and generating hypotheses at a pace far beyond human capability. This acceleration is particularly crucial in fields like genomics and astrophysics, where the volume of data is vast and complex. AI's ability to analyze data with precision leads to more accurate and efficient research outcomes. It reduces human error and biases, providing a more objective basis for discoveries and innovations.

The Challenges and Suggestions in AI-driven Discovery. The challenges in AI-driven discovery include missing latest data, the risk of generating inaccurate or biased results, and the need for substantial computational resources. Addressing these challenges involves implementing stringent data security measures, developing algorithms that can identify and correct biases, and investing in advanced computational infrastructure.

5.2 Generative AI in Defining

AI's Contribution to Conceptualization and Planning. Generative AI plays a pivotal role in the ideation phase of projects. It assists in generating a diverse array of ideas and concepts, far beyond the conventional human brainstorming process. For instance, Midjourney can generate inspiring solutions, combining ideas and trends that might be difficult to envision in detail in the human mind. Moreover, AI tools are capable of refining these ideas by simulating scenarios and predicting outcomes, leading to more informed decision-making.

AI's ability to process and analyze large volumes of data expedites the decision-making process. It provides data-driven insights that can validate or challenge the initial hypotheses or ideas. This aspect of AI is particularly beneficial in complex projects where multiple variables and potential outcomes must be considered. AI models can present various scenarios and their potential impacts, aiding stakeholders in making more informed choices.

Customization and Personalization the Idea Generation. Generative AI is instrumental in developing customized solutions. By analyzing user data and preferences, AI algorithms can create highly personalized products or services. This approach not only enhances user experience but also boosts the efficiency and effectiveness of the solution.

Various case studies across industries like healthcare, marketing, and product design illustrate the power of generative AI in customization. For example, in healthcare, AI systems design personalized treatment plans for patients based on their unique genetic makeup and medical history. In marketing, AI tools analyze consumer behavior to tailor advertising campaigns.

Overcoming Limitations in Defining Phase with AIGC. Generative AI addresses several limitations traditionally faced in the defining phase of projects. For instance, human bias and a limited perspective can often skew the defining phase. AI, with its expansive data processing capabilities, offers a more objective and comprehensive app-roach. Additionally, AI can identify potential risks and challenges early in the project lifecycle, allowing for proactive measures to be taken.

5.3   Generative AI in Development

AI in the Design and Prototyping Phases. Generative AI simplifies the design pro-cess by providing advanced tools capable of automatically generating multiple design solutions. Similar to ChatGPT, which utilizes extensive datasets to propose optimized designs based on specific parameters such as durability, aesthetics, or cost-effectiveness. This approach not only enhances creativity but also reduces the time and resources typ-ically required in the design phase. In terms of transformation in the realm of generative art, Stable Diffusion enhances user accuracy in prompt composition by offering a set of predefined prompts. Providing users with a filtering approach rather than a creative one increases the efficiency of the design process.

The integration of AI in the prototyping and testing stages has fundamentally trans-formed traditional approaches. Stable Diffusion can simulate various design scenarios based on user requests, predicting performance and functionality for different demo-graphics under different conditions, and identifying potential flaws. AI models like Midjourney and Stable Diffusion, which belong to the realm of generative art, enable the instant generation of simulated images for different scenarios. This allows users to intuitively experience the performance in various environments. This capability makes rapid prototyping feasible, enabling developers to iterate and refine designs quickly and efficiently.

Efficiency and Productivity Improvements. GAI not only automate operations, but also automates learning, which is the core of innovation [30]. Generative AI introduces automation and optimization into the development process. It can automate routine tasks such as code generation and testing, allowing developers to focus on more complex and creative aspects. Furthermore, AI's optimization techniques ensure higher qual-ity and more efficient outputs. For instance, fine-tuning models like Stable Diffusion with extensive data can optimize the quality and accuracy of images in the realm of conceptualization.

One of the most significant impacts of generative AI is the reduction in time-to-market for new products and services. By accelerating developing and prototyping phases, AI enables faster design iterations. This speed is crucial in industries where rapid innovation and quick response to market trends are vital for success.

Addressing Developmental Challenges with AI Solutions. Generative AI addresses various challenges faced during the development phase. It can handle complex data anal-ysis, predict market trends, and provide insights for strategic decisions. AI's predictive capabilities are particularly useful in identifying potential issues and mitigating risks before they become critical, ensuring smoother development processes. Designers view GAI tools as mediators between insufficiency and precision, particularly in early stages of a design project [32].

5.4 Generative AI in Delivery

Enhancing Product and Service Delivery. AI enables the personalization of customer experiences at an unprecedented scale. By analyzing customer data, AI can tailor recommendations, offers, and services to individual preferences. This personalization not only increases customer satisfaction but also fosters a deeper engagement with the brand.

AI's Role in Post-Launch Activities. After the launch of a product or service, generative AI plays a crucial role in monitoring performance and analyzing customer feedback. AI tools can sift through large volumes of data to glean insights on customer satisfaction, usage patterns, and potential areas for improvement.

AI facilitates continuous improvement and upgrades of products and services. By constantly analyzing performance data and customer feedback, AI can identify areas for enhancement and guide the development of new systems. This ongoing cycle ensures that products and services remain relevant and competitive.

Future Trends and Opportunities in AI-Enhanced Delivery. The future of AI in delivery is marked by significant trends and opportunities. AI is expected to become more autonomous, making decisions, and taking actions with minimal human intervention. The integration of AI with other emerging technologies like the Internet of Things and block chain will further enhance delivery processes. Additionally, AI's role in sustainability will gain prominence, influencing how products and services are delivered.

6 Conclusion

Novice designers were highly motivated to learn the emerging technologies (like GAI) as design tools and incorporate them into their design works for sustainability, as reveal by a similar study on soft robotics [33]. By chatting with GAI bots like ChatGPT, the novice designers were empowered to collect, analyze, and aggregate vast amounts of information with very high efficiency. By analyzing a number of cases provided by text-to-image models like Midjourney, the novice designers can gain abundant inspiration with little effort. By precisely manipulating the parameters of Diffusion models like Stable Diffusion, the novice designers can optimize their concepts with fine details, such as optimizing the building appearance, structure or material visualization, or optimizing the appearance and structural strengths. Furthermore, GAI might also be helpful in understanding user behavior and preferences, thereby improving the interactive interface and experience of product-service systems. This study contributes to the growing literature on AI in design and sustainable design, which delivers useful insights into future research and development of GAI tools for design.

Nevertheless, the controllability and learnability of GAI tools are the main thresholds along with the privacy, copyright, bias, and ethical issues that calls for further studies to make GAI an indispensable tool in design thinking processes.

Disclosure of Interests. The authors have no competing interests to declare that are relevant to the content of this article.

References

1. MIT Technology Review Insights. Sustainability Starts in the Design Process, and AI Can Help. Accessed 23 Jan 2024
2. Shi, Y., Gao, T., Jiao, X., Cao, N.: Understanding design collaboration between designers and artificial intelligence: a systematic literature review. Proc. ACM Hum.-Comput. Interact. 7(CSCW2), 368 (2023). https://doi.org/10.1145/3610217
3. Collaborative Creativity in AI. Nat. Mach. Intell. 4, 733 (2022). https://doi.org/10.1038/s42 256-022-00539-8
4. United Nation. https://sdgs.un.org/goals. Accessed 23 Jan 2024
5. Gao, Y.: Research on the sustainable design ascending path driven by Artificial Intelligence 2.0. Packag. Eng. 2, 200–210 (2022). https://doi.org/10.19554/j.cnki.1001-3563.2022.02.026
6. van Wynsberghe, A.: Sustainable AI: AI for sustainability and the sustainability of AI. AI Ethics 1, 213–218 (2021). https://doi.org/10.1007/s43681-021-00043-6
7. McDonough, S., Colucci, E.: People of immigrant and refugee background sharing experiences of mental health recovery: reflections and recommendations on using digital storytelling. Vis. Commun. 20(1), 134–156 (2021)
8. Shen, Y., Yu, F.: The influence of artificial intelligence on art design in the digital age. Sci. Program. 2021, 1–10 (2021). https://doi.org/10.1155/2021/4838957
9. Kimbell, L.: Rethinking design thinking: part II. Des. Cult. 4(2), 129–148 (2012). https://doi.org/10.2752/175470812X13281948975413
10. Zirou, Z.: Taking MidJourney as an example to explore the significance of artificial intelligence (AI) design application in the process of design thinking. Pearl River Transp. 15, 109–111 (2023)
11. Fuping, D.: On the deepening of design thinking by phenomenological methods and its inspiration to design education. Indust. Eng. Design 2(3), 14 (2020)
12. van Dis, E.A.M., Bollen, J., Zuidema, W., van Rooij, R., Bockting, C.L.: ChatGPT: five priorities for research. Nature 614(7947), 224–226 (2023). https://doi.org/10.1038/d41586-023-00288-7
13. Mansimov, E., Parisotto, E., Ba, J.L., Salakhutdinov, R.: Generating images from captions with attention. ICLR 1 (2016)
14. Reed, S., Akata, Z., Yan, X., Logeswaran, L., Schiele, B., Lee, H.: Generative adversarial text to image synthesis. In: International Conference on Machine Learning, pp. 1060–1069, vol. 1. PMLR (2016)
15. Zhang, H., et al.: Stackgan: text to photo-realistic image synthesis with stacked generative adversarial networks. In: Proceedings of the IEEE International Conference on Computer Vision, vol. 1, pp. 5907–5915 (2017)
16. Xu, T., et al.: Attngan: fine-grained text to image generation with attentional generative adversarial networks. Proc. IEEE Conf. Comput. Vis. Pattern Recognit. 1(6), 1316–1324 (2018)
17. Li, B., Qi, X., Lukasiewicz, T., Torr, P.: Controllable textto-image generation. Adv. Neural. Inf. Process. Syst. 32, 1 (2019)
18. Ramesh, A., et al.: Zero-shot text-to-image generation. In: Proceedings of the 38th International Conference on Machine Learning, pp. 8821–8831. PMLR (2021)
19. Ding, M., et al.: Cogview: mastering text-toimage generation via transformers. Adv. Neural. Inf. Process. Syst. 34, 19822–19835, 1, 6 (2021)
20. Wu, C., et al.: Nuwa: visual synthesis pre-training for neural visual world creation. In European Conference on Computer Vision, pp. 720–736. Springer, Cham (2022). https://doi.org/10.1007/978-3-031-19787-1_41

21. Yu, J., et al.: Scaling autoregressive models for content-rich text-to-image generation. arXiv preprint 1, 6, 7 arXiv:2206.10789 (2022)
22. Saharia, C., et al.: Photorealistic text-to-image diffusion models with deep language understanding. arXiv preprint arXiv:2205.11487 (2022)
23. Chen, L., Sun, L., Han, J.: A comparison study of human and machine-generated creativity. ASME. J. Comput. Inf. Sci. Eng. 23(5), 051012 (2023). https://doi.org/10.1115/1.4062232
24. Hu, E.J., et al.: LoRA: Low-Rank Adaptation of Large Language Models. arXiv preprint arXiv:2106.09685 (2021)
25. Design Council. Eleven Lessons: Managing Design in Eleven Global Companies-Desk Research Report. Design Council (2007)
26. Zhang, C., Zhang, C., Zhang, M., Kweon, I.S.: Text-to-Image Diffusion Models in Generative AI: A Survey (2023). https://doi.org/10.48550/arXiv.2303.07909
27. Kadow, C., Hall, D.M., Ulbrich, U.: Artificial intelligence reconstructs missing climate information. Nat. Geosci. 13, 408–413 (2020). https://doi.org/10.1038/s41561-020-0582-5
28. Lc, R., Tang, Y.Y.: Speculative design with generative AI: applying stable diffusion and Chat-GPT to imagine climate change futures. In: Proceedings of the 11th International Conference on Digital and Interactive Arts (ARTECH 2023), Faro, 28–30 November 2023. ACM, New York (2023)
29. Biswas, S.S.: Potential use of Chat GPT in global warming. Ann. Biomed. Eng. 51, 1126–1127 (2023). https://doi.org/10.1007/s10439-023-03171-8
30. Verganti, R., Vendraminelli, L., Iansiti, M.: Design in the Age of Artificial Intelligence. Harvard Business School, Working Paper, No. 20-091 (2020)
31. Horvath, A.-S., Löchtefeld, M., Heinrich, F., Bemman, B.: STEAM matters for sustainability: 10 years of art and technology student research on sustainability through problem-based learning. J. Prob. Based Learn. High. Educ. 11(2), 1–33 (2023)
32. Pouliou, P., Horvath, A.-S., Palamas, G.: Speculative hybrids: investigating the generation of conceptual architectural forms through the use of 3D generative adversarial networks. Int. J. Archit. Comput. 21(2), 315–336 (2023)
33. Horvath, A.S., Jochum, E., Löchtefeld, M., Vissonova, K., Merritt, T.: Soft robotics workshops: supporting experiential learning about design, movement, and sustainability. In: Dunstan, B.J., Koh, J.T.K.V., Turnbull Tillman, D., Brown, S.A. (eds.) Cultural Robotics: Social Robots and Their Emergent Cultural Ecologies. Springer Series on Cultural Computing. Springer, Cham (2023)
34. Wu, Z., Ji, D., Yu, K., Zeng, X., Wu, D., Shidujaman, M.: AI creativity and the human-AI co-creation model. In: Kurosu, M. (eds.) Human-Computer Interaction. Theory, Methods and Tools. HCII 2021. LNCS, vol. 12762. Springer, Cham (2021)
35. Song, X., Liu, M., Gong, L., Gu, Y., Shidujaman, M.: A review of human-computer interface evaluation research based on evaluation process elements. In: Kurosu, M., Hashizume, A. (eds.) Human-Computer Interaction. HCII 2023. LNCS, vol. 14011. Springer, Cham (2023)
36. Wang, J., Weng, Y., Shidujaman, M., Ahmed, S.U.: A multilevel perspective for social innovation: three exemplary case studies in collaborative communities toward sustainability. In: Kurosu, M., Hashizume, A. (eds.) Human-Computer Interaction. HCII 2023. LNCS, vol. 14014. Springer, Cham (2023)

Environmental Multisensory HCI Design Strategies: Molecules as Storytellers

Paula Neves[1,2]([✉]) [iD]

[1] IADE, Faculty of Design, Technology and Communication, European University of Lisbon,
Av. D. Carlos I, 4, 1200-649 Lisbon, Portugal
paula.neves@universidadeeuropeia.pt
[2] UNIDCOM/IADE, Research Unit in Design and Communication, Av. D. Carlos I, 4,
1200-649 Lisbon, Portugal

Abstract. Human health and well-being are intertwined with environmental health. Through breathing and ingestion, humans and the natural environment share molecules and atoms. Thereby, emerging environmental health problems impact human health, while human actions impact environmental conditions. These interdependencies are difficult to evidence because it permeates the understanding of complexity, multidimensionality and multi-perspective about environmental health problems. However, these are the challenges that designers embrace, in the context of today's global warming events, to explore possibilities for technology and human-environment communication strategies, to raise environmental health literacy. In a previous study, we ideated and investigated a multisensory HCI design strategy with smell and taste. Targeting non-scientific audiences, we explored how chemical sense perceptions could represent environmental problems within digital forms and how these could be applied to communicate interdependencies of environmental health themes, with mixed reality media. The results of our study validated our design strategy and mission. Building on the previous study, in this paper we describe our exploratory study that aims to verify our conceptual approach with stakeholders. Our goal is to answer the research question about how effective is our HCI design strategy for environmental health communication based on molecules as storytellers, from the stakeholder point of view. We presented videos of virtual reality demos and captured quali-quanti data about efficacy, pertinence and future ideations. Findings validated our design strategy, and provide insights about interdependency themes, interaction modes and application opportunities. We discuss our results in the context of environmental health communication HCI strategies.

Keywords: Multisensory HCI Design · Chemical Senses · Environmental Health Communication · Virtual Reality · Storytelling

1 Introduction

Human health and well-being are intertwined with environmental health conditions. In general, environmental health refers to all aspects of human health and disease that result from factors in the environment, as well to the theory and practice of identifying

M. Kurosu and A. Hashizume (Eds.): HCII 2024, LNCS 14687, pp. 79–97, 2024.
https://doi.org/10.1007/978-3-031-60441-6_6

and controlling factors in the environment that potentially affect human health. The field includes the direct pathological effects of hazard agents like chemicals, physical radiation and some biological components, as well as the effects on health and well-being of the physical, psychological, social and aesthetic environment [1]. Climate change and loss of ecosystem stability are having a major impact on human health. In general, environmental hazards are susceptible to transmission of food-borne, water-borne and zoonotic infectious diseases, besides for example, impacting food and water scarcity [2]. To mitigate these problems, the World Health Organization (WHO) reports the need for "global reinvigoration and broadening of the discipline of environmental health to address the scale and complexity of modern environmental health challenges", that implies, among other indications to "promote a vision of health with a longer-term perspective that focuses on health determinants" and "promote behavioral change towards more sustainable and healthier ways of living" [3, p. 15]. Accordingly, environmental health communication strategies should provide "societal awareness of the fundamental health threats posed by environmental risks and climate change, and their potential solutions" [4, p. 17], so that more sustainable and health-promoting development choices are integrated by citizens. In this context, environmental health literacy (EHL) is fundamental to raise awareness of health impacts, costs to society, and solutions. The baseline definition of EHL is "an understanding of the connection between environmental exposures and human health" [5].

1.1 The Mission of Environmental Health Communication

Environmental health literacy (EHL) objective is to prevent "illness by raising awareness of risks from environmental factors and by providing approaches that individuals and communities can take to avoid, mitigate, or reduce such exposures" [5]. Therefore, since its foundation, EHL has operated in risk communication. In the early days of EHL, graphic abstract forms were applied to warn about toxic materials, such as skull and crossbones symbols. Meanwhile, with World War II, symbolic communication needed to expand due to new dangerous and toxic events, while in the postwar these also had to consider high-risk situations of toxic chemicals, poison and nuclear energy warnings. In the late 20th century, further risk effects on human health were covered, such as pollutants and other environmental. Consequently, these increased levels of complexity demanded new communicated strategies, beyond icons or symbols. Hence, with the emergence of computer science technology, risk communication modalities evolved. Sensor technology were applied to measure environmental toxicants, while regulations where implemented of standards and for chemical exposures. The widespread use of technology in the 1990 s and the development of mapping software, such as geographic information systems (GIS), enabled connected visualization forms of geospatial data. In this line, risk calculation and representation could be linked to geographic locations and cost-effectively delivered to wider publics. Finally, with the emergence of the Internet and the World Wide Web (W3), new opportunities to access information and services were provided. Technologies, such as real-time electronic measurement and monitoring were applied in governance surveillance systems, as well as on public digital media platforms [6]. In this line, we highlight the "Digital Earth" concept, described by Albert Gore [7] in 1998, as a virtual globe platform, where the general public could interact with scientific data and results, and understand human problems, from climate change and natural disasters to warfare, hunger, and poverty. Gore claimed that information had to be displayed comprehensively and persuasively, by taking advantage of latest interaction modes that could display several information layers, on demand. Accordingly, Google Earth Engine [8], launched in 2010, democratized geo data access, by offering in one public platform, ready-to-use datasets of satellite images, maps, climate and remote sensing data type options, and other data sources, for analysis. Such evolving mixed media representation forms of environmental health topics, as the case of time-lapse views on maps [9], propelled environmental data dissemination. Insofar, as these systems help to disseminate environmental information, to impact awareness and pro-environmental action, they have to provide additional tools for individuals and communities to act on change. Hence, an effective Environmental Literacy Model proposed by Gray [10] unfolds along three interdependent dimensions: (1) awareness and understanding that environmental exposures and socio-cultural dynamics influence health; (2) skills & self-efficacy to enable individual's decision-making for health-protective decisions; (3) community change or collective action to reduce or remove harmful environmental exposures. The model suggests that beyond understanding environmental health information, individuals and communities should be provided with tools and skills for informed decisions and actions to prompt individual and community-level actions. Therefore, the inclusion of these dimensions in the design of environmental health communication strategies is crucial to address pro-environmental information and action. In this context, we infer that HCI design interdisciplinary framework is a key player outlining strategies that support EHL's mission, to fully reveal our entangled human-environmental health relationships.

1.2 The Importance of Chemical Sense Inclusion in HCI Design to Communicate Environmental Health

We consider that environmental health, human agency and technology should converge towards a holistic and inclusive frameset. Beyond exploiting geodata for surveillance purposes, it benefits environmental health literacy and action. In this line, we envision HCI design strategies that evidence the chemical senses, through which human-environmental relationships take place. Human organism is permeable to environmental exposure vectors through air, food, soil and water conditions [11]. Through breathing and ingestion, environmental pollutants reach the human body, potentially triggering health issues. Hence, to reveal these mostly invisible events, the chemical senses are the most relevant. However, engaging with the chemical senses, as design materials, is challenging as they encompass different functional domains. In general designing with the senses of smell and taste implies to consider its essential physiological, psychological and cultural dimensions. In the physiological realm, they comprise the senses of smell (olfaction), taste (gustation) and trigeminal stimulation. By "sniffing" air through the nostrils (orthonasal) or by swallowing reaching the back of the throat (retronasal), neural signals are sent to key areas of the brain involved in speech, emotions, memories and reward [12]. The molecular machinery that mediates olfactory and gustatory signal transduction, via orthonasal and retronasal route, contributes to strong interaction between the chemical senses. Considering the psychological domain, chemical senses are linked to affective experiences and perception [13], and to inter-modal sensory experiences. Cross modal correspondence research aims to map association mechanisms between smell and taste stimuli and different sensory perception domains [14], e.g., color, shape and sound [15, 16]. Finally, the cultural domain refers to the nature, significance and meaning of the embodied experience [17, 18]. Chemical sense functions signal identity and partner choice, among others [19], besides conveying verbal or non-verbal communication modes.

While the listed property dimensions make chemical sense inclusion in HCI a challenge, - mainly because of its highly inter-subject variability, spatial-temporal volatility and context dependency-, these represent design opportunities. Overall, multisensory HCI framework has evolved from the digitalization of smell and taste for delivery, transmission or substitution of senses [20–23], towards multisensory perception experiences [24]. As environmental health events are multisensory by nature, we envision chemical sense inclusion in HCI experiences, taking advantage of all its dimensions for environmental health communication.

2 Background

Fig. 1. Molecule Chlorophyll as Storyteller in VR environment.

To investigate multisensory HCI design strategies for environmental health communication, we conducted a previous exploratory study that aimed to answer research questions, (1) how can chemical sense experiences communicate environmental health information with digital systems and (2) how the design of such a multisensory HCI system could be [25]. Our conceptual baseline was built up on the concept of the molecule as the mediator to communicate the intertwined connections between living and non-living materials, places and systems. Therefore, we enact molecules as carriers of meaning and emotions. Through the embodied experience of smell and taste, breath and ingestion, we aimed to explore environmental health communication for information and educational purposes. Targeting the non-scientific public, our multisensory HCI design strategy aimed to enhance environmental literacy and foster pro-environmental behavior. To this end, we considered a set of problems and solutions in in their wholeness, as envisioned by Donella Meadows [26], regarding effective environmental education approaches. Accordingly, we developed an explorative HCI design process based on synesthetic design methodology [27] along two phases: the chemical sense experience for cross-sensory analogies and the digital media experience for meaning and communication purposes. The first design phase offered smell and taste experiences related to environmental topics. The participants in the study associated these sensorial perceptions with visual basic graphic forms, volumetric objects and textures, as well as descriptors and own words. The second phase considered Mobile Augmented Reality (MAR) and Mobile Virtual Reality (MVR) basic prototype concepts about chemical senses perception inclusion, informed by the first design phase exploration. Here the participant was enabled to engage with interactive contents that associated molecules to their previous sensory experience, linking them further to environmental health topics. In the first design phase, molecules stimulated perceptions and emotions (of smell and taste samples), which were translated through symbolic associations. In the second phase, we showed specific 3D molecule models related to the environmental health theme (Fig. 1). In the MAR prototype, 2D molecules appeared as an additional information layer related to the in situ geolocation. Whereas in the MVR prototype, the 3D molecule was embedded in the digital landscape. In the case of the MAR prototype concept, built on Figma platform [28], we provided functionalities that combined a symbolic chemical sense annotation system with geodata, with additional information layers and community-building features. Regarding the MVR prototype, we offered a 360° VR narrative content, that highlighted sensory perception as a mediator of specific locations and environmental topic interconnections. Assets comprised 360° imagery (GoPro Camera & Google Street View Studio), characteristic local sounds, and voice locution. It was implemented using the Unity game engine [29], with eye-gaze-based interaction as an input method.

For evaluation, we conducted a concept-of-proof study with 16 participants (M = 18.5 years, SD = 13.46). We collected quanti-qualitative data about heuristic and conceptual design dimensions. Synthesizing our findings, they showed that 87,5% (N = 14) participants, handling the symbolic annotation system allowed them to communicate their smell or taste perceptions. Near all (94%) stated that linking chemical senses with environmental topics provided an innovative perspective that increased their environmental awareness. The MAR prototype experience was rated by 94% (N = 15) of participants as highly relevant and useful, recommending it as an educational tool. Regarding the MVR prototype experience 75% (N = 12) of participants confirmed that a clear message was provided, and thereby was evaluated by 81% (n = 13) of participants as useful, while 75% (N = 12) would recommend it as an education tool. Moreover, 68,75% (N = 11) stated that the VR content experience improved awareness about the environment; impacting 75% (N = 12) their behavior awareness towards the environment, while 87,50% (N = 14) felt positively inspired to take pro-environmental action. In short, the results of our HCI design strategy were validated by a non-scientific public target. In this paper, we describe our exploratory study that aims to validate our communication key concept "Molecule as Storyteller" with stakeholders. Our exploratory study is based on research through design methodology that states "research artefacts provide the catalyst and subject matter for discourse in the community" to "produce knowledge for the research and practice communities" or "artifacts that demonstrate significant invention" (Zimmerman et al., 2007, p.499). Along this line, these artefacts instigate further explorations in design practices to enhance knowledge and innovation. Accordingly, we

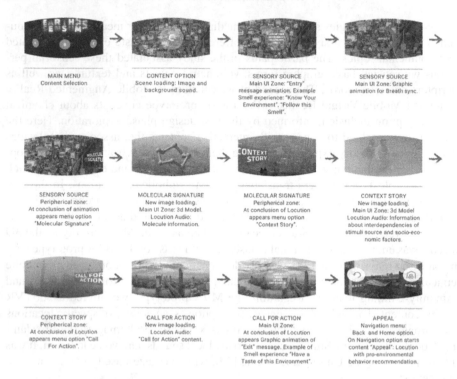

Fig. 2. VR Storyboard presenting the common structure of sequential main scene and navigation.

considered design thinking guidelines, that encompass empathize, definition, ideation, prototype and testing stages [31]. Each dimension represents different modes that inform the entire project, e.g., testing reveals insights that redefine the problem. Hence, having in the previous study tested User Interface (UI) and User experience (UX) aspects with a non-scientific public, we now aim to inquire about stakeholders' perspectives on our design concept. Engagement with stakeholders in research ensures that deliverables are useful and validate usable knowledge. Their unique expertise lens provides rich insights, that benefit design research outcomes.

Our goal is to answer the research question about how effective is an HCI design strategy for environmental health communication based on molecules as storytellers, from the stakeholder point of view. This is important to envision future developments of our multisensory HCI design approach. To investigate this topic, we designed and conducted a survey to capture quantitative and qualitative data [32] about the efficacy, pertinence and future ideations of our "Molecule as Storyteller" concept. We presented videos of four Virtual Reality scenarios and narratives to a panel of eight specialists in the domains of Ecology, Environmental Engineering, Psychology, and Design Education. Next, we collected quantitative and qualitative data and identified key factors related to our research topics. We discuss the overall findings and conclude with a summary of remaining design challenges and future design opportunities.

In summary, the main contributions of this paper are first, proposing a multisensory HCI design strategy that conceptualizes molecules as storytellers with immersive media for environmental health communication, that we used to augment and transform our perception of systemic interdependencies of environmental health topics. Secondly, our study aids the perspective of stakeholders, informing preferred interdependencies themes, interaction modes and application opportunities, around multisensory environmental HCI design. Taken together, we aim to inspire HCI researchers and designers to further explore chemical senses as a design medium for innovation around human-environmental interaction design. In the next sections, the paper unfolds describing related work topics followed by methods, results, discussion and conclusions.

3   Related Work

The main challenge of environmental health topics is to grasp the complexity of these problems and its wide range of interdependencies. Pioneering systems analysis studies, conducted in the 20th century by environmental scientist Donella Meadows [33], concluded that the earth's limited resources and systemic interdependencies could not sustain the economic quest of unlimited growth, leading to its inevitable system collapse. The actual climate change emergency echoes Meadow's warnings, propelling adaptation and mitigation strategies to endorse integrative approaches of a system, managed as separate units [34].

In fact, the multi-disciplinary researchers at the Stockholm Resilience Centre highlight how currently anthropogenic perturbations of the global environment are primarily addressed as if they were separate issues, e.g., climate change, biodiversity loss, or pollution [35], and therefore, ignore its effects of nonlinear interactions on the overall state of the Earth system. To grasp these interdependencies, Johan Rockström [36] conceptualized the "Planetary Boundaries" as a framework to communicate a scientific understanding of anthropogenic global environmental impacts [34] into a framework *"that calls for considering the state of the Earth system as a whole"* [35]. Such integrative envisioning is fundamental in solution-seeking for eminent problems, such as the loss of terrestrial biodiversity and its functional ecosystem, versus the food security of a growing human population [37].

In this context, design discipline is called to tackle problems and address major threats based on its interdisciplinary framework, by recognizing that an issue of one type is inextricable from many others [38]. Hence, the design space spreads beyond production and materiality towards systems [39]. An early attempt to communicate a systemic view, was Buckminster Fuller´s [40] description of Earth as a spaceship flying through space, without a user manual to help "Earthians" steward this ship and highlighting that it has a finite amount of resources that cannot be resupplied. Through this analogy, Fuller revealed Earth's fragility and spurred reflection on linked interdependencies for sustainability practices. Advances in technology have made it possible to reveal these complex relations and interactions of agents. Philosopher of technology Peter-Paul Verbeek [41] claims that technologies mediate perception and action, and therefore, shape both subject and object. This has consequences at the micro level of perception and the macro level of culture, as *"artefacts, help shape how humans can be presented in the world and how the world can be present for them"* [41, p. 195]. In this line, the field of Human-Computer-Interaction (HCI) design and its multidisciplinary approach, provide the ideal frameset to explore and reveal these relationships.

Following, we present HCI projects that applied design strategies to communicate complex systems using data visualization, metaphors, interactive multimedia storytelling and immersive media.

Unusual Suspects [42] is a work-in-progress prototype that aims to highlight the complex interdependencies between the Ukrainian war and climate change. Data visualization is applied to unfold intricate relationships between food, people, war support, raw materials and the environment. Its fluid interconnection of the distinct elements is represented by the metaphor of an assemblage that contains and agglomerates different components, enhanced by layers of text and numerical data.

Myriad [43] is an immersive multimedia experience about animal migration and climate change. Building block of the narrative is based on the element carbon, which forms the basis of all life in earth. By such means, the installation combines sculptural carbon modules covered by large-format projection mapping, multi-channel audio system, interactive floor projection and 3D documentation. Through interactions and tracking migrating animals on air, water and soil, the installation wants visitors to empathize with living animal species and raise awareness of global dependencies.

Breathing with the Forest [44] is an immersive video installation that augments the perception about reciprocity of the ecosystem that surrounds an Amazonian capinuri tree (Maquira coriacea). Visitors are invited to move around the space and to synchronize their breath with audiovisual cues. This reveals the network of interconnections that emerge from the forest, such as carbon sequestration, water cycles, nitrogen fixation and myriad mycorrhizal networks. Thereby, visitors' bodies extend to meet the forest as a whole system, insomuch the breathing planet becomes an extension of their self-perception. The installation aims to instigate reflection about the sense of human separateness of nature, conveying a sense of connection and interdependency with nature, by shifting the perspective of the viewer about the vibrancy of ecosystems.

BaguaMarsh [45] is an ongoing project whose central theme is the "Unity between Heaven and Man". It describes how man must follow universe laws, to respect and protect nature. The conceptual design dwells on Chinese philosophy *I ching* (Book of Changes) and combines the *Bagua* (eight trigrams) of the *I ching* as a metaphor, to present a novel form of narrative visualization. It takes a form of a virtual reality environment that integrates personal data, environmental data, and media materials to convey personal subjective perception and experience.

4 Methods

In this section, we present the methods and procedures used in our research study. We followed a mixed method approach [27]. A total of 8 participants (Females = 7; Male = 1) were recruited in Portugal, between ages 27 and 62 years (M = 58,50 years, SD = 12,08) to take part in the study. We contacted participants based on their specialization field related to our design concept: Psychology (P1, P3); Biophysics (P4); Marine Biology (P5); Ecology (P6); Environmental Engineering (P8); Circular Design Education (P2) and Tech Creative Direction (P8). First, we provided Video URLs of four VR content experiences, as well as the script text of each content demo, for clear narrative understanding support.

	SECTION 1 – CONTENT EVALUATION
Q1	In your words describe what we're communicating.
Q2	In your opinion, is this narrative understandable to the general public?
Q3	In your opinion, is this narrative impactful enough to provoke pro-environmental behavior?
	SECTION 2 – EFFICIENCY
Q4	How effective is this communication concept in explaining the systemic complexity of environmental health issues?
Q5	What did you like best about this design concept? Why?
Q6	What did you unlike most about this design concept? Why?
	SECTION 3 – PERTINENCE
Q7	How relevant is the use of the molecule as key concept? Why?
Q8	How relevant is it to exploit the senses of smell and taste to communicate environmental health? Why?
Q9	How relevant is this HCI design strategy to promote pro-environmental behavior? Why?
Q10	From your perspective, what could be the impact on the non-scientific public?
Q11	In your field of work, in what contexts or environments do you imagine interacting with this HCI design experience?
	SECTION 4 – FUTURE IDEATION
Q12	What content do you think is missing?
Q13	Considering the interactive experience concept, what kind of additional interactions would you like to experience?
Q14	From your perspective, what are the priority environmental health top-ics that we should design for?
Q15	Considering the systemic view of environmental health, which compo-nents or interdependencies should be highlighted?

Fig. 3. Set of questions asked in the questionnaire.

Following a common structure (Fig. 2), these videos presented two content experiences each, related to smell stimuli[1] and to taste stimuli[2], aligned with environmental health topics (Fig. 4). We asked the participant to view these contents at their own pace. Next, we conducted a structured interview based on an online survey (Fig. 3). The survey presented open-ended questions and a self-report questionnaire with a Likert evaluation scale (5-point). Each interview lasted for approximately 35 min. All feedback was provided in written form and was based on four main sections presented in sequential order: (1) Questions about content evaluation; (2) Questions about design concept efficiency; (3) Questions about multisensory HCI strategy pertinence and (4) Questions about future development ideation. We analyzed the data following inductive thematic analysis, which entails deriving meaning and identifying themes without expected outcomes [46]. Findings are presented and discussed in the next section.

---

[1] URL: https://vimeo.com/353220905 and URL: https://vimeo.com/353219095.

[2] URL: https://vimeo.com/353218005 and URL: https://vimeo.com/353218548.

VR SCENES	CONTENT NARRATIVE
	Hydrogen Sulfide - Pulp Industry (Leirosa, Portugal) https://vimeo.com/353220905
Source	Transformation process of Cellulose liberates Hydrogen Sulfide.
Molecular Signature	You are smelling Hydrogen Sulfide.
Context Story	The pulp and paper industry are one of the most successful in Portugal. In 2016 Portugal's Wood pulp export was $3,2M. Main Export partners are Spain and Turkey. Eucalyptus plan-tation contributes to soil erosion. Enhanced rainfall deficit can lead to desertification and therefor environmental health vulnerability.
Call for Action	How does Hydrogen Sulfide feel like? How does Hydrogen Sulfide tastes?
Appeal	What can you do for your environmental health? Use paper wisely!
	Dimethyl Sulfide - Fishing industry (Adraga, Portugal) https://vimeo.com/353219095
Source	In the ocean, dimethyl sulfide is emitted to the atmosphere by bacteria, when eating dying phytoplankton.
Molecular Signature	You are smelling Dimethyl Sulfide.
Context Story	Seabirds and other ocean animals use the smell of dimethyl sulfide to identify areas rich in phytoplankton, which attract fish. Dimethyl Sulfide is normally present at very low levels in the human body, namely in blood, urine and on expired breath. In the atmosphere, Dimethyl sulfide also helps to form clouds. Dimethyl sulfide is used in petroleum refining and in ethylene production. Ethylene is the chemical industry's pri-mary building block, with over 60% of the raw material pro-duced, being used in the plastic industry. Plastic pollution of marine-ecosystems leads into Fish eating micro plastic.
Call for Action	How does Dimethyl Sulfide feel like? How does Dimethyl Sulfide tastes?
Appeal	What can you do for your environmental health? Reduce plas-tic consumption! Always recycle plastic waste! Waste prevention and recycling reduce the amount of waste sent to incinerators, lowering the greenhouse gases emitted when waste burns. Buy sustainable seafood products. Always ask the person you buy fish from, where and how their fish is caught. Avoid bottom trawling and pair trawling fishing.
	Chlorophyll – Plastic industry (Tehran, Iran) https://vimeo.com/353218005
Source	You are tasting Spinach. Chlorophyll is responsible for its green pigment and minty flavor. Chlorophyll contains Hydrogen atoms.
Molecular Signature	Chlorophyll.
Context Story	Ancient Persia is considered the birthplace of spinach before it spread to India, China and Europe. Iran has a major Air Pollution Index from vehicle emissions, refinery operations and industrial effluents, especially in urban areas. Current issues contemplate also water pollution from raw sewage and industrial waste. Tehran is ranked high for severe fine particle air pollution globally, leading to unhealthy air pol-lution levels. Iran's main export trade is Crude Petroleum and the main import trade are Cars. Iran's second export trade is Ethylene Polymers for the chemical industry. Hy-drogen atoms are applied in Ethylene production, used for plastic bags, food containers, and packaging in general. American Federal data has listed Spinach to contain the highest levels of pesticides residues. Main fresh Spinach exporters are the United States, Spain and Italy where Ethylene is applied in Spinach leaves packaging. What you are tasting contains compounds which are found in materials which contributes to environmental stress of Tehran's and of global citizens.
Call for Action	How does Chlorophyll make you feel? How does Tehran tastes?
Appeal	What can you do for Tehran's environmental health? Use Public Transport and Car-sharing services! Reduce Plastic Consumption! Buy fresh Spinach from your local organic food producer.
	Water – Farming industry (Beijing, China) https://vimeo.com/353218548
Source	You are tasting Jiaozi. Soy sauce gives it a savory flavor. Soy sauce is made of fermented paste of Soybeans. 100grs of Soybeans contains 9% of water and 5% of ash.
Molecular Signature	Water
Context Story	Although the soybean originated in China, 60 % of all soy-beans entering international trade go to China. Main Soy-bean importers are the United States and Brazil. Explosive growth of soybean consumption in China is linking to soared consumption of pig meat, poultry and fish, which farming industry are feed by soybean meal. Only one tenth of the soybeans used in China is consumed directly as food such as tofu and soy sauce. But Soybeans world demand is rising, putting on pressure for more land requirement. But since the United States has no additional land to plant more soybeans, the Brazilian Amazon Basin is offering new land for plantation, facing deforestation, loss of biodiversity and increased carbon emissions. The same effects of deforestation, urbanization and industrial development causes Beijing to be listed as one of the most polluted cities in the world. What you are tasting contains compounds which are found in the air and the ground, hence contributes to environmental stress of Beijing's citizens and global citizens.
Call for Action	How does Soy sauce make you feel? How does Beijing tastes?
Appeal	What can you do for Beijing's environmental health? Reduce Meat Consumption!

Fig. 4. VR narrative content structure of smell and taste stimuli experiences.

5 Findings

In this section, we describe the findings of our data analysis, following the questionnaire structure. We summarize key feedback and provide representative quotes to illustrate the received feedback.

5.1 Section 1 – Questions About Content Evaluation

We started our inquiry by asking questions about content impact on experts. Q1 - Q3 aims to evaluate content comprehension, quality and impact on behavior. The first question asked experts to describe in their own words what we are communicating (Q1). All answers revealed that the design concept dimensions were comprehended, by participants' fields of expertise (Table 1).

Asking about experts' opinions about if this narrative is understandable to the general public (Q2), 50% (N = 4) validated it as very comprehensible, and 37,5%, as comprehensible (N = 3). Inquiring about how they evaluate if the narrative is impactful enough to provoke pro-environmental behavior, 62,5% (N = 5) agree that it is impactful and 25% (N = 2) strongly impactful.

5.2 Section 2 – Questions About Efficiency.

In this section, we asked questions about the efficiency of our environmental health communication design concept. Q4 - Q6 inquiries about our design strategy adequacy and its impact on experts. Investigating how effectively our communication concept explains the systemic complexity of environmental health issues (Q4), 50% (N = 4) agreed and 37,5% (N = 3) strongly agreed that interdependencies were understood. What experts liked best about the design concept (Q5), was (1) the idea of using sensory evocation to convey the complexity of environmental issues (P2, P3, P4, P6), and (2) the sense of immersion through visualization and auralization (P1, P5, P7, P8). What experts liked less (Q6), were the technical aspects of our early prototype demo, such as the basic sound quality (P1, P3, P4), the diction (P4, P5) and the fact that they weren't exploring virtual representations with the VR equipment (P3, P8).

Table 1. Participants descriptions with their own words of the content experience.

Experts	Quotes
P1	"Human action in the environment and its consequences for the planet, for living beings and the need to transform the perception and behavior that lead us to destruction."
P2	The relationship between sensory experiences and the place where they can occur; The link between a sensory phenomenon and its supporting molecular origin; The link between the different components identified and the historical and socio-cultural context in which they occur."
P3	"On environmental impacts and recommendations on how to reduce self-pollution."
P4	"The relationship and confrontation of environmental contexts with associated multi-sensory stimuli."
P5	"I understood that various aspects relating to our planet and the way we live and explore it are being addressed and at the same time as being made aware of the problems we are also given suggestions for trying to reduce them in some way."
P6	"Nature through the senses - uses place and landscape and tries to capture elements that promote the expression of connectivity."
P7	"Complex relationships between very disparate elements of the sensory world (food, pollution, geography, history, memory)."
P8	"This project communicates environmental problems detectable through smell and taste that highlight the non-recycling of plastic, the excessive use of paper, the exaggerated consumption of meat and the choice of unshared mobility. Communication using immersive images complemented by text leads to "calls to action" that could contribute to solving (or at least minimizing) these problems."

5.3 Section 3 - Questions About Pertinence

Next, we asked questions about the pertinence of our design approach. Q7 - Q11 explores expert's views about our key design concept, HCI design strategy and application opportunities for the non-scientific public. When asking about how relevant is the use of the molecule as a key concept (Q7), almost all experts emphasized it as strongly relevant (75%, N = 6). Overall, the conceptual strategy enabled them to perceive events holistically: "It evokes a degree of precision and scale in the organic human-earth-universe relationship (P2)"; as the invisible turns visible: "We don't usually see the molecules and that helps us understand the argument (P3)". The whole conceptual approach "is relevant mainly because of its originality. A molecule is a simple unit that has no associated value judgments and can integrate chemical processes and compounds with positive and negative connotations (P5)," while "we are intimately connected to everything that happens in environmental terms and all of this is reflected in our physical and even mental health (P6)". Additionally, P7 highlights how in this context, "the molecule is only relevant if it is given a key role in which it is deciphered or is an important element of the story. As a purely visual element, it seems unnecessary to me."

Inquiring about the exploitation of the senses of smell and taste to communicate environmental health (Q8), all experts strongly agreed as relevant (100%, N = 8). Arguments reveal two main reasons: this approach (1) provides comprehension of problem inter-relationships and (2) conveys a sense of immersion in the environment.

Comprehension of Problem Inter-relationships. As smell and taste are primarily sensorial and natural (P1, P6), "these are senses in which the seriousness of the problems manifests itself unquestionable" (P8); hence "they imply the establishment of a more visceral and intimate relationship between people and the issues in question" (P4). In this line, multisensory inclusion could take advantage of impacting experience embodiment and memory. One expert mentioned how memories linked to smell and taste, allow to compare current and past experiences which may reveal environmental health impacts over time (P5), while a second expert highlighted how these features enhance comprehension of interdependencies (P2).

Sensory Immersion with the Environment. One expert stated that in general higher quality environments are more comfortable and more sensorial stimulating, and therefore revealing opposite conditions may provide arguments for change: "Sensory immersion can be a good shortcut for communicating discomfort, danger and ephemerality" (P7). In this line, sensorial immersion discloses "the context as a whole, and how environmental health impacts on smells and tastes, besides the quality of what we consume" (P3); along with the fact that "the quality of the environment will impact the way you perceive yourself and the world. The quality of the environment reveals the quality of human mental health, which in turn creates a harmful environment for life" (P1).

Regarding our HCI design strategy to promote pro-environmental behavior (Q9), experts considered it strongly relevant (50%, N = 4) and relevant (25%, N = 2). Their opinions are based on (1) aspects of HCI design and (2) aspects of the conceptual strategy. It was recognized that the use of an interaction design strategy benefits cognition: "the digital environment allows actors to act and become aware of their actions" (P1), as well as the ease of interaction leading to understanding, and this, eventually to action (P7). Overall, the conceptual strategy was recognized as relevant because of multisensory integration being effective tin activating new behaviors (P2, P5); accomplishing a holistic view of system impact consequences (P3); by providing new connections with the environment and raising awareness (P4).

Asking about what impact could have our multisensory HCI design approach on the non-scientific public (Q10), half of the participants (N = 4) rated it as impactful and 37,5% (N = 3) as strongly impactful. Investigating the application opportunities, we asked in which contexts or environments the participants would imagine interacting with this HCI design experience (Q11). All participants identified education and environmental literacy as application domains, as well as "interpersonal dynamics that seek to broaden sensitivity in the relationship between people and between people and the environment, bearing in mind that the environment is not outside of us" (P1). Key locations were envisioned as schools, universities and interpretation centers that promote scientific dissemination actions. Additionally, P8 pointed out the Ocean as a key theme, because in this case "the representation of smell and taste are essential to demonstrate the seriousness of possible environmental problems".

5.4   Section 4 – Future Ideation

In the last section, we asked questions about future ideation, to gain insight about further concept developments. Q12 - Q15 instigates suggestions on content development, interaction design, preferred environmental topics and interdependencies. We asked about what content is missing, from the lens of their expertise field (Q12). Overall, responses indicated (1) design dimensions and (2) technological shortcomings. Synthetizing, missing aspects were the emotional dimension (P1, P2); the human presence as a guide (P3); content location-specific data (P4) and constant updated data (P5); higher level of detail demonstrating cause-effect events (P7, P8); and finally, more rich virtual environments in terms of diversity and color (P6).

Regarding the interactive experience concept, we inquired about what kind of additional interactions would they like to experience (Q13). Answers covered (1) interaction mode suggestions, besides (2) technological demands.

Interaction Modes. Interaction design insights comprise requests for enhanced interaction modes with the molecule model (P1, P3) and chemical sense experiences (P4). In addition, interaction modes with a human figure, that could allow a sort of dialogue (P3, P5) were suggested; as also "with objects that influence the narrative, for example through color" (P2).

Technological Demands. For a richer and more memorable user experience, one expert suggested real-time data inclusion (P8).

Inquiring about what are the priority environmental health topics that we should design for (Q14), the following themes emerged: global warming; biodiversity loss; species extinction such as pollinators; food security; deforestation; Air pollution; Ocean pollution; Water quality and management; Pathogen emergence and zoonotic diseases; mental health; as also, local and national action systems for global urgency.

Considering the systemic dimension of environmental health, we asked about which components or interdependencies should be highlighted (Q15). Answers analysis revealed the following main theme clusters: (1) systemic interdependencies, (2) health and (3) pro-environmental behavior.

Systemic Interdependencies. Experts suggested specific interrelationships between "demography; literacy; tradition and history" (P7), while P4 considers all the elements of the system, adding that there are no hierarchies between environmental, economic or social factors. P8 encapsulates the aforementioned visions disclosing: "Environmental health problems result from the interaction between disturbing agents and the environment. This interaction results in changes in the descriptor variables of the environment which, in turn, translate into impacts on environmental health. Emphasis should therefore be placed on the variables that describe the disturbing agents, the environment, the effects and the impacts".

Health. In this line, one expert mentioned the interdependency between human health and planetary health (P6), revealed through diseases "such as pandemics, respiratory problems and allergies" (P5).

Pro-environmental Behavior. Finally, the responsibility of the human individual and collective behavior in creating the environment in which we live (P1) should be highlighted. In this line, P2 suggests designing for aspects of biomimicry between nature and public space, while P3 mentions natural resource exploitation and technological component production.

6 Discussion

In this discussion, we reflect on our research question and address some potential developments fundamented by stakeholder insights. Concerning our goal, of validating the conceptual multisensory HCI design strategy based on "Molecule as Storyteller" with stakeholders, our findings suggest that the evaluation content provided does bring awareness and newness about systemic human-environmental health interdependencies and is impactful enough to provoke pro-environmental behavior. Additionally, findings showed that this design strategy is suitable for the non-scientific public, specifically for education and environmental literacy purposes. The design concept of using sensory evocation (smell and taste), to (1) guide the viewer through the web of complex cause-effect relationships of human-environmental health themes, as also (2) the sense of merging with the environment through the chemical senses, was held as the major conceptual innovation factors. Even while the evaluation process implied stakeholders to "view" the VR content demo on a web platform, instead of interacting with a head-mounted device that provides virtual reality for the wearer, participants of the study stated a sense of immersion with the environment was conveyed through visualization and auralization, that supported the conceptual intend.

These responses encourage multisensory HCI design strategies considering immersive media that evidence, beyond the units of the system, also the system as a whole. Such digital environments enable multiple experience design layers, in line with environmental health literacy guidelines: augmentation, information, education and action. Future developments were suggested by stakeholders in the realm of interaction modes, environmental health topics and interdependency themes. Therefore, our environmental multisensory HCI design solution should consider enhanced interaction modes with smell and taste dimensions, with the molecule and with emotion. Furthermore, prior environmental health topics to design for are global warming; biodiversity loss; zoonotic diseases; food and water security as also air and ocean pollution. Regarding interdependencies themes, they refer socio-cultural independencies with environmental variables; human and planetary health symptoms; besides human behavior impact. The final remarks refer to concerns about cognitive overload, as connecting all provided interdependencies was felt as demanding for a wider public, by two stakeholders (P6, P7). In addition, one stakeholder (P6) pointed out that success of our strategy would depend on the digital literacy of target audiences.

Our study echoes the challenges of designing impactful environmental health HCI communication strategies. In this line, our findings inform about design considerations and opportunities, around multisensory environmental HCI design. Opportunities for technological innovation were touched, upon when stakeholders suggested real time data inclusion in mixed media environments. In fact, these emergent technologies of recent developments in HCI, could sensorially augment single or collective experiences, in the context of environmental health information. At MIT Media Lab, the "Responsive Environment" Group [47] has been developing sensor networks to augment and mediate human interaction with built and natural environments. Its project portfolio includes AirSpecs [48], an eyewear platform that incorporates environmental sensing to estimate the composition of inhaled gases for a more accurate understanding of inhaled pollutants in real-time. In this context, we speculate that the application of such sensor network systems provides the means, to envision mixed media strategies for chemical sense inclusion in HCI design, as also for innovative environmental health communication strategies.

Limitations. Our VR demos present an early stage of prototype development. Image and sound assets present Mid-Fi quality. As mentioned previously, stakeholders viewed these content experiences on a web platform, instead with VR equipment. In this context, we consider comments about technological aspects, as indicators of what potential users expect, such as observations requiring a higher degree of immersion (P7).

7   Conclusion and Future Work

In this paper, we describe our exploratory study that aims to verify our design concept with a panel of stakeholders. Our goal was to answer the research question about how effective is an HCI design strategy for environmental health communication based on molecules as storytellers, from the stakeholder point of view. For that matter, we presented videos of virtual reality content demos, followed by a survey that collected quali-quanti data about efficacy, pertinence and future ideations. The study findings validated our conceptual baseline and design strategy of chemical sense inclusion. In summary, the main contributions of this paper are first, proposing a multisensory HCI design strategy that conceptualizes molecules as storytellers with immersive media for environmental health communication, that we used to augment and transform our perception of systemic interdependencies of environmental health topics. Secondly, our study aids the perspective of stakeholders, informing preferred interdependency themes, interaction modes and application opportunities, around multisensory environmental HCI design. Taken together, we aim to inspire HCI researchers and designers to further explore chemical senses as a design medium for innovation around human-environmental interaction design. Regarding future developments, we intend to evolve our HCI design strategy with smell and taste, by Gray's [10] Environmental Health Literacy guidelines. To this end, our goal is to apply HCI design methodology (1) to explore further representations of interdependencies dimensions; and (2) to examine tools that enable individual's decision-making.

Acknowledgments. This study was funded by Foundation for Science and Technology – grant UIDB/00711/2020.

Disclosure of Interests. The author declares that the research was conducted in the absence of any commercial or financial relationships that could be construed as a potential conflict of interest.

References

1. European Environment Agency. Environmental health. http://glossary.eea.europa.eu/EEAGlossary. Accessed 29 Jan 2024
2. Marselle, M.R., et al.: Pathways linking biodiversity to human health: a conceptual framework. Environ. Int. **150** (2021). https://doi.org/10.1016/J.ENVINT.2021.106420
3. World Health Organization. WHO global strategy on health, environment and climate change: the transformation needed to improve lives and wellbeing sustainably through healthy environments (2020)
4. World Health Organization. WHO Global Strategy on Health, Environment and Climate Change: the transformation needed to improve lives and well-being sustainably through healthy environments. World Health Organization (2020). https://www.jstor.org/stable/resrep32997. Accessed 29 Jan 2024
5. Finn, S., O'Fallon, L.: The emergence of environmental health literacy-from its roots to its future potential. Environ. Health Perspect. **125**(4), 495–501 (2017). https://doi.org/10.1289/ehp.1409337
6. Câmara, A.S.: Environmental Systems: A Multidimensional Approach. Oxford University Press (2002)
7. Gore, A.: The digital earth. Australian Surveyor **43**(2), 89–91 (1998). https://doi.org/10.1080/00050348.1998.10558728
8. Google Earth Engine. Google Earth Engine. https://earthengine.google.com/platform/. Accessed 22 Feb 2024
9. NASA. Global Warming from 1880 to 2022. https://climate.nasa.gov/climate_resources/139/video-global-warming-from-1880-to-2022/. Accessed 22 Feb 2024
10. Gray, K.M.: From content knowledge to community change: a review of representations of environmental health literacy. Int. J. Environ. Res. Public Health **15**, 466 (2018). https://doi.org/10.3390/IJERPH15030466
11. Landrigan, P.J., et al.: Health consequences of environmental exposures: changing global patterns of exposure and disease. Ann. Glob. Health **82**(1), 10–19 (2016). https://doi.org/10.1016/J.AOGH.2016.01.005
12. Lundström, J.N., Boesveldt, S., Albrecht, J.: Central processing of the chemical senses: an overview. ACS Chem. Neurosci. **2**(1), 5–16 (2011). https://doi.org/10.1021/cn1000843
13. Kontaris, I., East, B.S., Wilson, D.A.: Behavioral and neurobiological convergence of odor, mood and emotion: a review. Front. Behav. Neurosci. **14**, 506708 (2020). https://doi.org/10.3389/FNBEH.2020.00035/BIBTEX
14. Spence, C.: Crossmodal correspondences: a tutorial review. Attent. Percept. Psychophys. **73**(4), 971–995 (2011). https://doi.org/10.3758/s13414-010-0073-7
15. Spence, C.: On the relationship(s) between color and taste/flavor. Exp. Psychol. **66**(2), 99–111 (2019). https://doi.org/10.1027/1618-3169/a000439
16. Deroy, O., Crisinel, A.S., Spence, C.: Crossmodal correspondences between odors and contingent features: Odors, musical notes, and geometrical shapes. Psychon. Bull. Rev. **20**(5), 878–896 (2013). https://doi.org/10.3758/s13423-013-0397-0
17. Henshaw, V., McLean, K., Medway, D., Perkins, C., Warnaby, G.: Designing with Smell: Practices, Techniques and Challenges, 1st ed. Routledge (2017). https://doi.org/10.4324/9781315666273
18. Heywood, I.: Sensory Arts and Design, 1st ed. Bloomsbury Academic (2017)
19. Classen, C.: Foundations for an anthropology of the senses. Int. Soc. Sci. J. **49**(153), 401–412 (2010). https://doi.org/10.1111/j.1468-2451.1997.tb00032.x
20. Obrist, M.: Touch, taste, & smell user interfaces: the future of multisensory the future of multisensory HCI (2016). https://doi.org/10.1145/2851581.2856462

21. Obrist, M., Ranasinghe, N., Spence, C.: Special issue: Multisensory human–computer interaction. Int. J. Hum. Comput. Stud. **107**, 1–4 (2017). https://doi.org/10.1016/j.ijhcs.2017.06.002
22. Spence, C., Obrist, M., Velasco, C., Ranasinghe, N.: Digitizing the chemical senses: possibilities & Pitfalls. Int. J. Hum. Comput. Stud. **107**, 62–74 (2017). https://doi.org/10.1016/J.IJHCS.2017.06.003
23. Brooks, J., Lopes, P., Obrist, M., Amores Fernandez, J., Kaye, J.: Third wave or winter? The past and future of smell in HCI. In: Conference on Human Factors in Computing Systems - Proceedings, New York, NY, USA, pp. 1–4. Association for Computing Machinery (2023). https://doi.org/10.1145/3544549.3583749
24. Velasco, C., Obrist, M.: Multisensory Experiences: Where the Senses Meet Technology. Oxford University Press (2020)
25. Neves, P., Câmara, A.: Multisensory HCI design with smell and taste for environmental health communication. In: Stephanidis, C., Marcus, A., Rosenzweig, E., Rau, P.L.P., Moallem, A., Rauterberg, M. (eds.) HCII 2020, LNCS, vol. 12423, pp. 1–23. Springer, Cham (2020). https://doi.org/10.1007/978-3-030-60114-0_31
26. Meadows, D.H., UNEP: Harvesting one hundredfold: key concepts and case studies in environmental education /: by Donella H. Meadows. UNEP (1989). https://digitallibrary.un.org/record/147029. Accessed 22 Feb 2024
27. Haverkamp, M.: Synesthetic Design: Handbook for a Multi-Sensory Approach. Birkhäuser Verlag (2012)
28. "Figma". https://www.figma.com/. Accessed 21 Jul 2019
29. "Unity3D." https://unity3d.com/unity
30. Zimmerman, J., Forlizzi, J., Evenson, S.: Research through design as a method for interaction design research in HCI. In: Proceedings of the SIGCHI Conference on Human Factors in Computing Systems - CHI 2007, New York, New York, USA, pp. 493–502. ACM Press (2007). https://doi.org/10.1145/1240624.1240704
31. Brown, T.: Change by Design: How Design Thinking Transforms Organizations and Inspires Innovation. Harper Business (2009). https://www.amazon.com/Change-Design-Transforms-Organizations-Innovation/dp/0061766089. Accessed 01 Feb 2024
32. B. Laurel, *Design research: methods and perspectives.* MIT Press, 2003
33. Donella, W.M., Dennis, M., Jørgen, R., Behrens III, W.: The Limits to Growth. Potomac Associates - Universe Books (1972)
34. United Nations. UN Climate Change Conference. https://unfccc.int/cop28. Accessed 23 Dec 2023
35. Richardson, K., et al.: Earth beyond six of nine planetary boundaries. Sci. Adv. **9**(37) (2023). https://doi.org/10.1126/sciadv.adh2458
36. Steffen, W., et al.: Planetary boundaries: guiding human development on a changing planet. Science (1979) **347**(6223), 1259855 (2015). https://doi.org/10.1126/science.1259855
37. Leclère, D., et al.: Bending the curve of terrestrial biodiversity needs an integrated strategy. Nature **585**(7826), 551–556 (2020). https://doi.org/10.1038/s41586-020-2705-y
38. "Prototypes for Humanity". https://www.prototypesforhumanity.com/. Accessed 30 Jan 2024
39. Rawsthorn, A.: Design as an Attitude. JRP | RINGIER (2022)
40. Fuller, B.R.: Operating Manual for Spaceship Earth. Southern Illinois University Press, Carbondale (1969)
41. Verbeek, P.-P.: What Things Do: Philosophical Reflections on Technology, Agency, and Design. Penn State University Press (2005). https://philpapers.org/rec/VERWTD. Accessed 21 Aug 2020

42. Ceccarini, C., Ferreira, M., Prandi, C., Nunes, N., Nisi, V.: Unusual suspects - visualizing unusual relationships of complex social phenomena with climate change. In: ACM International Conference Proceeding Series, pp. 494–503 (2023). https://doi.org/10.1145/3582515. 3609572
43. Interactive Media Foundation. Myriad. Where we connect. https://myriad.earth/. Accessed 31 Jan 2024
44. Marshmallow Laser Feast, "Breathing with the Forest." Accessed: Jan. 31, 2024. [Online]. Available: https://marshmallowlaserfeast.com/project/breathing-with-the-forest/
45. MIT Media Lab and MIT Media Lab. "BaguaMarsh," Responsive Environments Group. https://www.media.mit.edu/projects/baguamarsh/overview/. Accessed 06 Feb 2024
46. Clarke, V., Braun, V.: Teaching thematic analysis: overcoming challenges and developing strategies for effective learning. Psychologist **26**(2) (2013)
47. MIT Media Lab. Responsive Environments. https://www.media.mit.edu/groups/responsive-environments/projects/. Accessed 17 Feb 2024
48. MIT Media Lab. AirSpecs. https://www.media.mit.edu/projects/airspecs/overview/. Accessed 17 Feb 2024

A Hybrid Framework for Long-Term Photovoltaic Power Generation Forecasting

Eunseop Park[ID], Jahwan Koo[(✉)][ID], and Ungmo Kim[ID]

Graduate School of Information and Communications, Sungkyunkwan University, 12-2, Seonggyungwan-ro, Jongno-gu, Seoul, Republic of Korea
{jhkoo,ukim}@skku.edu

Abstract. Recent extreme weather events around the world have increased interest in renewable energy. As Photovoltaic power grows in importance, so does the need for long-term forecasting. Generally, the data related to Photovoltaic power generation consists of many variables with multi-periodicity. In this study, we propose a new architecture that combines TimesNet and iTransformer models to maximize the performance of long-term Photovoltaic power generation forecasting. First, the TimesNet model is used to identify intra- and inter-period variations and to transform 1D information into 2D to effectively model different time series patterns in temporal data. Second, the iTransformer model is utilized to capture multivariate correlations using the Attention mechanism to reflect relationships across the entire time series. The proposed model outperformed the existing models in Photovoltaic power generation forecasting.

Keywords: Photovoltaic Power Generation · Long-Term Forecasting · TimesNet · iTransformer

1 Introduction

In recent times, the use of fossil fuels and the resulting environmental pollution have led to an increase in abnormal climate patterns and natural disasters. Consequently, many countries are emphasizing the importance of renewable energy, with a notable surge in Photovoltaic power development. Globally, it is anticipated that solar energy will account for a significant portion of the total energy generation by 2050 [1]. However, as the Photovoltaic power business expands, the volatile nature of renewable energy, coupled with the asynchronous nature of renewable power generation, is impacting the grid and creating economic challenges. Therefore, accurate prediction of Photovoltaic power production is essential for ensuring stable renewable energy supply and optimizing operations [2,3]. Various studies on predicting Photovoltaic power production leverage machine learning and deep learning technologies [4–7]. Models such as SVM/SVR, XGBoost, CNN, ANN, Stacked LSTM, LSTM, GRU are widely employed, and recently, models based on Transformer architecture for time series forecasting have gained attention [8]. These prediction models predominantly utilize meteorological data, incorporating information from equipment sensors and module data from Photovoltaic power facilities. The data consists of diverse variables, exhibiting periodic variations on daily, monthly, and yearly cycles. In this paper, a proposed structure combines the TimesNet model [9], which considers various periodicities in time series data, with the iTransformer [10] model known for shortening training time and demonstrating high performance in long-term predictions. The structure was tested using datasets from observed Photovoltaic power inverter data and Numerical Weather Prediction (NWP) models. The proposed structure in this paper has the best performance among the existing time series models including Transformer-based method, Linear-based method, and TCN-based method in the long term Photovoltaic power generation prediction experiment.

2 Related Work

In addition to using a single model to make short-term, medium-term, and long-term forecasts using time-series datasets, many studies have used a combination of multiple machine learning models, deep learning models, probabilistic methods, and numerical analysis-based forecasting methods to achieve better results. The paper [11] presents a hybrid structure of a machine learning model and a numerical simulation model based on numerical analysis. It proposes a hybrid structure that can overcome the disadvantages of machine learning models, such as difficulty in collecting data and difficulty in interpreting results, through data simulation models, and increase reliability by combining the advantages of simulation models. The paper [12] studied the prediction of minute-to-minute solar irradiance variability from hourly NWP meteorological data by using machine learning like the Light Gradient Boosting (LGMB) and applying statistical post-processing techniques to improve the grid integration efficiency and reduce the instability of minute-to-minute photovoltaic power generation systems. The paper [13] was the first to apply TimesNet to the El Niño/La Niña phenomenon. They proposed a hybrid forecasting method to improve accuracy over existing single-model forecasts. They first decomposed the sea surface temperature data through a feature extraction process, and then combined TImesNet and ARIMA models to make forecasts, showing better forecasting ability than the current best performing single forecaster, the ConvLSTM model.

The paper [14] proposed a novel hybrid model combining TimesNet and Temporal Convolutional Network(TCN) for short-term electricity load forecasting. proposed a novel hybrid model combining TimesNet and Temporal Convolutional Network (TCN) for short-term power load forecasting. TimesNet is used to transform a one-dimensional time series based on multiple cycles into a set of two-dimensional tensors to capture the dependencies and relationships between different time units in the power load data. Temporal Convolutional Network is then used to further extract the temporal features and long-term dependencies of the load data to obtain a more holistic pattern of temporal information. The proposed model showed significantly better performance compared to LSTM, TCN, TimesNet, TCN-LSTM, and TimesNet-LSTM models.

Based on the above studies, the core of this study involves combining the TimesNet model, which reflects time series patterns to capture the inherent multiple periodicities in time series datasets, with the iTransformer model, which understands the interdependencies among multiple variables to enhance predictive performance. The combined hybrid model aims to achieve superior predictive performance by reflecting time series patterns and capturing complex relationships among variables in photovoltaic power generation datasets.

The rest of the paper is organized as follows: in "Datasets and Methods" section, We describe the description and analysis of the dataset. Therefore, we describe the TimesNet and iTransformer models along with the structure of our proposed hybrid framework. The results of long-term forecasts of photovoltaic power generation and comparisons between the models are in the "Experiments" section. Finally, the "Conclusions and Future Work" section contains the conclusions of this study.

3   Datasets and Methods

3.1   Datasets

In this paper, two datasets are used to study photovoltaic power generation forecasting. The first dataset is observed data from inverters at actual photovoltaic power sites. It consists of 12 variables that contain information about the inverter and actual observed temperature and horizontal radiation data. The data is observed hourly from January 1, 2022 to May 31, 2023, and is described in Table 1.

Table 1. Photovoltaic Power Inverter Data Description.

no	variable	unit	no	variable	unit
1	AC Power	kW	2	AC Voltage	V
3	AC Current	I	4	DC Power	kW
5	DC Voltage	V	6	DC Current	I
7	AC frequency	Hz	8	Date	an hour
9	The slope of the day	W/m2	10	Horizontal radiation	W/m2
11	Temperature	°C	12	Module temperature	°C
13	Photovoltaic power generationZ	kW			

Figure 1 shows the inverter dataset demonstrates that inverter information exhibits similar patterns to solar power generation. This shows that inverters are

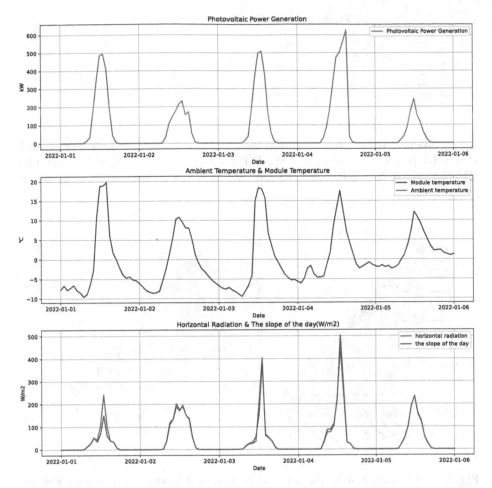

Fig. 1. Daily values of solar power generation, temperature, module temperature, horizontal radiation, and slope of the day in the inverter dataset for 5 d.

directly affected by weather conditions and possess multi-periodicity, including daily, monthly, and seasonal cycles. The second dataset is the NWP dataset. Numerical Weather Prediction (NWP) is a model that uses numerical models to predict future atmospheric conditions. Many existing solar power forecasting studies have been based on the NWP dataset [15,16]. We used the Local Data Assimilation and Prediction System(LDAPS) model, a Unified Model(UM) published by the UK Met Office, which has a horizontal resolution of 1.5 km and provides hourly data with a 48-hour forecast period. The NWP dataset was collected from January 1, 2022 to December 31, 2022, and The NWP dataset consists of over 100 weather variables, the main ones are shown in Table 2.

In Fig. 2, we can see the correlation between the inverter dataset and the NWP dataset with solar power generation. Since the inverter dataset is the

Table 2. NWP Key Data Description.

no	variable	description	no	variable	description	no	variable	description
1	NDNSW	Net Down Surface short wave Flux	6	OULWT	Outgoing long wave Flux	11	HFSFC	surface Heat Flux
2	SWDIR	Direct Flux	7	DLWS	Downward Long wave radiation Flux	12	TMP	Temperature
3	SWDIF	Diffuse short wave radiation Flux	8	SHFLT	Surface sensible Heat Flux on Tiles	13	HCDC	High Cloud Cover
4	TDSWS	Total Downward surface Short wave Flux	9	TOMFS	Total Surf Moisture Flux per times step	14	MCDC	Medium Cloud Cover
5	NDNLW	Net Downward surface Long wave Flux	10	HFSOIL	Heat Flux from surface To Deep Soil level 1	15	LCDC	Low Cloud Cover

actual observed data, we can see that most of the variables are highly correlated with solar power generation. In the NWP dataset, we can see that the variables HFSFC, TDSWS, TMP, and NDNLW are highly correlated with solar power generation.

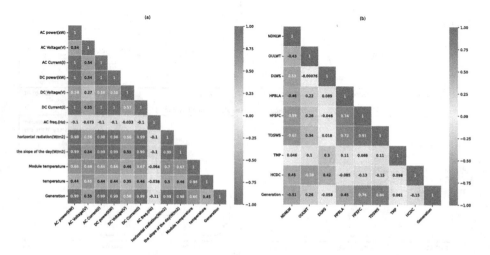

Fig. 2. The visualization of the correlations among datasets. (a) represents the correlation of the observed dataset from the inverter. (b) shows the correlation between NWP variables and Photovoltaic power generation.

3.2 TimesNet

TimesNet is a model that effectively models the complex temporal variation of time series data by exploiting polyperiodicity and enhances its representational power through two-dimensional transformation. The proposed TimesNet achieved SOTA performance in five major time series analysis tasks, including short-term and long-term forecasting, missingness imputation, classification, and outlier detection. The datasets used for solar power generation forecasting are also multivariate and have multiple time series patterns. TimesNet performs well on these datasets. The overall structure of TimesNet is shown in the Fig. 3.

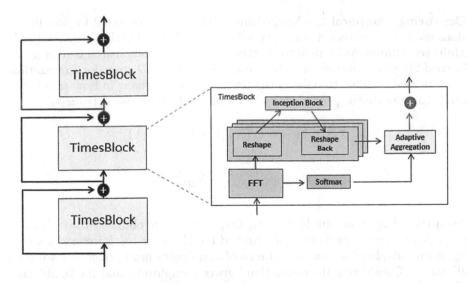

Fig. 3. Overall structure of TimesNet.

Transform 1D-Variations into 2D-Variations. To reflect the multi-periodicity characteristic of time-series data, timesnet converts the existing one-dimensional time series data into a two-dimensional space to simultaneously identify the inter-period, which reflects the short-term temporal pattern, and the intra-period, which reflects the long-term trend of successive periods.

First, use the Fast Fourier Transform (FFT) to derive the frequencies in the one-dimensional time series data. Find k periods using the top k frequencies with the largest amplitude among the FFT-derived frequencies as follows:

$$A = \text{Avg}\left(\text{Amp}\left(\text{FFT}\left(X_{1D}\right)\right)\right) \qquad (1)$$

$$\{f_1, \cdots, f_k\} = \underset{f_* \in \{1, \cdots, \lfloor \frac{T}{2} \rfloor\}}{\arg\text{Topk}}(A) \qquad (2)$$

$$\{p_1, \cdots, p_k\} = \left[\frac{T}{f_1}, \cdots, \frac{T}{f_k}\right] \qquad (3)$$

It represents the Fast Fourier Transform (FFT) and amplitude calculation as FFT(·) and Amp(·), respectively. For each frequency, the calculated amplitude $A \in \mathbb{R}^T$ is the average of C dimensions obtained using the Avg(·) function. Therefore, it selects the top-k amplitude values to obtain the corresponding frequencies $\{f_1, \cdots, f_k\}$. Each frequency is calculated as periods. To leverage the symmetry of the frequency domain, we only consider frequencies within the positive range, from 1 to $\lfloor \frac{T}{2} \rfloor$. After we get the periods, we transform them into 2D tensors using the reshape function. To simplify the reshaping process, we first use Padding(·) to ensure all periods have the same size. Then, we apply the following equation to convert them into 2D tensors by the following equation:

$$X_{2D}^i = \text{Reshape}_{pi, fi}\left(\text{Padding}\left(X_{1D}\right)\right), i \in \{1, \cdots, k\} \qquad (4)$$

Capturing Temporal 2D-Variations. The tensors converted to two dimensions are feature extracted using a two-dimensional kernel in the inception block. Multi-scale filters can be used to effectively extract various spatial features. The learned 2D representations are then reshaped back to 1D space for aggregation. Since it used Padding to reshape the tensor into a 2D shape in Equation (4), it needs to truncate the padded series to its original length using Trunc(·).

$$\hat{X}_{2D}^{l,i} = \text{Inception}\left(X_{2D}^i\right), i \in \{1, \cdots, k\} \tag{5}$$

$$\hat{X}_{1D}^{l,i} = \text{Trunc}\left(\text{Reshape}_{1,(p_i \times f_i)}\left(\hat{X}_{2D}^i\right)\right), i \in \{1, \cdots, k\} \tag{6}$$

Adaptive Aggregation. In Eq. (1), frequencies were obtained through FFT, and among them, periods were determined based on the top k frequencies with significant amplitudes. The importance of amplitudes lies in their role within a 2D tensor. Considering the correlation between amplitudes and the significance of the 2D tensor, aggregation of 1D tensors is performed based on these amplitudes. The amplitudes obtained through FFT are subjected to softmax, and the result is then aggregated through inner product and summation with the 1D tensors resulting from Eq. (6).

$$\hat{A}_{f_1}^{l-1}, \cdots, \hat{A}_{f_k}^{l-1} = \text{Softmax}\left(A_{f_1}^{l-1}, \cdots, A_{f_k}^{l-1}\right) \tag{7}$$

$$X_{1D}^l = \sum_{i=1}^{k} \hat{A}_{f_i}^{l-1} \times \hat{X}_{1D}^{l,i} \tag{8}$$

3.3   iTransformer

To perform well in time series forecasting, itransformer applies attentions and feedforward networks in an inverted dimension. The time points of individual

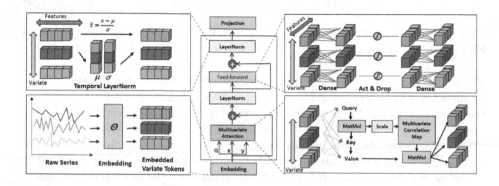

Fig. 4. Overall structure of iTransformer.

series are embedded in variable tokens that the attentional mechanism uses to capture multivariate correlations, while the feedforward network is applied to each variable token to learn a nonlinear representation. The datasets used in the study to predict solar power generation have a large number of variables, and by using itransformer to capture multivariate correlations, we have seen more efficient prediction performance. In layer normalization, iTransformer applies normalization to individual variable time series, as shown in Eq. (9) (Fig. 4).

$$\text{LayerNorm}(\mathbf{H}) = \left\{ \frac{h_n - \text{Mean}(h_n)}{\sqrt{\text{Var}(h_n)}} \mid n = 1, \cdots, N \right\} \tag{9}$$

In a typical transformer-based predictor, this module normalizes multivariate representations of the same timestamp, progressively fusing each variable to the other. However, the computation can introduce noise from interactions between the cause and the delayed process when the collected time points do not represent the same event. In the inverted version of normalization, normalization is applied to the series representation of each variable. This is effective for dealing with non-stationary problems. In the feedforward network, iTransformer achieves more accurate and generalized time series predictions due to differences in the application position of the feedforward network (FFN). FFN, by learning the unique characteristics of time series, outperforms self-attention mechanisms in linear tasks, leading to improved performance and generalization abilities.

In self-attention, iTransformer applies the self-attention mechanism to the entire variable time series, incorporating normalization during query, key, and value calculations. This approach implicitly includes correlation information among variables, making iTransformer more suitable and interpretable for multivariate time series predictions compared to traditional models.

3.4   Hybrid Framework

The model's architecture, depicted in the Fig. 5, can be broadly divided into three key components. First, it incorporates the TimesNet architecture, characterized by its ability to extract multi-periodicities from a normalized input sequence. As the normalized input sequence passes through the TimesNet model, it acquires essential temporal patterns inherent in the data. The output is a learned sequence that effectively captures the intricate structures of the time series. Second, the model integrates the iTransformer component. Building on the output of the TimesNet model, the iTransformer takes on the task of capturing multivariate correlations. By applying its distinctive features, the iTransformer enhances the overall performance of multivariate time series predictions. The model thus leverages the strengths of TimesNet in understanding temporal patterns and combines them with the capabilities of iTransformer to effectively model and predict multivariate relationships in time series data.

Finally, the network architecture undergoes optimization with the introduction of residual modules and feed-forward layers. This refinement aims to enhance

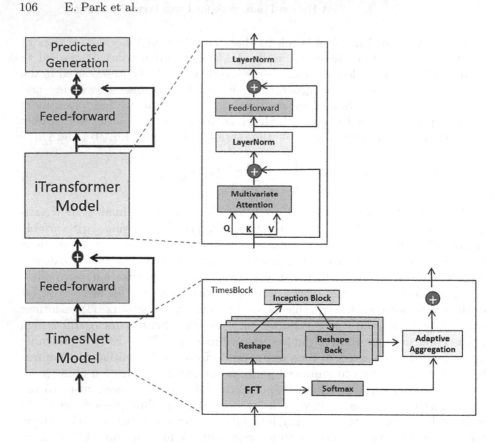

Fig. 5. Hybrid Model Structure

the overall nonlinear representations within the network, leading to an improvement in its performance. Residual modules contribute by mitigating the vanishing gradient problem and facilitating the flow of information through the network, while feed-forward layers further refine the learned representations, collectively contributing to the model's enhanced capabilities and overall effectiveness.

4   Experiments

As mentioned in Sect. 3.1, two datasets were utilized in this study: the dataset observed from the inverter and the NWP dataset. For performance comparison, we selected 9 well-established temporal forecasting models, including Informer [17], Pyraformer [18], Autoformer [19], LightTS [20], FEDformer [21], Dlinear [22], TimesNet [9], PatchTST [23], and iTransformer [10]. The evaluation metrics employed for assessing performance are Mean Squared Error (MSE) and Mean Absolute Error (MAE). The formulas for MSE and MAE are defined as follows:

$$MAE = \frac{1}{n} \sum_{i=1}^{n} |y_i - \hat{y}_i| \tag{10}$$

$$MSE = \frac{1}{n} \sum_{i=1}^{n} (y_i - \hat{y}_i)^2 \tag{11}$$

The dataset was normalized and divided into train, valid, and test sets for training and evaluation. Each dataset was trained with the input sequence length fixed at 96 and the window size of moving average fixed at 25, and various prediction lengths were used. First, the experimental results of the inverter dataset show that the proposed model structure has the best MSE performance for all prediction lengths, and the best MAE performance for prediction lengths of 120 and 192. Next, the TimesNet model performed well, followed by the Dlinear model, which also performed well. Second, on the NWP dataset, the proposed model structure performs the best in terms of MSE and MAE for all prediction lengths. TimesNet is the second best performer. When we experimented on the inverter dataset, there was a small difference in the metrics with the second best model, but when we experimented on the NWP dataset, there was a approximately significant difference of 0.7 with the second best model. Details are provided in Table 3. The Fig. 6 illustrates the results obtained from a 3-day long-term forecast using the NWP dataset. From this visualization, it can be seen that the forecasts made with the model structure proposed in this study most closely match the observed maximum solar power generation for each day. This agreement shows that the proposed model effectively captures the underlying patterns and trends in the data. In addition, the proposed hybrid model structure, which performed the best based on the above experiment, and the timesnet, itransformer, Dlinear, and patchTST models, which performed the next best, were experimented with input sequence lengths of 120 144 192 and prediction lengths of 96 120 144 192. As in the above experiment, the window

Table 3. Results for the long-term forecasting task. We compare ten competitive models extensively across various prediction lengths, specifically 96, 120, 144, 196. The input sequence length is fixed at 96. The "Avg" column represents the average performance across all four prediction lengths. For each dataset, we counted the occurrences of the top-performing and second-top-performing models, and the total count was computed.

Dataset	Models	Ours		iTransformer (2023)		PatchTST (2023)		TimesNet (2023)		Dlinear (2023)		FEDformer (2022)		LigthTS (2022)		Autoformer (2021)		Pyraformer (2021)		Informer (2021)	
Metric		MSE	MAE	MSE	MAE	MSE	MAE	MSE	MAE	MSE	MAE	MSE	MAE	MSE	MAE	MSE	MAE	MSE	MAE	MSE	MAE
Inverter	96	0.478	0.419	0.527	0.458	0.496	0.419	0.497	0.417	0.495	0.426	0.518	0.481	0.593	0.519	0.536	0.509	0.910	0.636	0.930	0.694
	120	0.457	0.404	0.533	0.466	0.502	0.423	0.500	0.418	0.500	0.429	0.529	0.489	0.599	0.524	0.545	0.516	0.889	0.634	1.041	0.750
	144	0.491	0.427	0.538	0.469	0.508	0.427	0.506	0.422	0.505	0.431	0.570	0.517	0.610	0.529	0.582	0.545	0.910	0.641	1.097	0.775
	192	0.467	0.407	0.547	0.477	0.514	0.431	0.499	0.417	0.510	0.434	0.522	0.481	0.611	0.531	0.659	0.589	0.881	0.637	1.093	0.803
	Avg	0.473	0.414	0.536	0.467	0.505	0.425	0.500	0.418	0.502	0.430	0.534	0.492	0.603	0.525	0.580	0.539	0.897	0.637	1.040	0.755
1st | 2st Count		8 / 2		0 / 0		0 / 0		2 / 4		0 / 2		0 / 0		0 / 0		0 / 0		0 / 0		0 / 0	
NWP	96	0.607	0.525	0.757	0.591	0.754	0.589	0.709	0.569	0.754	0.601	0.778	0.616	0.762	0.604	0.749	0.602	0.732	0.605	0.864	0.683
	120	0.637	0.541	0.769	0.597	0.767	0.595	0.728	0.577	0.763	0.606	0.785	0.620	0.768	0.608	0.766	0.611	0.737	0.607	0.902	0.708
	144	0.656	0.552	0.779	0.602	0.777	0.600	0.747	0.588	0.769	0.610	0.797	0.627	0.78	0.615	0.78	0.617	0.744	0.611	0.892	0.701
	192	0.674	0.563	0.799	0.611	0.795	0.609	0.772	0.600	0.781	0.617	0.804	0.632	0.793	0.622	0.777	0.615	0.759	0.623	0.903	0.707
	Avg	0.643	0.545	0.776	0.600	0.773	0.598	0.739	0.583	0.766	0.608	0.791	0.623	0.775	0.612	0.768	0.611	0.743	0.611	0.890	0.699
1st | 2st Count		10 / 0		0 / 0		0 / 0		0 / 10		0 / 0		0 / 0		0 / 0		0 / 0		0 / 0		0 / 0	
Total Count		20		0		0		16		2		0		0		0		0		0	

Table 4. The result of experiments on the inverter dataset, where the input sequence length was extended to 120, 144, 196, while prediction lengths of 96, 120, 144, 196. The "Avg" column indicates the average performance across all four prediction lengths. The model exhibiting the best performance in each experiment was counted.

Dataset	Models	Ours		iTransformer (2023)		PatchTST (2023)		TimesNet (2023)		Dlinear (2023)	
Metric		MSE	MAE	MSE	MAE	MSE	MAE	MSE	MAE	MSE	MAE
Inverter (120)	96	0.4453	0.4046	0.5020	0.4496	0.4795	0.4144	0.4837	0.4130	0.4784	0.4189
	120	0.4502	0.3971	0.5109	0.4564	0.4868	0.4185	0.4878	0.4155	0.4846	0.4221
	144	0.4578	0.4021	0.5188	0.4623	0.4924	0.4214	0.5279	0.4423	0.4887	0.4241
	192	0.4704	0.4124	0.5273	0.4705	0.4968	0.4242	0.5030	0.4225	0.4915	0.4264
	Avg	0.4559	0.4041	0.5148	0.4597	0.4889	0.4196	0.5006	0.4233	0.4858	0.4229
Inverter (144)	96	0.4420	0.3937	0.4946	0.4483	0.4696	0.4103	0.4763	0.4121	0.4698	0.4145
	120	0.4466	0.4002	0.5020	0.4538	0.4760	0.4138	0.5004	0.4268	0.4748	0.4170
	144	0.4522	0.3989	0.5061	0.4578	0.4796	0.4161	0.4726	0.4058	0.4773	0.4188
	192	0.4662	0.4098	0.5130	0.4640	0.4840	0.4188	0.4889	0.4137	0.4796	0.4208
	Avg	0.4518	0.4007	0.5039	0.4560	0.4773	0.4148	0.4845	0.4146	0.4754	0.4178
Inverter (192)	96	0.4416	0.4037	0.4843	0.4443	0.4594	0.4062	0.4640	0.4002	0.4576	0.4075
	120	0.4550	0.4103	0.4879	0.4472	0.4632	0.4088	0.4629	0.4009	0.4602	0.4094
	144	0.4574	0.4118	0.4904	0.4502	0.4658	0.4105	0.4741	0.4061	0.4622	0.4109
	192	0.4999	0.4347	0.4940	0.4535	0.4699	0.4127	0.4831	0.4121	0.4656	0.4131
	Avg	0.4635	0.4151	0.4891	0.4488	0.4646	0.4095	0.4710	0.4048	0.4614	0.4102
1st Count		24		0		1		5		0	

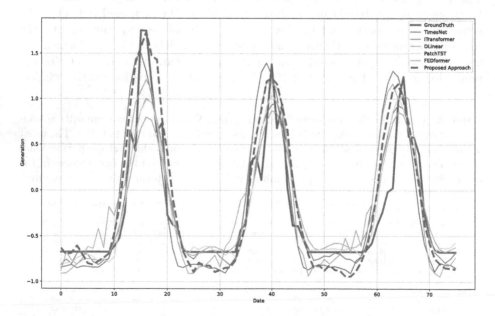

Fig. 6. The predicted values of photovoltaic power generation for a period of three days, generated by all models based on the NWP dataset.

size of moving average was fixed at 25, and In most of the experiments, The proposed model structure performs best in all evaluations when the input sequence length is 120,144, and performs well with TimesNet when the input sequence length is 192. We can also see that the proposed model structure performs significantly better than the other models when the input sequence is larger than 96. Details are provided in Table 4.

5   Conclusion and Future Work

The proposed model structure demonstrated superior performance in long-term photovoltaic power generation prediction tasks compared to existing time series prediction models. Particularly, experimental results using NWP meteorological data showed significantly better performance than other models. This can be attributed to the NWP dataset containing more variables than the dataset observed from the inverter, enabling the proposed model to exhibit enhanced performance. Utilizing the proposed model structure by combining datasets from both the inverter observations and NWP is expected to yield improved predictive accuracy. Based on the research findings in long-term photovoltaic power generation prediction, there is a need for future studies to enhance the efficiency of photovoltaic power projects from an economic perspective and stabilize power supply.

References

1. Nikitha, M.S., et al.: Solar PV forecasting using machine learning models. In: 2022 Second International Conference on Artificial Intelligence and Smart Energy (ICAIS). IEEE (2022)
2. Erdiwansyah, et al. A critical review of the integration of renewable energy sources with various technologies. Protection Control Modern Power Syst. **6**, 1–18 (2021)
3. Lee, W., et al.: Forecasting solar power using long-short term memory and convolutional neural networks. IEEE Access **6**, 73068–73080 (2018)
4. Alkhayat, G., Mehmood, R.: A review and taxonomy of wind and solar energy forecasting methods based on deep learning. Energy AI **4**, 100060 (2021)
5. Voyant, C., et al.: Machine learning methods for solar radiation forecasting: a review. Renewable Energy **105**, 569–582 (2017)
6. Vennila, C., et al.: Forecasting solar energy production using machine learning. Int. J. Photoenergy **2022**, 1–7 (2022)
7. Sharma, N., et al.: Predicting solar generation from weather forecasts using machine learning. In: 2011 IEEE International Conference on Smart Grid Communications (SmartGridComm). IEEE (2011)
8. Vaswani, A., et al.: Attention is all you need. Advances in neural information processing systems 30 (2017)
9. Wu, H., et al.: Timesnet: temporal 2d-variation modeling for general time series analysis. arXiv preprint arXiv:2210.02186 (2022)
10. Liu, Y., et al.: itransformer: inverted transformers are effective for time series forecasting. arXiv preprint arXiv:2310.06625 (2023)

11. von Rueden, L., et al.: Combining machine learning and simulation to a hybrid modelling approach: Current and future directions. In: Advances in Intelligent Data Analysis XVIII: 18th International Symposium on Intelligent Data Analysis, IDA 2020, Konstanz, Germany, April 27-29, 2020, Proceedings 18. Springer International Publishing (2020)
12. Kreuwel, Frank PM, et al. "Forecasting day-ahead 1-minute irradiance variability from numerical weather predictions." Solar Energy 258 (2023): 57-71
13. Du, Y., Li, Y., Liu, H.: A new hybrid prediction method of El Niño/La Niña events by Combining TimesNet and ARIMA. IEEE Access (2023)
14. Zuo, C., et al.: An ensemble framework for short-term load forecasting based on timesnet and tcn. Energies **16**(14), 5330 (2023)
15. Zhang, G., et al.: Solar forecasting with hourly updated numerical weather prediction. Renewable Sustainable Energy Rev. **154**, 111768 (2022)
16. Bakker, K., et al.: Comparison of statistical post-processing methods for probabilistic NWP forecasts of solar radiation. Solar Energy **191**, 138–150 (2019)
17. Zhou, H., et al.: Informer: beyond efficient transformer for long sequence time-series forecasting. In: Proceedings of the AAAI Conference on Artificial Intelligence, vol. 35. No. 12 (2021)
18. Liu, S., et al.: Pyraformer: low-complexity pyramidal attention for long-range time series modeling and forecasting. In: International Conference on Learning Representations (2021)
19. Wu, H., et al.: Autoformer: decomposition transformers with auto-correlation for long-term series forecasting. In: Advances in Neural Information Processing Systems 34, pp. 22419–22430 (2021)
20. Zhang, T., et al.: Less is more: Fast multivariate time series forecasting with light sampling-oriented mlp structures. arXiv preprint arXiv:2207.01186 (2022)
21. Zhou, T., et al.: Fedformer: frequency enhanced decomposed transformer for long-term series forecasting. In: International Conference on Machine Learning. PMLR (2022)
22. Zeng, A., et al.: Are transformers effective for time series forecasting? In: Proceedings of the AAAI Conference on Artificial Intelligence, vol. 37. No. 9 (2023)
23. Nie, Y., et al.: A time series is worth 64 words: long-term forecasting with transformers. arXiv preprint arXiv:2211.14730 (2022)

Design Futures, Ecological Citizenship and Public Interest Technologies = HCI Regenerative Interaction Opportunities …?

Robert Phillips[1]([✉]), John V. Wilshire[1], Elise Hodson[1], Sharon Baurley[1], Emily Boxall[1], Luke Gooding[2], Daniel Knox[3], Charlotte Nordmoen[1], Alec Shepley[3], Tracy Simpson[3], and Tom Simmons[1]

[1] The Royal College of Art, Design Futures, 1 Hester Road, London SW11 4AY, UK
robert.phillips@rca.ac.uk
[2] Stockholm Environmental Institute, Environment Building Department of Environment and Geography University of York, York YO10 5NG GB, UK
[3] School of Arts, Wrexham University, 49 Regent Street, Wrexham LL11 1PF, UK

Abstract. Design practice(s) improve circumstances applying foresight, instigating creative *Human Computer Interaction* (HCI) proposals within systems. HCI physically and digitally embodies technologies through human touchpoints. We refer to HCI points as *Public-Interest Technology* (PITs), a growing field comprising expertise working to ensure technology is created, deployed, and used responsibly. This article reports on design-led opportunities combining *Design Futures* (Domain 1) and *Ecological Citizenship* (Domain 2), questioning *Public-Interest Technologies* (Domain 3).

Design Futures navigates 'preferable futures' based on real-world, tangible situations within the context of climate futures and stewardship of environment(s) we rely upon for 'all life'. *Ecological Citizen(s)* catalyzes empowered agents, informing *Public-Interest Technologies* as (at this point in history) the people of the UK have never been so excluded, disconnected, and deprived from our natural world(s). Interested parties do both actions; calling out where technologies improve the public good, and questioning whether certain technologies should be created. Insights are appropriate to the HCI community as they cultivate design and community-led opportunities for technologies in the field, through design practice-led approaches.

We report on a *Regenerative Design Field Kit* with *Smithery* consultancy, deployment with Royal College of Art MDes Design Futures students. We highlight the toolkit's development, precedents, leading to a *Field Kit*. The parts: a viewing frame, (teaching tool) facilitating the examination of worlds and 40 core questions based on The Design Council's systemic design framework and the RSA's 10 core capabilities. Work yields valuable insights from Domains (1–3), mapping HCI opportunities for *Ecological Citizenship* within PITs.

Keywords: Ecological Citizenship · Design Principles · Regenerative Design

M. Kurosu and A. Hashizume (Eds.): HCII 2024, LNCS 14687, pp. 111–127, 2024.
https://doi.org/10.1007/978-3-031-60441-6_8

1   Introduction

This article reports on a *Regenerative Design Field Kit* combining; design futures, eco-logical citizenship with the means for students to instigate, question and cultivate *Public-Interest Technologies* (PITs). We specifically report on the use of a bespoke *Regenerative Design Field Kit* (Field Kit) with Design Futures students, mapping HCI opportunities for Ecological Citizenship, within PITs. *Public-Interest Technology* comprises "tech-nologists [and designers] working to ensure technology is created and used responsi-bly. [Parties] call out where technology can improve for the public good, question[ing] whether certain technologies should be created at all. PITs combine perspectives with a knowledge of the way technology works and an understanding of the ethical, legal, policy and societal concerns that shape our world" [1].

Modelled after public-interest law, PITs work to ensure technology is designed, deployed, and regulated, protect[ing] and improv[ing] the lives of people, centering values of equity, inclusion, and accountability where public interest is a priority. PITs are simultaneously a positive catalyst juxtaposed with serious (unseen) negative ram-ifications requiring review, not polarisation. A contemporary example, *'Hello Barbie'* (technological child's toy) "carried everywhere [children] and their parents go, could be the ultimate in audio surveillance device for miscreant hackers" [2]. In the early days of social media, particularly *Facebook*, security agencies advised publics against "post[ing] social media status update[s] indicating their vacations, as [you may as well] leave your home's front door open" [3].

Strava fitness geo-locating app, not only helps people "navigate air pollution whilst exercising" [4], but also required review as (historically) "its heatmap feature enable[d] stalkers and predators to track users to their home addresses and commit felonies" [5]. Even *'find my phone'*, a useful smartphone feature, (historically) caused implications for domestic violence [6]. Finally, technologies, i.e., 3D printers (the championed 'make anything anywhere tech'), have been used to fabricate untraceable working firearms [7].

These well-intentioned technologies require contextualisation, care, inverse ques-tioning, empathy, culture, deployment and unpicking for applications and continuously questioning activities post techno-solutionism [8]. It is not our desire to populate spaces with 'future' technologies, but to unpick potential pitfalls, benefits, and opportunities within this space to mitigate against unsustainable challenges. This article navigates three domains: *Design Futures (DF)* (Domain 1), *Ecological Citizenship (EC)* (Domain 2) and PITs (Domain 3). It shares the rationale, methodology and HCI opportunities, specifically identifying touchpoints for future interventions and proposals.

1.1   (D1) Design Futures

DF has many definitions, design fiction [9] or speculative design, but it is not a metaphor-ical crystal ball or science-fiction tool. We view DF alongside Hopkins [10] from *What Is to What If?* – navigating preferable futures. In a turbulent era for nature, planet, and people, how we navigate futures is paramount. DF (at the Royal College of Art) "is designed to enable work across all disciplines and beyond, build future-shaping knowl-edge and skills, address the challenges we face, envision and then navigate towards a preferred future through design-led interventions" [11]. Preferable as in "those we think 'should' or 'ought to' happen: normative value judgements as opposed to the mostly cognitive" and preferred futures encompass "what 'should' or 'ought to' happen – can take in any or all of the classes from preposterous to projected, because these futures must be at least imaginable" [12]. We see it as steps to progress, unpick and navigate unsustainable consequences of our global actions.

The 'craft' of DF is navigating; "inquisitiveness over predictability, bridging today and tomorrow, crafting future narratives, being champions for a better future and tackling long-term challenges" [13]. Futures are seen by businesses as foresight tools, bringing strategic resilience and means to navigate challenges and opportunities. Foresight "tools can use hard evidence or exploit creativity and imagination. They may be based on insights from an expert pool or collective thinking and promote participation" [14]. DF methods can include comprehensive qualitative or quantitative studies or lighter touch *Headlines from the Future* activities [15]. DF is not bound by one 'industry' or skill-set, but a craft, applying what is happening contextually, and identifying emergence in between the things that currently exist.

DF focuses on resilience and how that translates to sustainable practices, using design as a means to explore positive action within climate futures [16] – in a world where islands are taking countries to court [17], young people are advocating for change [18] and governments refuse to seek nature-based solutions [19]. At the moment our human existence (not technologies) are constant as technologies change – the difference is, in time we often think differently; for example the unknown health impacts of diets [20], that smoking tobacco was considered (historically) 'cool' [21], the need to keep 'plastics' on a tighter leash [22], questioning global travel [23] and the historical life of 'ultra-processed foods' [24].

1.2 (D2) Ecological Citizenship

EC is defined as accessible activities and skills establishing sustainable practice(s) and/or addressing ecological inequalities. This is encompassed in our approach—to our contextual surroundings, materials we use (and more) as an act of citizenship towards each other and the ecosystem. We "are (all) citizens of the world, with the natural environment sustaining all life on earth. Our human existence is intertwined with our environment; we live in, and are 'citizens' of, that environment. EC fosters positive, ecological behaviours involving and benefiting communities through individual and collective action(s)" [25]. The domain constantly questions 'what being a citizen means.' Unconcerned with place, or judicial waters, but with what it means to be empowered in place(s) you live, work, and contribute to… yielding 'better' for all. Citizen is a contentious term, we frame it as an opportunity for interested parties to have agency, enabling new sustainable practices. Stepping into the "citizen story, we recognise that context not only cannot be ignored, but that context is all. As citizens we must develop a sense of belonging in community, cultivate relationships with one another, help heal each other, and collectively build the world" [26]. *The Royal Society for the Encouragement of Arts, Manufactures and Commerce* (RSA) believes we are in an "economic, social and environmental crisis that has placed our world in a fragile, unbalanced and degenerative state" [27]. Their strategic aims are moving from 'sustain' "to 'do less harm' to the planet" to regenerate "seek[ing] to learn from Earth's living systems and look to regenerative future[s]" [28].

Regenerative design "has the goal of producing [outputs] with a net-positive impact on surroundings – restoring or improving their locales rather than aiming for less harm" [29]. Regenerative futures [30] are both; 1) a way of seeing the world, long rooted in many cultures, religions, and wisdom traditions around the globe, which is less present in dominant economic and social systems today; 2) An emerging paradigm, which looks to deepen notions of sustainability by taking a holistic approach to address current challenges [27]. Regenerative approaches are interlinked with Ecological Citizen(s), as they foster long-term agency in post-sustainable futures [31]. Sustainable futures are organizationaly run and top-down, post sustainable futures enable autonomy and decision making to its intended audience.

1.3 (D3) Public-Interest Technologies

Public-Interest Technology "is a growing field of technologists who work to ensure technology is created and used responsibly. Technologists call out where technology can improve for the public good, and sometimes question whether certain technologies should be created at all" [1]. In a leading *Freedman* report PIT challenges "are real and numerous, they are surpassed by the tremendous opportunities for action" [32]. Beyond access, "the challenge of PITs is the urgent need to create a new level of literacy, one that empowers [learners] not only to have access, but to be more selective and more integrative in information they receive" [33]. PITs are defined as the "application of design, data, and delivery to advance the public interest and promote the public good in the digital age" [34]. A "common mistake people make when trying to improve or modernise something is believing that digital will always be better. Digitising a broken paper process does not make it better" [34]. We see PITs as a means for collaborative, ethical and democratised action, providing technologies that protect individual rights and improve people's lives.

1.4 Uniting Domains

These domains coalesce, creating more ecologically, environmentally, and sustainably preferable futures. A contemporary approach is citizen science, for example "proving the River Wye was polluted" [35], or volunteer anglers monitoring for water quality as there is "limited government funding" with citizens looking after spaces they occupy [36]. The concept of "regeneration is inherently layered, complex, and evolving. It can have spiritual, ecological, and even medical connotations. Regardless of context, however, regeneration evokes hopeful themes of renewal, revival, rebirth, and restoration" [37]. Prospective design is a means of 'futures' believing that "Prospective Design is, in itself, a relation that discovers new possible relations in alternative presents, here and now" [38]. Figure 1, maps (known) analogue and digital intervention exemplars. We do not believe that 'technology' or futures only uses 'high-tech', but is appropriate and contextual to its surroundings, as represented in the following examples:

1. Historic Analogue Technology: a *Crinkle Crankle Wall 1}* "a curved structure taking fewer bricks to build than straight ones, gaining structural support from its sinuous shape, whilst a straight wall needs to be strengthened using buttresses" [39]. A process and technological knowledge that crosses domains.

2. Analogue Technology, Facilitating Digital; *Coast Snap 2}* hosts camera mount points around the Southwest coastline. Public smartphones are (momentarily) placed in camera mounts. Captured photos (taken from the mount) are shared with scientists offering "insights to a changing coastal environment including; beach erosion/accretion events to weather conditions, seasonal fluctuations and extreme storm events" [40]. A design mechanism that is cost and contextually effective.

3. Digital Technology: *Smart Citizens Kit 3}* "comprises various sensors measuring environmental parameters like temperature, humidity, noise levels, and air quality. This versatile tool empowers citizens to monitor surroundings, generate valuable data, and actively participate in creating solutions for their communities" [41]. A great resource that creates 'informed citizens'.

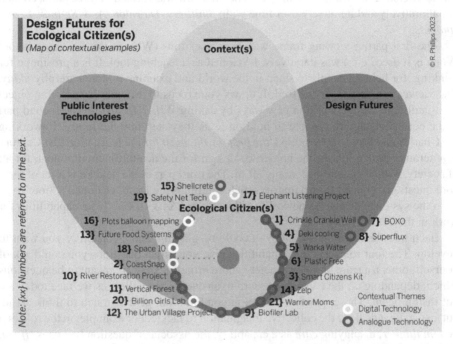

Fig. 1. Wider context of the design space. References and links within the map; **4}** Deki cooling [42], **5}** Warka Water [43], **6}** Plastic Free [44], **7}** BOXO [45], **8}** Superflux [46], **9}** Biofilter Lab [47], **10}** River Restoration Project [48], **11}** Vertical Forest [49], **12}** The Urban Village Project [50], **13}** Future Food Systems [51], **14}** Zelp [52], **15}** Shellcrete [53], **16}** Plots balloon mapping [54], **17}** Elephant Listening Project [55], **18}** Space 10 [56], **19}** Safety Net Tech [57], **20}** Billion Girls Lab [58], **21}** Warrior Moms [59].

2 Method

Toolkit Design. Design toolkits are means to help frame propositions, proposals, and prototypes. They are a set of parameters that operate as boundary objects [60]. Topics covered in our literature review included stewardship [61], play [62], circular design and more. We reviewed all and built on their processes, means and tools. Finally, we built on practitioner examples of a "resources audit", something that *Local Works Studio* do, navigating material mechanisms that are local to the building site [63]. Toolkits are "boundary tools" to help define and provide focus [64]. This article combines the domains (previously outlined) to show that they are accessible and provocative. It provides a framework for regenerative thinking, prototyping, and doing. The bespoke *Regenerative Design Field Kit (Field Kit)* offered *Design Futures* students mapping HCI opportunities for *Ecological Citizenship*, within PITs. The *Field Kit* was formed of three parts, created collaboratively and iteratively over time with: *Smithery, Thornton, A, & Shupak, L, and students.*

The first part, a viewing frame with core questions (What is this? What is it for? When is it used? etc.) was iteratively developed as a teaching tool. It is a prosthetic for thinking, for helping people to stand in the world and examine it more carefully *today.* The viewer is an *obliquiscope* [65]. It draws your focus to different layers of an object or situation, to see the world in new ways by asking *WHAT IS THIS?* The second part is the core challenge for people to hold on to as they step into the future. Reworking the Charles and Ray Eames motto (*'the best for the most for the least'*) for 21st Century regenerative design, it asks the holder to "design for the healthiest environment, for all of society, with the greatest economy" [66]. The third part of the field kit is a set of forty core questions, created from a matrix which combines the Design Council's "four roles from the systemic design framework" [67], and the *RSA's 10 C's*, "core capabilities for work in the 21st Century" [27].

Each question combines a role you could be playing, and a capability you want to develop. The four roles and ten capabilities give you direct questions you could ask of yourself, others, a team or indeed society, more broadly. They are meant to be questions which, depending on the context, are hard to answer. The challenges we face today are not insignificant. These questions, taken in combination, give us much to think about, but also a great deal for the collective imagination to tackle. For example, in the role of a *system thinker*, displaying *care* as a capability, the associated question becomes *'If you make the first change you think of, who won't benefit?'*. Participant demographic (MDes), was a mix of UK and international students, many of whom have have completed 2–3 years in industry in appropriate design industries from UX, service, product, industrial etc. The tensions around trying to hold all three of these ideas together in the same place is where people can start to find new points for intervention.

Participants were issued with a *Field Kit*, readings, and contexts to explore over three weeks. The main challenge, on the reverse of each card, is; 1) how do you design the healthiest environment, 2) with the greatest economy, and 3) for all in society. Participants were trained in the use of the *Field Kit* and underwent an orientation exercise before they started to map 'opportunities for what [they] viewed (through the obliquiscope) and how it could inform ecological citizenship'. Students were given support and asked to catalogue six images per person, to restrict the scope, specifically explaining the image identifying the opportunity for *"what you viewed and how it could inform ecological citizenship"*.

Over 55 participants contributed towards the gathered evidence. This was achieved through upload-able content, in the form of photographs and 100-word explanations of each image. Imagery was collected through an online portal over the course of one month. Thematic analysis was used by authors to map HCI opportunities for *Ecological Citizenship*, within PITs. The observations and notes through the DF students, were gathered on a digital platform, then mapped thematically against the following themes; *Embedded Interactions*, *Resource Access*, *Sustainable Alternatives*, and *Background System(s)*. Outlying data/images were removed or discounted from the thematic analysis if there was no description (provided by participants) or if it was repeated by another individual. These themes are specific with direct 'functionality' tangible for HCI communities/practitioners to scaffold off in multiple contexts.

3   Results

1. Embedded *Interactions:* are defined as "the technological and conceptual phenomena of seamlessly integrating the means for interaction into everyday artefacts. Technically, this requires embedding sensing, actuation, processing, and networking into common objects. Conceptually, it requires embedding interaction into users' everyday tasks" [68]. These are interactions that are built 'into' our environment, are accessible and not reliant on sole individuals, or siloed organisations. Examples of *Embedded Interactions* are train-ticket machines, public toilets, or supermarket self-checkouts.

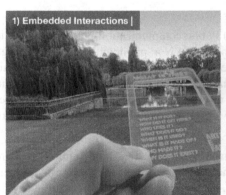 

Public rainwater harvesting, that is used for irrigation. *Image Credit ©Qiqi 2023* |

Self navigation within the context of efficient journeys, experiences. *Image Credit ©Trisha 2023* |

Fig. 2. Examples of embedded interactions.

Participant insights included (Fig. 2); i) Rainwater harvesting in public / private buildings and how community resources can be shared. Scenarios included potential models of how you would rent your roof to organisations for rain harvesting, a parallel to solar power. ii) Food inventories (based on retail activity) and how that information can be stored, shared, or used to reduce waste. iii) Reviewing 'ticket machines' as financial assets. These are embedded systems holding other functions (i.e., charitable donation, or local payment where digital/physical finance is an issue). iv) Water use /consumption and how that can be beneficial to know / share local resources.

2. *Resource Access:* we define it as the access to resources within ethical and inclusive means, rather than hierarchical structures. Resources refer to useful or valuable possession or quality of a country, organisation, or person.

Perception of waste. *Credit ©Ibrahim 2023* | Open resources for wider situations. *Credit ©Trisha 2023* | Biodiversity resources for all. *Credit ©Maria 2023* |

Fig. 3. Examples of resource access

Participant insights included (Fig. 3); i) Public communication points, e.g., public phone booths, charging stations and wayfinding. ii) Non-public/public resources e.g., sports clubs, wildlife properties, sports pitches, and libraries are public assets with amenities worthy of opening or consideration of how they can regenerate their environment. iii) Increasing biodiversity and how we can use digital means to perform transects, create accessible ecological records and positive parallel examples where we can all learn internationally from diverse cultures.

3. Regenerative Alternatives: defined as materials, sources and interventions that are proactively rejuvenating areas, means, materials or locations involved. To "regenerate" means to be formed or created again, restored to a better, higher, or more worthy state, to generate or produce anew, or to restore to original strength or properties" [69].

Participant insights included (Fig. 4); i) Public Transportation, and optimisation of resources not from a cost-benefit, but from a journey or engine efficiency perspective. ii) Personal Navigation, looking at footfall and complimentary subsidiary services, for example community delivery services or similar. iii) Scenario Impact Mitigation, foreseeing and unpicking certain actions to find probable impacts on resources and how

Integrated personal navigation.   Equitable & inclusive policy?   Exploring from different views.
Credit ©Trisha 2023 | Credit ©Trisha 2023 | Credit ©Maria 2023 |

Fig. 4. Examples of regenerative alternatives

those could be benefitted, for example water use or ethical purchasing. iv) Parallel Growing Conditions, comprehending international food growing conditions so growers can benefit from prior knowledge in ever-changing emerging conditions. New Economies, alternate means of trading, earning based on non-conventional constructs. For example, time sharing, skills exchange, non-financial transactions or digital 'Saturday jobs'.

Background System(s): we define this as a process that runs behind the scenes (i.e., in the background) but can leverage other interventions for interested parties. More specifically clearly communicating how systems operate and their subsidiary interconnections. These things are imperative so that more ecological and sustainable choices can be made (where possible). It is a series of interactions and touchpoints that can bring agency to decision makers.

When is something truly waste?   Material passports and the depth of everything
Credit ©Shaivi 2023 | 'made'Credit ©Shaivi 2023 |

Fig. 5. Examples of background systems.

Participant insights included (Fig. 5); i) Ethical Material Passports, a means to comprehend all details of materiality, sustainability, and production even after its third or fourth owner, entering a material custody model for easy repair and more. ii) Ethical End of Life, how we (our bodies) and the goods we own transition into the next stage of life. Iii) Public Food, the concept of using every space, location, and surface to grow accessible food within infrastructures. Something that is utopian, yet works with total logic. iv) Amenity Location & Distribution.

4 Discussion I

The researchers are aware of our biases and within design we often look for opportunities, and we are also aware of the desire for "techno-solutionism" within the discipline [70]. Within the domains (1–3) we identified and framed the responses in the analysed results. Authors perceive the following areas that are worthy of deeper research work as they are rich territories for HCI practices that can result in HCI opportunities for *Ecological Citizenship,* within *Public Interest Technologies.* The authors are also aware that the participants observed norms of "public to private", rather than private to public, meaning that participants explored how public systems benefit individuals.

4.1 Opportunities

HCI includes many technological means to make propositions. Within these we include; Augmented Reality, Virtual Reality, Data Repositories, Digital Sensing, Artificial Intelligence, Machine Learning, Mixed Reality, Embedded Technologies, Interconnectivity, and Internet of Things developments. We see these technologies as tools that can relay the following themes enabling Ecological Citizen PITs, although we are also aware of the 'carbon divide' and the appropriateness of these technologies to certain contexts [71].

Based on the participants' insights, discussions, and reflections while using the Field Kit, we have identified key touchpoints where HCI can be used to develop themes from our analysis, and where HCI design propositions could be created to benefit this space. This includes HCI for more sustainable choice(s); from product specifications, deconstruction and spare-part repositories, to looking at more socially led propositions. Within the context of the three domains explained above, it is critical not to create "a culture of blame" [72] around decisions regarding sustainability; people are making choices about their family statuses, e.g., not having children [73], while other decisions should be made by governments rather than burdening individuals.

Including Future Generations: We need to include younger generations and children in choices about PITs, as they will inherit the impacts of these new technologies [74]. How do we/should we cultivate HCI systems for the bigger picture, for preferable futures? Or indeed how do we provide training or systems to onboard younger generations to the future systems we will need?

Decision making: more informed decision-making and diagnosis tools, for example AI decision-making that can help with everything from making journeys, supply chains, reducing food waste, to foreseeing the impacts of city construction and infrastructure change. The opportunity here is linking systems and improving communication between parties.

Inventory management: waste optimisation in all manner of systems, from domiciles to parts records on physical / digital systems etc.

Shared conditions: we are a connected world, somewhere in the world there are communities experiencing similar weather conditions to us/you. Digitally sharing those experiences; how they are growing food, how they live their lives, can be shared, and learnt from and are an amazing opportunity.

Interactive Material Passports: Repositories of items, washing instructions, identifying materials' compliance, artefacts that can talk to each other for easy replacement, repair/deconstruction, and key interactions. This could aid provenance tracing and encourage more locally based consumption.

Provenance: Burton (snowboards) are building material passports within high-end sports equipment [75]. Not only do these open-up cultures of repair and material provenance but they could also e.g., open up how buildings are recycled [76] and planning is co-opted with links to 'decision-making' applications. Fairphone has also set the bar in using ethically sourced materials that are dictating best practices for how materials should be sourced and communicated.

Sub-assemblies: products are built off common batteries and parts you will find in many items. There are digital opportunities for deconstruction, repair, reconstruction, and parts distribution.

Systems: the interconnection between things is vast, i.e., clothes labelling informing washing machines, to ensure optimum washing cycles etc.

Purchasing power; people are changing their purchasing choices informed by ethical sourcing and sustainable impacts, often badged (rightly so) as 'green washing', however sustainable practices are good for business.

Interactions that Yield New Economies and Public Regeneration. Saturday jobs, means of gathering data / citizen science that is validated and worthy of finance, new means of sharing tools, digitally mapping regenerative assets parks etc., interactive biodiversity corridor connectors, and connecting local skills bases.

Healthy world: there are so many opportunities now to create health-based interactions that can inform and protect citizens, for example detecting heart irregularities in shopping trolley handles [77] or via toilets monitoring our health [78]. The question at hand is: do we opt-in, and how is that ethically managed?

Citizen Science: opportunities are in full and existing operation, however the bigger opportunity for HCI is in ground truthing data, and enhancing how we protect the natural world through monitoring and data collection. Often this is built from dual motivations or across sectors, but building 'citizen-led' processes with rigorous data is a continuous interaction and HCI opportunity.

Cottage Data Industries: we are already in the domain of cottage makers and online selling, but akin to YouTube 'selling content' there is a model for selling your home's CO_2 footprint for optimisation, albeit a tiny market; a street-scale documentation of 'real-world' living could be shared and optimised.

Hubs: we see public resources as, eg. Libraries, however, imagine if football clubs/venues could have regenerative effects on their surroundings. In peak Premier League season, 30,943 visitors go to Brighton & Hove Albion every week [79]. HCI interactions created for scenarios could yield scale. Knepp Estate (infamous rewilding site in Sussex, UK) was often thought of as unprofitable. Now, Knepp's nature tourism business – comprising 'wild safaris', camping, glamping, and a shop –has a turnover of around £800,000 per year, with a 22% profit margin (£190,000) [80]. It has cultivated; local volunteering, wellbeing, policy and social change, sustainable means, and species recovery and reintroduction (some of which have not been found in the UK since the Mediaeval period). This in turn connects communities to places, and provides opportunities for connection and creation of digital and physical interactions in the space.

4.2 Pitfalls

From our insights, the authors see spaces where more fundamental changes are required before the identified themes can be developed. Our current economic models are driven by capitalism [81] and this new typology of work requires the uptake of more distributed means. The ethical dimension and related security issues (e.g., of information) need to be unpicked and are only just being publically understood. The challenges of interested parties' motivation(s), outside of financial gain, are a further consideration. These models should be accessible to all, not just those that can afford the time. The kit did not identify economic means to support activities.

5   Conclusion

This field is new to design, but it is post-sustainability and requires deeper investigation, especially as our participants explored 'public to private' resources and not vice versa. This is an ongoing process, however we feel that learning how to look and unpick and identify HCI interactions/systems for regenerative opportunities can unite Product, Service, Systems. Whilst this requires refinement, it is an impactful process/tool for questioning how we can interlink HCI assets. Here we have identified several domains that can be explored for HCI purposes.

Acknowledgements. Rights Retention Statement: This work was funded by UKRI grant (EP/W020610/1). For the purpose of open access, the author has applied a Creative Commons Attribution (CC BY) licence to any Author Accepted Manuscript version arising. We thank the students of the *Design Futures* (MDes) programme at the Royal College of Art particularly; *Arushi, Feng, Fliss, Ibrahim, Lin, Maria, Martha, Mehek, Qingyi, Qiqi, Rafael, Shaivi, Tanushree, Trisha* who shared their imagery. The Ecological Citizen(s) is a cross-RCA research network led by Dr. Rob Phillips, with Professor Sharon Baurley, and Tom Simmonds, in partnership with Professor Sarah West of the Stockholm Environment Institute (SEI) at the University of York, and Professor Alec Shepley of the Faculty of Arts, Science and Technology at Wrexham Glyndŵr University, and partners from industry, third sector, NGO. Ecological Citizens is a Digital Economy Network+ project funded by the UKRI Digital Economy Programme, that is focused on digital interventions that would create 'the conditions to make change' towards a sustainable post-industrial society. The work was supported by the EPSRC Network+ award (EP/W020610/1). We acknowledge the proofing work of colleague Dan Price.

Disclosure of Interests. The authors have no competing interests to declare that are relevant to the content of this article.

References

1. Ford Foundation. Public interest technology and its origins - Ford Foundation (2023). https://www.fordfoundation.org/work/challenging-inequality/technology-and-society/public-int erest-technology-and-its-origins/. Accessed 4 Oct 2023
2. Gibbs, S.: Hackers can hijack Wi-Fi Hello Barbie to spy on your children. The Guardian (2019). https://www.theguardian.com/technology/2015/nov/26/hackers-can-hijack-wi-fi-hello-barbie-to-spy-on-your-children. Accessed 4 Oct 2023
3. NBC News. Social Media Status Updates Tip Off Burglars, Study Shows (2011). https://www.nbcnews.com/id/wbna45195926. Accessed 4 Oct 2023
4. Sun, Y., Mobasheri, A.: Utilizing crowdsourced data for studies of cycling and air pollution exposure: a case study using Strava data. Int. J. Environ. Res. Public Health **14**(3), 274 (2017)
5. Ngila, F.: Researchers found that Strava's heatmap feature could lead stalkers to users' homes. Quartz (2023). https://qz.com/strava-s-heatmap-feature-could-expose-users-to-stalkers-185 0532840. Accessed 4 Oct 2023
6. Woodlock, D.: The abuse of technology in domestic violence and stalking. Violence Against Women **23**(5), 584–602 (2017)
7. Ghost Gunner. Ghost Gunner (2019). https://ghostgunner.net/. Accessed 4 Oct 2023
8. Avle, S., Li, D., Lindtner, S.: Responsible IoT after techno-solutionism. ThingsCon Report: The State of Responsible Internet of Things 2018 (2018)
9. Dunne, A., Raby, F.: Speculative Everything: Design, Fiction, and Social Dreaming. MIT Press (2013)
10. Hopkins, R.: From What is to What If: Unleashing the Power of Imagination to Create the Future We Want. Chelsea Green Publishing (2019)
11. Design futures. RCA Website (2023). https://www.rca.ac.uk/study/programme-finder/design-futures/. Accessed 4 Oct 2023
12. Voros, A.J.: The Futures Cone, use and history. The Voroscope (2023). https://thevoroscope.com/2017/02/24/the-futures-cone-use-and-history/. Accessed 4 Oct 2023
13. Schindler, T.: Why every organization needs a futurist in residence — Tanja Schindler ǀ Futurist. Tanja Schindler ǀ Futurist (2023). https://www.tanjaschindler.com/blog/why-every-organization-needs-a-futurist-in-residence. Accessed 4 Oct 2023
14. Digital, S.: The Future Is Ours: Strategic Foresight toolkit – making better decisions ǀ Save the Children's Resource Centre. Save the Children's Resource Centre (2023). https://resourcec entre.savethechildren.net/pdf/strategic_foresight_toolkit_online.pdf/. Accessed 4 Oct 2023
15. Session Lab. Headlines from the Future (2019). https://www.sessionlab.com/methods/headli nes-from-the-future. Accessed 4 Oct 2023
16. Flood, S., Cradock-Henry, N.A., Blackett, P., Edwards, P.: Adaptive and interactive climate futures: systematic review of 'serious games' for engagement and decision-making. Environ. Res. Lett. **13**(6), 063005 (2018)
17. McVeigh, K.: Small island nations take high-emitting countries to court to protect the ocean. The Guardian (2023). https://www.theguardian.com/environment/2023/sep/10/small-island-nations-take-high-emitting-countries-to-court-to-protect-the-ocean#:~:text=During%20the%20two%2Dday%20hearing,environment%20should%20be%20considered%20poll ution. Accessed 4 Oct 2023
18. Laville, S.: Young people to take 32 European countries to court over climate policies. The Guardian (2023). https://www.theguardian.com/environment/2023/sep/14/young-people-to-take-32-european-countries-to-court-over-climate-policies. Accessed 4 Oct 2023

19. Greenfield, P., Horton, H.: Ministers 'ignored' own adviser over weak targets for restoring English nature. The Guardian (2023). https://www.theguardian.com/environment/2023/mar/16/ministers-ignored-own-adviser-over-weak-targets-for-restoring-english-nature. Accessed 4 Oct 2023
20. Bali, A., Naik, R.: The impact of a vegan diet on many aspects of health: the overlooked side of veganism. Cureus 15(2) (2023)
21. Sangole, O.M.: A study on teenage and college culture: why substance abuse is considered as cool? Int. J. Indian Psychol. 11(1) (2023)
22. Holmberg, K., Persson, S.: Keep plastics on a tight leash: Swedish public opinion on plastic policies. Environ Sci Policy 141, 109–116 (2023)
23. Aaditya, B., Rahul, T.M.: Long-term impacts of COVID-19 pandemic on travel behaviour. Travel Behaviour Soc. 30, 262–270 (2023)
24. Hall, K.D.: From dearth to excess: the rise of obesity in an ultra-processed food system. Philos. Trans. R. Soc. B 378(1885), 20220214 (2023)
25. Phillips, R., et al.: Defining ecological citizenship; Case-studies, projects & perspectives; analysed through a design-led lens, positioning 'preferable future (s)'. In: Design for Adaptation Cumulus Conference Proceedings Detroit 2022, pp. 264–288. Cumulus Association (2023)
26. Alexander, J., Conrad, A., Eno, B.: Citizens: Why the Key to Fixing Everything is All of Us. Canbury Press
27. RSA. Regenerative futures (2023). https://www.thersa.org/regenerative-futures. Accessed 4 Oct 2023
28. RSA. Shifting towards a life-centric business - The RSA Blog (2023). https://www.thersa.org/blog/2023/07/shifting-towards-a-life-centric-business. Accessed 4 Oct 2023
29. Sto Corp. Regenerative design: Going beyond sustainability (2022). https://www.stocorp.com/regenerative-design-going-beyond-sustainability/. Accessed 4 Oct 2023
30. Arup. Regenerative design (2023). https://www.arup.com/perspectives/regenerative-design. Accessed 4 Oct 2023
31. Global Ecovillage Network. Ecovillage Design Course - Design with all dimensions of Sustainability (2023). https://ecovillage.org/sustainability-education/ecovillage-design-course/?gad=1&gclid=CjwKCAjwyNSoBhA9EiwA5aYlb72qmWJNJQt7_kAROUfFExJyMrOlZ1LBIBgxrQxfauzKNaum2f9UoRoCoEIQAvD_BwE. Accessed 4 Oct 2023
32. Freedman Consulting. A pivotal moment - Squarespace (2016). https://static1.squarespace.com/static/5a5e62b02aeba5a8b337504b/t/5a86ff58e2c48398a124a0c5/1518796635450/pivotalmoment.pdf. Additionally, program staff from several foundations, including the Ford Foundation, the John D. and Catherine T. MacArthur Foundation, the John S. and James L. Knight Foundation, the Open Society Foundations, the Mozilla Foundation, the Media Democracy Fund, the Omidyar Network, and the William and Flora Hewlett Foundation, informed the shape and direction of this research
33. Boyer, E.L.: New technologies and the public interest. Leonardo 29(3), 248–250 (1996)
34. McGuinness, T.D., Schank, H.: Power to the Public: The Promise of Public Interest Technology. Princeton University Press (2021)
35. Ungoed-T, J.: 'Citizen scientists make a vital difference': the locals who proved the River Wye was polluted. The Guardian (2023). https://www.theguardian.com/global/2023/aug/12/citizen-scientists-make-a-vital-difference-the-locals-who-proved-the-river-wye-was-polluted. Accessed 4 Oct 2023
36. Horton, H.: 'We are not going away': the volunteers fighting back against England's polluted rivers. The Guardian (2022). https://www.theguardian.com/environment/2022/sep/14/we-are-not-going-away-the-volunteers-fighting-back-against-englands-polluted-rivers. Accessed 4 Oct 2023

37. Camrass, K.: Regenerative futures: eight principles for thinking and practice. J. Fut. Stud. (2022)
38. Van Amstel, F.: Designing relations in Prospective Design. Frederick Van Amstel (2023). https://fredvanamstel.com/talks/designing-relations-in-prospective-design
39. Jenkins, P.: The Crinkle-Crankle Wall explained | Blog | ALCO Properties (2023). ALCO Properties. https://alcoltd.co.uk/alco-news/crinkle-crankle-wall-explained/ [Accessed 4 Oct. 2023]
40. CoastSnap. SWRCMP (2022). https://southwest.coastalmonitoring.org/coastsnap-home/. Accessed 4 Oct 2023
41. Smart Citizens. Smart Citizen empowers communities to better understand their environment (2019). https://smartcitizen.me/. Accessed 4 Oct 2023
42. Siripurapu, M.: Deki cooling installation. Ant Studio (2018). http://ant.studio/beehive/kf5xbx dw7lcg0nll8j1omv18tebcr6. Accessed 4 Oct 2023
43. Vittori, A.: Projects. Warka Water (2019). https://warkawater.org/projects/. Accessed 4 Oct 2023
44. PlasticFreeDotCom Limited. Create what's next. PlasticFree (2020). https://plasticfree.com/. Accessed 4 Oct 2023
45. Boxo. Boxo, Herbruikbare Verzendverpakkingen voor webshops. Herbruikbare verzendver-pakkingen voor webshops (2023). https://boxo.nu/. Accessed 4 Oct 2023
46. Jain, A.: Refuge for resurgence. Superflux (2023). https://superflux.in/index.php/work/ref uge-for-resurgence/#. Accessed 4 Oct 2023
47. SPACE 10. Biofilter Lab. Esteban Gomez. https://estebangomez.co/Biofilter-Lab. Accessed 4 Oct 2023
48. Marshall, C.: Story of cities #50: The Reclaimed Stream Bringing Life to the Heart of Seoul. The Guardian (2016). https://www.theguardian.com/cities/2016/may/25/story-cities-reclaimed-stream-heart-seoul-cheonggyecheon. Accessed 4 Oct 2023
49. SPACE 10. How can we meet the needs and dreams of the many people while remaining within the boundaries of the planet? Space10 Mexico City: Beyond human-centred design (2019). https://space10.com/projects/space10-mexico-city. Accessed 4 Oct 2023
50. Bakker, J.: Future Food System Future Food System. Future Food System (2018). https://www.futurefoodsystem.com/. Accessed 4 Oct 2023
51. Boeri, S.: Vertical Forest: Milan. Stefano Boeri Architetti (2023). https://www.stefanoboeri architetti.net/en/project/vertical-forest/. Accessed 4 Oct 2023
52. Zelp. Reduce methane emissions while improving animal welfare (2016). https://www.zel p.co/. Accessed 4 Oct 2023
53. Bosence, B.: Building materials from shells. Local Works Studio (2021). https://localwork sstudio.com/projects/shellcrete-transforming-sea-shells-into-low-carbon-materials/#:~:text= Shellcrete%20is%20an%20on%2Dgoing,and%20landscape%20materials%20and%20feat ures. Accessed 4 Oct 2023
54. Warren, J.: Public lab: Balloon & kite mapping (2012). https://publiclab.org/wiki/balloon-mapping. Accessed 4 Oct 2023
55. Payne, K.: Elephant Listening Project Home. Elephant Listening Project. https://www.elepha ntlisteningproject.org/. Accessed 4 Oct 2023
56. SPACE 10. Could flat-pack housing pave the way for better everyday living in the city? The Urban Village Project: Re-envisioning our homes (2019). https://space10.com/projects/ urban-village. Accessed 4 Oct 2023
57. Watson, D.: Enabling precision fishing. SafetyNet Technologies (2023). https://sntech.co.uk/. Accessed 4 Oct 2023
58. IDEO.org. Billion girls collab. Billion Girls Collab (2020). https://www.billiongirlscolab.des ign/. Accessed 4 Oct 2023

59. Carrington, D.: "Put kids first": India's warrior moms fight for clean air at COP27. The Guardian (2022). https://www.theguardian.com/environment/2022/nov/11/india-warrior-moms-cop27-egypt-climate. Accessed 4 Oct 2023

60. Akkerman, S.F., Bakker, A.: Boundary crossing and boundary objects. Rev. Educ. Res. **81**(2), 132–169 (2011). https://doi.org/10.3102/0034654311404435

61. Anon. Toolkit for Steward-Ownership. Purpose (2021). https://purpose-economy.org/en/workbook-steward-ownership/. Accessed 4 Oct 2023

62. Falaydesign. A toolkit for play: The Environmental Citizen's Playbook. Falay Transition Design (2019). https://www.falaydesign.com/news-events/a-toolkit-for-play. Accessed 4 Oct 2023

63. Local Works Studio. Services. Local Works Studio (2018). https://localworksstudio.com/practice/services-2/#:~:text=Resource%20mapping%20and%20material%20audits. Accessed 4 Oct 2023

64. Rhinow, H., Köppen, E., Meinel, C.: Design prototypes as boundary objects in innovation processes (2012)

65. Willshire, J.V.: Obliquiscopes: setting aperture for reality. Smithery (2023). https://smithery.com/2023/09/22/obliquiscopes-setting-aperture-for-reality/

66. Raworth, K.: About doughnut economics. [online] Doughnut Economics Action Lab (2021). https://doughnuteconomics.org/about-doughnut-economics. Accessed 4 Oct 2023

67. Design Council. Systemic Design Framework - Design Council (2023). https://www.designcouncil.org.uk/our-resources/systemic-design-framework/

68. Kranz, M., Holleis, P., Schmidt, A.: Embedded interaction: Interacting with the internet of things. IEEE Internet Comput. **14**(2), 46–53 (2009)

69. Greener World. What is "Regenerative"? 9 Reasons You Should Care (2022). https://agreenerworld.org/a-greener-world/what-is-regenerative-9-reasons-you-should-care/

70. Selwyn, N.: Lessons to Be Learnt? Education, Techno-solutionism, and Sustainable Development. Technol. Sustain. Dev. **71** (2023)

71. Watts, J., Wishart, E., Amitrano, A., Burkett, P., Cousins, R.: The great carbon divide. The Guardian (2023). https://www.theguardian.com/environment/ng-interactive/2023/nov/20/the-great-carbon-divide-climate-chasm-rich-poor

72. Petersson McIntyre, M.: Shame, blame, and passion: Affects of (un) sustainable wardrobes. Fash. Theory **25**(6), 735–755 (2021)

73. Gayle, D.: More people not having children due to climate breakdown fears, finds research. The Guardian (2023). https://www.theguardian.com/environment/2023/nov/09/more-people-not-having-children-due-to-climate-breakdown-fears-finds-research#:~:text=But%20what%20had%20seemed%20an,their%20fears%20of%20climate%20breakdown

74. Kaminski, I.: Stop locking young people out of legal process in climate cases, say experts. The Guardian (2023). https://www.theguardian.com/environment/2023/oct/26/stop-locking-young-people-out-of-legal-process-in-climate-cases-say-experts

75. Nishimura, K.: Sourcing Journal. Sourcing Journal (2023). https://sourcingjournal.com/topics/compliance/avery-dennison-digital-product-passport-as-a-service-burton-snowboards-circular-economy-action-plan-463383/

76. Metabolic. Materials passport for a circular economy (2019). https://www.metabolic.nl/news/circular-economy-materials-passports/?gad_source=1&gclid=CjwKCAiAu9yqBhBmEiwAHTx5p9OuIDbuG7VgBywCzZPV6ulv1My8DaAu0xSYcMOkesRQEbVDFwNp9xoC7ScQAvD_BwE

77. Roberts, B.M.: Supermarket trolleys reveal heart problems in shoppers. BBC News (2023). https://www.bbc.co.uk/news/health-65983627#:~:text=Supermarket%20trolleys%20with%20a%20special,any%20irregularities%20while%20they%20shop.

78. Zhou, J., et al.: Stool image analysis for digital health monitoring by smart toilets. IEEE Internet Things J. **10**(5), 3720–3734 (2022)

79. Transfermarkt. Brighton & Hove Albion - Change in attendance figures (2023). https://www. transfermarkt.co.uk/brighton-amp-hove-albion/besucherzahlenentwicklung/verein/1237
80. Rewilding Britain: Case study: Knepp Estate (2023). https://www.rewildingbritain.org.uk/ why-rewild/rewilding-success-stories/case-studies/knepp-estate
81. Bell, D.: The cultural contradictions of capitalism. J. Aesthetic Educ. **6**(1/2), 11–38 (1972)

Human Factors Design of Electric Bicycle Charging Shed Based on STAMP

Shiqi Tang, Xuanyue Wang, and Zhijuan Zhu(✉)

School of Mechanical Science and Engineering, Huazhong University of Science and Technology, Wuhan, People's Republic of China
zhuzhijuan@hust.edu.cn

Abstract. This study was conducted to address the problems of non-standard charging time and vehicle stacking that may lead to fire accidents, focusing on the usage process of campus electric bicycle charging sheds. The safety constraint within electric bicycle charging system was determined, and a hierarchical model based on human factors for the control on the risk of electric bicycle charging accident was constructed. Potential unsafe control behaviors were identified in the control model, and their comprehensive weights were calculated and ranked by using AHP (Analytic Hierarchy Process). Human factors analysis and design optimization were performed to obtain the optimal solution. In addition, the feasibility and effectiveness of this approach through the design practice of the campus electric bicycle charging shed were verified. This implementation demonstrated that incorporating the STAMP model and human factors engineering theory in the early stages of electric bicycle charging shed design could improve the safety and comfort of user charging processes and provide new ideas for the design of charging shed structures and charging interaction systems, such as electric bicycle charging shed design.

Keywords: System theory accident model and process · Ergonomics · Electric bicycle charging pile · Security · Accident prevention

1 Introduction

Charging shed is one of the most important public facilities to provide charging places and shelter for electric bicycles on campus [1]. The advantages and disadvantages of its design directly affect the charging safety, charging efficiency, user comfort and satisfaction of the charging shed. With the emergence of potential unsafe factors such as unattended charging behavior, weather influence, and different brands of electric bicycle chargers, the probability of danger when charging users is greatly increased. At present, the charging shed has been studied in the parking environment [2] and the charging program [3]. However, there are few designs from the aspects of fire hazard prevention and human-computer interaction. Therefore, the purpose of this paper is to design a campus electric bicycle charging shed system that can realize safe and comfortable charging based on the risk control-human factors model of electric bicycle charging accident [4].

© The Author(s), under exclusive license to Springer Nature Switzerland AG 2024
M. Kurosu and A. Hashizume (Eds.): HCII 2024, LNCS 14687, pp. 128–143, 2024.
https://doi.org/10.1007/978-3-031-60441-6_9

2 Related Research

2.1 STAMP Model Theory

STAMP (System Theory Accident Model and Process) is an accident analysis model proposed by Leveson [5], also known as accident prevention and risk control model. It is mainly used to investigate the causes of safety accidents in the system, verify the safety of the system, and present the executing agencies and processes of risk prevention and control in the system through the model [6].

In the research field of charging shed design, scholars have done a lot of research on the charging environment, charging technology and charging process of electric bicycles. Wan Mingshuai et al. [7] analyzed the parking environment and user charging process of the charging shed. Luo Yunqing et al. [8] designed an intelligent charging management system with overload protection, automatic start and stop functions for the characteristics of centralized charging, unattended and complex environment of electric bicycles. Zhu Zhe [3] et al. studied the charging applet and control components. Liao Yang et al. [2] studied the size, parking space and layout of electric bicycles. Shen Jianliang et al. [9] believed that the frequent charging accidents of electric bicycles are due to the uneven quality of batteries and chargers and the unoptimized charging technology, and innovatively proposed a charging mode that uses a DC output charging method and can automatically adjust the output and protection according to the parameters of the charged battery [10].

Based on the above literature analysis, academic research of China on the human factors of electric bicycle charging sheds is relatively scattered, and it pays more attention to the research on the causes of charging accidents and intelligent management, which cannot meet the needs of users for the safety and comfort of electric bicycle charging sheds [11]. Therefore, the STAMP [12] model and human factors design method are introduced to increase the security of the system and the comfort of users in the system requirement design stage.

2.2 Research Status of Human Factors of Electric Bicycle Charging Shed

The design of the charging shed directly affects the satisfaction of users with the charging shed, and also greatly affects the probability of danger during charging [13]. According to the data of China Fire Bulletin, there were 15,000 electric moped fire accidents from January to October 2022, far exceeding the total number of last year. A total of 18,000 fires occurred, an increase of 25.7% over the same period last year. According to the above data research, it can be seen that there are many safety hazards in the charging process of electric bicycles, which threaten property and life safety of people. It is of great significance to analyze the causes of electric bicycle fires and preventive measures, and optimize the design of charging sheds to curb fire casualties and ensure people's safe life.

3 Research on the Design of Charging Shed Based on STAMP Model

STAMP system theory regards the system as a whole, which can identify the cause of danger more comprehensively, to reduce the risk of accidents. Because the campus charging shed is common in residential areas, the safety requirements are high, and the consequences of the accident will be very serious. Therefore, it is necessary to combine the STAMP model with the human factor design method, and ensure the system security as the emergence from the system level, so as to achieve the design purpose of improving the comfort of charging users and the safety of charging shed.

3.1 Theoretical Model

The STAMP analysis process includes the following four steps [14], see Fig. 1: (1) Identify system security constraints; (2) Determine the safety control structure; (3) Identify potential control defects; (4) Evaluate the system security status. Based on the above steps, this paper redesigns the campus charging shed.

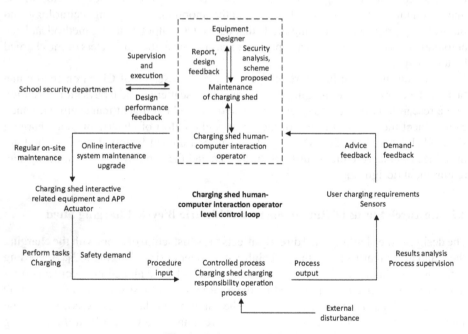

Fig. 1. Safety control circuit

Firstly, System Security Constraint Identification. In order to ensure the security of the system performance, the security constraints are identified and analyzed. The safety constraints include: the user operates the charging according to the specified safety code of conduct; design and maintenance personnel set up safety measures for the interaction process of the charging shed; ensure the normal operation of the charging shed during use.

Secondly, the STAMP-Human Factor Model of Charging Shed Interaction System is Constructed. By using the advantages of this model in system design, the charging shed interaction system is substituted into the analysis, and the core structure of the control loop is analyzed emphatically, so that the control feedback interaction between levels emerges the characteristics of the overall safety of the system. The control loop and local control structure of the use phase are shown in Figs. 2 and 3.

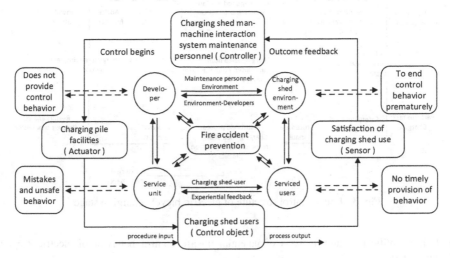

Fig. 2. Electric bicycle charging STAMP-human factor control loop model

Thirdly, Unsafe Behavior Recognition in STAMP-Human Factors Model. The local control loop and safety constraints of the charging shed in the use stage of the STAMP-human control loop model are analyzed in depth, and the unsafe control behavior in the hierarchical system of the charging shed is summarized. Six elements in the human-machine-environment system are introduced for analysis. The research results are shown in Table 1.

Fourthly, Based on the KPCA-AHP Model to Evaluate Unsafe Behavior. That is to say, the kernel principal component analysis (KPCA) is introduced to reduce the dimension of the variable data of the unsafe control behavior that should be avoided in the design process of the charging shed interaction system, and then the analytic hierarchy process (AHP) [15] is used to sort the synthetic weights of each level. Finally, the behavior with larger weights is selected for optimization. Firstly, the chromatographic structure is constructed based on kernel principal component analysis-analytic hierarchy process for the above 'possible behavioral processes'. In order to facilitate the expression, A is used to represent the importance of unsafe control behavior in the target layer, Bi is used to represent the criterion layer, and Bii is used to represent the element layer. According to the relative scale of 1~9, the assignment is shown in Fig. 4, with a total of 23 dimensions.

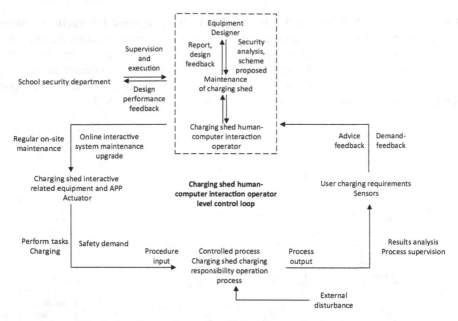

Fig. 3. Local control structure of electric bicycle charging stage

Table 1. Identification and analysis of potential unsafe control behavior of electric bicycle charging shed

Types of unsafe control behaviors	Unsafe control behavior	Probable process	Human factor relation
The required control behavior was not provided	①Charging shed unable to provide service ②Unable to use charging shed for continuous charging	①The main power supply switch of the charging shed is not opened	computer
		②Insufficient number of charging ports are all occupied	computer–human
		③ Loose or dropped plug during charging process	computer–human
		④The charging port has malfunctioned during the charging process	computer–human
		⑤Other users unplug the charging plug during the charging process	computer–human
		⑥Insufficient battery pack selection by users resulting in not being fully charged	human–computer

(*continued*)

Table 1. (*continued*)

Types of unsafe control behaviors	Unsafe control behavior	Probable process	Human factor relation
The provision of erroneous or unsafe control behaviors	①There is a malfunction in the charging shed ②Unsafe control behavior during charging process	①Timely maintenance was not carried out in the charging shed	human–computer
		② The charging shed itself has not set up an error mechanism	computer
		③Aging or other faults in the charging shed circuit	computer
		④The supporting design of charging stations and apps is incomplete	computer
		⑤The charging shed itself has not been designed with protective devices and programs	computer
		⑥The user did not follow the correct operating procedures to use the charging shed	human
		⑦Electric vehicle batteries charged by users pose safety hazards	human
		⑧Inconvenient use of charging shed interaction system leads to increased error rate	computer–human
		⑨Misoperation leading to malfunctions during use	human–computer
Delay in controlling behavior	①The delay in response during the feedback process in the usage state	①Delayed charging shed power supply	computer
		②There is a delay between the operation of the charging station and the display of the APP	computer
		③Lack of timely user feedback design	computer–human
		④Full of untimely power outage and cashback of remaining usage	computer–human
Premature termination of control behavior	①End the operation of using the charging shed for charging in advance	①The charging plug is loose from the socket during charging	environment-human
		②Lack of feedback prompt of insufficient power	computer–human
		③Failure of charging shed during use	computer

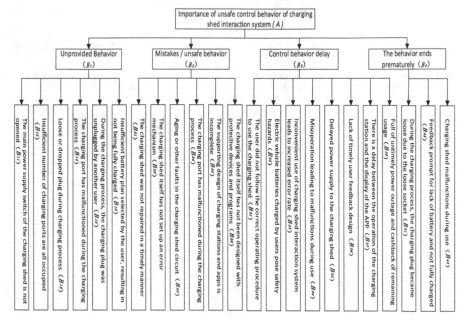

Fig. 4. Local control structure and control loop of electric bicycle charging stage

However, because of too many control factors and too high dimensions, it is not realistic to design an all-round system. In this paper, kernel principal component analysis

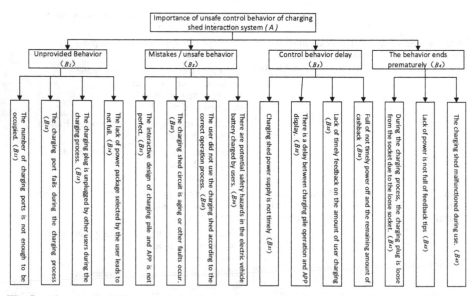

Fig. 5. After the simplification, the local control structure and control loop of the electric bicycle charging stage are simplified

(KPCA) is used to reduce the dimension. KPCA is a nonlinear data processing method. Its core idea is to project the data of the original space into the high-dimensional feature space through a nonlinear mapping, and then perform data processing based on principal component analysis (PCA) in the high-dimensional feature space. A total of 85 college students aged 18–22 who have been using the questionnaire for more than 3 years were collected for point measurement. Then KPCA in SPSS software was used to reduce the dimension of data, and the original 23 variables were reduced to 15 variables, which made the analysis data of AHP [16] more streamlined. The variables after dimension reduction are shown in Fig. 5.

3.2 Questionnaire Design

Based on the model of STAMP model charging shed design in Fig. 4, a questionnaire was designed for college students aged 18–22, including 4 test variables and 23 measurement items. Among them, 'unprovided behavior' is used to measure the user's evaluation of the system's unresponsiveness; the 'error/unsafe behavior' is used to measure the user's evaluation of the accident in the charging shed. The 'control behavior delay' is used to measure the user's evaluation of the control system response delay. 'Premature end of behavior' is used to measure the user's evaluation of premature power failure of the charging shed.

Table 2 is the result of Cronbach's α coefficient of the questionnaire, which is used to measure the reliability quality level of the data. Generally, if the Cronbα coefficient (or the half-fold coefficient) is above 0.7, the reliability of the test or scale is good, and the reliability below 0.5 indicates that the reliability is very low. SPSS software was used for analysis, and the coefficient was 0.887, indicating that the reliability of the questionnaire was high.

Table 2. Cronbach's α coefficient table.

Cronbach's α coefficient	Standardized Cronbach's α coefficient	Number of terms	Number of samples
0.888	0.887	15	81

3.3 Data Analysis

By constructing the judgment matrix, see the formula (1), and using the analytic hierarchy software (Yaahp) to calculate the synthetic weight of each level to the system target, the consistency test is passed by the platform calculation, and the weight ranking is shown in Table 3. There are four important potential unsafe control behaviors that may lead to accidents: 'insufficient number of charging sockets are occupied', 'lack of feedback prompts for unfilled power', 'lack of timely feedback on user charging', and 'charging shed power supply is not timely'.

Table 3. Comprehensive weight ranking table of unsafe control behavior of charging shed interaction system

$$
A = \begin{bmatrix} 1 & 2 & 1 & 1 \\ \frac{1}{2} & 1 & \frac{1}{2} & \frac{1}{2} \\ 1 & 2 & 1 & 1 \\ 1 & 2 & 1 & 1 \end{bmatrix}, \; B_1 = \begin{bmatrix} 1 & 3 & 2 & 7 \\ \frac{1}{3} & 1 & \frac{1}{2} & 6 \\ \frac{1}{2} & 2 & 1 & 7 \\ \frac{1}{7} & \frac{1}{6} & \frac{1}{7} & 1 \end{bmatrix}, \; B_2 = \begin{bmatrix} 1 & 2 & 6 & 4 \\ \frac{1}{2} & 1 & 4 & 2 \\ \frac{1}{6} & \frac{1}{4} & 1 & \frac{1}{2} \\ \frac{1}{4} & \frac{1}{2} & 2 & 1 \end{bmatrix}, \; B_3 = \begin{bmatrix} 1 & 4 & 1 & 2 \\ \frac{1}{4} & 1 & \frac{1}{4} & \frac{1}{2} \\ 1 & 4 & 1 & 2 \\ \frac{1}{2} & 2 & \frac{1}{2} & 1 \end{bmatrix}, \; B_4 = \begin{bmatrix} 1 & \frac{1}{2} & 1 \\ 2 & 1 & 1 \\ 1 & 1 & 1 \end{bmatrix} \tag{1}
$$

Because AHP is a subjective judgment based on certain objective reality, there are some limitations. The principal component analysis (PCA) of SPSS software was used to verify the conclusions of AHP. There is a certain correlation between the variables of the coefficient correlation matrix of this group of data, and some of the correlation coefficients are large. The KMO statistic is greater than 0.7 and the significance is less than 0.05, so this sample is suitable for principal component analysis. The four principal components obtained from the analysis of this group of data are shown in Table 4. Among them, the larger the variance of the common factor is, the greater the proportion of the extracted variables is. From Table 5, it can be seen that the four principal components analyzed are consistent with the results of the analytic hierarchy process, indicating that the weight ranking is more reliable. The first four unsafe behaviors are subjected to human factors analysis and design optimization.

Criterion layer factor weight	Decision-making factors	Decision-making level factor weight	comprehe nsive rank
No behavior provided (B₁) 0.2857	①The number of charging ports is not enough to be occupied.	0.1348	1
	②The charging socket failed to complete the charging during the charging process.	0.053	8
	③The charging plug is unplugged by other users during the charging process.	0.0849	6
	④The power package selected by the user is not full of electricity.	0.0129	13
Mistakes /Unsafe behavior (B₂) 0.1429	①The interactive design of charging pile and APP is not perfect.	0.0733	10
	②The charging shed itself has not designed safety maintenance devices and procedures.	0.0393	12
	③The user did not use the charging shed according to the correct operation process.	0.0106	15
	④There are potential safety hazards in the electric bicycle battery charged by users.	0.0197	14
Control behavior delay (B₃) 0.2857	①Charging shed power supply is not timely	0.1039	3
	②There is a delay between charging pile operation and APP display.	0.026	11
	③Lack of timely feedback on the amount of user charging	0.1039	4
	④Full of not timely power off and the remaining amount of cashback	0.0519	9
The charging behavior ends prematurely. (B₄) 0.2857	①During the charging process, the charging plug is loose from the socket due to the loose socket.	0.0743	7
	②Lack of power is not full of feedback tips	0.1179	2
	③The charging shed malfunctioned during use.	0.0936	5

Table 4. The variance interpretation of AHP analysis conclusion

Component	Initial Eigenvalue			Extracting the sum of squared loads		
	total	variance percentage	accumulate %	total	variance percentage	Accumulate%
1	5.947	39.648	39.648	5.947	39.648	39.648
2	1.562	10.411	50.059	1.562	10.411	50.059
3	1.423	9.487	59.546	1.423	9.487	59.546
4	1.240	8.265	67.810	1.240	8.265	67.810

Table 5. The common factor of AHP analysis conclusion

common factor		initial	extract
F1	Insufficient number of charging ports are all occupied	1.000	0.827
F2	Delayed power supply to the charging shed	1.000	0.754
F3	Lack of timely feedback on user charging volume	1.000	0.756
F4	Feedback prompt for lack of battery and not fully charged	1.000	0.759

4 Design Practice of Campus Electric Bicycle Charging Shed

4.1 Human Factors Analysis and Design Optimization of Unsafe Behavior

Human Factors Analysis and Optimization of 'Insufficient Number of Charging Sockets are Occupied'. There are five problems in this aspects as below:

1. The height and spacing of the charging socket

    The electric bicycle charging shed is a common public product for 18–25 years old men and women. Combined with the requirements of the national standard for the layout height range of the charging socket, the best value of the charging socket height is 1100 mm, and the best value of the spacing is 1000 mm [17].

2. Charging socket

    In this paper, the international requirements of the two-hole plus three-hole 10A safety socket. In order to prompt whether the user's charging port is in a normal operating state, two light modes of red and green are set for reminding. The reason of man-machine analysis [18] is shown in Table 7. At the same time, starting from the principle of anatomy, the board is tilted 20 ° from the vertical direction, and the wrist is kept in a vertical state to reduce the discomfort of the user's plug action and reduce the probability of accidental plug shedding.

3. The layout height of the intelligent charging box

    Combined with the law that the best reading method of Ergonomics should be horizontal reading and the natural line of sight of people standing is 10 ° lower, the optimal value of the height of the middle of the intelligent charging box is determined to be 1500 mm, and the optimal value of the height of the upper end from the ground is 1685 mm.

4. The size of the shed and the width of the road

    Because there are more electric bicycles on the campus, the electric lane for one-way driving is narrower. If the national standard 60 ° diagonal can effectively increase the width of at least 600 mm, so that the original road at least widened to 1600. This is in line with the requirements of the national standard road at least 1500 mm wide. Therefore, combined with international requirements and Ergonomics principles, the best value of shed width is 1700 mm, and the best value of height is 2200 mm.

5. Improve the effective utilization rate of charging socket

There is a problem that the charging port still occupies a place after the use is completed. In order to reduce the occupancy phenomenon, control elements are added to the socket design [2]. The vehicle is full of electricity to issue instructions to pop up the charger inserted into the socket in time and empty the charging socket. At the same time, the charger that is charging will be controlled by the components and not easy to fall off.

Table 6. Man–machine color analysis table.

The color of the light	color analysis
Green（5G5.5/6）	① Safety: guide people to walk the color of safety exit signs ② Hygiene: this color is commonly used in ambulance stations and protective equipment boxes ③ Indicates safe operation of the device
Red（7.5R4.5/14）	① Stop: Traffic requires parking, equipment requires emergency braking ② Prohibited: indicates no operation, no movement, no passage ③ Highly dangerous: such as high voltage, sewage outlets, highly toxic substances, intersections, etc ④ Fire prevention: Fire trucks and firefighting equipment are mainly colored in red

Human Factors Analysis and Optimization of 'Charging Shed Power Supply is not Timely' and 'Lack of Timely User Charging Amount Feedback'. The 'charging shed power supply is not timely' and 'lack of timely user charging amount feedback' can be subdivided into the following four pain points: ① the user does not know whether the electric bicycle is full when the package is completed; ② the user cannot know the working state of the charging pile in time for charging use; ③ The real-time feedback design of the user's power is not perfect (including the use state, the amount of charge, the length of time, the feedback after filling, etc.); 4 When the unattended charging encounters an accident, the user cannot receive message feedback and return the package amount in time (Table 6).

To this end, through the improvement of the interaction design between the charging pile and the APP, on the premise of retaining the reasonable part of the original interaction system design, the 'product package' and 'charging details' interfaces are modified, and the functions are added, and four new interfaces are added. See Figs. 6, 7, 8, and 9 to solve these two problems.

In the improvement interface, the following functions are added to the APP for the four problems: ① When selecting the charging package in the 'product package', the 'pay after charging' option is provided. For users who cannot determine the length of charging after the trial package, the choice of whether to continue charging is provided; ② Users can view the selected package, the amount of electricity that has been charged, and the amount of electricity that needs to be charged and the duration through the 'in

Fig. 6. Improved interface contact 1   **Fig. 7.** Improved interface contact 2   **Fig. 8.** Improved interface contact 3   **Fig. 9.** Improved interface contact 4

use' interface. After charging, the APP will remind the user to pick up the car in time in the form of a pop-up window; ③ when a fault occurs during the charging process, the small program interface will display the cause of the fault and inform the user in the form of a pop-up window. At the same time, the charging port will be temporarily closed, waiting for the user to choose to continue charging or return the amount.

Lack of Power is not Full of Feedback Tips 'Human Factors Analysis. In the process of using the charging shed, there is a problem that the user relies too much on the mobile phone APP to know whether the charging port is available. Therefore, the charging pile itself has great defects in the visualization of the use situation, and it is extremely important to solve the problem of human-computer interaction through visual means. Therefore, this defect can be solved by lighting a four-grid light scheme representing electricity in the horizontal direction. According to the user's habits, the eye moves faster in the horizontal direction than in the vertical direction [19], and the horizontal arrangement can optimize the user experience. Secondly, white, yellow and blue are a wide range of colors in people's color vision [18]. Combined with the cultural atmosphere of the campus, blue is selected to indicate the charging state.

4.2 Design Scheme Display

Based on the above analysis, the final design scheme of electric bicycle charging shed interaction system based on STAMP-human factors is formed. The appearance of the continuation of the modern industrial style of the campus dormitory is shown in Fig. 11, and the appearance color matching of the APP scheme continues the charging shed charging interactive APP style is shown in Fig. 10. Due to the imperfect fire fighting facilities of the existing charging piles, although there are hanging fire extinguishers in the shed, when a fire occurs in the shed, the fire extinguisher will be quickly covered by the fire and inconvenient for people to use. The design uses a suspended dry powder fire extinguisher as shown in Fig. 12 [20]. It does not need to lay pipelines and lines, and the structure is light and small and reasonable. It is suitable as an auxiliary fire fighting equipment for the electric bicycle charging shed fire fighting system. In terms of material selection, this paper investigates a large number of charging shed component materials, and finally selects high-strength aluminum alloy frame, galvanized steel pipe and polycarbonate plate as the use materials, which can achieve good light transmittance, strong flame retardancy, impact resistance, mute effect and so on. The final optimization scheme and usage scenario are shown in Figs. 13, 14 and 15.

Fig. 10. Existing charging interactive APP interface of charging shed

Fig. 11. Campus dormitory real shot

Fig. 12. Hanging dry powder fire extinguisher

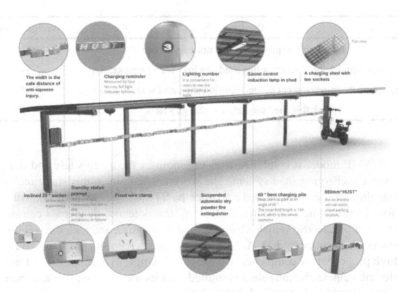

Fig. 13. Charging shed final optimization scheme model

Fig. 14. Use Scene Showcase 1

Fig. 15. Use Scene Showcase 2

4.3 Feedback

The optimized design of the campus electric bicycle charging shed was sent to the 18-22-year-old college students who have used the charging shed for more than 3 years in the form of a questionnaire survey to perceive its feasibility. A total of 101 samples were collected. Through the combination of pictures and texts to help users understand the product to improve the validity of the questionnaire, the combination of positive and negative directions is used to set the topic, and the scale is used to measure the user's recognition of the scheme. The results are as follows: Table 7, the results show that the design optimization of the scheme is feasible.

Table 7. Feasibility analysis of scheme.

Question	Average Score
I think this improved shed is not easy to use.	2.81
I 'm skeptical about whether this shed can help me charge safely.	2.63
I recognize the improvement of this charging shed and want to be a user.	3.67
I think this shed can help me charge safely.	3.85

The STAMP model is combined with Ergonomics theory to study and design the electric vehicle charging shed system. The work carried out in this study includes: 1) Determine the safety constraints and construct the STAMP human factor control process model for electric vehicle charging; 2) Identify the potential dangerous causes in the control loop of the electric vehicle charging shed during use, and rank the weight values of the dangerous causes by KPCA-AHP model, and screen out the dangerous causes with a high proportion of comprehensive weight rankings; 3) The human factors design of the electric vehicle charging shed is studied, and its use process, size and interaction system are designed and optimized. Through the above research process, the risk causes are accurately identified, and effective control measures are designed. On the one hand, the design of the existing electric vehicle charging shed can be optimized to reduce fire hazards and improve the safety of use. On the other hand, it can also provide new ideas for the structural design and charging interaction design of electric vehicle charging piles, to enhance the application dimension and value of the design.

References

1. Pan, J., Xia, P., Ma, X.: Evaluation of carbon reduction potential and economic performance of photovoltaic charging system for campus electric bicycles. In: Journal of Physics: Conference Series, vol. 1 (2023)
2. Yang, L.: Research on the design of E-bicycle parking space–Taking Nanning as an example. Guangxi University, Nanning (2020). (in Chinese)
3. Zhe, Z., Sheng, Z., Hao, G.: Research on charging small program design of electric bicycle in smart campus. Inf. Record. Mater. **24**, 207–213 (2023). (in Chinese)
4. Zeleskidis, A., Charalampidou, S., Dokas, I.M., Papadopoulos, B.: A preparedness drill scenario development and system safety competency assessment based on the STAMP Model. In: HCII 2023: Engineering Psychology and Cognitive Ergonomics, pp. 484–500 (2023)
5. Hans, J.O.: Physical workload of flight attendants when pushing and pulling trolleys aboard aircraft. Int. J. Ind. Ergon. **37**, 845–854 (2007)
6. Rad, M.A., Lefsrud, L.M., Hendry, M.T.:. Application of systems thinking accident analysis methods: a review for railways. Saf. Sci. **160**, 106066 (2023)
7. Shuai, W.M.: Research on Charging System Design of Electric Bicycle Based on Scenario Analysis. Wuhan University of Technology, Wuhan (2020). (in Chinese)
8. Qing, L.Y., Xin, D.: Research on intelligent charging management system for electric bicycles. Fire Sci. Technol. **38**, 151–153 (2019). (in Chinese)
9. Liang, S.J.: Cause analysis of electric bicycle charging fire and research on new intelligent charging station. In: 2022 Annual Conference of Science and Technology of China Fire Protection Association, Hangzhou (2022). (in Chinese).
10. Avina-Bravo, E.G.: Design and validity of a smart healthcare and control system for electric bikes. Sensors **23**(8), 4079 (2023). (Basel, Switzerland)
11. Zhang, Z., Liu, X., Hu, H.: Passenger rail station safety improvement and analysis of end-of-track collisions based on systems-theoretic accident modeling and processes (STAMP).Smart Resilient Transp. **3**(2), 94–117 (2021)
12. Han, X., Tang, T., Lv, J.: A hierarchical verification approach to verify complex safety control systems based on STAMP. Sci. Comput. Program. **172**, 117–134 (2018)
13. Min, Z.W., Ping, H.J., Yong, Y.X.: Analysis of the causes of electric vehicle fire and counter measures. Fire Sci. Technol. **30**, 870–872 (2011). (in Chinese)
14. Xu, J.H., Guo, H.L.: Human factors design of civil aviation dining cart based on STAMP. Package Eng. **43**, 283–292 (2022). (in Chinese)
15. Wang, Y.T.: The APP Design of community medical service based on analytic hierarchy process. Des. Art Res. **12**, 137–141 (2022). (in Chinese)
16. Li, Y., Guo, Y.: Interaction design of wrist health prevention products based on persuasive design and AHP-entropy weight method. In: Kurosu, M., Hashizume, A. (eds.) Human-Computer Interaction. HCII 2023, LNCS, vol. 14014, pp. 30–49. Springer, Cham (2023). https://doi.org/10.1007/978-3-031-35572-1_3
17. Zhou, Q., Li, J., Liu, D., Wang, Z., Wang, Q.: Charging pile used for shared electric bicycle and interface thereof (2017)
18. Ding, Y.L.: Ergonomics. Beijing Institute of Technology Press, Beijing (2017). (in Chinese)
19. Zhang, L., Zhou, R., Yang, J., Shao, Z., Wang, X.: How information influences the way we perceive unfamiliar objects – an eye movement study. In: Mori, H., Asahi, Y. (eds.) Human Interface and the Management of Information. HCII 2023, Human Interface and the Management of Information, pp. 196–208 (2023)
20. Manikath, E., Li, W.C., Piotrowski, P., Zhang, J.: Usability evaluation of an emergency alerting system to improve discrete communication during emergencies. HCII 2023, Engineering Psychology and Cognitive Ergonomics, pp. 120–134 (2023)

Design and User Experience Evaluation Case Studies

Optimization Design of Fresh e-Commerce Platform for the Elderly

Yi Ding(✉) [iD] and Mingxi Wang

Nanjing University of Science and Technology, Xiaolingweistr. 200, Nanjing 210094, China
dingyiblue@qq.com

Abstract. The primary objective of this study is to address the concern of the extensive utilization of dark patterns in the fresh e-commerce platform in the Chinese market, which may have a negative impact on user experience. Specifically, the research focuses on the information requirements of the elderly population in relation to these fresh e-commerce platforms. To accomplish this, a comprehensive research approach incorporating case studies, user surveys utilizing the KANO Model, design implementation, and in-depth interviews is adopted. The findings derived from this study offer valuable insights into the specific information needs of elderly users within the realm of fresh e-commerce platforms. Moreover, optimization strategies for user interface design are proposed based on these discerned needs, thereby contributing to enhanced user experience among the elderly users.

Keywords: UI Optimization Design · Dark Pattern · E-Commerce Platform

1 Introduction

With the increasing aging trend in Chinese society, the proportion of elderly population is on the rise and is expected to stay higher than the global average for an extended period. This demographic shift poses a significant burden on the society [1], sparking growing concerns in both industry and academia about the models of elderly care and support services. Among them, home-based care for the elderly is considered the primary mode for future provision due to its compatibility with China's national conditions and public sentiment [2]. Within the realm of home-based elderly care, culinary activities and their associated tasks have been recognized as crucial aspects of daily life, substantiated by several studies [3–5]. However, due to the rapid urbanization in recent years, urban planning has not kept up with the pace, presenting challenges for the elderly in terms of food procurement [6]. Not only do long-term residents of urban areas face these inconveniences, but also a substantial number of elderly individuals who have relocated from rural regions in recent years, making their daily activities, including shopping, more cumbersome [7]. Confronted with this reality, the establishment of fresh e-commerce platforms has emerged as an important alternative [8, 9]. Consequently, it is imperative to enhance the design of aging-friendly fresh e-commerce platforms and provide design-based support for the elderly's daily activities related to cooking.

M. Kurosu and A. Hashizume (Eds.): HCII 2024, LNCS 14687, pp. 147–162, 2024.
https://doi.org/10.1007/978-3-031-60441-6_10

Despite experiencing rapid growth, the elderly population in China has historically accounted for a relatively small portion of the online shopping market [10]. However, the COVID-19 pandemic, which emerged in 2020, unexpectedly provided an opportunity to encourage elderly individuals to purchase fresh ingredients through online platforms [11, 12]. Recent research indicates that there is no significant difference in attitudes towards online shopping between the elderly and younger age groups [13]. Nevertheless, even with the pandemic's influence on driving food purchases online, the number of elderly individuals who choose to learn how to shop for groceries on the internet remains lower compared to younger age groups [14]. This observation not only highlights the potential for growth in kitchen services that cater to elderly users, but also suggests areas for improvement within the current fresh e-commerce platforms. By focusing on enhancing the user interface (UI) and user experience (UX) specifically designed for the elderly, it is possible to increase the appeal of fresh e-commerce platforms among this demographic. This, in turn, can enhance food accessibility for the elderly, particularly during home-based care, and mitigate the inconveniences they face when venturing out for traditional shopping methods.

2　Literature Review

Since the turn of the century, research on the impact of UI/UX design on e-commerce platforms has been steadily growing. Early studies have emphasized the significance of consumers' comprehension and trust in relevant information as crucial factors in maintaining user engagement [15, 16]. The success of an e-commerce platform greatly relies on how designers structure and organize information within the constraints of limited screen space, a notion that has been substantiated by prior investigations [17]. It is important to note that a well-designed information structure should avoid overwhelming platform users with excessive data. Information overload theory suggests that an excess of information can impede decision-making in consumption [18]. Consequently, researchers have sought ways to optimize the design of information prompts in smartphone interfaces from a UI perspective, aiming to alleviate the information burden on older adults [19]. If the information presented on an e-commerce platform is not adequately planned, such as the extravagant display of irrelevant and complicated product recommendations, it may hinder the elderly from mastering the art of online shopping effectively [11]. Furthermore, additional research has indicated that while information overload may initially encourage impulse buying, consumers often experience regret once the initial excitement subsides, leading to higher product return rates [20, 21]. Thus, it becomes evident that information overload is not conducive to the sustainable growth of e-commerce.

Merchants are driven by sales incentives to provide extensive information on fresh e-commerce platforms. Previous research has indicated that scarcity-based and bandwagon-based information, such as indications of limited stock or the popularity of products, can lead customers to engage in unexpected consumption [22]. Moreover, studies have highlighted the manipulation and deliberate presentation of information as influential factors in consumer behavior. Various visual inducement techniques, including low-stock messages (e.g., "Only 7 items left in stock"), activity messages (e.g., "68 people purchased this product in the past day"), countdown timers (e.g., "Only 10 min remaining for the product discount"), and limited-time messages (e.g., "Today-only sale"), are often employed. Such manipulative strategies, known as dark patterns, serve as means to stimulate sales. Specifically, time-limited activities have been proven through experimentation to significantly influence consumption behavior in young and middle-aged individuals [24]. Furthermore, it has been suggested that dark patterns have a more pronounced effect on elderly individuals compared to younger individuals [25].

Numerous implementations of dark patterns may give rise to a phenomenon known as information overload, which in turn can result in confusion and negatively impact the overall consumer experience [26]. The convolution and convoluted operations brought about by aggressive dark patterns easily elicit negative emotional responses, even powerful backlash from consumers. Although it is acknowledged that such aggressive practices may generate increased business opportunities [27], consumers themselves express a clear reluctance to have designers incorporate dark patterns into the platform [28, 29]. Moreover, even when considering the platform's UI/UX design from a business standpoint, studies have pointed out that enhancing Perceived Usability is a more effective method of driving unplanned consumption [30]. Thus, promoting consumption alone cannot justify the widespread integration of dark patterns into the platform's UI design and compromising the user experience. When discussing strategies to enhance the popularity and development of fresh e-commerce platforms through UI/UX design, particular attention should be given to the target user segment, ensuring that the conveyed product information is properly curated and organized. The objective of this study is to explore the type of information that should be provided by fresh e-commerce platforms from the standpoint of the elderly, and subsequently validate it through UI design practice.

3 Research Method and Results

This research paper aims to provide a comprehensive analysis of the design and functional attributes of fresh e-commerce platforms in the Chinese market through a case study approach. Moreover, it delves into the crucial information and design strategies pertaining to dark patterns found in its primary interface. Furthermore, to validate the findings and draw insights specific to the elderly population, a set of samples were developed and questionnaires were administered.

3.1 Case Study: Fresh e-Commerce Platforms in Chinese Market

This case study examines four prominent fresh e-commerce platforms in China's market, namely Ding Dong Grocery Shopping (Chinese name: 叮咚买菜), Fresh Hema (Chinese name: 盒马鲜生), Meituan Grocery Shopping (Chinese name: 美团买菜), and JD.COM Home (Chinese name: 京东到家). The study focuses on analyzing the product-related information showcased on their respective app homepages and product columns (refer to Fig. 1). Notably, both Ding Dong Grocery Shopping and Fresh Hema offer an easy mode feature tailored for the elderly. Therefore, the analysis takes into account the interface content when set to easy mode.

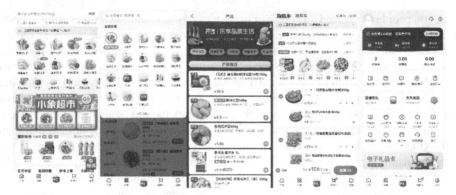

Fig. 1. An illustration of UI for a new e-commerce platform in the Chinese market.

In terms of the layout of UI, there exists a remarkable similarity among the three fresh e-commerce platforms. These platforms including the home page, product column, shopping cart, and settlement page. Notably, the home page and product column, positioned at the first left and the second left correspondingly, assume a critical role in shaping users' consumption behaviors and preferences.

From the topmost section to the lowermost part, the homepage is comprised of several distinct components. These include an address bar, a search bar that offers word recommendations, a sliding selection mechanism for classifying merchandise, a bar displaying recommended goods, and a navigation bar. Within the navigation bar, five items are present. The homepage, product classification bar, shopping cart, and personal page possess identical attributes. Conversely, the middle section accommodates distinct functionalities in accordance with the business strategy adopted by the enterprise. For instance, Ding Dong Grocery Shopping manifests an online menu, while Fresh Hema and Meituan Grocery Shopping exhibits either enterprise-specific or member-exclusive product recommendations.

In addition to the shared elements observed across various online shopping platforms, such as the address bar, search bar, shopping cart, and personal settings, the homepage of this platform showcases pertinent information pertaining to products. These include product promotion details, seasonal ingredients that are highly recommended, home-cooked recipes that are endorsed (the menu page allows for the acquisition of ingredients associated with the recipes), a comprehensive sales ranking list of commonly purchased ingredients, and various non-edible household sundries. Detailed descriptions and supplementary functionalities associated with the Graphics User Interface (GUI) for the aforementioned product-related information are presented in Table 1.

Based on the information presented in the product column, the product columns on the four fresh e-commerce platforms are categorized into three hierarchical menus. This includes the primary menu, which is horizontally positioned beneath the top search column, the secondary menu, which is vertically placed on the right side of the screen, and the third-level menu, which is horizontally located below the primary menu.

Table 1. Information on the homepage of the platform.

Product information	GUI Design				Additional function
	Buy Button	Badge Icon	Enhance Text Color	Weaken Text Color	
Product promotion column	●				
Recommended recent seasonal ingredients	●				
Recommended home-cooked recipes	●	●			Link to related ingredients
Sales ranking list of common ingredients	●				Link to related ingredients
Recommend products other than ingredients	●	●			

When showcasing various commodities within the product column, in addition to the essential details such as product name, photo, and price, frozen and chilled foods are distinctly labeled. Moreover, the display unit of commodities provides further information depending on the specific types of commodities and sales conditions. These additional details incorporate the taste and flavor of ingredients, production dates, options for personal ingredient selection, discounts on ingredients, commonly used cooking techniques, ingredient sales rankings, and sales performance within a defined time period.

To demonstrate the various forms and supplementary functionalities associated with the information related to commodities, graphical user interface design principles are employed. A comprehensive depiction of these elements, along with their specific formats, is outlined in Table 2.

Based on the analysis of current products, it is evident that the page information display strategy employed by leading fresh e-commerce platforms in the Chinese market bears strong resemblance to that of other online shopping platforms. The objective is to stimulate consumer behavior through the provision of scarcity and bandwagon-related information associated with the available goods [21]. Distinguishing themselves from ordinary products, fresh commodities necessitate particular attention on factors such as shelf life and cooking methods. Consequently, these aspects are highlighted individually within the product section, being prominently displayed below the commodity name in vibrant colors such as red, gold, and gray. The utilization of such display technique effectively occupies a significant portion of the right-aligned side within the entirety of the commodity display unit.

Although both Dingdong Grocery Shopping and Fresh Hema have implemented the "easy mode" feature, which aims to enhance the visibility and usability of their app interfaces for elderly users, the primary method employed is simply increasing the font size. Several studies have highlighted the potential of dark patterns in e-commerce platforms to induce impulsive consumer behavior [24]. However, as discussed in the second chapter of this paper, marketing elements concealed within the user interface design should not come at the expense of user experience. To effectively promote the widespread adoption of fresh e-commerce platforms among the elderly population, it is crucial to prioritize their unique needs and tailor the platform accordingly.

3.2 User Survey Based on KANO Model

To investigate the indispensability and significance of various commodity-related information on the homepage and commodity column of a fresh e-commerce platform for elderly users, this study employs the KANO model for user research. Developed by Japanese scholar Noriaki Kano, the KANO model serves as an analytical framework for classifying and prioritizing user requirements, thereby delineating the nonlinear correlation between product or service quality characteristics and user satisfaction. In the KANO model, quality characteristics are categorized into five types: one-dimensional (or performance) quality, Attractive quality, Must-be quality, Indirect quality, and Reverse quality. Specifically, one-dimensional quality denotes that a particular attribute of a product or service exhibits a positive correlation with user satisfaction. If the presence of a feature significantly enhances user satisfaction while its absence does not evoke substantial dissatisfaction, the feature falls under the category of Attractive quality. Conversely, if the absence of a feature leads to notable dissatisfaction despite its limited impact on user satisfaction, it qualifies as a Must-be quality aspect. Indifferent quality characterizes a specific feature whose existence or absence bears no substantial impact on user satisfaction, while Reverse quality attributes a negative relation between a feature of a product or service and people's overall contentment.

Table 2. Information in the platform product column

Product information		GUI Design			Additional function
	Buy Button	Badge Icon	Enhance Text Color	Weaken Text Color	
The taste and flavor of ingredients				●	
Production dates			●		
Options for personal ingredient selection			●		
Discounts on ingredients		●	●		
Commonly used cooking techniques				●	
Ingredient sales ranking	●	●	●		Link to related ingredients
Ingredient sales performance			●		

This study employs the KANO model to examine a wide range of commodity-related information found on the homepage and product column of fresh e-commerce platforms.

With a focus on individuals aged 50 and above, a questionnaire was designed based on the commodity information presented in Tables 1 and 2, as well as the corresponding GUI design strategies. Respondents were presented with various common information provided by the fresh e-commerce platform on its homepage and product column and were asked to express their preferences towards the provision of specific information by the platform. Each question elicited responses along the following five-point Likert scale: "I like it that way," "It must be that way," "I am neutral," "I can live with it that way," and "I dislike it that way."

In order to capture the necessity of certain information being provided by the platform, respondents' answers were recorded in Table 3, which outlines the attributes of the information and functions offered by the fresh e-commerce platform. Specifically, the attribute positioned at "M" represents Must-be quality, the attribute at "O" represents One-dimensional quality, the attribute at "A" represents Attractive quality, the attribute at "I" represents Indifferent quality, and the attribute at "R" represents Reverse quality. Additionally, the designation "Q" implies that the question was deemed unreasonable or that the respondents made mistakes in understanding or completing the questionnaire.

Based on the results obtained, we calculate the satisfaction improvement (SI) and dissatisfaction (DIS) metrics. SI measures the extent to which user satisfaction improves when the fresh e-commerce platform provides information on the homepage or commodity column. On the other hand, DIS quantifies the decrease in user satisfaction when such information is not provided. The calculation formula for these metrics is as follows:

$$SI = (A + O)/(A + O + M + I) \tag{1}$$

$$DSI = -1 * (O + M)/(A + O + M + I) \tag{2}$$

3.3   Results of User Survey

For the survey conducted in November 2023, a professional online sample service was utilized to gather data. A total of 228 questionnaires were distributed among individuals who were approximately 60 years old. After removing non-standard responses and those from individuals who had not used the fresh e-commerce platform before, 124 valid questionnaires were obtained.

The results of the questionnaire survey on the necessity of all kinds of information in the homepage of fresh e-commerce platforms were extracted for statistical analysis, and the percentage of the answers in each box in the questionnaire to the total number of people was filled in the statistical table. Among the six attributes of M, O, A, I, R and Q, the attribute with the largest number of answers on the necessity of providing certain information on the homepage of fresh e-commerce platform was selected as the attitude of users. Statistics and calculation results are shown in Table 4:

The results of the questionnaire survey on the necessity of all kinds of information in the product column of fresh e-commerce platforms were extracted for statistical analysis, and the percentage of the answers in each box in the questionnaire to the total number of people was filled in the statistical table. Among the six attributes of M, O, A, I, R and Q, the attribute with the largest number of answers on the necessity of providing certain

Table 3. KANO evaluation table.

Functional Form		If the fresh e-commerce platform does not provide some information				
My attitude	I like it that way	I like it that way	It must be that way	I am neutral	I can live with it that way	I dislike it that way
If the fresh e-commerce platform provides some information	It must be that way	Q	A	A	A	O
	I am neutral	R	I	I	I	M
	I can live with it that way	R	I	I	I	M
	I dislike it that way	R	I	I	I	M
	I like it that way	R	R	R	R	Q

Table 4. The necessity of providing all kinds of information on the homepage of fresh e-commerce platforms

Information	M	O	A	I	R	Q	Attribute	SI	DSI
Product promotion column	10.48%	30.65%	33.87%	24.19%	0.81%	0%	A	54.55%	-21.14%
Recommended recent seasonal ingredients	8.06%	9.68%	37.1%	45.16%	0.00%	0.00%	I	76.42%	-64.23%
Recommended home-cooked recipes	1.61%	13.71%	61.61%	33.06%	0.00%	0.00%	A	34.15%	-10.57%
Sales ranking list of common ingredients	5.65%	7.26%	31.45%	55.65%	0.00%	0.00%	I	57.26%	-29.84%
Recommended products other than ingredients	27.03%	18.02%	5.41%	47.75%	1.80%	0.00%	I	53.23%	-12.1%

information on the product column of fresh e-commerce platform was selected as the attitude of users. Statistics and calculation results are shown in Table 5:

4 Discussion

4.1 The Information Needs of the Elderly in the Context of Fresh E-commerce Platforms

According to the survey results of KANO model, from the perspective of the elderly, although the homepage of the platform provides a variety of activity pages including promotional activities, food sales list, seasonal food and so on around the products for consumers to browse and buy after clicking, only the promotion column of the products and the home-cooked recipes with links to food are attractive to the elderly, and there is basically no difference as to whether to provide other contents; The product column of the platform provides various information around each product, such as the taste/flavor of ingredients, production date, preferential methods, sales and repurchase, etc. Interestingly, the elderly demographic exhibits a particular interest in the production dates. Although such information can be accessed on the product details page, senior users express a desire to ascertain this crucial information at a glance, without navigating further. Additionally, the taste and flavor of ingredients and the provision of commonly used cooking methods also serve as alluring factors for elderly users.

Subsequent paragraphs, however, are indented.

Upon comparing the findings derived from both the User Survey and literature review conducted within this study, it becomes evident that dark patterns, as supported by previous studies [23, 24, 27], do indeed create more business opportunities for emerging e-commerce platforms. However, it is crucial to note that such patterns have a greater propensity for influencing the elderly population [25]. Regrettably, the elderly populace lacks significant demand for most information presented through these dark patterns. In essence, the fresh e-commerce platform's information pertaining to commodities fails to offer convenience to the elderly, instead merely serving as a catalyst for their consumption. Furthermore, research demonstrates that, unlike their younger counterparts, the elderly face challenges in recognizing the manipulative tactics employed by dark patterns and fail to realize the potential manipulations and influences exerted upon their behaviors [31]. Consequently, these factors exacerbate numerous inherent risks originating from unscrupulous UI design [32].

The fresh e-commerce platform has received favorable reception from the elderly regarding certain aspects. An instance of this is the inclusion of a promotional section on the homepage that offers discounted prices, providing economic benefits for the elderly. Consequently, this feature is perceived as an appealing component of the platform's homepage. Conversely, the inclusion of logos such as "limited time discount" or "discount when meeting a certain amount" beneath the names of ingredients in the product section, accompanied by design elements like icons or badges to emphasize relevant information, has failed to gain recognition from the elderly. It is plausible that a promotional section alone suffices for the elderly to shop and obtain pertinent information, or perhaps the pricing information itself (including highlighting the original price in a larger red font) is sufficient for their needs. Further research is required to ascertain the specific reasons behind this.

Another notable aspect is the display of home-cooked recipes on the homepage, along with indications of taste, mouthfeel, and cooking methods under the ingredient names in the product section. The elderly also view these as praiseworthy indicators. While it may be logical to assume that most elderly individuals possess sufficient cooking experience, these informational tips can offer convenience and introduce new cooking experiences. As a result, the fresh e-commerce platform has the opportunity to showcase its added value.

Furthermore, the elderly express concern regarding the production dates of ingredients. Although it has been explicitly stated in the questionnaire that the production date is accessible by clicking on the product details page, this aspect may be considered one of the primary decision-making factors for the elderly when purchasing ingredients. Consequently, they hope to receive relevant information promptly.

Through the juxtaposition of user survey findings and a comprehensive literature review, it becomes evident that the prevailing information recommendations on China's

Table 5. The necessity of providing all kinds of information on the product column of fresh e-commerce platforms

Information	M	O	A	I	R	Q	Attribute	SI	DSI
The taste and flavor of ingredients	3.23%	17.74%	40.32%	37.9%	0.81%	0.00%	A	54.55%	-21.14%
Production dates	12.1%	51.61%	24.19%	11.29%	0.81%	0.00%	O	76.42%	-64.23%
Options for personal ingredient selection	2.42%	8.06%	25.81%	62.9%	0. 81%	0%	I	34.15%	-10.57%
Discounts on ingredients	4.84%	25%	32.6%	37.9%	0%	0%	I	57.26%	-29.84%
Commonly used cooking techniques	3.23%	8.87%	44.35%	43.55%	0%	0%	A	53.23%	-12.1%
Ingredient sales rankings	8.06%	15.32%	30.65%	45.97%	0%	0%	I	45.97%	-23.39%
Ingredient sales performance	5.65%	12.9%	30.65%	50.81%	0%	0%	I	43.55%	-18.55%

prominent fresh e-commerce platforms originate from the potential business benefits stemming from the implementation of dark patterns. While select platforms have introduced simplified modes catered to the elderly demographic, these adjustments primarily revolve around superficial elements such as the user interface architecture, font size, color schemes, and icon dimensions. Regrettably, the issue of information overload arising from pervasive dark patterns remains unaddressed. By embracing a pragmatic user experience (UX) methodology, designers have the opportunity to extract invaluable insights from the results of the aforementioned user survey. These insights will serve as a foundation for crafting a platform that seamlessly caters to the needs of the elder population, while also providing an aesthetically pleasing interface. To achieve this goal, it is imperative to optimize the delivery of information, meticulously avoiding the detrimental impact of deceptive user interface designs commonly known as dark patterns.

It is noteworthy that the practitioners and creators of emerging e-commerce platforms have displayed a propensity for employing dark patterns, which aim to manipulate consumers and generate profits. While the efficacy of such strategies has been reaffirmed through a series of research and business endeavors, it is crucial to recognize that their applicability and long-term viability might not prevail universally. Notably, legislations in Europe and certain regions of the United States have imposed limitations on the utilization of dark patterns [27, 33, 34]. Therefore, the evaluation of the platform's long-term prospects in the Chinese market must encompass the potential legal risks involved. Furthermore, given the detrimental impact of manipulative techniques on user experience, many professionals in the industry have adopted a cautious and evasive stance [35].

4.2   UI Optimization Design Strategy and Verification of Fresh E-Commerce Platform

Based on the findings from the case study and user survey conducted in this research, insights have been gained into the current state of UI design for fresh e-commerce platforms in the mainstream Chinese market. Moreover, the study has uncovered the information requirements of elderly users and identified design flaws in existing platforms at the information level. Building upon these findings, the study focuses on addressing the prominent issues concerning product information. By eliminating irrelevant information and enhancing relevant information, it is anticipated that the optimized UI design will receive favorable evaluations from elderly users in terms of user experience. Consequently, this study endeavors to create a prototype for an easily accessible mode of the fresh e-commerce platform and verifies its effectiveness through in-depth interviews.

This study summarizes various optimization design methods related to information and propose the following design strategies:

- User-Centric Approach: The primary task of a fresh e-commerce platform is to provide information that meets the real needs of its target users. It is crucial to prioritize user satisfaction over inducing unnecessary consumption through using dark patterns.
- Emphasize Ingredient Freshness: When displaying information on the platform, the freshness of ingredients should be prominently highlighted. This not only assures consumers of the quality of the products but also helps to build trust and credibility.
- Provide Additional Information about Ingredients: To enhance the overall experience of consumers using the fresh e-commerce platform, it is recommended to label additional information such as taste, texture, and cooking methods of ingredients. This enables users to make informed decisions and better utilize the platform's offerings.
- Clear Expression of Price Concessions: While information on price concessions is important for consumers, it should be presented in a concise and clear manner. Avoid complex combination purchase schemes that may confuse or overwhelm users. Instead, focus on simple and straightforward messaging to improve consumer satisfaction.

These design strategies are essential for optimizing the information provided by a fresh e-commerce platform and improving the overall user experience. By implementing these approaches, the platform can cater to the needs of its users and build a strong foundation for success.

To validate the strategies mentioned above, this study focuses on the information optimization design of a user-friendly mode for a fresh e-commerce platform. Our goal is to create a prototype and conduct initial validation through in-depth interviews. The information optimization design encompasses the following key areas. Regarding the overall tone, it should be noted that some existing fresh e-commerce platforms employ an excessive amount of blue, which is not visually appealing to elderly users in UI design [36]. In order to cater to the preferences of the elderly, the high-fidelity prototype in this study adopted orange as the primary color [37]. Additionally, various colors associated with appetite were incorporated into the design of certain UI elements [38]. Furthermore, the discount area on the platform's homepage was retained, with a focus on enhancing the visual representation of discounts and their corresponding amounts.

The design of the home-cooked menu was improved accordingly. In the product column, certain information was either eliminated or reinforced based on the results of the user survey. The UI of the platform following the optimization of information can be observed in Fig. 2.

When assessing the user experience of the UI following the optimization design, it is crucial to examine beyond the conventional A/B testing approach. Relying solely on A/B testing may lead to an amplification of dark patterns and related information, as commercial interests often take precedence [27, 28]. To overcome this limitation, in-depth interviews were conducted. Prior to the interviews, the information-optimized platform prototype was prepared and deployed onto the terminal devices. Two platforms were randomly chosen from the four widely used fresh e-commerce platforms in the Chinese market, and three distinct sample groups were compared. To ensure a comprehensive evaluation, a group of 12 elderly individuals aged 60 and above were recruited for the interviews, who were randomly assigned to utilize the three platforms in order to purchase two different types of ingredients. Once the respondents completed all assigned tasks, they engaged in one-on-one semi-structured interviews, wherein they were asked to share their experiences using both the existing platform and the optimized platform prototype. The main feedback received from the respondents is outlined as follows:

- After removing the commodity information, respondents did not report experiencing any inconvenience while operating the prototype. This observation indicates that there were no noticeable disparities in the subjective evaluation of task completion difficulty when compared to the existing platforms available in the market.
- The majority of interviewees perceive purchasing a specific quantity of discounted items or availing a "buy two, get one free" offer as of little significance. The complex process involved in these activities and the difficulty in actually obtaining the discounts mentioned on the signs diminishes the credibility associated with such promotions.
- Respondents generally prioritize the freshness, nutritional value, and safety of certain ingredients over the popularity or frequency of their purchase.
- While the respondents had no prior experience using recipes in the prototype, they believe they would not frequently utilize this feature. However, they all took note of this functionality when they first encountered it. Almost half of the respondents acknowledged that the inclusion of this feature enhanced their overall experience and motivated them to select ingredients they typically wouldn't purchase.
- In contrast to the ability to access detailed information on the platform, respondents generally emphasize the importance of information authenticity, UI visibility, and operational convenience.
- Whether it is the existing platform or a platform with optimized information design, most interviewees stated that they can recall the basic operational methods after using it once or twice. The main challenge they face is relying on corrective lenses to enhance their visual clarity and operational accuracy when utilizing the platform on their mobile phone screens.

Based on the findings of in-depth interviews, it can be concluded that the application of the KANO model in investigating user needs and implementing targeted optimization design based on survey results can contribute to enhancing the user experience.

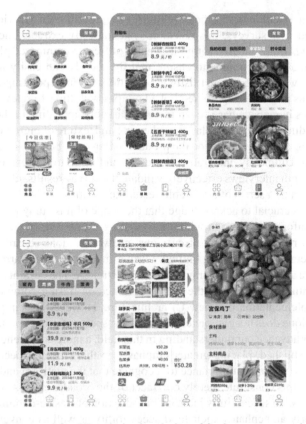

Fig. 2. Prototype after UI optimization design of fresh e-commerce platforms.

The optimization of information pertaining to products does not impede users from acquiring essential information. Among various types of information, the elderly population demonstrates a heightened interest in details relating to ingredient freshness, nutrition, taste, and cooking methods. While some older individuals do not completely disregard promotions and sales related to other ingredients, they express a certain level of skepticism towards a considerable amount of information. Enhancing the credibility of information could potentially increase their motivation to make purchases, albeit this enhancement may require improvements beyond design modifications alone. Additionally, while information optimization design positively affects the user experience, the extent of optimization is constrained by limited visibility during time-limited interactions. Therefore, whenever feasible, information optimization should be coordinated with UI visibility optimization.

5 Conclusion

Given the relatively low adoption rate of fresh e-commerce platforms among the elderly in the Chinese market, this study aims to address the issue of information overload resulting from the widespread use of dark patterns. It is evident that the resulting confusion and cumbersome operations significantly impact the overall user experience. Through case studies and user surveys, this research systematically extracts and analyzes the information needs of the elderly within the realm of fresh e-commerce platforms. Consequently, it becomes imperative to ensure that the elderly can easily access product expiration dates within the product listings. Additionally, incorporating attractive promotional sections and featuring home-cooked recipes with links to relevant ingredients on the platform's homepage has proven to be remarkably appealing to the elderly. Furthermore, providing information relating to the taste and texture of ingredients, as well as common cooking methods, alongside the product listings, has been observed to enhance user satisfaction. Ultimately, integrating these key findings into UI design practices and conducting in-depth interviews effectively validate the survey results, ultimately leading to the formulation of a series of actionable recommendations.

However, it is crucial to acknowledge that the scope of this study primarily focuses on optimizing information design within the existing framework of fresh e-commerce platforms. As a result, theoretical discussions and verifications regarding interaction forms and UI details are somewhat limited. Further investigation is warranted to devise a comprehensive and exceedingly pragmatic design strategy. The current study acknowledges the potential for enhancing the user experience on fresh e-commerce platforms through the implementation of a new UI architecture. However, it is important to note that this study alone does not completely address all aspects of user experience improvement. To further advance our understanding in this field, a more comprehensive research plan will be established, placing greater emphasis on this crucial aspect in the future. Additionally, it is of utmost importance to recognize that the platform and its associated information prompts constitute merely one facet of the broader expanse of fresh online shopping services. To successfully increase the adoption of fresh e-commerce platforms among the elderly and enhance their food accessibility as well as convenience in their daily lives, an expanded discourse encompassing service design from a more holistic standpoint is imperative.

Disclosure of Interests. The authors have no competing interests to declare that are relevant to the content of this article.

References

1. Bao, J., et al.: Current state of care for the elderly in China in the context of an aging population. BioSci. Trends **16**(2), 107–118 (2022). https://doi.org/10.5582/bst.2022.01068
2. Krings, M.F., van Wijngaarden, J.D.H., Yuan, S., Huijsman, R.: China's elder care policies 1994–2020: a narrative document analysis. Int. J. Environ. Res. Public Health **19**(10), 6141 (2022). https://doi.org/10.3390/ijerph19106141
3. Wilhelmson, K., Andersson, C., Waern, M., Allebeck, P.: Elderly people's perspectives on quality of life. Ageing Soc. **25**(4), 585–600 (2005)
4. Chen, R.C.Y., Lee, M.S., Chang, Y.H., Wahlqvist, M.L.: Cooking frequency may enhance survival in Taiwanese elderly. Public Health Nutr. **15**(7), 1142–1149 (2012)
5. Iinuma, T., et al.: Satisfaction with dietary life affects oral health-related quality of life and subjective well-being in very elderly people. J. Oral Sci. **59**(2), 207–213 (2017). https://doi.org/10.2334/josnusd.16-0414

6. Wei, Y., Yang, D.F.: Exploring the impact of built environment on usage frequency of food market from the perspective of elderly healthy life. J. Hunan Settlements West China **36**(4), 66–74 (2021) (in Chinese)

7. Li, G.F.: Research on the urban integration on the elderly immigrating to the city from the rural in the course of the urbanization. J. Zhengzhou Univ. Aeronaut. (Social Science Edition) **41**(4), 106–112 (2022) (in Chinese)

8. Bezirgani, A., Lachapelle, U.: Online grocery shopping for the elderly in Quebec, Canada: the role of mobility impediments and past online shopping experience. Travel Behav. Soc. **25**, 133–143 (2021)

9. Geurden, B., Cant, J., Beckers, J.: Food accessibility in the suburbs of the metropolitan city of Antwerp (Belgium): a factor of concern in local public health and active and healthy aging. Int. J. Environ. Res. Public Health **19**(23), 15754 (2022)

10. Wang, X., Jiang, L.: Research on online shopping demand of Chinese elderly under the background of aging. Int. J. Educ. Humanit. **1**(1), 16–20 (2021)

11. Yao, Y., Zhang, H., Liu, X., Liu, X., Chu, T., Zeng, Y.: Bridging the digital divide between old and young people in China: challenges and opportunities. The Lancet Healthy Longevity **2**(3), e125–e126 (2021)

12. Chen, D., Wang, C., Liu, Y.: How household food shopping behaviors changed during COVID-19 lockdown period: evidence from Beijing, China. J. Retail. Consum. Serv. **75**, 103513 (2023)

13. Gao, X., Shi, X., Guo, H., Liu, Y.: To buy or not buy food online: the impact of the COVID-19 epidemic on the adoption of e-commerce in China. PLoS ONE **15**(8), e0237900 (2020)

14. Feng, R., Ivanov, A.: Does a generational gap exist in online shopping attitudes? A comparison of Chinese consumer generations from the media system dependency perspective. Telematics Inform. Rep. **12**, 100106 (2023)

15. Chau, P.Y., Au, G., Tam, K.Y.: Impact of information presentation modes on online shopping: an empirical evaluation of a broadband interactive shopping service. J. Organ. Comput. Electron. Commer. **10**(1), 1–22 (2000)

16. Egger, F.N.: Affective design of e-commerce user interfaces: how to maximise perceived trustworthiness. In: Helander, M.G., Khalid, H.M., Tham, M.P. (eds.) Proceedings of the International Conference Affective Human Factors Design, pp. 317–324. ASEAN Academic Press, London (2001)

17. Lurie, N.H.: Decision making in information-rich environments: the role of information structure. J. Consum. Res. **30**(4), 473–486 (2004)

18. Jacoby, J., Speller, D.E., Kohn, C.A.: Brand choice behavior as a function of information load. J. Mark. Res. **11**(1), 63–69 (1974)

19. Salman, H.M., Ahmad, W.F.W., Sulaiman, S.: Usability evaluation of the smartphone user interface in supporting elderly users from experts' perspective. IEEE Access **6**, 22578–22591 (2018)

20. Soto-Acosta, P., Jose Molina-Castillo, F., Lopez-Nicolas, C., Colomo-Palacios, R.: The effect of information overload and disorganisation on intention to purchase online: the role of perceived risk and internet experience. Online Inf. Rev. **38**(4), 543–561 (2014)

21. Lv, J., Liu, X.: The impact of information overload of e-commerce platform on consumer return intention: considering the moderating role of perceived environmental effectiveness. Int. J. Environ. Res. Public Health **19**(13), 8060 (2022)

22. Browne, W., Jones, M.S.: What works in e-commerce-a meta-analysis of 6700 online experiments. Qubit Digital Ltd, 21 (2017)

23. Mathur, A., Kshirsagar, M., Mayer, J.: What makes a dark pattern... dark? Design attributes, normative considerations, and measurement methods. In: Kitamura, Y. (ed.) Conference on Human Factors in Computing Systems, Proceedings of 2021 CHI, pp. 1–18. SIGCHI, Association for Computing Machinery, New York (2021)

24. Koh, W.C., Seah, Y.Z.: Unintended consumption: The effects of four e-commerce dark patterns. Cleaner Responsible Consumption **11**, 100145 (2023)
25. van Nimwegen, C., de Wit, J.: Shopping in the dark: effects of platform choice on dark pattern recognition. In: 24th International Conference on Human-Computer Interaction on Proceedings, pp. 462–475. Springer International Publishing, Cham (2022). https://doi.org/10.1007/978-3-031-05412-9_32
26. Lucian, R., Farias, S.A.: Effects of information overload on Brazilian e-consumers. Am. J. Econ. Bus. Adm. **1**(1), 21–26 (2009)
27. Luguri, J., Strahilevitz, L.J.: Shining a light on dark patterns. J. Legal Anal. **13**(1), 43–109 (2021)
28. Narayanan, A., Mathur, A., Chetty, M., Kshirsagar, M.: Dark patterns: past, present, and future: the evolution of tricky user interfaces. Queue **18**(2), 67–92 (2020)
29. Duane, J.N.: Digital Nudges: An Investigation of Both Consumer and Designer Perspectives (Doctoral dissertation, Bentley University) (2023)
30. Ying, Z., Caixia, C., Wen, G., Xiaogang, L.: Impact of recommender systems on unplanned purchase behaviours in e-commerce. In: 5th International Conference on Industrial Engineering and Applications on Proceedings, pp. 21–30. IEEE, Singapore (2020)
31. Bongard-Blanchy, K., Rossi, A., Rivas, S., Doublet, S., Koenig, V., Lenzini, G.: "I am definitely manipulated, even when i am aware of it. it's ridiculous!"-dark patterns from the end-user perspective. In: Ju, W., Oehlberg, L., Follmer, S., Kuznetsov S. (eds.) Designing Interactive Systems Conference 2021, Proceedings of DIS 2021, pp. 763–776. ACM, New York (2021)
32. Anaraky, R.G., et al.: Older and younger adults are influenced differently by dark pattern designs. arXiv preprint arXiv: 2310.03830 (2023)
33. Sin, R., Harris, T., Nilsson, S., Beck, T.: Dark patterns in online shopping: do they work and can nudges help mitigate impulse buying? Behavioural Public Policy 1–27 (2022)
34. Zac, A., Huang, Y.C., von Moltke, A., Decker, C., Ezrachi, A.: Dark patterns and online consumer vulnerability. Available at: SSRN 4547964 (2023)
35. Sánchez Chamorro, L., Bongard-Blanchy, K., Koenig, V. Ethical tensions in UX design practice: exploring the fine line between persuasion and manipulation in online interfaces. In: 2023 ACM Designing Interactive Systems Conference on Proceedings, pp. 2408–2422. ACM, New York (2023)
36. Balata, J., Mikovec, Z., Slavicek, T.: KoalaPhone: touchscreen mobile phone UI for active seniors. J. Multimodal User Interfaces **9**(4), 263–273 (2015)
37. Men, D., Wang, D., Hu, X.: The analysis and research of the smart phone's user interface based on Chinese elderly's cognitive character. In: Stephanidis, C., Antona, M. (eds.) UAHCI 2014. LNCS, vol. 8515, pp. 138–146. Springer, Cham (2014). https://doi.org/10.1007/978-3-319-07446-7_14
38. Sugano, N., Shinomiya, I.: Fuzzy set theoretical analysis of semantic data as human membership values on the color triangle. In: SCIS & ISIS 2010 on Proceedings, pp. 681–686, Japan Society for Fuzzy Theory and Intelligent Informatics, Fukuoka (2010)

Usability Assessment and Design Proposal for the Web Platform for Curriculum Registration at a Peruvian University

Kaytlin Drew Espinoza Concha⬤, Eder Quispe Vilchez(✉)⬤,
and Claudia Zapata Del Río⬤

Pontificia Universidad Católica del Perú, San Miguel, Lima 32, Perú
{kaytlin.espinoza,eder.quispe,zapata.cmp}@pucp.edu.pe

Abstract. Usability has been recognized as a fundamental element in ensuring the quality of a software. Moreover, the lack of adequate usability can be decisive in the success or failure of the system. This study focuses on the web platform responsible for managing curriculum proposals at a university in Peru. It is acknowledged that the current platform lacks usability considerations, leading users to rely on manuals, technical assistance, or personal notes for operation, which is non-intuitive and prone to being forgotten over time. Therefore, the main objective of this project is to develop a design proposal aimed at improving the platform's usability. Initially, user evaluations of the current platform are conducted using the Think-aloud technique, along with interviews to understand user needs and define required usability guidelines. Subsequently, canvases such as User Persona, Empathy Map, User Journey Map, and Product Vision Board are employed to investigate user experience and identify their needs. With this collected information, a high-fidelity prototype is developed and tested with users to assess usability improvements. The results establish usability guidelines for curriculum proposal management, emphasizing the importance of periodically updating user requirements. A high-fidelity prototype is created with enhancements in element layout and icon clarification, aiming to enhance user effectiveness and satisfaction, directly addressing identified needs. In conclusion, user testing proves beneficial in addressing user dissatisfaction, involving them throughout the project development.

Keywords: User evaluation · Usability · High fidelity prototypes

1 Introduction

Currently, web platforms play a fundamental role in the competitiveness of any organization. Beyond visual aesthetics, the usability of a web platform is a determining factor for user satisfaction [1].

In the context of a university in Peru, the web platform dedicated to the registration of curriculum proposals plays a crucial role in the approval process of such plans. However, it faces usability challenges due to the omission of fundamental guidelines in design,

M. Kurosu and A. Hashizume (Eds.): HCII 2024, LNCS 14687, pp. 163–177, 2024.
https://doi.org/10.1007/978-3-031-60441-6_11

lack of consideration for user needs, and inherent issues with the current design. Consequently, the current platform design negatively impacts the process of registering new study plans or modifications, leading to dissatisfaction among users. They often resort to manuals, consult with technical personnel whose availability is often challenging, or rely on personal notes to carry out these actions, as registering a curriculum proposal typically occurs after some time, and it is common to forget the procedure due to the lack of intuitiveness in the platform.

Therefore, the main objective of this project is to develop a design proposal aimed at improving the usability of the curriculum registration web platform, ensuring user satisfaction, and consequently enhancing its usability.

A systematic review was conducted to identify the most appropriate usability techniques, methods, and tools for the project. This review provided crucial information that allowed selecting user evaluation as the most suitable approach. Furthermore, by identifying common usability errors, a basis was established to detect the problems present in the platform, as well as the most important features considered. These findings were fundamental in considering key aspects when designing the high-fidelity prototype. Additionally, the systematic review allowed choosing tools such as User Persona, Empathy Map, User Journey Map, and Product Vision Board, all focused on users, to ensure their satisfaction with the design proposal.

The sections of this document address the problem arising from the lack of usability, the selection of techniques and tools to address this challenge, the methodology employed in the project, the application of this methodology and the results obtained, followed by final conclusions and bibliographic references.

2 Lack of Usability

2.1 Usability

The concept of usability has been defined by several authors in the literature [2]. In this project, primarily rely on the most referenced approach, which characterizes it as a quality attribute assessing the ease of use of user interfaces [3].

Furthermore, Nielsen, an eminent expert in the field, identifies five key components that define usability:

- Learning: Evaluates how easily users can learn to perform basic tasks the first time they interact with the system.
- Efficiency: Once users have learned to use the system, it focuses on the speed with which they can carry out tasks.
- Memory: Refers to the ease with which users can regain their proficiency when using the system after a period of inactivity.
- Errors: Analyzes the quantity and severity of errors users make, as well as how easily they can recover from them.
- Satisfaction: Assesses the overall user experience and how pleasant it is for users to use the system.

These components provide a comprehensive framework for evaluating and enhancing the usability of an information system from various perspectives, thereby contributing to a more effective and satisfying user experience.

2.2 Problem

In the currently used web platform, the needs of users who submit proposals were not considered, as expressed by system users. However, literature indicates the importance of identifying and considering the needs of all users, which in this case are academic and administrative staff, aiming to optimize the system's utility, usability, and acceptance [4].

Unfortunately, sometimes software developers do not invest in usability evaluations during design or development because it is believed that testing is costly in time and money. Nevertheless, there are low-cost and time-efficient usability tests available. Furthermore, it has been shown to be less expensive to invest in usability in early stages of the process than to rebuild or redesign a website when it does not perform as expected [5].

The lack of emphasis on usability during system development leads to the omission of usability guidelines in web platform design, as seen in the platform studied in this project, evidenced by users having to rely on manuals or technical support for guidance on performing tasks, thus delaying the proposal registration process because technical staff availability is limited. This creates a serious issue, as usability is linked to worker productivity. Additionally, the time users spend deciphering difficult instructions translates to money lost by the company [3].

When registering a new curriculum proposal, inputting information into a system is crucial, yet usability principles are not applied in this function. An example of a usability problem encountered during information registration is the lack of supportive prompts for filling out information and uncertainty about distinguishing mandatory fields [6]. This mentioned example is a problem on the web platform because users must rely on notes they have taken to recall how to perform an action since, after some months, they return to the platform and do not remember due to its lack of intuitiveness.

For the reasons stated, the design of the curriculum registration web platform presents issues that negatively impact the curriculum registration process, consequently leading to user dissatisfaction.

3 Selection of Techniques and Tools

In this section, a systematic review is conducted using the PICOC method, abbreviating Population, Intervention, Comparison, Outcome, and Context [7] (see Table 1). The main objective of this systematic review is to identify relevant studies on usability techniques, methods, and tools used, in order to properly select those pertinent to the current project and thus develop a design proposal that significantly improves usability.

The primary studies were obtained using the following search engines: Scopus and IEEE Xplore.

The search string used is as follows: ("technological platform" OR "software" OR "website") AND ("techniques" OR "methods" OR "usability evaluation" OR "heuristics" OR "software design" OR "usability test" OR "usability engineering") AND ("academic" OR "educational").

Here are the responses to research questions formulated based on the selected documents.

Table 1. The PICOC method for question formulation.

Population	Technological platform, Software, Website
Intervention	Curriculum registration, Curriculum management
Comparison	Not apply because the aim is not to compare usability evaluation methods
Outcome	Techniques, Methods, Usability evaluation, Heuristics, Software design, Usability test, Usability engineering
Context	Academic, Educational

Q1. What techniques or methods are currently applied in the usability evaluations of educational web platforms, and how do they help identify existing problems?

A1. According to primary studies, inspection methods are conducted by experts, while inquiry and testing methods are carried out by users [8]. Heuristic evaluation, a form of inspection method, is the most widely used in usability evaluations according to the selected documents [9–11]. The goal of these evaluations is to identify issues affecting usability in a system, and the results are used to make recommendations for addressing problems and improving usability design [12]. Another inspection method used is cognitive walkthrough evaluation, which involves problem identification through simulation, evaluating the difficulty of tasks, and determining the goals and activities constituting each task [13].

On the other hand, user evaluations, a form of inquiry method, are the second most commonly used in usability tests conducted on academic management websites [14, 15]. Other techniques employed in usability tests on educational web platforms include:

- Think Aloud Evaluations.
- Questionnaire-based evaluations using tools such as System Usability Scale [4, 16], User Experience Questionnaire [17, 18], or online questionnaires and Google Analytics reports [19].
- Performance-based evaluations.

In heuristic evaluations, the evaluators are usability experts and may not truly reflect the opinions of real users. Therefore, it is recommended that heuristic evaluations be conducted alongside user testing to complement each other [6]. In conclusion, a combination of methods or techniques is suggested to obtain more effective results [20–22].

Q2. What are the most common errors found in the results of usability evaluations of educational systems, and how do they impact usability?

A2. The most common errors identified in the results of usability evaluations of educational systems can be categorized into three main areas:

The first error is related to the incorrect organization and structure of the system's information, along with issues with content quality. These aspects hinder the user's ability to locate and comprehend information [11, 12, 15, 23].

The second frequent error is associated with minimalist design and aesthetics [17, 24]. This error occurs when users express dissatisfaction with the colors, fonts, and images used on websites [22], resulting in an unattractive system [18].

The third most recurrent error is linked to navigation issues [11]. An example of this is hyperlinks on the website that do not function efficiently and quickly [14], affecting the user's orientation within the system [13].

These errors contribute to making the system complicated and challenging to use [10], impacting user performance and leading to inappropriate task development times [8]. Therefore, correcting these errors is crucial to enhance system efficiency and achieve user satisfaction [20].

Q3. What characteristics are considered relevant in the design of interfaces for curriculum or academic management software, and what is the basis for their importance?

A3. On one hand, two fundamental characteristics stand out that curriculum or academic management software should possess, both mentioned together in various documents. One of them is the correct organization and quality of the software's content [25, 26]. The content should be grouped and ordered according to the potential objectives of the user [9]. This characteristic is crucial as it facilitates task completion, aids in remembering the website's structure, and contributes to user satisfaction when using it [24]. The other relevant characteristic is associated with the visual design and coherence of the user interface [1, 6, 13, 19]. Its importance lies in its connection to the visual appeal of the site's design, the proper use of images, fonts, and colors, elements that elicit approval or disapproval from the user [22].

In conclusion, having the aforementioned characteristics allows the system to be efficient and effective [10], easy to use and understand [4], as information becomes accessible, and navigation is simplified [14].

Q4. What techniques or design tools are used to identify the perceived needs of users, focusing on them as the protagonists?

A4. One of the mentioned tools is the creation of User Personas, which are hypothetical archetypes developed to identify the profile, needs, and goals of real users. These representations can guide decisions related to functionality, navigation, interaction, and even visual design [27]. User profiles are not invented but constructed from data collected in previous research. However, the name and associated personal data are fictitious [28]. This tool is used to foster empathy from the development team towards end-users [29].

Another prominent tool in these studies is the Empathy Map. This technique is used to externalize and synthesize the information gathered about the end-user, enabling the identification and understanding of their needs more effectively [30]. Empathy maps traditionally are divided into four quadrants (what they say, what they think, what they do, and what they feel), with an avatar or image of the user in the middle [31].

Additionally, reference is made to the User Journey Map, which is described as a visual representation of the sequence of events that a user experiences during their interaction with a product or service [32]. This map visualizes significant changes in user needs, satisfaction with the software, and other usage metrics throughout the different stages of the user experience [33].

Furthermore, the Product Vision Board, this visual technique helps to present more comprehensibly the vision and the needs that the product must [34].

These techniques allow visualizing the software from the user's perspective, facilitating the identification of their needs, thus ensuring their satisfaction.

4 Methodology

The primary objective is to define the usability guidelines that should be present in the curriculum proposal registration system to apply them in the design proposal. For this objective, the functionalities of the web platform and user needs regarding the system were first identified. This was accomplished through an interview conducted via Zoom with a representative user of the system. Given that this system is tailored for an educational institution and not a widely used commercial product, only one user was considered. Consequently, it's crucial to provide user training to ensure proficiency in the system's domain knowledge and application of relevant rules and restrictions. The interview utilized the unstructured interview method, aiming to gather valuable data about participants' experiences without imposing restrictions on their expressions [35].

Subsequently, usability tests were designed, considering the product under evaluation, the test objectives, and the appropriate materials, recommended from usability evaluation literature such as Rubin & Chisnell's book [36]. Pre-test questionnaires were administered to gather users' personal data and evaluate their familiarity with the system, while post-test questionnaires were employed to solicit feedback regarding users' impressions upon completing the test. Additionally, a detailed list of tasks was provided to identify usability issues.

Following the preparation phase, usability tests were conducted with users using Zoom. Initially, a pilot test was executed to refine the testing plan. Subsequently, tests were conducted with five users, a number deemed significant by usability pioneers like Nielsen, Lewis, and Virzi, who argue that 80% of usability problems can be identified with a sample of five users [37]. During the user testing sessions, the Thinking Aloud approach, specifically the Concurrent Thinking Aloud (CTA) method, was employed. This method instructed users to verbalize their thoughts, actions, and feelings as they performed tasks, allowing observers to comprehend the cognitive processes associated with task execution [38].

Finally, a comprehensive report on the user tests was developed. Each task on the list was analyzed to identify both positive aspects and improvement opportunities within the platform. Responses from questionnaires were also scrutinized, leading to the formulation of conclusive usability guidelines.

The second objective is to conduct a user experience research to identify the needs related to the curriculum proposal registration process. For all the techniques, the required information was obtained from interviews and tests with users.

It was decided to create a User Persona, as it allows the development of a reliable and realistic representation of users, facilitating the visualization of how they might react to a new interaction flow and proving useful in the design process [39]. The creation of a single canvas was considered because it represents the only type of users who perform the registration. For the canvas design, a simple format was used containing only the most relevant points, inspired by the graphic design of the UXPressia page [40], which includes the following points: Name, avatar, position, gender, age, place of residence, personality, knowledge, goals, frustrations.

Subsequently, an Empathy Map was developed, which helps to understand and prioritize user needs, as well as verify that there is sufficient knowledge about the users [31]. The format used was a traditional format presented on the Nielsen Norman Group website [31], which is divided into four quadrants: what they say, what they think, what they do, and what they feel.

After this, a User Experience Journey Map was created, allowing the visualization of the complete user experience and serving as a basis for decision-making [41]. The format used was the one indicated on the Nielsen Norman Group website [42]. This format mentions 3 zones: in the first, the person and the scenario in which the journey takes place are mentioned; in the second, the journey actions that are in phases and the user's emotions at each phase; and in the third, the improvement opportunities resulting from the journey.

Finally, a Product Vision Board was elaborated, as it is a tool that captures the vision and strategy of the product, guiding the development of high-fidelity prototypes. The format used was the one presented on the RomanPichler website [43], which is divided into 5 sections: the vision, the target group, the users' needs, the product, and its value.

The third objective aims to develop a design proposal for the web platform interfaces based on the results obtained from previous objectives. To achieve this, the Figma tool was employed to create a high-fidelity prototype. Each screen of the prototype was designed, addressing previously identified issues and considering user needs expressed in the canvases, as well as established usability guidelines and principles from ISO 9241–210:2019. Subsequently, colors were defined for the various components of each screen, buttons, and notifications.

Afterward, a testing plan was developed based on the one used previously. Similar to previous tests, a pilot test was conducted, followed by usability evaluations with users on the proposed high-fidelity prototype, aiming to identify areas for improvement. Following the implementation of suggested improvements, final approval was obtained from the users.

Finally, a qualitative report of the usability evaluation results was created to compare the new interfaces with the original ones (See Fig. 1).

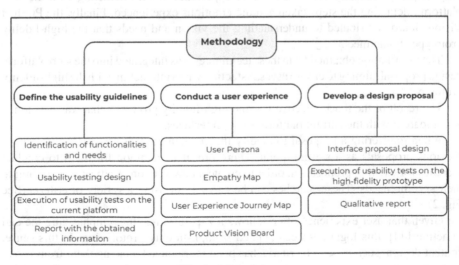

Fig. 1. Methodology

5 Results

Based on the findings of the first objective, the following usability guidelines have been defined:

- Periodically request updates to the requirements from real users, as workers, academic processes, and consequently, needs may change over time.
- Due to the lack of knowledge transfer between incoming and outgoing workers, it is crucial to document all agreements and key standards, as well as explain the meaning of options in the process and how each choice affects the final curriculum, subject to approval from the relevant authorities.
- The system should provide captions and help messages so that any user can understand and remember each functionality. This is especially important as users interact with the platform when modifications to the curriculum are required, often occurring each semester. Therefore, it is essential that they can easily recall the aspects learned from the platform.
- Use icons that are representative of reality to ensure understanding by any user.
- Display the most recent records first, as these are commonly used by users, thus avoiding the need for an additional step to organize information.
- Indicate the "Loading" status during ongoing actions, providing users with information about the process that is taking place.

The results of the second objective are reflected in the canvases, which were useful for understanding the profile of users and identifying their usability needs, focusing primarily on ease of finding functionalities, registration efficiency, and error prevention.

The User Persona allowed the identification of users' profiles, needs, and goals for the web platform. Likewise, the Empathy Map facilitated the ability to empathize with the user and understand their perspective. Additionally, the User Experience Journey Map helped graphically visualize the user experience when interacting with the web platform, depicting the steps taken and the emotions experienced. Finally, the Product Vision Board contributed to understanding the vision and needs that the high-fidelity prototype should meet.

The information obtained from these techniques was integrated into the web platform design proposal, aiming to ensure user satisfaction when interacting with the high-fidelity prototype.

The result of the third objective was the high-fidelity prototype that was developed to compare it with the current platform's user interfaces.

When registering a proposal to modify the curriculum, it is essential to base it on previous proposals as a starting point. Therefore, it is common for users to conduct searches for existing proposals in order to create a new version or adjust it according to their specific needs. These searches can be carried out using a variety of criteria (See Fig. 2).

Given that user experience often follows a Z-pattern reading, emphasizing the call to action [44], this logic has been applied in high-fidelity prototyping. In this sense, content design, such as search criteria, has been reorganized, placing them from left to right and from top to bottom according to their importance and frequency of use. This improvement aims to enhance the user experience by naturally guiding them towards the most relevant information and expected actions.

Another crucial aspect to consider is that new users or those returning to the system after a prolonged period may face difficulties in understanding or remembering certain fields. To address this issue, a contextual help feature has been implemented. This feature is presented through a question mark icon, indicating the availability of assistance. By clicking on this icon, a pop-up window appears offering detailed information about the meaning of each field, possible search options, and a complete description of its purpose. This functionality has been designed with the aim of improving accessibility and understanding for users who are getting acquainted with the system.

During searches or proposal creations, since the process may take some time, the current platform lacks clear notification about the loading progress, leaving the user in uncertainty. To address this issue, a loading icon has been incorporated alongside an informative message in the high-fidelity prototype. This provides the user with necessary information and significantly enhances the system's transparency by keeping them informed about the process's status.

In the current platform, search results are presented from oldest to newest, which is not convenient given users' tendency to prioritize the most recent proposals. This is a crucial consideration, whether presenting a new proposal based on current circumstances or reviewing those requiring approval. In response to this need, the order of proposal visualization has been rearranged in the high-fidelity prototype, presenting them from newest to oldest.

To effectively register a curriculum, it's essential to complete several sections with detailed and relevant information, among which the Justification stands out (See Fig. 3). In the current platform, entering the justification reason is restricted to a single text box, without clearly specifying the points to be addressed in this section. Therefore, in the high-fidelity prototype, the users' needs have been taken into account, and two text boxes have been added. This is because there are two fundamental aspects to consider: the reason for the justification and the main changes made. Additionally, examples and necessary information will be provided in the help icons to guide users in writing the justification, thus eliminating the need to seek external help to complete this section properly.

In the current platform, sections with mandatory fields lack a logical order, which may cause users to overlook the requirements. In the high-fidelity prototype, these sections have been relocated to the beginning, and a clear informative notice about the sections with mandatory fields has been added. Furthermore, a preventive error message is introduced when attempting to finalize the proposal without completing these sections, thus avoiding subsequent errors and enhancing the process's effectiveness.

After confirming an action such as saving in the current platform, another confirmation message appears, slowing down the process. In the high-fidelity prototype, a temporary success notification has been implemented that disappears after an appropriate time, informing the user about successful saving and avoiding unnecessary clicks. This improves efficiency and interaction flow.

Another important section is the Curriculum (See Fig. 4), where some icons proved difficult for users to interpret. In the high-fidelity prototype, unconventional icons have been replaced with underlined text, such as "Add row" and "Add course," aiming to improve understanding and facilitate the identification of actions associated with these elements.

Regarding informative notices, in the current platform, they are presented in yellow, which may not catch the user's attention and go unnoticed. In contrast, in the high-fidelity prototype, a specific color has been assigned to each type of notice: light blue tones for informative notifications, yellow tones for warnings, green tones for success notifications, and red tones for error notifications. Additionally, each notice includes a representative icon of its type, aiding in highlighting them and facilitating their identification.

Other considered aspects encompass multiple screens, some of which in the current platform display large white spaces at the bottom, resulting in underutilization of the total space and overwhelming presentation of information. In contrast, in the high-fidelity prototype, this issue is addressed by ensuring that the information utilizes the entire screen, thus significantly improving readability and visual experience.

Furthermore, the current platform displays button redundancy on all screens, potentially causing confusion in the interface. In the high-fidelity prototype, button design has been optimized to ensure they appear only once per screen, aiming to simplify navigation and reduce perceived complexity for the user.

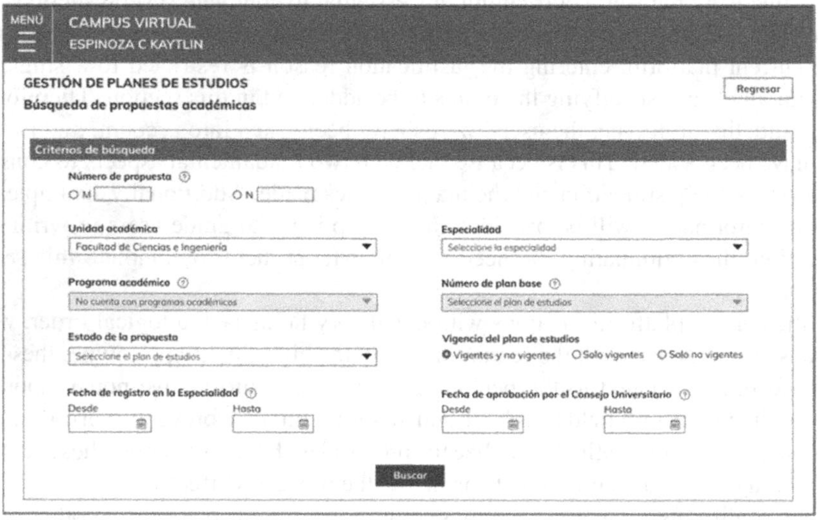

Fig. 2. Proposal Search Screen

Fig. 3. Justification Screen

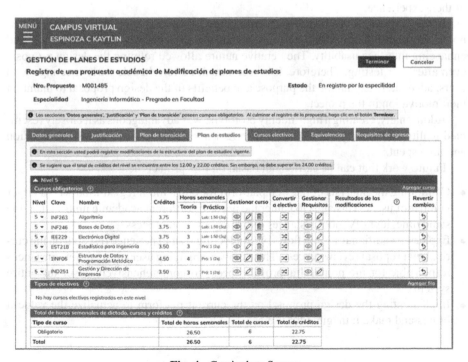

Fig. 4. Curriculum Screen

6   Conclusions and Future Work

User testing proved to be beneficial as it addressed the prior dissatisfaction of users with the web platform, involving them from the project's inception and considering their needs. Conducting a pilot test was advantageous in refining the testing plan and estimating the total duration of the evaluation. A key takeaway was the need to emphasize the explanation of the thinking-aloud method to ensure users understood and executed it correctly, particularly in remote usability tests where screen sharing is essential for observation.

As a result, the methods employed to achieve the first objective were effective in analyzing user interaction with the web platform, defining usability guidelines to be considered in high-fidelity prototyping, and addressing positive and negative aspects of the platform, resolved in the design proposal.

Overall, the four techniques used— User Persona, Empathy Map, User Journey Map, and Product Vision Board—complemented each other, enabling a comprehensive investigation of the user experience to gather crucial information considered in the design proposal. It's important to mention that the Empathy Map technique stands out because it contributes to a deeper understanding of users' emotions, thoughts, needs, and concerns, which is reflected in decision-making during the development of the high-fidelity prototype. The Empathy Map could be integrated alongside the User Persona, with a more concise approach to facilitate visualization and understanding of the user. Furthermore, the User Journey has proven to be a valuable tool for identifying friction areas and designing user-centered solutions, enabling a more effective approach in critical stages of their experience.

In the third and final objective, the utilization of user experience research in developing the high-fidelity prototype proved valuable in achieving user satisfaction and enhancing interface usability. The iterative nature allowed refining the design proposal even after user testing. Therefore, it is recommended to schedule early meetings with users, adequately explaining the purpose and benefits of the design proposal to maintain their motivation in the project.

Additionally, creating a high-fidelity prototype was advantageous as it closely resembled reality, facilitating a comparison with real interfaces in terms of task completion and time spent.

Future work that can be carried out based on this project includes:

- Continuing the analysis of the web platform for curriculum registration with a larger number of users. This aims to gather the needs of different academic units and, at the same time, identify more instances of the registration process.
- Exploring additional system flows by conducting user experience research on the curriculum proposal review process. This involves engaging users from various instances responsible for the proposal approval process to comprehensively cover the entire system.
- Implementing the design proposal on the current platform to actualize the value it brings and make it tangible for users.

References

1. Roy, S., Pattnaik, P.K., Mall, R.: A quantitative approach to evaluate usability of academic websites based on human perception. Egypt. Inform. J. **15**(3), 159–167 (2014). https://doi.org/10.1016/j.eij.2014.08.002
2. Paz Espinoza, F.A.: Método para la evaluación de usabilidad de sitios web transaccionales basado en el proceso de inspección heurística. Pontificia Universidad Católica Del Perú (2018). http://hdl.handle.net/20.500.12404/9903
3. Nielsen, J.: Usability 101: Introduction to Usability. All Usability (2012). https://www.nngroup.com/articles/usability-101-introduction-to-usability/
4. Al-Omar, K.: Evaluating the Usability and Learnability of the "Blackboard" LMS Using SUS and Data Mining (2018). https://doi.org/10.1109/iccmc.2018.8488038
5. Liu, F.: Usability evaluation on websites. In: 9th International Conference on Computer-Aided Industrial Design and Conceptual Design: Multicultural Creation and Design - CAIDCD 2008 (2008). https://doi.org/10.1109/CAIDCD.2008.4730538
6. Alotaibi, M.B.: Assessing the usability of university websites in Saudi Arabia: A heuristic evaluation approach. In: Proceedings of the 2013 10th International Conference on Information Technology: New Generations, ITNG 2013 (2013). https://doi.org/10.1109/ITNG.2013.26
7. Petticrew, M., Roberts, H.: Systematic Reviews in the Social Sciences: A Practical Guide (2008). https://doi.org/10.1002/9780470754887
8. Rosmasari, et al.: Usability study of student academic portal from a user's perspective. In: Proceedings - 2nd East Indonesia Conference on Computer and Information Technology: Internet of Things for Industry, EIConCIT 2018, pp. 108–113 (2018). https://doi.org/10.1109/EIConCIT.2018.8878618
9. Silvis, I.M., Bothma, T.J.D., de Beer, K.J.W.: Evaluating the usability of the information architecture of academic library websites. Libr. Hi Tech **37**(3), 566–590 (2019). https://doi.org/10.1108/LHT-07-2017-0151
10. Almarashdeh, I.A., Sahari, N., Zin, N.A.M.: Heuristic Evaluation of distance learning management system interface. In: Proceedings of the 2011 International Conference on Electrical Engineering and Informatics, ICEEI 2011 (2011). https://doi.org/10.1109/ICEEI.2011.6021542
11. Hasan, L.: Heuristic evaluation of three jordanian university websites. Inf. Educ. **12**(2), 231–251 (2013). https://www.scopus.com/inward/record.uri?eid=2-s2.0-84888403610&partnerID=40&md5=8fd964718df1a28c089342a6bed7cad9
12. Salas, J., et al.: Guidelines to evaluate the usability and user experience of learning support platforms: a systematic review. In: Ruiz, P.H., Agredo-Delgado, V. (eds.) Human-Computer Interaction: 5th Iberoamerican Workshop, HCI-Collab 2019, Puebla, Mexico, June 19–21, 2019, Revised Selected Papers, pp. 238–254. Springer International Publishing, Cham (2019). https://doi.org/10.1007/978-3-030-37386-3_18
13. Habibi, S., Seyed-Akbari, L., Torab-Miandoab, A., Samad-Soltani, T.: Usability of central library websites of iranian universities of medical sciences: an evaluation. DESIDOC J. Libr. Inf. Technol. **39**(4), 162–168 (2019). https://doi.org/10.14429/djlit.39.4.14462
14. Baroudi, M., Alia, M., Marashdih, A.W.: Evaluation of accessibility and usability of higher education institutions' websites of Jordan. In: 2020 11th International Conference on Information and Communication Systems, ICICS 2020 (2020). https://doi.org/10.1109/ICICS49469.2020.239565
15. Halim, F., Elly, H.: Usability evaluation for digital library: a case study of library websites, Mikroskil. In: Proceedings of 2019 4th International Conference on Informatics and Computing, ICIC 2019 (2019). https://doi.org/10.1109/ICIC47613.2019.8985768

16. González-Puetate, P., Fernández-Peña, F., Urrutia-Urrutia, P.: Hybrid procedure for measuring usability of management systems in higher education. In: Iberian Conference on Information Systems and Technologies, CISTI (2019). https://doi.org/10.23919/CISTI.2019.8760905

17. Paramitha, A.A.I.I., Dantes, G.R., Indrawan, G.: The evaluation of web based academic progress information system using heuristic evaluation and user experience questionnaire (UEQ). In: Proceedings of the 3rd International Conference on Informatics and Computing, ICIC 2018 (2018). https://doi.org/10.1109/IAC.2018.8780430

18. Valerian, A., Santoso, H.B., Schrepp, M., Guarddin, G.: Usability evaluation and development of a university staff website. In: Proceedings of the 3rd International Conference on Informatics and Computing, ICIC 2018 (2018). https://doi.org/10.1109/IAC.2018.8780456

19. Sheikh, A.: Evaluating the usability of COMSATS institute of information technology library website: a case study. Electron. Libr. **35**(1), 121–136 (2017). https://doi.org/10.1108/EL-08-2015-0149

20. Reyes Vera, J.M., Berdugo Torres, M.I., Villegas, L.M.: Usability evaluation of a course management system based on lingweb platform [Evaluación de usabilidad de un sistema de administraciónde cursos basado en la plataforma Lingweb]. Ingeniare **24**(3), 435–444 (2016). https://doi.org/10.4067/S0718-33052016000300008

21. Stergioulas, L., et al.: Evaluating e-learning platforms for schools: use and usability, user acceptance, and impact on learning. Proceedings - IEEE 14th International Conference on Advanced Learning Technologies, ICALT 2014, pp. 19–21 (2014). https://doi.org/10.1109/ICALT.2014.16

22. Hasan, L.: Evaluating the usability of nine Jordanian university websites. In: International Conference on Communications and Information Technology - Proceedings, pp. 91–96 (2012).https://doi.org/10.1109/ICCITechnol.2012.6285849

23. Hassan, W.A.W., Teridi, N.A., Abdullah, K.A., Hamid, A., Zainuddin, N.M.M.: An assessment study on usability of academic management system. In: Proceedings - 2010 International Conference on User Science and Engineering, i-USEr 2010, pp. 199–202 (2010). https://doi.org/10.1109/IUSER.2010.5716751

24. Rosas-Chavez, P., Mora-Fernandez, J., Suarez, C.: Comparative analysis of usability of the public universities' web sites of Riobamba city in ecuador. Adv. Intell. Syst. Comput. **972**, 742–752 (2020). https://doi.org/10.1007/978-3-030-19135-1_73

25. Sagar, K., Saha, A.: Qualitative usability feature selection with ranking: a novel approach for ranking the identified usability problematic attributes for academic websites using data-mining techniques. Hum. Centric Comput. Inf. Sci. **7**, 1–24 (2017). https://doi.org/10.1186/s13673-017-0111-8

26. Yerlikaya, Z., Durdu, P.O.: Usability of university websites: a systematic review. In: Antona, M., Stephanidis, C. (eds.) Universal Access in Human–Computer Interaction. Design and Development Approaches and Methods: 11th International Conference, UAHCI 2017, Held as Part of HCI International 2017, Vancouver, BC, Canada, July 9–14, 2017, Proceedings, Part I, pp. 277–287. Springer International Publishing, Cham (2017). https://doi.org/10.1007/978-3-319-58706-6_22

27. Nieters, J.E., Ivaturi, S., Ahmed, I.: Making personas memorable. In: CHI 2007 Extended Abstracts on Human Factors in Computing Systems, pp. 1817–1824. ACM Press, New York, NY (2007)

28. Cooper, A.: The Inmates are Running the Asylum (1999). https://doi.org/10.1007/978-3-322-99786-9_1

29. Wolkerstorfer, P., et al.: Probing an agile usability process. In: Proceedings of the Twenty-Sixth Annual CHI Conference Extended Abstracts on Human Factors in Computing Systems - CHI 2008 (2008). https://doi.org/10.1145/1358628.1358648

30. Gray, D., Brown, S., Macanufo, J.: Gamestorming: A Playbook for Innovators, Rulebreakers, and Changemakers. O'Reilly Media, Inc. (2010) https://www.oreilly.com/library/view/gam estorming/9781449391195/
31. Gibbons, S.: Empathy Mapping: The First Step in Design Thinking (2018). https://www.nng roup.com/articles/empathy-mapping/
32. Rosenbaum, M.S., Otalora, M.L., Ramírez, G.C.: How to create a realistic customer journey map. Bus. Horiz. **60**, 143–150 (2017)
33. Howard, T.: Journey mapping. Commun. Des. Q. **2**(3), 10–13 (2014)
34. Pichler, R.: Strategize: Product Strategy and Product Roadmap Practices for the Digital Age. Pichler Consulting (2016). https://www.romanpichler.com/romans-books/strategize/
35. Wilson, C.: Chapter 3 - Unstructured Interviews. Interview Techniques for Ux Practitioners, pp. 43–62 (2014). http://www.sciencedirect.com/science/article/pii/B97801241039310 0003X
36. Rubin, J., Chisnell, D.: Handbook of Usability Testing, Second Edition: How to Plan, Design, and Conduct Effective Tests. Wiley (2008). https://www.amazon.com/-/es/Jeffrey-Rubin/dp/ 0470185481
37. Alroobaea, R., Mayhew, P.J.: How many participants are really enough for usability studies? In: Proceedings of 2014 Science and Information Conference, SAI 2014, pp. 48–56 (2014). https://doi.org/10.1109/SAI.2014.6918171
38. Yen, P.Y., Bakken, S.: A comparison of usability evaluation methods: heuristic evaluation versus end-user think-aloud protocol - an example from a web-based communication tool for nurse scheduling. In: AMIA Annual Symposium Proceedings / AMIA Symposium. AMIA Symposium (2009). https://www.researchgate.net/publication/42639800_A_Comparison_ of_Usability_Evaluation_Methods_Heuristic_Evaluation_versus_End-User_Think-Aloud_ Protocol_-_An_Example_from_a_Web-based_Communication_Tool_for_Nurse_Schedu ling
39. Kertesz, J.: Introduction to user personas (n.d.). https://miro.com/blog/introduction-user-per sonas/
40. UXPressia: Create Personas Online (2014). https://uxpressia.com/personas-online-tool
41. Gibbons, S.: Journey Mapping 101 (2018b). https://www.nngroup.com/articles/journey-map ping-101/
42. Kaplan, K.: When and How to Create Customer Journey Maps (2016). https://www.nngroup. com/articles/customer-journey-mapping/
43. Pichler, R.: The Product Vision Board (2011). https://www.romanpichler.com/blog/the-pro duct-vision-board/?ref=https://product-frameworks.com
44. Cao, J., Zieba, K., Stryjewski, K., Ellis, M.: Web UI Design for the Human Eye: Content Patterns and Typography — Part 2 (2020). https://uxpin.medium.com/web-ui-design-for-the-human-eye-color-space-contrast-part-2-6661091c347f

Discovering Authentic Self: Coaching Agent for Job-Hunting Students

Ekai Hashimoto[1]([✉]), Kohei Nagira[2], Takeshi Mizumoto[2],
and Shun Shiramatsu[1]

[1] Nagoya Institute of Technology, Nagoya, Aichi 466-8555, Japan
`e.hashimoto.611@stn.nitech.ac.jp`
[2] Hylable Inc., Tokyo 170-0005, Japan
`https://www.hylable.com/`

Abstract. This study addresses the social issue in Japan where the unique recruitment system often leads to a mismatch between students' vague career goals and job requirements, impacting their motivation and productivity. Our solution is a pioneering coaching agent integrated into the recruiting process, designed to prompt users to reflect on their future, thereby enhancing their self-understanding and clarifying their career direction. This approach aims to shift the focus of job-hunting students from the immediate to a long-term perspective. Experimental results demonstrate the effectiveness of our agent in boosting career awareness and self-reflection among engineering students, particularly through sections that probe into their goals, offering fresh insights into their career paths. The significant innovation of this research lies in its novel method for career exploration, challenging conventional job-hunting approaches by enabling students to deeply ponder their career desires. Future research should expand the agent's application to a wider array of academic fields to broaden its impact.

Keywords: Job-Hunting Support · Coaching · Dialogue System · Large-Language-Model

1 Introduction

1.1 Job-Hunting in Japan

The lack of career vision has become a social problem in Japan due to its unique recruiting format [1]. Unlike companies in other countries, Japanese companies tend to expect employees to be able to have in various cross-disciplinary roles in their job [2]. Thus, they prioritize students' personality and communication skills over them having specific expertise. This recruiting approach gives students an incentive to focus on their short-term benefits, overlooking expertise and long-term aspirations. Therefore, students choose jobs on the basis of the company reputation and salary, instead of their career vision and professional development.

The unique recruiting format in Japan can result in mismatches between the student's unarticulated goals and the requirements of the position, affecting motivation and productivity [3]. To prevent mismatches, students conduct "self-analysis" before job searching [4]. While "self-analysis" is encouraged, it demands high meta-cognition, and conventional methods, e.g., worksheets, often fall short due to their lack of personalization.

1.2 Contribution

The main contribution of this paper is incorporating a coaching agent in the recruiting system that encourages reflection on the future to deepen the user's self-understanding and clarify career direction [5]. This will allow the agent to encourage users to think about the future and provide them with a long-term perspective. Our coaching agent will solve the problem of job-hunting-students only thinking about the present and immediate future. Specifically, it is designed to help users improve their meta-cognition and clarify their career goals through questions that encourage them to think deeply about their ideal future and what they would like to do after achieving it.

2 Related Work

2.1 Need for Career Advice Agents

Lee et al. [6] evaluated the feasibility and need for using chatbots in college-student career advising. They conducted interviews using chatbots with 350 undergraduate students at an American university. The results indicated the potential for chatbots to provide services at four levels: information provision, career- development intervention, counselor-task supplementation, and career counseling. Fouad et al. [7] found that college students exhibit difficulty in career decision-making, high levels of psychological distress, and low levels of psychological well-being, with about half the students being aware of career services but far fewer having used these services. The study also demonstrated a correlation between psychological distress and career-related variables for students who had not decided on a career path. Palade et al. [8] highlighted the necessity of counseling services in universities and the usefulness of such services for students and graduates. Students highly value these services and wish to benefit from them, but often find it challenging due to factors such as economic.

Therefore, our proposed coaching agent clarifies individual user's values and career directions. A key advantage of this agent is the use of large-scale language models to provide just-in-time personalized services.

2.2 Student Life and Chatbots

Chatbots, a form of conversational technology, have primarily been used for commercial purposes such as customer support [9]. Researchers have begun expanding the value of chatbots to promote collaboration [10], improve performance

[11], and encourage healthy lifestyles [12]. These developments have been further expanded by GPT-4 [13]. Some universities have deployed chatbots to support student life. The system by Kosuga et al. [14] identifies areas of confusion in students' lessons, which are then explained by professors or teaching assistants in subsequent classes.

However, there is a lack of chatbots aiding in higher education career assistance. Therefore, our aim is to use chatbots in providing career advice to college students.

2.3   Coaching and Chatbots

Passmore et al. [15] predicted that with the advent of artificial intelligence (AI) and machine learning, chatbots might revolutionize the coaching industry over the next decade, becoming the primary providers of coaching conversations in place of humans. Terblanche et al. [16] demonstrated that AI coaches can be as effective as human coaches. However, they concluded that AI currently lacks empathy and emotional intelligence, thus cannot mimic human coaches. D'silva et al. [17] created a chatbot using cognitive science to mimic human conversations. Their chatbot aims to provide clients with suitable job listings and other services through psychological tests.

Our coaching agent enhances empathy by providing users with positive feedback from its persona. Instead of finding suitable jobs for users, it assists users in discovering the jobs they truly desire.

3   Method: Coaching Agent that Supports Self-analysis

Our coaching agent assists job-seeking students in their self-analysis using a large-scale language model, with the aim of addressing challenges in job hunting. This agent is an agenda-based dialogue system [18]. Such a system is one in which each agenda (stage) has a set goal, and upon achieving that goal, moves to the next agenda and offers a different topic of conversation. Each agenda has its prompts, meaning the theme of the questions changes as the stage progresses. All prompts are listed in Table 4.

This agent confronts job-seeking students with their values, aiding in the understanding of these values and supporting their career paths. Kato et al. [19] have shown that the criteria job-seeking students use in selecting companies are related to their values. In developing this agent, we prepared eight perspectives considered important in choosing a company. The agent initially encompasses the eight perspectives of "Occupation," "Salary," "Work-Life Balance," "Skill Up," "Company Brand," "Company Sustainability," "Transfer and Company's Address," and "Company's Culture and Philosophy". as the evaluation axes for choosing a company.

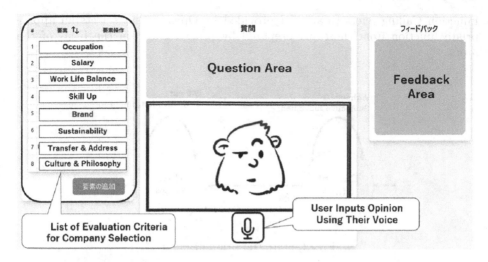

Fig. 1. User interface of coaching agent

3.1   Agent User Interface

Figure 1 shows the agent's user interface (UI). It has a table of evaluation axes on the left side of the screen, which can be rearranged and added to during use. The upper center and right of the screen display windows for questions and feedback. Feedback is based on the user's previous response and sometimes leads into the next question. An animation plays while waiting for the response from the server, indicating to the user that the system is processing. Additionally, feedback is displayed one character at a time to encourage the user to read it. A microphone button is located at the bottom center of the screen.

Initially, the user ranks the priorities of the eight evaluation axes for company selection in Japan. The system processes the user's input with the GPT-4 application programming interface (API), generating light feedback and questions for the user. The user then responds to the system-generated questions via voice, repeating this procedure. After completing all dialogue sections, the user again sends their prioritized evaluation axes for company selection to the agent. Finally, the user receives comprehensive feedback from the system.

3.2   Features of Agent

To delve deeper into the user's responses, the coaching agent possesses the following features.

1. Classification of spoken content using Function Calling
   - Utterance classification based on coaching techniques
   - Avoidance of errors for unclear inputs
2. User- emotion analysis
   - Emotional labeling based on voice features
   - Measurement of the time between question display and response. (Interval)

Function Calling refers to an API provided by OpenAI that selects an appropriate function from those pre-prepared by programmers on the basis of the input.

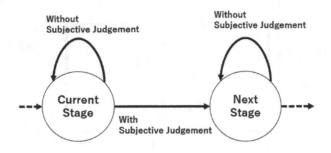

Fig. 2. State transition diagram

Utterance Classification. Figure 2 shows the state transition diagram for the agent.

Hamada et al. [20] patterned dialogues in career coaching that make the user aware of values they had not realized. To replicate these dialogue patterns, we used Function Calling. In our agent, Function Calling classifies input utterances into three categories: utterances that include subjective judgment and the reasons/experiences behind them, utterances that include only subjective judgment, and utterances that include neither. As shown in Fig. 2, if the agent determines that the user's utterance includes subjective judgment and the reasons/experiences behind it, it moves to the next stage. Otherwise, it remains in the current stage and encourages the user to delve deeper into their response, especially asking for reasons if the user's response lacks them.

Emotion Analysis. Non-verbal elements are also important in coaching. Our coaching agent conducts emotion analysis and labeling using Speechbrain [21], which is used to analyze emotions from voice features using prosody and labels them as angry, sad, happy, or neutral with respective probabilities. It then measures the interval from when the question is displayed on the UI until the user clicks the microphone button, determining whether the user is pondering.

If three out of these five types of numerical values (angry, sad, happy, neutral and interval) are detected as outliers from the interquartile range, the agent processes this as the user being unsettled by the question. In this case, the agent does not execute utterance classification using Function Calling and remains in the current stage, continuing to ask questions about the current conversation theme (Fig. 3).

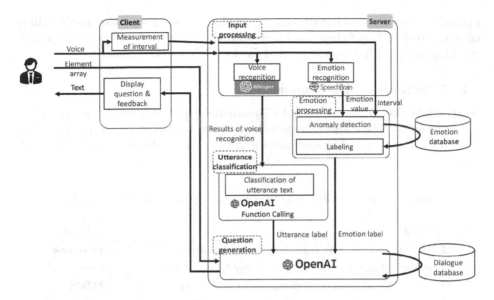

Fig. 3. System architecture

3.3   System Architecture

The following describes the system architecture of our coaching agent The client sends either the user's voice response or table of prioritized evaluation axes to the server using Flask.

In the case of a voice response, voice recognition is conducted using OpenAI's Whisper, and emotion recognition is conducted using Speechbrain. From the fourth response onwards, the user's data stored in the database are compared, and an outlier detection using the interquartile range is executed. If an anomaly is detected, as described in Sect. 3.2, the agent remains in the current stage and generates questions. If no anomalies are detected, utterance classification is executed, as illustrated in Fig. 2, and question generation is conducted using the results of voice recognition and pre-prepared prompts. In the case of a table of prioritized evaluation axes, question generation is executed using the table and pre-prepared prompts. These generated questions and feedback are ultimately sent to the client.

4   Experimental Design

We conducted an experiment to evaluate our coaching agent in terms of encouraging users to consider their future and enhance their self-understanding and clarify their career goals by comparing it with a coaching agent that does not ask about the future. Our agent consists of five dialogue sections, three of which are about the present and the other two about the future. The section asking about the future includes a subsection asking about the user's values up to the realization of their ideal state and subsection asking about the user's values after the realization of their ideal state. The baseline for the experiment was a coaching agent with five sections that focuses only on the present.

4.1 Experimental Questionnaire

As shown in Table 1, we conducted a 7-point-scale questionnaire before and after using the agent. The questionnaire includes items related to career maturity and depth of self-understanding and uses the Adult Career Maturity Scales (ACMS) [22].

Table 1. Questionnaire used in experiment (translated into English)

No.	Question	Category
1	I have my own outlook regarding my future career	Job-Career
7	There are things I want to tackle in my future career	from
5	I have personal goals concerning my future career	ACMS
9	I have my own vision for my future personal life	Life-Career
2	I have several things I want to attempt in my future personal life	from
4	I have personal goals concerning my future personal life	ACMS
6	I can explain my values and thoughts to others with reasons	
3	I understand the background of how my thoughts were formed	Metacognition
8	I can explain my career direction to others	
10	After using the agent, I could reconsider my values deeply	After
11	After using the system, I gained a new perspective on my career and values	Experiment
12	After using the agent, there was a change in my way of thinking	Questionnaire

4.2 Experimental Participants

The participants were 13 job-hunting undergraduate university students from the engineering department of a Japanese university. The agent was used from November to December 2023. This period falls after the typical phase of internships and company briefings in August and September for job-seeking students, and before the preparation period for internships and early selection processes in February and March [23].

5   Results and Discussion

Table 2 shows the average changes in responses to each question, and Table 3 presents the average values of responses to each question.

Table 2. Comparison of average changes in evaluation items before and after using agent

No.	Question	Proposed	Baseline	p-value
1	I have my own outlook regarding my future career	+0.60	+0.25	0.252
7	There are things I want to tackle for my future career	+0.60	+0.38	0.362
5	I have personal goals concerning my future career	+1.2	−0.38	0.0461*
9	I have my own vision for my future personal life	+0.60	+0.13	0.222
2	I have several things I want to attempt for my future personal life	+1.0	−0.13	0.0252*
4	I have personal goals concerning my future personal life	−0.40	+1.3	0.0802*
6	I can explain my thoughts to others with reasons	+0.60	+0.75	0.397
3	I understand the background of how my thoughts were formed	+0.80	+1.4	0.272
8	I can explain my career direction to others	+0.80	+1.4	0.0164**

** $p > 0.05$, * $p > 0.1$

Table 3. Comparison of average scores after using agent

#	.Question	Proposed	Baseline	p-value
10	I could reconsider my values more in depth	5.2	4.6	0.313
11	I gained a new perspective on my career and values	5.4	3.9	0.0838*
12	There was a change in my way of thinking	4.8	3.3	0.0865*

* $p > 0.1$

5.1 New Perspectives

As shown in Table 3, those who used our coaching agent were able to gain new perspectives on their values and experienced changes in their thinking and awareness. This can be attributed to our agent supporting users in contemplating their ideal career.

The use of our agent in November and December coincides with the process of gaining new perspectives through job-hunting activities such as internships. In job hunting, it is crucial to break free from entrenched thoughts and images and become aware of various career paths. In this regard, our agent is able to provide job-seeking students with new perspectives and ways of thinking. This suggests that our agent can positively impact job hunting when used by students who cannot participate in internships, or during periods such as May and June when internships are not typically held.

5.2 Self-understanding

In terms of self-understanding and the ability to articulate one's career, the baseline achieved higher scores compared with our agent. This is likely because the baseline has more stages focused on current thoughts, making it more effective for understanding oneself. This is believed to be due to the process, as shown in Fig. 2, where the agent requires clear reasons for the user's responses.

Table 4. Prompts (translated into English)

system	You are a professional providing career advice to job-seeking students, assisting them in self-analysis. The user (student) prioritizes eight elements on the UI (Occupation, Salary, Work- Life Balance, Skill Up, Company Brand, Company Sustainability, Transfer and Company's Address, and Company's Culture and Philosophy). - The student may discover new elements during the coaching process and add them to the list. It's important to listen carefully to their feedback and questions. - You should provide feedback and ask questions on the basis of the user's responses. - Feedback: Provide positive feedback on the user's opinions and thoughts. This should include praise for their unique perspective and solid values. - Question: Ask questions that challenge their values, helping them delve deeper into their thoughts. These questions should make the student re-evaluate and deeply understand their opinions and thoughts. Questions should be based on the feedback provided. Always ask about the eight elements and do not repeat the same question twice or ask about the same matter more than three times. Limit the question to one per output, within 100 characters, and ensure it's easy to understand. - The output should be as follows: [Feedback] (Feedback) [Question] (Question)
assistant	Select one of the elements prioritized by the job-seeking student and directly ask for the reason behind its ranking
assistant	Change the topic and inquire about the elements the student struggled to prioritize and the reasons behind it
assistant	Change the topic and ask one value-challenging comparative question without assumptions about an element not yet mentioned in the conversation
assistant	Change the topic and suggest the user re-evaluate their values list on the basis of the coaching results. Inform them that adding new elements is also an option. Always generate a question. Example question: "Would you like to modify any elements?"
assistant	Change the topic and ask the user about their ideal lifestyle or life goals. Example output: [Feedback] Your thoughts are wonderful. Now, let's change the topic. Everyone has various goals, such as "Wanting to see the NBA" or "Wishing to marry by age 35". [Question] So, what are your specific goals?
assistant	Change the topic and, on the basis of the user's dreams, ask a value-challenging question about whether their current list of values can achieve those goals, citing one element from the array without assumptions. Example: Desiring marriage but having low company stability
assistant	Change the topic and ask a value-challenging question about the possibility of changes in values or thoughts, even if the user's goals have been specifically achieved or completed, while maintaining the current array of elements. Example: Considering the possibility of transfer even after getting married and having 20 years until retirement
assistant	Change the topic and clearly and concretely organize the main points or themes that emerged during the dialogue, highlighting the user's change in values or recognition process. Then, provide specific feedback on actionable items or areas for improvement. It's not necessary to generate a question in this process, but make sure to explicitly state the points that form the basis of the feedback

5.3   Career Plan

As shown in Table 2, in terms of occupational career items, our coaching agent scored higher than the baseline across all items. This can be attributed to users of our agent having a higher tendency to respond about their career goals during stages where their goals are inquired about. Conversely, for personal life items, the baseline scored higher. This may be due to our agent asking users about their life after achieving their goals, i.e., when users' responses were related to their occupational career, the opportunity to inquire about their personal life decreased. Therefore, setting separate stages for inquiring about users' occupational and personal goals might lead to improvements in both areas.

6   Conclusion

We introduced a coaching agent designed to foster a long-term career perspective among students, addressing a prevalent issue in Japanese job-hunting practices. Our agent, by incorporating reflections on the future, aims to assist students in developing a long-term career perspectives and directions.

The experimental results validated the efficacy of our agent in enhancing students' career consciousness and self-understanding. Specifically, sections of the agent that involve inquiring about goals provided users with new perspectives on their careers. Feedback from post-experiment open-ended questions included remarks such as, "Being made to think about what comes after achieving my goals, a point I had not considered, allowed me to rethink about myself". These findings indicate that incorporating stages about the future can help clarify users' long-term career perspectives and directions.

The most pivotal contribution of this research is its groundbreaking approach to career exploration. Using our unique self-analysis coaching agent, we revealed a transformative method for students to delve deeper into and reflect more consciously on their career aspirations, challenging traditional job-hunting paradigms.

This study catered exclusively to engineering students. Therefore, extending the applicability of our agent to students from a broader range of disciplines and backgrounds is important for subsequent studies [24].

Acknowledgements. This study is partially supported by JST CREST (JPMJCR20D1) and NEDO (JPNP20006). We greatly appreciate the kind advices and help by members of the job-hunting NPO en-courage.

References

1. PERSOL Research and Consulting Co., Ltd: Quantitative survey on job hunting and the actual situation after joining the company results report (2019)
2. Hamaguchi, K.: Employment and Labor Law in Japan, p. 16. Nikkei Inc. (2011)
3. Sato, M.: The relationship between satisfaction with a workplace and overall satisfaction with a result of job hunting. In: Japanese Psychological Association Conference, vol. 78, p. 1EV–2–037 (2014)
4. Ukai, Y.: "What I want to do" fueled by business: from an examination of self-analysis during job hunting. Annu. Rep. Hum. Sci. **28**, 79–98 (2007)
5. Sato, M.: The change of undergraduates' time attitude toward their future. In: Japanese Psychological Association Conference, vol. 76, pp. 1PMB12–1PMB12 (2012)
6. Lee, T., et al.: Intelligent career advisers in your pocket? A need assessment study of chatbots for student career advising. In: Americas Conference on Information Systems (2019)

7. Fouad, N.A., et al.: Need, awareness, and use of career services for college students. J. Career Assess. **14**, 407–420 (2006)
8. Palade, A., Constantin, C.P.: The necessity of counselling and vocational orientation in students' career management. Bull. Transilvania Univ. Brasov. Seri. V: Econ. Sci. 61–68 (2012)
9. Johannsen, F., Leist, S., Konadl, D., Basche, M.: Comparison of commercial chatbot solutions for supporting customer interaction. In: European Conference on Information Systems (2018)
10. Avula, S., Chadwick, G., Arguello, J., Capra, R.G.: Searchbots: user engagement with chatbots during collaborative search. In: Proceedings of the 2018 Conference on Human Information Interaction and Retrieval (2018)
11. Williams, A.C., Kaur, H., Mark, G., Thompson, A.L., Iqbal, S.T., Teevan, J.: Supporting workplace detachment and reattachment with conversational intelligence. In: Proceedings of the 2018 CHI Conference on Human Factors in Computing Systems (2018)
12. Schroeder, J., et al.: Pocket skills: a conversational mobile web app to support dialectical behavioral therapy. In: Proceedings of the 2018 CHI Conference on Human Factors in Computing Systems (2018)
13. OpenAI: Gpt-4 technical report (2023)
14. Kosuge, R., Takagi, M., Ichikawa, H.: Development and evaluation of a learning support system for identifying and addressing areas of misunderstanding through dialogue with learners using chatbots. Technical report 4, Graduate School of Software and Information Science, Iwate Prefectural University, September 2019
15. Passmore, J., Tee, D.: Can chatbots replace human coaches? Issues and dilemmas for the coaching profession, coaching clients and for organisations. The Coaching Psychologist (2023)
16. Terblanche, N., Molyn, J., De Haan, E., Nilsson, V.O.: Coaching at scale: investigating the efficacy of artificial intelligence coaching. Int. J. Evidence Based Coach. Mentor. **20**(2), 20–36 (2022). Publisher Copyright: 2022. the Author(s) Published by Oxford Brookes University
17. D'silva, G.M., Jani, M., Jadhav, V., Bhoir, A., Amin, P.N.: Career counselling chatbot using cognitive science and artificial intelligence (2020)
18. Hiroaki, S., Hiromi, N., Masahiro, M., Tsunehiro, A.: Agenda-based chat-oriented dialogue systems that talk along the dialogue flow. JSAI SLUD **87**, 12 (2019)
19. Kato, S.: Preference of university student job choice-conjoint analysis. Jpn. Maneg. Diagn. Assoc. **8**, 56–59 (2008)
20. Hamada, Y., Shoji, Y.: Extracting value creation patterns in career coaching. Proceedings of the Japan Society of Kansei Engineering (2016)
21. Ravanelli, M., et al. SpeechBrain: a general-purpose speech toolkit (2021). arXiv:2106.04624
22. Sakai, T.: Examination of reliability and validity of adult career maturity scales (ACMs). Bull. Aichi Univ. Educ. (Educ. Sci.) **48**, 115–122 (1999)
23. Cabinet Office Government of Japan and Ltd.: Marketing Communications. Survey report on the timing of students' job hunting and recruitment activities (2022)
24. Notsuda, M.I.Y., Takahashi, K.: Analysis on features of university students in humanity and science courses from the questionnaire. TCE **1**(4), 83–92 (2015)

Reproducibility Challenges of External Computational Experiments in Scientific Workflow Management Systems

Muhammad Mainul Hossain[✉][iD], Banani Roy[iD], Chanchal Roy[iD], and Kevin Schneider[iD]

University of Saskatchewan, Saskatoon, SK, Canada
{mainul.hossain,banani.roy,chanchal.roy,kevin.schneider}@usask.ca
https://www.usask.ca/

Abstract. Reproducibility is essential in scientific experiments to ensure that results can be consistently obtained using new data and methods across studies to answer the same scientific question. It evaluates the validity and robustness of the results. A scientific workflow management system (SWfMS) offers specialized tools for data analysis, modelling, and visualization, streamlining complex analyses and accelerating discoveries. It facilitates reproducibility by providing a standardized environment for executing scientific experiments. However, external scientific experiments often utilize tools developed independently by researchers, employing diverse programming languages and operating systems. Reproducing these experiments within an SWfMS requires installation, configuration, and incorporation of the tools into the SWfMS environment for composition, execution, and analysis of workflows. Managing a multi-user SWfMS is challenging, especially when integrating and configuring a diverse array of scientific tools. Many tools require elevated privileges either during installation or execution, creating roadblocks for efficient onboarding and potentially compromising security. Dissimilarities between the SWfMS and individual tool environments can render straightforward installation impossible, requiring time-consuming workarounds. These challenges burden administrators and impede research progress by hindering the seamless reproduction of critical scientific experiments. Our research addressed the critical challenge of reproducing external scientific experiments within SWfMSs. The complex process of integrating diverse software tools and executing them within the SWfMS runtime infrastructure often hinders reproducibility. We conducted a user study to investigate researchers' challenges during experiment reproduction in SWfMSs. Based on the identified pain points, we propose a solution that empowers domain experts to package their tools within self-contained, isolated Docker containers. These containers can then be seamlessly uploaded to the system via a user-friendly graphical interface, eliminating installation obstacles and facilitating integration with the SWfMS runtime environment. Furthermore, we conducted another user study to evaluate the effectiveness of our proposed method, ensuring its practical utility for researchers in real-world scenarios.

© The Author(s), under exclusive license to Springer Nature Switzerland AG 2024
M. Kurosu and A. Hashizume (Eds.): HCII 2024, LNCS 14687, pp. 189–207, 2024.
https://doi.org/10.1007/978-3-031-60441-6_13

Keywords: Reproducibility · Scientific Workflow · SWfMS · Tool Integration

1   Introduction

In complex scientific experiments and simulations, scientists seamlessly integrate diverse tools, orchestrating their executions within a meticulously designed scientific workflow. Each step in this workflow entails data transformation and analysis operations based on a set of rules and instructions for execution [16]. Provenance information is systematically captured and queried throughout the process, culminating in comprehensive visualization for later analysis. Scientific Workflow Management Systems (SWfMSs) streamline the specification, registration, execution, visualization, and monitoring of scientific workflows [1,7,8,15]. Many scientific domains such as astronomy, bioinformatics, gravitational wave physics, geoinformatics, and chemoinformatics extensively use SWfMSs.

Scientific experiments need reproducibility, the ability to achieve consistent results with new data and methods, ensuring the validity and robustness of findings. However, achieving reproducibility becomes complex in the realm of scientific software development. Researchers or programmers typically create software tools independently, employing diverse programming languages, libraries, and frameworks to tackle specific scientific challenges [13]. While these tools serve their intended purposes well, integrating them into Scientific Workflow Management Systems (SWfMSs) poses formidable challenges, primarily due to their lack of portability, which impedes smooth movement and integration. Time and budget constraints often lead developers to prioritize solving specific problems over adhering to software engineering principles for robustness [3,20], making integration with other tools challenging. Large-scale, web-based systems often restrict end-user administrative access, adding complexity to experiment reproduction within the system. These challenges slow scientific progress and raise concerns about the validity and reliability of research findings. Addressing these issues is crucial for unlocking the full potential of SWfMS in accelerating scientific discovery.

Modern scientific workflow management systems (SWfMSs) like Galaxy [8] and KNIME [7] are multi-user, web-based platforms designed for collaborative research. However, this web-based approach often restricts end-user access to installing and configuring tools directly, presenting a hurdle for achieving thorough scientific reproducibility. The limited administrative privileges in such systems create challenges when transferring experiments and tools. Ideally, users would have a user-friendly interface to upload and configure their tools seamlessly within the SWfMS. Systems like VizSciFlow [13] demonstrate progress in this area with their web-based interface for tool integration. While straightforward tools can be easily integrated, the pursuit of scientific reproducibility necessitates grappling with the installation and configuration complexities of sophisticated software tools, alongside the transfer of entire experiments to the workflow server, which requires advanced administrative measures such as custom installation, source compilation, system configuration, and system repository dependency. Facilitating end-users to reproduce such experiments without compromising security poses an exceptional challenge, if not a formidable task altogether. Providing researchers with a user-friendly interface to effectively manage numerous software tools' diverse installation and configuration parameters adds another layer of complexity to the endeavour.

We adopted a user-centric approach to explore the challenges associated with reproducing scientific experiments within a SWfMS, gathering insights from researchers regarding their requirements and experiences in this process. Participants underwent training on integrating their experiments into VizSciFlow, a generic scientific workflow management system [12], before being tasked with the integration process. Subsequently, we utilized the NASA-TLX [11] post-task questionnaire to capture participants' opinions on their integration experience. Based on the identified challenges, we proposed isolated execution environments for external experiments. This approach leverages containerization to abstract complexity, enhance security, and simplify the integration of external tools. To gauge the effectiveness of this solution, we revisited the tool integration process with containerized experiments and gathered feedback from researchers using the NASA-TLX questionnaire. This provided valuable insights into the user experience and perceived benefits of the solution. Additionally, we conducted a software analytics case study using NiCad clone detection [4] and BigCloneEval evaluation [18] toolkits within docker containers to assess overhead introduced by this approach.

We formulate the following research questions for this work:

1. **RQ1**: What are the challenges of reproducing external scientific experiments in Scientific Workflow Management Systems?
2. **RQ2**: What measures can SWfMS take to address those challenges?
3. **RQ3**: How effective is the proposed solution at reproducing external experiments in a SWfMS?

The remainder of this document is organized as follows. In Sect. 2, we delve into the reproducibility of scientific experiments in SWfMS. Section 3 outlines the challenges associated with reproducing external computational experiments in SWfMSs. The proposed solutions to these challenges are discussed in Sect. 4. The evaluation and experimentation to understand the effectiveness of our proposed solution are presented in Sect. 5. Potential threats to validity are described in Sect. 6. Finally, we conclude the paper in Sect. 7.

2   Reproducibility of Scientific Experiments

Reproducibility of scientific experiments refers to obtaining consistent results of a study using the same procedure, condition, and new or same data as the original study. Two critical aspects of reproducibility are – repeatability and replicability. Repeatability indicates whether the same researchers can achieve the same results using the same data and methods. At the same time, replicability refers to the ability of other researchers to arrive at similar conclusions using new data and possibly different methods.

Scientific workflow management systems (SWfMSs) offer a platform for scientific computing, but their adaptability is crucial for keeping pace with ever-evolving research needs. Extensibility comes to the rescue, empowering users to seamlessly integrate specialized tools within the SWfMS, augmenting its capabilities, and tailoring it to specific domains and challenges. This ability strikes a delicate balance – maintaining the system's intuitive usability while allowing it to incorporate novel tools as they emerge. Researchers constantly push the boundaries, developing innovative tools for targeted scientific problems. SWfMSs facilitate the seamless registration of these tools, expanding the language of workflows to incorporate them into experiments seamlessly. While security often necessitates restricting initial tool registration to administrators or superusers, this extensibility unlocks immense potential. User communities can leverage it to customize the SWfMS to their specific needs and adapt it to new scientific demands. This capability enhances reproducibility by incorporating complex external experiments into the SWfMS framework, promoting transparency and facilitating future scientific advancements. The extensibility mechanism through tool integration operates in the following four phases:

1. *Registration*: In this phase, the tool is uploaded to the system, installed, and configured. The language system is extended for the new tool.
2. *Composition*: Users connect tools with datasets to build the workflow pipeline during this phase. This process serves to bridge input and output datasets, facilitating the flow of data throughout the pipeline.
3. *Execution*: Input datasets are made accessible to the tool's environment, where the tool is subsequently executed within the designated runtime environment.
4. *Provenance*: External tools and experiments participate in provenance capture by providing essential information about the origin, quality, authorship, and evolution of data and processes [5].

A scientific workflow management system must seamlessly coordinate all these phases to reproduce an external scientific experiment successfully. However, the reproducibility of external experiments is not well supported in scientific workflow management systems. While the extensibility mechanism enables seamless integration of simple tools that require minimal configuration and installation, more complex tasks such as custom installations or source code compilation remain challenging [13]. End-users still face significant hurdles when integrating tools to facilitate experiment reproducibility. We conducted a user study to delve deeper into the reproducibility challenges encountered in VizSciFlow. We gathered participants' insights using the NASA Task Load Index (NASA-TLX) workload assessment tool [10,11]. Developed by NASA, the Task Load Index (TLX) is a post-task questionnaire that helps researchers understand the cognitive, physical, and temporal demands placed on users by complex products and tasks. It comprises six rating scales - mental demand, physical demand, temporal demand, performance, effort, and frustration - to gauge users' workload during a task. Participants rate their experience on each scale using a 1 (very low) to 7 (very high) range for all dimensions except performance, where 1 denotes perfect and 7 signifies failure. Using a standardized coding system, these raw scores were then transformed and mapped to a hundred-point scale. The TLX offers raw scores calculated from direct user ratings and weighted scores where participants prioritize the relative importance of each dimension for their specific experience. For this preliminary assessment, we use raw scores.

Five graduate students with extensive research experience in software analytics participated in the user study. Before the study, they received training on integrating their tools into the VizSciFlow system and composing workflows using them. Furthermore, they were introduced to the NASA-TLX questionnaire to familiarize themselves with its usage. Following this preparatory phase, the participants began integrating their experiments into VizSciFlow and constructed workflows employing the integrated tools. Subsequently, the participants' perceived workload was captured through the NASA-TLX questionnaire.

The NASA-TLX responses from participants are depicted in Fig. 1. The average raw (non-weighted) NASA-TLX score stands at 86, signalling a *very high* perceived workload level among participants. While three participants managed to integrate their tools using the extensibility interface independently, the remaining participants required assistance from the administrator. We also gathered additional data regarding the challenges participants encountered, their previous experience with SWfMS, Python, or other languages, as well as details about their experiments and tools. The findings indicate a need for potential improvements to enhance the user-friendliness of the framework and reduce reliance on administrator assistance.

3   Reproducibility Challenges of External Experiments in Scientific Workflow Management Systems

While scientific workflow management systems (SWfMSs) can excel at running and reproducing internal experiments where data and resources are readily available, reproducing external experiments presents a significant challenge. Traditionally, this has been achieved by integrating the experiment's software tools into the SWfMS execution environment.

Reproducing external experiments that use numerous software tools can be challenging for scientific workflow management systems (SWfMSs). VizSciFlow addresses this limitation by introducing a novel extensibility framework based on tool integration, as described in [13]. This framework leverages a JSON mapper to establish connections between the functionalities provided by various tools and the workflow's Domain Specific Language (DSL) vocabulary while also furnishing a Python adapter to facilitate communication between workflow runtime and tool execution. The tools may necessitate one or more of the supports outlined in Table 1 for their execution.

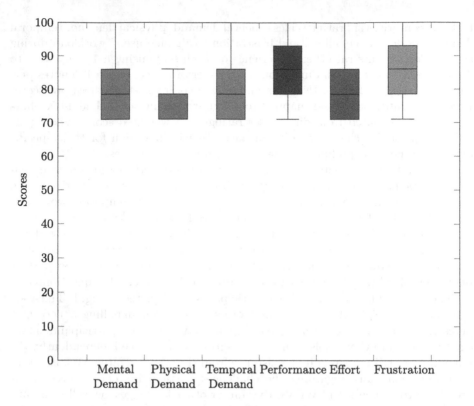

Fig. 1. NASA-TLX Reproducibility of External Tools

Table 1. Extensibility Challenges of VizSciFlow

No.	Challenges	Tools
1	Function	Tool is implemented as additional Python functions to the adapter
2	Program	An executable program
3	Shell Script	Shell scripts call an executable or tool is implemented directly in a shell script
4	Library Dependency	Tool depends on one or more non-default Python packages
5	Virtual Environment Dependency	Tool needs a virtual environment for execution
6	Separate SWfMS and Tool Languages	Tool and SWfMS are developed using different languages and the tool may run only as an external executable
7	System Configuration Dependency	Tool needs to configure system properties e.g. environment variables

(*continued*)

Table 1. (*continued*)

No.	Challenges	Tools
8	Containerization and Virtualization	Tool needs an isolated environment for execution
9	Web Service Tool	Tool is deployed as a web service in an external/internal server
10	Custom Installation	Tool must be installed in a customized way
11	Source Compilation	Source code of the tool must be compiled in the target machine
12	System Repository Dependency	Tool needs to install system packaged e.g., using apt-get)
13	Elevated privileges	Tool needs elevated access privileges e.g., sudo to execute

Assisting end-users in meeting these requirements for integrating tools and reproducing external experiments poses considerable challenges and cannot be uniformly supported. While specific requirements for tool integration have been identified and evaluated using case studies (No. 1–7) [13], addressing the complexities of requirements (No. 8–13) necessitates further exploration. In the subsequent subsections, we delve into the intricacies surrounding the support for the reproducibility of complex external scientific experiments in SWfMS.

3.1 System Configuration Dependency

Some tools may necessitate specific configuration adjustments to operate effectively. For instance, setting environment variables or paths is a prerequisite for many tools. Some tools may need to set a particular directory (often the executable or data source directory) as the current directory before execution. Linux distinguishes between system-wide and user-specific configuration files. System-wide files typically contain sensitive information and should only be modified by administrators or super users with elevated privileges. Modifying system-wide configurations without a thorough understanding can potentially introduce security vulnerabilities.

3.2 Containerization and Virtualization

Certain software tools might not be compatible with the same runtime infrastructure on which SWfMS operates. Occasionally, a software tool may only function properly on a specific operating system or architecture, whereas the SWfMS operates on a different platform. These interoperability challenges between disparate execution environments can impact the reliability and performance of data and resource sharing. Transferring in-memory data from one environment to another can result in serialization overhead, compatibility issues with data formats, potential data loss and corruption, as well as concurrency and synchronization problems.

3.3 Web Service Tool

SWfMSs benefit from incorporating a wide array of tools, which may include web services accessible either locally or remotely. Each web service often possesses unique input and output parameter types, requiring careful mapping and adaptation for seamless integration within the SWfMS workflow. Additionally, transferring large data volumes between remote web services and the SWfMS can significantly impact performance, especially in data-intensive applications.

3.4 Custom Installation

Custom installation is the procedure of installing software in a manner that aligns with the particular needs and specifications of both the user and the tool. This tailored installation approach is indispensable for numerous software tools. However, custom installation often involves interactive procedures that enable users to make choices regarding specific configurations. Additionally, it often requires administrative privileges, granting users elevated control over the system. Allowing end-users unrestricted access to install tools with administrative privileges can pose significant security risks by introducing vulnerabilities or disrupting system stability by making unintended changes.

3.5 Source Compilation

Compiling certain tools from their source code is a necessary step for their installation. Similar to custom installations, source compilation often entails interactive processes and demands technical expertise. However, end-users typically need administrative access rights to execute these tasks, which can potentially expose vulnerabilities or destabilize the system. Consequently, enabling end-users to integrate such software tools into a SWfMS seamlessly poses significant challenges.

3.6 System Repository Dependency

Some tools may rely on specific system repositories that are not installed on the system or require different versions of installed repositories to function properly. However, only system administrators or superusers possess the authority to update these repositories. Granting end-users the ability to add, remove, or update system repositories can potentially introduce security vulnerabilities and may lead to compatibility issues if an incorrect repository version is installed.

3.7 Elevated Privileges

Granting elevated access privileges, often required for certain tools to install and operate effectively, poses significant security risks within SWfMSs. End-users with elevated privileges may inadvertently or intentionally modify system settings, introduce vulnerabilities, or compromise sensitive data. Expanding user access rights creates a wider attack surface, potentially making the system more susceptible to unauthorized access and exploitation.

Answer to RQ1

RQ1: What are the challenges of reproducing external scientific experiments in Scientific Workflow Management Systems?

Answer: The challenges associated with reproducing external computational experiments in scientific workflow management systems stem from transferring, installing, and configuring complex software tools within the SWfMS environment, inconsistencies caused by the differences between the original experiment's execution environment and that of the SWfMS, dependencies on external system packages, the need for elevated user privileges for installation or execution posing security concerns, and the necessity for tool source compilation.

---

4   Proposed Solutions for Reproducing External Experiments in a SWfMS

Reproducing experiments within Scientific Workflow Management Systems can be challenging. To better understand these challenges, we analyzed the key obstacles hindering successful reproduction and explored the root causes and contributing factors. By combining this analysis with researcher needs, we developed strategies to address these issues and enhance SWfMS support for reproducible research. These strategies will be further elaborated upon and categorized based on their impact on different aspects of the SWfMS architecture and various phases of the extensibility framework.

SWfMSs typically follow a layered architectural pattern [12,16] with multiple layers such as presentation, domain, execution, and infrastructure. The reproducibility of an external computational experiment in a SWfMS depends on its requirements on the host SWfMS. One significant obstacle to reproducibility identified is the lack of administrative access for end-users. While granting elevated privileges raises security and stability concerns, it is often necessary for tool execution. To address this, we explored container-based deployments. Researchers have complete control over the containers of their experiments. Containers isolate entire experiment environments, including specific tools and dependencies. This ensures consistent execution across different SWfMSs and mitigates potential execution environment-related reproducibility issues. In this section, we delve into the enhancement of different phases of extensibility within a SWfMS to seamlessly implement containerized reproducibility strategies.

Containerization, with technologies like Docker and Singularity, is a method of packaging and running software applications and their dependencies in a portable, isolated environment called a container. Containers offer numerous benefits such as packaging (self-contained units that encapsulate everything an application needs to run), portability (easily shared and deployed across different systems), isolation (run in isolated environments, separate from the host system and other containers), efficiency (lightweight and share the host system's resources), scalability (scaled up or down by creating new instances), consistency (ensures consistency between development, testing, and production environments), security (hard for security vulnerabilities due to isolation between applications). One promising approach to mitigate the challenges of reproducing external experiments in SWfMSs is by enabling researchers to transfer their experiments into isolated containers seamlessly. Figure 2 illustrates how containerization can play a pivotal role in the enhancement of the VizSciFlow extensibility framework to support the reproducibility of external experiments.

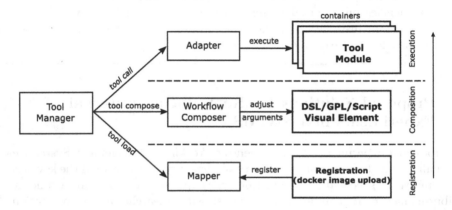

Fig. 2. Reproducibility Framework of VizSciFlow

4.1   Enhancements to Registration Phase

We propose developing user-friendly interfaces that enable researchers to seamlessly upload, register, and execute self-contained Docker containers encapsulating their external experiments. These containers encapsulate researchers' entire experiment environments, ensuring consistent execution across different SWfMS instances. In this pursuit, the tool integration interface of VizSciFlow has been extended with intuitive elements specifically designed for Docker container integration. VizSciFlow utilizes a JSON mapper to link the tool with the DSL vocabulary, binding the input and output datasets of a tool with the language vocabulary. Researchers compile and execute their scientific experiments within a Docker container and have the option to create a Docker image from it. Subsequently, they can save the Docker image in a local file or push it to Docker Hub [6]. Researchers can attach their experiments with a docker container in one of the following ways:

1. *Upload Image*: The web interface is enhanced with a drag-and-drop file uploader for uploading a Docker image to the server.
2. *Pull Image*: Researchers can specify the tag name of a Docker image. If the docker image exists on the server, it is immediately utilized. If the image is

unavailable on the server, the system automatically fetches it from the Docker Hub repository.

3. *Specify Container*: Researchers can insert a container name. A new container is instantiated with this name either by utilizing an uploaded image or by pulling the image from a Docker repository.

The enhanced user interface for reproducibility is depicted in Fig. 3.

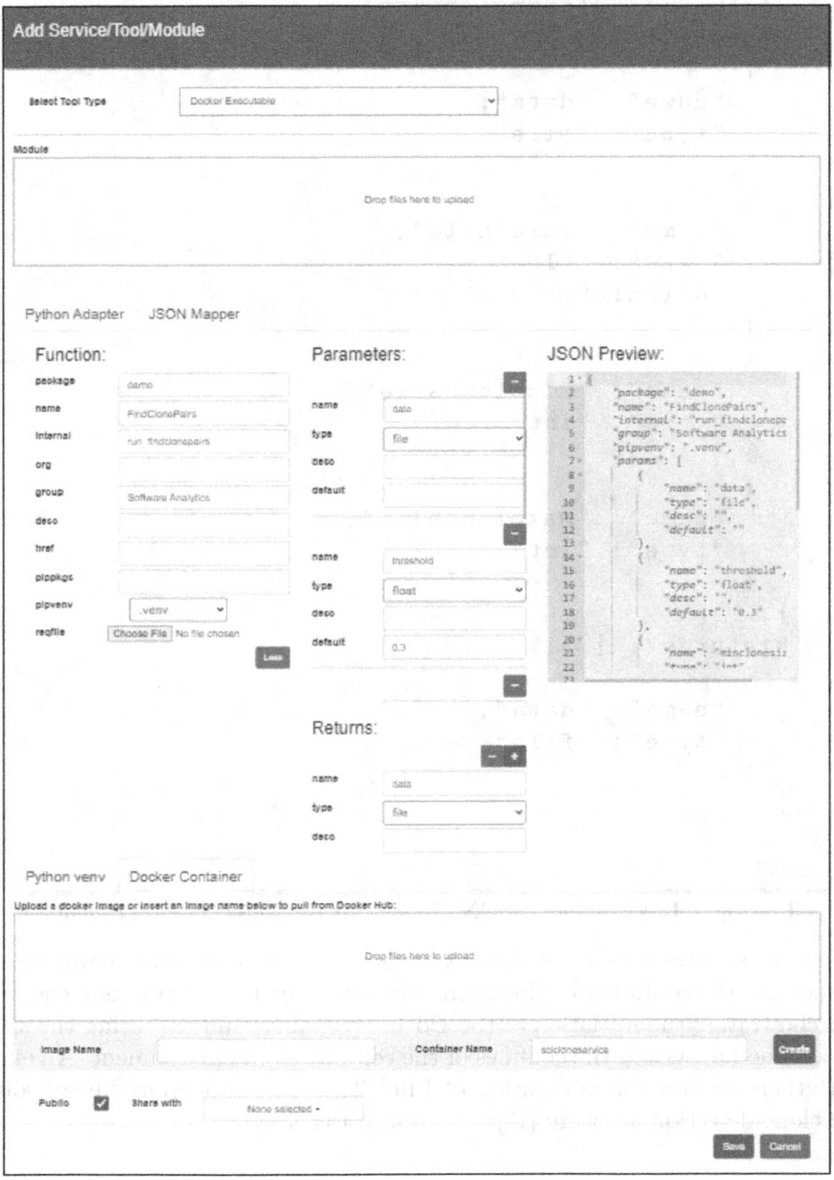

Fig. 3. Mapper Interface for Reproducing External Experiments in VizSciFlow

Listing 1.1 shows an example JSON mapper for FindClonePairs tool of NiCad source code clone detection software stack [17].

```
1   {
2     "package": "demo",
3     "name": "FindClonePairs",
4     "internal": "run_findclonepairs",
5     "group": "Software Analytics",
6     "params": [
7       {
8         "name": "data",
9         "type": "file"
10      },
11      {
12        "name": "threshold",
13        "type": "float",
14        "default": "0.3"
15      },
16      {
17        "name": "minclonesize",
18        "type": "int"
19      },
20      {
21        "name": "maxclonesize",
22        "type": "int"
23      }
24    ],
25    "returns": [
26      {
27        "name": "data",
28        "type": "file"
29      }
30    ]
31  }
```

Listing 1.1. VizSciFlow JSON Mapper for Reproducing Experiment

Python adapter facilitates the connection between the input parameters of the tool and the container environment. Additionally, the adapter is responsible for orchestrating the initiation of the Docker container and executing the specified tool module within the confines of the containerized environment. An example Python adapter for integration of FindClonePairs tool from NiCad source code clone detection software [17] is shown in Fig. 4.

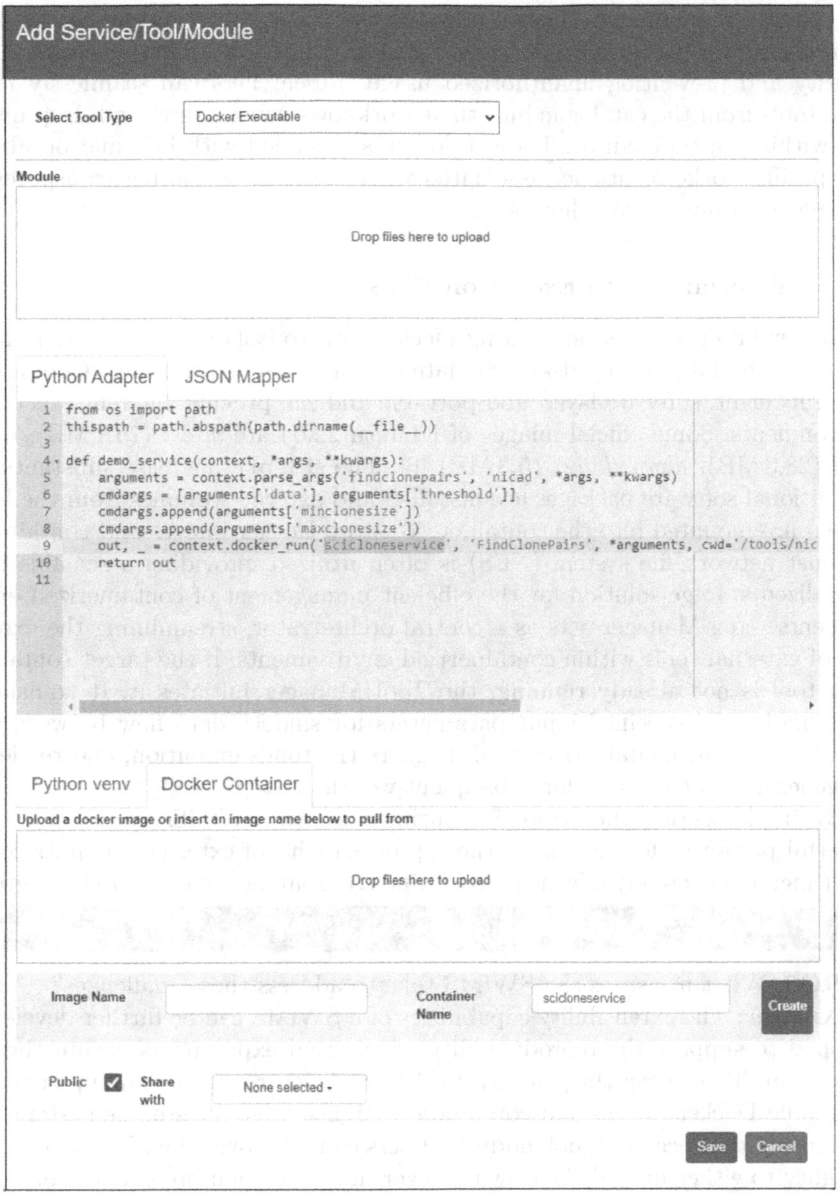

Fig. 4. Python Adapter for Reproducing External Experiments in VizSciFlow

4.2   Enhancements to Composition Phase

The system maintains a database of Docker images: those uploaded by users and those pulled from Docker Hub [6]. This database also stores information about the containers to be launched for tool execution, including configuration details and resource requirements. The system enforces access control permissions based on ownership or execution rights associated with each container, ensuring data security and preventing unauthorized usage. Researchers can seamlessly integrate tools from the catalogue into their workflows using a drag-and-drop interface within the code editor. The catalogue is extended with information about the specific Docker container associated with the tool, promoting transparency and informed integration choices.

4.3   Enhancements to Execution Phase

Containerization utilizes sandboxing mechanisms to isolate tool execution, mitigating potential security risks associated with elevated privileges. Containers are lightweight, software-layer, and portable and can provide different execution environments. Some official images of Ubuntu 22.04 are *latest* (79.1 MB), *minimal* (28.3 MB), *alpine:latest* (5.3 MB) [6]. The size may increase substantially if additional software packages are installed and external volumes from the host system are mounted into the container. To store Docker images and containers, a robust network file system (NFS) is often utilized, providing a scalable and centralized storage solution for the efficient management of containerized environments. Tool Manager acts as a central orchestrator, streamlining the execution of external tools within containerized environments. If the target container for a tool is not already running, the Tool Manager initiates it. It translates and bundles the specified input parameters for smooth data flow between the workflow and the containerized tool, triggers the tool's execution, and retrieves the generated output data for subsequent workflow steps.

By implementing the strategies outlined above, SWfMSs can evolve into powerful platforms for enhancing the reproducibility of external computational experiments, ultimately advancing scientific transparency and research progress.

Answer to RQ2

RQ2: What measures can SWfMS take to address those challenges?
Answer: The extensibility capabilities of a SWfMS can be further developed to support the reproducibility of external experiments within the system. To achieve this, the SWfMS infrastructure can be equipped to handle Docker images and containers within a large file storage system, housing the necessary tool modules. Users can be provided with the capability to either upload their own Docker images or pull pre-existing ones from Docker Hub. SWfMS can launch a corresponding Docker container and forward the tool execution request to the containerized environment.

---

5   Experiments and Evaluation

In this section, we elaborate on the experiments conducted to assess our framework for the reproducibility of external experiments in SWfMS.

5.1   Evaluation of Usability

We first enhanced VizSciFlow by implementing the proposed solutions outlined in Sect. 4, tailoring it for code clone detection experiments. This enhanced version is hosted at https://www.sciclone.usask.ca. To assess the impact of these enhancements, we conducted a user evaluation with the five researchers who evaluated the extensibility framework (cf. Sect. 2). In this case, participants were instructed to encapsulate their experiments within a Docker container and save the container as a .tar image. Then they followed the tool integration steps of VizSciFlow as outlined in [13], but this time, they uploaded Docker images through the "Add Tool" window. Participants were requested to provide feedback on their experience using the NASA-TLX workload assessment tool [11].

5.2   Results and Discussion

This approach allowed us to gather valuable insights into the perceived effectiveness of our enhancements in the reproducibility of external experiments within VizSciFlow. The NASA-TLX responses of the researchers are shown in Fig. 5. With an average NASA-TLX score of 23, it is evident that the researchers experienced a *very low* perceived workload when integrating their experiments into VizSciFlow. Moreover, all five participants were able to integrate their experiments using the enhanced framework successfully.

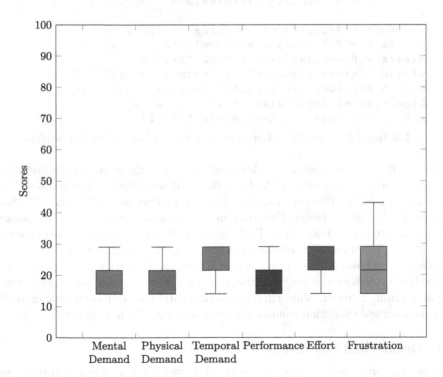

Fig. 5. Usability of Reproducing External Experiments in SWfMS

5.3   Evaluation of Performance

In a case study, we evaluate if the containerized execution has any overhead over the host execution of an experiment. To evaluate the performance of experiment execution within a container compared to the host environment, we customized VizSciFlow by integrating tools from the NiCad [4], Simcad [21], and Simian [9] clone detection toolkits, along with the BigCloneEval evaluation framework [18]. Additionally, we uploaded the dependency of BigCloneEval, the IJaDataset source system repository [19], to the VizSciFlow data storage. The VizSciFlow server is hosted in a container created from the Python:3.10-bullseye docker image (with a base size of 338.26 MB).

We devised three workflows to detect clones within a source code system using the three clone detection toolkits. They detect clone pairs from the source system, convert the clone results into the specific formats required for the evaluation tool, register the corresponding tool for evaluation, import the detected clones into the evaluation database, and finally compare the clones against the known clone pairs of BigCloneBench to evaluate the tool's performance. The NiCad workflow is depicted in Listing 1.2.

```
data = Extract(data,granularity='blocks',language='java'
      )
if normalize != 'none':
    data = Normalize(data)
    data = Abstract(nonterminals='condition')
else:
    data = Rename(data,renaming='blind')
    data = Filter(data,nonterminals='declaration')
clones = FindClone(data,threshold=0.3)
clones = nicad.BigCloneEvalConvert(clones)
tool = bigcloneeval.RegisterTool(name='NiCad')
bigcloneeval.ImportClones(clones, tool)
return bigcloneeval.EvaluateTool(tool)
```

Listing 1.2. Code Clone Detection and Evaluation Workflow Template

Subsequently, we created a docker container from the same docker image on our local machine and installed the tools from NiCad, SimCad, Simian, and Big-CloneEval within it. The Java Runtime Environment version 17 (JRE v. 17) was also installed in the container. The container was saved as a compressed .tar docker image, and we utilized our "Add Tool" interface to integrate the experiments in VizSciFlow. We then adjusted the workflow template to utilize these tools and ran these workflows. Table 2 provides a comparison between workflow execution on the host system and execution within a container. The data is showing the average of ten runs. The last column in the table indicates the additional time required for containerized execution compared to execution on the host system.

5.4   Results and Discussion

The performance evaluation experiment compares the execution of three clone detection software packages – NiCad, SimCad, and Simian – using BigCloneEval,

Table 2. Comparison of Host Execution vs. Container Execution

Clone Detection Toolset	Host Execution	Container Execution	Overhead
NiCad	5842.632 s	5848.274 s	5.642 s
SimCad	328.58 s	329.826	1.246 s
Simian	770.818 s	772.281 s	1.463

BigCloneBench, and IJaDataset. This evaluation is conducted both in the host environment and within a containerized setup. Despite the large dataset size of IJaDataset (250 m LoC and 8 m clone pairs), the overhead of running clone detection workflows within a Docker container proves to be negligible. The execution time for a tool remains consistent whether it is run within the SWfMS host system or a separate container. Any observed overhead primarily stems from starting the docker container, forwarding input parameters, and context switching to the container process. Additionally, Docker deployment empowers the system to migrate the container to a network system, thereby enabling distributed execution capabilities, which can further improve execution time for large-scale experiments.

Answer to RQ3

RQ3: How effective is the proposed solution at reproducing external experiments in a SWfMS?
Answer: Our user study reveals that researchers can effortlessly upload their containerized experiments and tools to the SWfMS, compose workflows utilizing these tools, and execute them within the containers. The case study further demonstrates that the performance overhead associated with containerized execution, as opposed to host execution, is negligible.

---

6   Threats to Validity

One potential threat to validity is the relatively small number of participants involved in our user studies. We specifically sought out experienced researchers actively engaged in developing computational scientific experiments for evaluation purposes. While an initial evaluation with a limited number of participants can be insightful, as observed in previous studies [2], we acknowledge the need for a larger participant pool to achieve statistical significance in our results, a goal we intend to pursue in future research to ensure the generalizability of our findings. Another concern is the limited sample size and operations in our performance tests. It is important to note that the primary focus of these studies was to evaluate the overhead associated with executing tool modules within a Docker container as opposed to the host system. Furthermore, a validity concern arises regarding the substantial data storage capacity required for Docker images of experiments. This concern can be partially addressed by sharing Docker images across multiple experiments that require similar runtime environments. Additionally, researchers can select Docker images with minimal sizes containing their necessary environments to optimize storage utilization.

7　Conclusion

Reproducing external computational experiments within a scientific workflow management system presents numerous challenges, such as incompatible execution platforms between tools and workflow systems, disparities in development languages and libraries, the necessity for elevated access privileges, and dependencies of tools on external software packages. Addressing these obstacles is crucial for fostering wider acceptance of SWfMS within the research community. In our work, we conducted a survey to evaluate the usability of web-based SWfMS for reproducing researchers' local experiments within the system. To tackle these challenges, we proposed strategies centred around implementing an isolated environment within a Docker container for these experiments. We enhanced the extensibility framework of SWfMS with user interface features to facilitate the transfer, installation, and configuration of external experiments within the SWfMS. After implementing these strategies as part of a case study, we conducted a survey, which yielded promising results. Nonetheless, challenges persist, particularly regarding the need for substantial data storage capacity for Docker images, highlighting an area open for future research.

References

1. Altintas, I., Berkley, C., Jaeger, E., Jones, M., Ludascher, B., Mock, S.: Kepler: an extensible system for design and execution of scientific workflows. In: Proceedings of the 16th International Conference on Scientific and Statistical Database Management, pp. 423– (2004). http://dx.doi.org/10.1109/SSDBM.2004.44
2. Barišic, A., Amaral, V., Goulão, M., Barroca, B.: Evaluating the usability of domain-specific languages. In: Software Design and Development: Concepts, Methodologies, Tools, and Applications, pp. 2120–2141 (2014)
3. Brack, P., et al.: Ten simple rules for making a software tool workflow-ready. Public Library of Science San Francisco, CA USA (2022)
4. Cordy, J., Roy, C.: The NiCad clone detector. In: 2011 IEEE 19th International Conference on Program Comprehension, pp. 219–220 (2011)
5. Cruz, S., Campos, M., Mattoso, M.: Towards a taxonomy of provenance in scientific workflow management systems. In: 2009 Congress on Services-I, pp. 259–266 (2009)
6. Docker, I.: Docker hub (2024). https://hub.Docker.Com/
7. Fillbrunn, A., Dietz, C., Pfeuffer, J., Rahn, R., Landrum, G., Berthold, M.: KNIME for reproducible cross-domain analysis of life science data. J. Biotechnol. **261**, 149–156 (2017)
8. Giardine, B., et al.: Galaxy: a platform for interactive large-scale genome analysis. Genome Res. **15**, 1451–1455 (2005)
9. Harris, S.: Simian-similarity analyser (2003). http://www.Harukizaemon.Com/simian/index.Html

10. Hart, S.: NASA-task load index (NASA-TLX); 20 years later. In: Proceedings of the Human Factors and Ergonomics Society Annual Meeting, vol. 50, pp. 904–908 (2006)
11. Hart, S., Staveland, L.: Development of NASA-TLX (task load index): results of empirical and theoretical research. Adv. Psychol. **52**, 139–183 (1988)
12. Hossain, M.M., Roy, B., Roy, C.K., Schneider, K.A.: VizSciFlow: a visually guided scripting framework for supporting complex scientific data analysis. Proc. ACM Hum.-Comput. Interact. **4**, 1–37 (2020)
13. Hossain, M., Roy, B., Roy, C., Schneider, K.: Extensibility challenges of scientific workflow management systems. In: International Conference on Human-Computer Interaction, pp. 51–70 (2023)
14. Kurtzer, G., Sochat, V., Bauer, M.: Singularity: scientific containers for mobility of compute. PLoS ONE **12**, e0177459 (2017)
15. Lawrence, P.: Workflow Handbook 1997. Wiley, New York (1997)
16. Liu, J., Pacitti, E., Valduriez, P., Mattoso, M.: A survey of data-intensive scientific workflow management. J. Grid Comput. **13**, 457–493 (2015)
17. Roy, C., Cordy, J.: NICAD: accurate detection of near-miss intentional clones using flexible pretty-printing and code normalization. In: 2008 16th IEEE International Conference on Program Comprehension, pp. 172–181 (2008)
18. Svajlenko, J., Roy, C.: Bigcloneeval: a clone detection tool evaluation framework with bigclonebench. In: 2016 IEEE International Conference on Software Maintenance and Evolution (ICSME), pp. 596–600 (2016)
19. Svajlenko, J., Roy, C.: Evaluating clone detection tools with bigclonebench. In: 2015 IEEE International Conference on Software Maintenance and Evolution (ICSME), pp. 131–140 (2015)
20. Taschuk, M., Wilson, G.: Ten simple rules for making research software more robust. Public Library of Science San Francisco, CA USA (2017)
21. Uddin, M., Roy, C., Schneider, K.: SIMCAD: an extensible and faster clone detection tool for large scale software systems. In: 2013 21st International Conference on Program Comprehension (ICPC), pp. 236–238 (2013)

Social Usability Evaluation of Douyin and TikTok

Yu-Hsiu Hung[(✉)] and Pei-Ching Chiang

Department of Industrial Design, National Cheng Kung University, Tainan, Taiwan
idhfhung@gmail.com, p36114107@gs.ncku.edu.tw

Abstract. Social usability is an indicator of how easily social activities are performed on a platform. It also determines user motivations to engage in community software over the long term. Douyin and TikTok are two popular mobile social networking applications. Douyin is the original version of the application, available only in China, while TikTok is its international counterpart. The purpose of this study was twofold: (1) to examine the social usability of Douyin and TikTok from the perspectives of social atmosphere, purposes and interests, richness of interaction, self-presentation, and support for formal interaction; and (2) to propose design recommendations to increase user engagement. In this study, forty Douyin/TikTok users were recruited to complete the social usability questionnaire and received follow-up semi-structured interviews. Independent sample t-tests were conducted on the rating score of each questionnaire item. Content analysis was conducted on participants' verbal responses in the interview. Results showed that both applications received high ratings (over four on a scale of one to five) for "media richness in communication," "ease of building identity," and "ease of operation," and low ratings (less than three) for "users feeling close to each other," "users treating each other with mutual respect and courtesy," and "accuracy of information." Results also showed a significant difference in the rating score of "Return on efforts." To enhance social usability and further foster customer loyalty, this study made design recommendations to address user experience issues in social atmosphere and accuracy of information.

Keywords: Douyin · TikTok · and social usability

1 Introduction

1.1 Research Background

In recent years, with the development of the internet, it has become integrated into the lives of every individual, particularly in social interactions. People can now connect with others and interact through social networking platforms [1]. There is a growing demand for online socialization, leading to the emergence of numerous social media platforms. Douyin/TikTok is a prime example, with the former being the Chinese version and the latter being the international version. According to the 40th China Internet Development Status Statistics Report in 2017, as of June 2017, Douyin had a user base of 751

M. Kurosu and A. Hashizume (Eds.): HCII 2024, LNCS 14687, pp. 208–218, 2024.
https://doi.org/10.1007/978-3-031-60441-6_14

million [2], Since its release in 2017, TikTok has surpassed 1.5 billion downloads globally [3],which has successfully attracted young demographics from various cultures [4], Both are short video social networking applications that can quickly increase download rates and may present interfaces differently across cultures. Users can record, publish, and view short videos and live broadcasts on Douyin/TikTok, as well as interact with other users [5].The AI algorithms of Douyin/TikTok enable users to see topics of interest, with creative video content being the primary social object, followed by features such as commenting, liking, and following, enticing users worldwide. However, major media platforms like Instagram, YouTube, etc., have also begun to introduce short video and live broadcasting features, posing a threat to Douyin and TikTok [6].How to make users participate in the long term and become loyal customers is still a challenge that Douyin/TikTok needs to face [3]. Social features are crucial factors in encouraging users to return to the community [7]. Therefore, this study focuses on social usability as its research objective.

1.2 Research Goal

Social usability refers to the attribute that assesses the ease of social interaction. If the social usability of a platform is removed, it is equivalent to removing the entire social momentum of the platform, which becomes a significant factor affecting user retention. Once interpersonal interaction and connections are established, they will inevitably influence the design of social interaction on the platform. It is necessary to strengthen useful social behaviors and eliminate harmful social behaviors (Gianandrea and Davide 2010). A successful social media platform needs to have effective and engaging social features to encourage long-term user participation. Additionally, cultural differences can influence interface design. To expand user demographics and capture global markets, a software platform needs to adapt to the design preferences of specific cultures [8]. In order to understand the differences of a software across different cultures and increase user engagement with Douyin/TikTok, this study aims to analyze the social usability of the Douyin/TikTok interface (social atmosphere, purposes and interests, richness of interaction, self-presentation, support for formal interaction) [9] identify its strengths and weaknesses, and propose strategies to improve the social usability of the interface. This will enhance user engagement, assist in converting potential users into loyal customers, and ultimately increase platform revenue.

2   Literature Review

2.1   The Impact of Social Features on Media

The addition of social features in media has changed the way individuals consume and share news. Specifically, a piece of news can be disseminated across various societies and discussed by people worldwide through social media platforms in a matter of minutes [10]. Information is sourced more rapidly compared to traditional media, as social media users can stumble upon the latest dynamic news due to accidental exposure. Moreover, this type of news holds greater influence on users because it is filtered by trusted individuals [11]. Furthermore, the social features of media can facilitate the parallelism of online and offline activities, forming connections between individuals. The dissemination of events occurs through links between people or groups, thereby promoting interaction and coordination among individuals [12]. Therefore, user participation is an indispensable element in sustaining online communities. Increased user engagement enhances users' willingness to revisit online communities. Moreover, users are driven to contribute on social media platforms based on their desire for income sharing, exposure, and reputation [7].

2.2 Social Usability

Sociality is defined as the degree to which a communication environment facilitates social interaction and strengthens social connections. Sociality supports common goals and social interactions among group members [13].Members find the communication and interaction process enjoyable, achieving community-shared goals through technologically-supported spaces. Sociality focuses on how participants connect for common goals, organize and implement, and how they present their identities [14]. To connect with others, users engage in various social activities. Studies have found that individuals adept at social activities correlate positively with the development of peer networks and the time spent on social networks. Furthermore, sociality is closely associated with positive emotions and life satisfaction. Individuals who engage less in social activities tend to experience high levels of loneliness and anxiety [15]. Sociality is a characteristic of the online interaction environment and a crucial factor in the success of a community media platform. The quality of sociality is influenced by social atmosphere, purposes and interests, demographics, richness of interaction, self-presentation, and support for formal interaction [9].Social atmosphere encompasses privacy and security issues in the online environment as well as the practice of a friendly atmosphere. Purposes and interests refer to whether the platform meets users' needs, such as identity verification, emotional interaction, information acquisition, and relationship management. The intimacy level and size of the user base also affect the quality of social usability. Specifically, people may try using software they haven't used before because their close contacts use it or because it is widely used by the general public [16]. Richness of interaction includes the diversity of information media content and formats, as well as the richness of interaction between people. Self-presentation involves conveying one's self-image to others and establishing self-reputation. Support for formal interaction involves supporting and facilitating formal communication, such as initiating discussions, organizing meetings, etc.

2.3 Culture Impact on Media Design

Culture refers to the characteristics of a group of people with common values, moral standards, language (written or spoken), customs, and ways of life. Culture is divided into two types: individualistic cultures, such as those found in Western countries, emphasize independence, personal goals, and self-reliance; collectivistic cultures, such as those found in Eastern countries, emphasize collective achievement, teamwork, and interdependence. These two types of cultures also exhibit differences in their intentions for continued use of social media platforms. Users from individualistic cultures tend to continue using social media for information seeking purposes, while users from collectivistic cultures tend to continue using social media for socialization and self-presentation needs [17]. Interface design can vary based on different cultures. In order to accommodate the design preferences of various cultures, elements such as text, numbers, date and time representations, images, symbols, colors, etc., need to adapt to cultural differences [8]. In terms of icon design, "thumbs up" signifies "good" to users in American culture, but to Australians, it can be interpreted as an insult [18].Therefore, culture also plays an important role in human-machine interaction.

3 Research Methodology

3.1 Research Framework

This study aims to explore the social usability of the interface design of Douyin and TikTok, analyzing its five dimensions of social usability (social atmosphere, purposes and interests, richness of interaction, self-presentation, support for formal interaction), and proposing methods to improve the social usability of the interface. The study is divided into two phases. The first phase involves the initial development of the research, proposing analysis directions, and designing experiments. Initial analysis of the study includes literature review and data collection, forming preliminary concepts based on literature collection, and referencing the framework of social usability questionnaires. Experiment design includes the process design of questionnaires and interviews, setting research focuses and questions based on the five dimensions of social usability. The second phase involves questionnaire surveys, interviews, qualitative data analysis, and quantitative data analysis.

3.2 Participants

To gain a deeper understanding of real user usage patterns, this study recruited 20 Douyin users and 20 TikTok users (a total of 40 participants), divided into Douyin and TikTok groups. A total of 40 valid questionnaires and 40 interview transcripts were collected, with 20 from each platform group.

3.3 The Design of Douyin and TikTok

The main functions of both are the same, allowing users to upload and view short videos and live streams, but there are significant differences in interface design and detailed feature design. Below is a comparison chart of the main pages (Fig. 1).

Observing the top navigation bar, it can be noted that Douyin offers significantly more features and categories compared to TikTok. In addition to "For You" and "Following," Douyin includes categories such as "Friends," "Experiences," "Nearby," "Live," and "Trending." The functionality, icon design, and naming conventions of the bottom navigation bar also differ between the two platforms. TikTok's icon design presents visual graphics alongside text, while Douyin only displays text. Douyin also includes

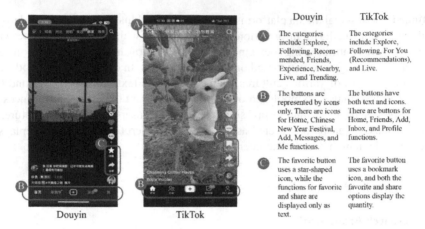

	Douyin	TikTok
(A)	The categories include Explore, Following, Recommended, Friends, Experience, Nearby, Live, and Trending.	The categories include Explore, Following, For You (Recommendations), and Live.
(B)	The buttons are represented by icons only. There are icons for Home, Chinese New Year Festival, Add, Messages, and Me functions.	The buttons have both text and icons. There are buttons for Home, Friends, Add, Inbox, and Profile functions.
(C)	The favorite button uses a star-shaped icon, while the functions for favorite and share are displayed only as text.	The favorite button uses a bookmark icon, and both the favorite and share options display the quantity.

Douyin   TikTok

Fig 1. Comparison chart of the main pages

a shopping feature, allowing users to make transactions within the app. Furthermore, Douyin offers a feature to search for similar products using images. Apart from differences in interface design, there are significant variations in registration methods, account types, traffic pools, operation methods, monetization methods, content management, and recommendation systems (WARM2023).

3.4 Questionnaires

This study references the social usability questionnaire items proposed by Gao [9] Each question has five options, with one indicating "very poor performance" and five indicating "very good performance". (Table 1)The questionnaire content is as follows:

3.5 Data Analysis

The survey results will be quantitatively analyzed using independent samples t-tests, and the interview results will undergo qualitative analysis to evaluate strengths and weaknesses and propose improvement methods for reference by live streaming platforms.To understand the differences between Douyin and TikTok in different cultural contexts, independent samples t-tests will be conducted to compare the average scores of social usability. Data will be collected using a Likert five-point scale questionnaire, with respondents completing the questionnaire in the presence of the researcher. Subsequently, the researcher will conduct interviews with the respondents to discuss the reasons behind their scores for each questionnaire item, aiming to understand the users' true thoughts. The verbal data will then undergo qualitative analysis using the KJ method to identify the root causes of the strengths and weaknesses.

Table 1. Questionare of social usability

Questions
Social Climate
1. Do users on Douyin/TikTok discuss different opinions with each other?
2. Do you feel that users on Douyin/TikTok are close to each other?
3. Do you think users on Douyin/TikTok respect and treat each other politely?
4. Do you feel that social activities on Douyin/TikTok are safe (in terms of personal and property safety)?
5. Do you feel that you can express emotions and provide support to others on Douyin/TikTok?
Purpose and Benefits
6. Do you think social activities on Douyin/TikTok contribute to real-world people and things?
7. Do you think that efforts and time invested in Douyin/TikTok will have returns?
8. Do you think that efforts and time invested in Douyin/TikTok can lead to tangible rewards (physical rewards)?
9. Do you think Douyin/TikTok review the information transmitted in social activities (text, images, audio, video)?
Interaction Richness
10. Is it easy to edit content (text, images, audio, or video) on Douyin/TikTok?
11. How rich is the variety of communication media such as text, images, audio, or video on Douyin/TikTok?
12. Can users obtain intangible rewards (social-emotional rewards) from the efforts and time invested on Douyin/TikTok?
Self-presentation
13. Can users easily establish and display their virtual image on Douyin/TikTok?
14. Can users obtain and display a good reputation on TikTok?
Support for formal interaction
15. How do you rate the authenticity of content and information on Douyin/TikTok?
16. How do you rate the ease of operation of various methods such as sliding and clicking on TikTok?
17. Can TikTok easily establish and maintain group activities?

4 Research Result

4.1 Result

The table below presents the questionnaire results, including the mean, standard deviation, and p-value for each question. According to the descriptive statistics, most of the scores fall between 3 and 4 points (fair to good). Only the richness of interaction achieves a good level, while the performance of the other four aspects (social atmosphere, purposes and interests, self-presentation, support for interaction) is not satisfactory (Table 2).

According to the independent samples t-test analysis, there is a significant difference between Douyin and TikTok in the question "Do you feel that the effort and time you put into Douyin will pay off?" However, there are no significant differences in the other

Table 2. Descriptive statistics and independent test results

Questions	抖音		TikTok		
	mean	sd	mean	sd	p-value
Social Climate					
1. Do users on Douyin/TikTok discuss different opinions with each other?	3.8	1.05	3.75	1.33	0.89
2. Do you feel that users on Douyin/TikTok are close to each other?	2.6	1.23	3.1	1.25	0.21
3. Do you think users on Douyin/TikTok respect and treat each other politely?	3.1	1.20	2.9	0.91	0.55
4. Do you feel that social activities on Douyin/TikTok are safe (in terms of personal and property safety)?	3.25	0.71	3.4	1.09	0.61
5. Do you feel that you can express emotions and provide support to others on Douyin/Tik-Tok?	3.9	1.02	4	0.79	0.73
Purpose and Benefits					
6. Do you think social activities on Douyin/Tik-Tok contribute to real-world people and things?	3.65	1.22	3.4	1.09	0.50
7. Do you think that efforts and time invested in Douyin/TikTok will have returns?	3.9	0.96	3.1	1.25	0.02
8. Do you think that efforts and time invested in Douyin/TikTok can lead to tangible rewards (physical rewards)?	3.2	1.00	2.5	1.27	0.06
9. Do you think Douyin/TikTok review the information transmitted in social activities (text, images, audio, video)?	3.75	0.96	3.95	1.14	0.55
Interaction Richness					
10. Is it easy to edit content (text, images, audio, or video) on Douyin/TikTok?	3.8	1.10	4.15	0.81	0.26
11. How rich is the variety of communication media such as text, images, audio, or video on Douyin/TikTok?	4.6	0.68	4.55	0.60	0.80
12. Can users obtain intangible rewards (social-emotional rewards) from the efforts and time invested on Douyin/TikTok?	3.6	0.99	3.45	0.88	0.61
Self-presentation					
13. Can users easily establish and display their virtual image on Douyin/TikTok?	4	0.85	4.2	1.00	0.50
14. Can users obtain and display a good reputation on TikTok?	3.15	1.26	3.1	1.20	0.89
Support for formal interaction					
15. How do you rate the authenticity of content and information on Douyin/TikTok?	2.9	0.91	2.8	0.89	0.72
16. How do you rate the ease of operation of various methods such as sliding and clicking on TikTok?	4.75	0.44	4.95	0.22	0.08
17. Can TikTok easily establish and maintain group activities?	3.25	1.25	3.5	1.23	0.52

Table 3. Descriptive statistics and independent test results of five dimensions

Dimensions	Douyin		TikTok		
	mean	sd	mean	sd	p-value
Social Climate	3.43	0.4	3.33	0.47	0.37
Purpose and Benefits	3.23	0.52	3.62	0.26	0.15
Interaction Richness	4.05	0.45	4	0.43	0.45
Self-presentation	3.65	0.55	3.57	0.42	0.46
Support for formal interaction	3.75	0.89	3.63	0.80	0.44

questions and the five major aspects. One potential reason for this difference could be the varying lengths of videos on TikTok and Douyin. TikTok restricts videos to 60 s or less, emphasizing concise and quick video content creation. On the other hand, Douyin allows videos up to 5 min, placing more emphasis on the quality of video content. This difference means TikTok users can create and ride trends quickly, making it relatively easier for content to go viral compared to Douyin (Table 3).

Both Douyin and TikTok scored above 4 points in "Richness of Media Exchange," "Ease of Creating Virtual Image," and "Ease of Operation." Diverse themes such as music, beauty, medicine, healthcare, and more can be explored within both applications, providing users with abundant media information. Additionally, both platforms offer a wide variety of filters and effects, allowing users to adjust facial details to create the desired virtual image effortlessly. The basic operation involves only swiping up and down and tapping, all within the reach of one hand, indicating user-friendly design. This suggests that both applications perform well in terms of media richness, the ability to create virtual images, and ease of operation.

However, the scores for "User Intimacy," "Mutual Respect and Politeness Among Users," and "Truthfulness of Information" are below 2 points. While users may leave comments in the comment section, they often only express their thoughts on the video and have less interaction with other users, resulting in a lack of intimacy. Some users may engage in heated debates in the comment section when encountering opinions different from their own, making it difficult to cultivate a polite and respectful community environment. Content on Douyin and TikTok includes both real and fictional information, requiring viewers to rely on their own judgment to discern authenticity, as the platforms currently lack features to verify the truthfulness of information. This indicates lower levels of user intimacy and respect, as well as truthfulness of information, which are pain points that can be improved. Therefore, it is determined that there is room for improvement in the details of the comment section, reporting mechanisms, presentation of reputation scores, and establishment of group activities in both interfaces. For example, the comment section does not encourage users to engage in deeper social interaction, the reporting mechanism is located under the share button, making it less noticeable and intuitive for users to associate sharing with reporting, and neither platform currently has features for reputation scores or creating group activities.

5   Discussion

5.1   Culture Impact on Douyin and TikTok

According to user interviews, cultural differences were found to influence responses to questions such as "Do you think the social activities on Douyin/TikTok contribute to real-world people and things?" "Do you think the effort and time invested in Douyin/TikTok will be rewarded?" and "Do you think the effort and time invested in Douyin/TikTok can lead to tangible/intangible rewards?" International users tend to post entertainment-focused videos, while Chinese users post a variety of content types including entertainment, educational, and life hacks. Therefore, users believe that Douyin's activities are relatively more beneficial to the real world. Regarding the return rate, TikTok users believe that efforts and creativity will be rewarded. Responses from Douyin users were polarized, with some supporting the idea of rewards for effort while others believed that the high time cost makes it difficult to achieve rewards. Additionally, the possibility of rewards is also related to the management approach. Western individualistic culture users mostly manage their accounts individually, focusing on creative themes. Eastern collectivist culture users often manage accounts together in groups, with a more detailed content release plan. Regarding the possibility of rewards, TikTok users believe that serious management can easily lead to traffic and fan feedback, which can be exchanged for cash rewards. Douyin users believe that even though traffic can be exchanged for cash, it takes too much time to become a well-known anchor before the chance of receiving physical rewards. Furthermore, it was found that content creators will adjust their video content, language, and customs to gain more fans from different cultures. Douyin users share food and customs related to their hometown, thus there is a "same city" category to resonate with viewers from the same city. TikTok content creators learn languages and jokes from various cultures to interact with fans and gain favor from fans of different cultures.

6   Conclusion

6.1   Summary

In this study, it was found that there was no significant difference in the overall social usability between Douyin and TikTok, and their strengths and weaknesses were quite similar. The strengths of both platforms lie in their rich content, easy usability, and the ability to create a virtual identity effortlessly. On the downside, users may not feel close to each other, there may be a lack of mutual respect in interactions, and the authenticity of information may be questionable. Cultural differences were also found to influence the social usability of Douyin and TikTok. For example, users from different cultures may produce different types of content, and cultural differences in management practices can affect account promotion and the adjustment of content by creators to cater to different cultural audiences.

To understand the differences in design and social usability among different cultures and to increase user engagement, it was found that there is room for improvement in the social atmosphere, purpose and benefits, self-presentation, and support for formal interaction aspects of both Douyin and TikTok. Therefore, creating a friendly online environment and supporting the transmission of genuine information will increase user trust in the platform's social atmosphere and the need for authentic information. This will enhance social usability performance, turning potential users into loyal users, and ultimately increasing platform revenue.

6.2 Research Limitation and Future Research

The study primarily focused on viewers' perceptions of the interface design, content, and features of Douyin and TikTok. Due to time and account level limitations, it did not delve into the opinions of live streamers regarding interface content and features, as well as the design of the backend for live streamers. In the future, research could investigate the social usability from the perspective of live streamers and increase the sample size for more comprehensive data analysis.

References

1. Amichai-Hamburger, Y., Vinitzky, G.: Social network use and personality. Comput. Hum. Behav. **26**(6), 1289–1295 (2010)
2. Feng, Y.L., Chen, C.C., Shu-Ming, Wu.: Evaluation of charm factors of short video user experience using FAHP – a case study of Tik Tok app. IOP Conf. Ser. Mater. Sci. Eng. **688**(5), 055068 (2019). https://doi.org/10.1088/1757-899X/688/5/055068
3. Bhandari, A., Bimo, S.: TikTok and the "algorithmized self": a new model of online interaction. AoIR Sel. Papers Internet Res. (2020).https://doi.org/10.5210/spir.v2020i0.11172
4. Auxier, B., Anderson, M.: Social media use in 2021. Pew Res. Cent. **1**, 1–4 (2021)
5. Omar, B., Dequan, W.: Watch, share or create: the influence of personality traits and user motivation on TikTok mobile video usage. Int. J. Interact. Mobile Technol. (IJIM) **14**(04), 121 (2020). https://doi.org/10.3991/ijim.v14i04.12429
6. Li, Xu., Yan, X., Zhang, Z.: Research on the causes of the TikTok app becoming popular and the existing problems. J. Adv. Manag. Sci. **7**(2), 59–63 (2019). https://doi.org/10.18178/joams.7.2.59-63
7. Kapoor, K.K., et al.: Advances in social media research: past, present and future. Inf. Syst. Front. **20**(3), 531–558 (2018)
8. Evers, V., Day, D.: The role of culture in interface acceptance. In: Howard, S., Hammond, J., Lindgaard, G. (eds.) Human-Computer Interaction INTERACT 1997, pp. 260–267. Springer US, Boston, MA (1997). https://doi.org/10.1007/978-0-387-35175-9_44
9. Gao, Q., et al.: Understanding factors affecting perceived sociability of social software. Comput. Hum. Behav. **26**(6), 1846–1861 (2010)
10. Lee, C.S., Ma, L.: News sharing in social media: the effect of gratifications and prior experience. Comput. Hum. Behav. **28**(2), 331–339 (2012)
11. Boulianne, S.: Social media use and participation: a meta-analysis of current research. Inf. Commun. Soc. **18**(5), 524–538 (2015)
12. Grabowicz, P.A., et al.: Social features of online networks: the strength of intermediary ties in online social media. PLoS ONE **7**(1), e29358 (2012)
13. Li, C.-Y., Ku, Y.-C.: The power of a thumbs-up: will e-commerce switch to social commerce? Inf. Manage. **55**(3), 340–357 (2018)
14. Phang, C., Kankanhalli, A., Sabherwal, R.: Usability and sociability in online communities: a comparative study of knowledge seeking and contribution. J. Assoc. Inf. Syst. **10**(10), 721–747 (2009)

15. Li, D.C.: Online social network acceptance: a social perspective. Internet Res. **21**(5), 562–580 (2011)
16. Nadeau, R., Cloutier, E., Guay, J.H.: New evidence about the existence of a bandwagon effect in the opinion formation process. Int. Polit. Sci. Rev. **14**(2), 203–213 (1993)
17. Hsu, M.-H., et al.: Understanding the roles of cultural differences and socio-economic status in social media continuance intention. Inf. Technol. People **28**(1), 224–241 (2015)
18. Khaddam, I., Vanderdonckt, J.: Towards a culture-adaptable user-interface architecture. Int. J. User-Syst. Inter. **7**(2), 161 (2014)
19. Giacoma, G., Casali, D F.: Social Usability Workshop at Frontiers of Interaction (2010)
20. Frontiers of Interaction 2010. Retrieved 27 Jun 2010. https://www.slideshare.net/folletto/social-usability-workshop-at-frontiers-of-interaction-2010
21. WARM: The difference between TikTok and Douyin is actually quite significant? Get to know these two different traffic pools. Retrieved 31 Aug 2023 (2023). https://tiktok01.com/article/tiktok-vibrato-difference/

Optimizing Urban e-Commerce Experiences: A Cross-Cultural Interface Design Approach for Enhanced Connectivity and Consumer Engagement

Wenhua Li[1], Jia Xin Xiao[2], and Meng Ting Zhang[3(✉)]

[1] Guangzhou Academy of Fine Arts, No. 168, Waihuan West Road, Panyu District, Guangzhou, China

[2] Guangdong University of Technology, Yuexiu District, No. 729, Dongfeng East Road, Guangzhou, China
cynthia.xiao@gdut.edu.cn

[3] Macau University of Science and Technology, Avenida Wai Long, Taipa, Macau, China
mtzhang@must.edu.mo

Abstract. This research paper presents an in-depth analysis of the Canton Fair's B2B e-commerce platform, with a focus on optimizing user experience in the context of urban e-commerce environments. The study employs a multi-method approach, incorporating heuristic evaluations, usability testing, and user interviews, to identify key areas for improvement in the platform's design. Central findings highlight significant issues with navigation complexity, limited search functionality, and the platform's lack of mobile optimization—elements that are critical for success in fast-paced urban markets. In response to these challenges, the paper proposes a set of comprehensive interface design guidelines. These guidelines emphasize a user-centric design philosophy, enhanced search capabilities, streamlined checkout processes, and the integration of advanced technologies such as AI for personalization. The research also underscores the importance of culturally and linguistically inclusive design to cater to the diverse urban user base. The paper concludes with strategic recommendations for the Canton Fair, aiming to transform its platform into a more efficient, accessible, and user-friendly e-commerce environment. This study contributes to the field of electronic commerce by offering insights and practical approaches for adapting traditional trade platforms to meet the evolving demands of the urban digital marketplace.

Keywords: Electronic Commerce · interface design · user experience · usability challenges · Canton Fair

1 Introduction

E-commerce has become an integral part of the urban landscape, shaping the way metropolitan consumers interact with digital marketplaces. The evolution of e-commerce in urban settings brings to the fore the necessity for interfaces that cater to diverse, tech-savvy urban populations. However, many business-to-business (B2B) platforms, such

M. Kurosu and A. Hashizume (Eds.): HCII 2024, LNCS 14687, pp. 219–234, 2024.
https://doi.org/10.1007/978-3-031-60441-6_15

as the Canton Fair, are grappling with the challenge of aligning their interface designs with the evolving needs of these users.

The Canton Fair, a cornerstone of China's trade landscape since 1957, exemplifies this struggle. While it effectively facilitates trade between Chinese manufacturers and global buyers, its e-commerce interface remains rooted in its traditional in-person fair format. The platform's design, characterized by text-heavy pages and convoluted navigation, reflects its physical trade show origins rather than contemporary e-commerce practices. This disconnect is particularly pronounced in the urban context, where users expect seamless and intuitive online shopping experiences.

This paper critically evaluates the user interface of the Canton Fair's e-commerce platform, employing methodologies, including usability assessments, surveys, and competitive analysis. The objective is to identify gaps in findability, usability, and mobile responsiveness, comparing these elements against B2B market leaders like Alibaba. The study reveals significant disparities in meeting the expectations of a diverse urban user base, including both foreign buyers and domestic Chinese suppliers, who each bring unique expectations to e-commerce interactions.

In response to these findings, this research proposes a series of key recommendations aimed at enhancing the Canton Fair's interface design. These recommendations are informed by a cross-cultural, user-centric approach that considers the specific demands of urban e-commerce environments. Emphasizing improved connectivity, user engagement, and trust-building measures, the paper offers a roadmap for legacy trade fair systems to adapt and thrive in the digital age, particularly in metropolitan settings.

By providing insights into the creation of adaptable, user-friendly B2B e-commerce interfaces, this paper contributes to the broader discourse on optimizing e-commerce experiences in urban contexts. It underscores the importance of understanding and bridging the localization gaps that exist in these digitally evolving marketplaces, especially in emerging markets.

2 Literature Review

2.1 Research on e-Commerce Interface Design Principles

E-commerce interfaces serve as the critical connection point between users and online shopping experiences. Their design significantly impacts user engagement and commercial outcomes [1]. Established guidelines and theories exist for developing usable, user-centric e-commerce interfaces. Several studies emphasize simplicity, findability, and efficiency as core attributes of effective e-commerce user interfaces. Presenting too many options or overloading pages hinders findability and frustrates users, aligning with Cognitive Load Theory principles [2]. Clean, minimalist interfaces with clear visual hierarchy enhance perceived usability, consistent with Gestalt psychology [3]. Gestalt theory explains how people perceive objects and patterns as unified wholes rather than just individual elements. Core principles such as similarity, continuity, and closure influence visual processing and can inform effective interface layouts. The principle of similarity states that items with shared visual characteristics are grouped together. E-commerce sites can leverage this through consistent branding elements, matching colors for CTAs, and aligning stylistic aspects like fonts across pages. This creates a cohesive identity. Continuity refers to the tendency to perceive smooth, continuous forms rather than disjointed elements. Strategies like using clear visual lines to connect navigation items, images with implied motion, and minimal visual interruptions can improve continuity perceptions [4]. This enhances usability by guiding users between interface areas. Closure describes the mind's tendency to fill in missing information to complete a whole form or pattern. E-commerce sites can apply closure principles by minimizing unnecessary visual gaps in layouts and using recognizable but incomplete icons and imagery [5]. User perception fills the blanks. Robust search functionality and filtering boost findability, reducing search complexity [6].

Personalization and consistency also aid interactions, relating to Technology Acceptance Model perceived usefulness and ease of use [7]. The Technology Acceptance Model (TAM) proposed by Davis [7] provides a theoretical framework for understanding user acceptance and adoption of new technologies. Two core constructs of TAM are perceived usefulness and perceived ease of use. According to TAM, users are more likely to accept and use a technology if they perceive it to be useful and easy to use. This directly applies to e-commerce interfaces, as shoppers must find the website or app useful for making purchases and perceive the interface as easy to navigate in order to fully engage with the platform.

E-commerce interfaces can enhance perceived usefulness through features like personalized recommendations, robust search and filters, detailed product information, seamless checkout, order tracking, and historical data on past purchases. These allow shoppers to easily evaluate and purchase products that suit their needs [8]. Providing abundant, high-quality information sources and enabling efficient transactions enhances the site's usefulness. Regarding perceived ease of use, principles like clean and consistent navigation, intuitive taxonomy, seamless flows between pages, informative feedback, and visually guided journeys can minimize complexity. Adhering to usability heuristics reduces mental effort for users. Responsiveness across devices also improves perceived ease of use. Lowering learning curves and interaction barriers enhances the feeling of usability. By focusing interface design decisions on usefulness and ease of use per TAM, e-commerce platforms can drive adoption and loyalty among consumers. This theoretical model provides guiding principles for user-centric design. Features like saved carts, recommendations, and unified experiences across devices enhance continuity and satisfaction [9]. Adhering to platform conventions builds user familiarity over time [10].

Cross-device responsiveness is also critical, tying into perceived mobility and flexibility [11]. Mobile optimization and minimizing risk cues aligns with Prospect Theory adoption factors [12]. Iterative A/B testing of new features balances novelty with familiarity [13].

In summary, simplicity, findability, consistency, personalization, and omnichannel responsiveness are key e-commerce interface design priorities based on accepted models. Further validation in emerging contexts is warranted.

2.2 Cross-Cultural Interface Design Considerations

As e-commerce expands globally, effectively catering to culturally diverse users through inclusive interface design grows increasingly relevant. Extensive research has explored cross-cultural considerations in crafting user experiences.

Hofstede's cultural dimensions' theory [14] provides a framework for understanding cultural variability. Hofstede identified six dimensions along which cultures differ - individualism vs collectivism, power distance, masculinity vs femininity, uncertainty avoidance, long term vs short term orientation, and indulgence vs restraint. Adapting e-commerce interfaces to align with cultural values on these dimensions is crucial. For instance, collectivist cultures like China prioritize community and relationships versus individualist Western cultures. E-commerce platforms can provide more social features and recommendations tailored to this. Languages also differ in power distance and formality. Direct translations may be inappropriate. Masculine cultures emphasize performance versus feminine cultures focused on quality of life - requiring nuanced messaging. Other tactical localizations may involve colors, visuals, currencies, date formats, using appropriate slang, and tailoring content tone. While globalizing core functionality, these surface adaptations resonate better with local users across Hofstede's cultural dimensions. Ongoing testing is key to refinement. Localization aligned with cultural dimensions theory can allow e-commerce firms to gain adoption in diverse international markets by adapting platforms to match user expectations and values. This demonstrates the importance of cross-cultural considerations.

Other studies emphasize localizing cultural markers like color, spatial organization, fonts, imagery and language in alignment with user preferences [15]. Adapting navigation models to align with mental models of different cultures also proves critical for usability [16]. For instance, Chinese interfaces commonly leverage hierarchical, text-heavy menus while Western users favor flat, icon-driven navigation.

However, surface-level localization alone is insufficient. Deeper structural differences between cultures significantly impact interfaces [14]. High-context cultures like China emphasize indirect, implicit communication versus the directness of Western low-context cultures. Thus, Chinese e-commerce sites rely heavily on contextual cues versus explicit classifications more suitable to Western mental models [17]. Adapting information architecture and content presentation to such differences is vital.

Rigorously evaluating interfaces using representative users from target cultures helps reveal preferences and pain points [15]. Quantitative performance metrics can further diagnose struggles specific to certain user segments. Iterative refinement then allows moving towards culturally inclusive experiences.

Therefore, thorough cross-cultural assessments and adaptations spanning visual, content, and interaction design elements are key to crafting globally successful e-commerce platforms. Progressing beyond superficial localization to reflect deeper cultural values and styles is critical based on existing literature.

2.3 Standards for B2B e-Commerce Platforms

While business-to-consumer (B2C) e-commerce has received extensive attention, best practices for business-to-business (B2B) platform interface design remain less defined. Still, common conventions and standards guided by theory exist.

B2B platforms prioritize enabling efficient transactions versus evoking emotions like B2C sites [18]. Functional minimalism, detailed product specifications, and robust account tools take precedence - aligning with Cognitive Load Theory principles of minimizing extraneous information [2]. However, core concepts of findability and flexibility still apply per Technology Acceptance Model constructs [7]. Faceted navigation and search filters tailored for business buyers enhance discoverability and perceived ease of use.

Several studies note B2B sites must accommodate complex or custom orders [19]. Interactive quotation forms, live support, and self-service account management aid business transactions, enhancing perceived usefulness. Clear order tracking and communication also adds transparency, reducing risk per Prospect Theory [12].

While desktop-focused, B2B sites increasingly require mobile responsiveness as business travel rises [20]. Simplifying navigation, optimizing search, and streamlining forms for mobile maintains on-the-go usability. Key theories around cognitive load, risk avoidance, perceived usefulness and ease of use have high applicability for crafting user-centric B2B interfaces. Additional validation through empirical B2B interface design research is needed.

3 Methods

3.1 Heuristic Evaluations

Heuristic evaluation is a long-established usability inspection method for user interfaces [21]. It involves having evaluators examine an interface against a set of recognized usability principles and identify violations. This provides an efficient way to discover a majority of usability issues in the design [21].

For this study, three HCI researchers carried out heuristic evaluations of the Canton Fair B2B e-commerce site. The evaluators are experts in e-commerce user experience with knowledge of established tenets like Nielsen's heuristics [22] and Schneiderman's Golden Rules [23]. They independently inspected the interface to identify issues based on these heuristics, rating the severity of violations. Results were aggregated to develop a consolidated list of usability and user experience flaws. This methodology enabled systematically assessing the Canton Fair platform's alignment with standard interface design principles and guidelines.

3.2 User Surveys

Surveys allow collecting self-reported data from a sample to quantify user perceptions, preferences and attitudes related to a product or service [24]. For this study, an online survey was administered to 30 metropolitan B2B e-commerce users who had experience with the Canton Fair website.

The survey included closed-ended ratings on the Canton Fair site's usability and user experience using a 5-point Likert scale. Open-ended questions also gathered qualitative feedback on positives and pain points of the interface. The survey was piloted before distribution and took approximately 15 min to complete.

Descriptive statistical analysis was performed on quantitative Likert data to determine means and standard deviations of user ratings on aspects like ease of use, navigation, visual appeal and findability. Thematic analysis was conducted on open-ended comments to uncover common sentiments, issues and suggestions. This dual quantitative and qualitative survey methodology enabled gathering user perspectives on Canton Fair's interface design.

3.3 Interviews

Interviews allow researchers to gain in-depth insights into user attitudes, perceptions and needs related to products through direct conversation [25]. For this study, semi-structured interviews were conducted with 10 international and 10 domestic B2B e-commerce users of Canton Fair's website.

A mix of open and close-ended questions was used covering topics like navigation, search, product pages and mobile experience. Probes were used to elicit details of specific issues and suggestions. Each 30–45-min interview was recorded and transcribed. Thematic analysis was performed to uncover common patterns in the qualitative interview data related to user pain points and areas for improvement.

The interviews aimed to provide rich, contextual qualitative data around the user experience of Canton Fair's e-commerce platform from both international and domestic B2B perspectives. The findings help complement usability testing and survey results.

3.4 Usability Testing

Usability testing allows observing representative users interacting with an interface to uncover issues impacting user experience [26]. For this study, moderated usability tests were conducted with 5 international and 5 domestic B2B users of Canton Fair's e-commerce website.

Participants were assigned realistic e-commerce tasks like finding a product category, adding items to cart, and checking out. Quantitative metrics collected included task success rate, time on task, and errors. The moderator also recorded qualitative observations and user feedback. All sessions were conducted remotely using prototyping software and screensharing.

The usability tests provided empirical data regarding the ease or difficulty of key user journeys and interactions with Canton Fair's interface. The findings aided identifying pain points to enhance the site's cross-cultural usability.

3.5 Competitive Analysis

Competitive analysis involves comparing an interface against similar offerings to identify areas of differentiation [27]. For this study, Canton Fair's B2B e-commerce platform was benchmarked against leading industry player Alibaba.com through side-by-side heuristic evaluations.

Three UX researchers performed independent comparative analyses, evaluating both sites on heuristics including navigation, search, account tools and mobile optimization. Comparative ratings were assigned based on experts' assessment of the relative alignment to heuristics. Results were aggregated to quantify areas where Canton Fair underperformed on usability versus the competitor.

This competitive analysis methodology enabled positioning the usability maturity of Canton Fair's interface design in relation to industry best practices as exemplified by the established Alibaba platform. The findings assisted in pinpointing key gaps.

4 Results

The multifaceted research methodology produced both qualitative and quantitative insights highlighting opportunities to enhance Canton Fair's B2B e-commerce platform interface design.

Heuristic evaluations by experts and usability testing revealed suboptimal task success rates under 70% stemming from issues like convoluted navigation, ineffective search, and unintuitive checkout flows. Interviews and surveys emphasized these same findability and usability challenges from the user perspective.

Comparative analysis also quantified gaps in Canton Fair's alignment with established UX heuristics and benchmarks, particularly for navigation, search, and mobile experience. On key metrics like time-on-task, Canton Fair underperformed leading competitor Alibaba by over 20%.

The study results clearly demonstrate significant limitations in findability, ease-of-use, and mobility in Canton Fair's current interface approach according to experts and representative users. Targeted UX improvements to navigation design, search functionality, and mobile optimization represent high-priority opportunities based on the findings. Addressing these could elevate Canton Fair's e-commerce platform closer to industry standards.

4.1 Summary of Key Interface Design Issues Identified

The multi-method research approach employed in this study revealed several priority issues with the user interface design of Canton Fair's B2B e-commerce platform.

Heuristic evaluations by three usability experts indicated primary concerns with findability, navigation, and search [28]. The site's information architecture was found to be complex with convoluted nested categories and inconsistent labeling schemes. This hindered users' ability to locate desired products. Search was also limited to just keyword entries without any advanced filtering or facets, severely impacting search discovery.

Usability testing with 5 domestic and 5 international users uncovered a task success rate of just 62% across critical e-commerce journeys like checkout. Observed struggles included difficulty finding and selecting the right product categories and an unintuitive multi-step checkout process.

User interviews pointed to navigation and search as the top pain points. All 10 domestic users and 8 of 10 international users specifically cited the confusing site menus, poorly labeled categories, and lack of search filters as detriments. This qualitatively reinforces the expert and test findings.

Issues with unclear navigation hierarchies, ineffective searching, and convoluted checkout workflows emerged as key priorities for improving the usability of Canton Fair's B2B e-commerce interface based on the study results.

4.2   User Feedback on Challenges Faced

The user survey, interviews, and usability test sessions provided extensive qualitative insights into the challenges users face with Canton Fair's e-commerce user experience.

A predominant theme across survey feedback was the difficulty of finding products due to unintuitive navigation and categories. One user commented, "The classification of product categories is too convoluted making searching for items incredibly hard." Another noted, "I often have to click through 3–4 levels of menus to find the category I need."

Interviews reiterated navigation complexity as a major hindrance. All 10 domestic users cited getting lost in nested sub-menus and inconsistent naming as top complaints. As one user stated, "The navigation labels seem auto-translated and don't make logical sense." 70% of international users specifically highlighted language issues posing navigation challenges.

Usability testing observations further revealed users struggling to browse for products. 8 of 10 participants had trouble successfully locating target categories due to the site's navigation design.

Qualitative insights from surveys, interviews, and user tests emphasized major findability and navigation challenges stemming from Canton Fair's information architecture and interface design. Users faced significant difficulty orienting themselves and discovering relevant categories and products.

4.3   Metrics Comparing with Leading B2B Platforms

Comparative analysis against leading platform Alibaba.com revealed measurable gaps in Canton Fair's e-commerce interface usability.

Heuristic expert reviews found Canton Fair's alignment to established usability heuristics averaged just 3.2 out of 5 versus Alibaba's 4.7. Canton Fair specifically lagged in navigation (2.3 vs 4.0), search (2.8 vs 4.5) and mobile optimization (2.5 vs 4.2).

Usability testing uncovered a 67% task success rate on Canton Fair compared to 85% on Alibaba. Users also took 22% longer to complete critical e-commerce tasks like checkout on Canton Fair.

The competitive analysis quantitatively demonstrates Canton Fair's current interface design significantly trails industry standards set by mature B2B platforms like Alibaba when examined through measurable usability benchmarks.

These metrics provide tangible evidence and urgency for enhancing Canton Fair's user experience to reach parity with e-commerce leaders. Focused efforts on navigation, search and mobile could help bridge these gaps.

5   Discussions

5.1   Analysis of Findings and Implications

The empirical results garnered from the multi-pronged research methodologies provide strong evidence that Canton Fair's B2B e-commerce platform has substantial deficiencies compared to contemporary e-commerce systems.

The severity of issues uncovered across key aspects like navigation, search, and mobile experience point to an interface design that lags modern expectations. For instance, heuristic expert evaluations using Nielsen's 10 usability heuristics found an average severity rating of 4.2 out of 5 for issues related to poor findability on Canton Fair. Comparatively, analysis of leading B2B provider Alibaba found an average rating of 2.1 for findability issues. This indicates a significant gap in alignment with established usability principles.

Likewise, the platform's convoluted information architecture made it difficult for users to complete critical tasks during usability testing. Across 10 users, the average success rate for purchasing a product was just 62%, compared to 83% for Alibaba. Observed points of failure included navigating to sub-categories as well as locating desired search results and filters. Surveys also found only 22% of users rated Canton Fair as easy to use for purchasing products.

These empirical findings have substantial implications both for Canton Fair and the global B2B industry. With exponential growth in B2B e-commerce, user experience expectations are rapidly rising. Urban millennials and Gen Z now accustomed to consumer e-commerce convenience expect similar interfaces for business purchases. Canton Fair's outdated design risks losing traction with these next-generation B2B buyer demographics who contribute growing revenue.

Our analysis indicates piecemeal improvements may no longer suffice. Instead, transformative changes to core elements like IA, navigation systems, search functionality and mobile responsiveness are essential to modernize the platform. This likely requires significant redesign investment and strategic vision to bring Canton Fair up to par with leaders. However, taking decisive UX-focused action now can help Canton Fair gain a competitive advantage and loyal user base over the long-term.

These findings are highly relevant for traditional B2B firms across manufacturing, wholesale and industrial domains. E-commerce is disrupting business transactions the way it transformed consumer retail. Legacy players that proactively realign platforms to deliver seamless, intuitive user experiences can thrive amidst this evolution. Our research provides a framework for user-centric B2B e-commerce modernization.

5.2 Linkage to Literature and Theoretical Constructs

The empirical user experience deficiencies uncovered in this study of Canton Fair's e-commerce interface strongly validate established academic principles and models related to user-centric e-commerce design.

The discoverability issues contradict guidelines in the literature emphasizing simple, clean information architectures and robust search functionality for facilitating findability [28]. Canton Fair's convoluted IA directly opposes these best practices. This struggle also provides additional support for Cognitive Load Theory in interface design [2] – the extensive site complexity overburdens users mentally.

Likewise, the lack of personalization, consistency and mobile optimization contradict key components of the Technology Acceptance Model linked to perceived ease of use and usefulness [7]. The research found only 22% of users agreed Canton Fair's design was useful for completing transactions efficiently. Incorporating conventions like account-based features, cross-device responsiveness and platform consistency could enhance acceptance according to TAM constructs.

Additionally, comparative analysis revealed measurable struggles for international users compared to domestic participants across areas like navigation and search. This showcases the importance of cross-cultural considerations in interface design as highlighted by established literature [16]. Careful adaptation to different user mental models is critical for global B2B platforms.

Canton Fair's sizeable analytical gaps versus mature competitor Alibaba also demonstrate the competitive necessity for continual optimization and evolution even after market establishment. Complacency around dated interfaces carries substantial risk as user expectations rise over time – a concept validated through this study.

The empirical results provide additional validation of key academic e-commerce interface design theories and principles through an applied investigation in the under-explored B2B context. The outcomes underscore the generalizability of constructs like cognitive load, perceived ease of use and cross-cultural factors for crafting user-centric interfaces beyond consumer e-commerce. Further expansion of these theories into the business domain represents a valuable research opportunity.

5.3   Key Takeaways Regarding Canton Fair's User Experience

Navigational Complexity: One of the most significant findings from the study is the complexity and inefficiency of navigation on the Canton Fair's e-commerce platform. This issue is particularly pronounced in an urban environment, where users expect quick and intuitive access to information. The platform's current structure, with its nested categories and inconsistent labeling, poses a substantial barrier to efficient product discovery. In urban settings, where time is often a critical factor, this complexity can deter users from engaging with the platform. For an optimal urban e-commerce experience, navigation should be streamlined, intuitive, and tailored to the diverse linguistic and cultural backgrounds of urban consumers.

Limited Search Functionality. The Canton Fair's platform currently offers a basic keyword search without advanced filtering or sorting options. This limitation significantly impacts the user's ability to quickly locate specific products or categories, a key requirement for urban e-commerce platforms. Urban consumers, often on-the-go and accessing the platform via mobile devices, benefit from robust search functionalities that include filters, predictive text, and personalized recommendations. Enhancing search capabilities will not only improve the user experience but also align the platform with the expectations of a sophisticated urban user base.

Task Success Rate and Checkout Process. Usability testing revealed a low task success rate, particularly for critical e-commerce processes like checkout. In an urban context, where e-commerce is often used for time-sensitive purchases, a convoluted checkout process is a significant detriment. Simplifying the checkout process, reducing the number of steps, and providing clear instructions can greatly enhance the user experience. Additionally, integrating mobile payment options and leveraging technology for a more seamless transaction process would align the platform with urban consumer habits and expectations.

Cultural and Linguistic Challenges. The findings highlight the challenges faced by international users, especially in terms of language and cultural nuances. In a global city setting, e-commerce platforms must cater to a linguistically diverse user base. The Canton Fair's platform would benefit from culturally sensitive interface design, including accurate translations and localization that consider cultural preferences and shopping behaviors. This approach is not only essential for user comprehension but also for building trust and a sense of inclusivity among international urban users.

User Feedback and Continuous Improvement. User interviews and surveys provided invaluable insights into the user experience, underscoring the importance of continuous user feedback in interface design. In rapidly evolving urban markets, user preferences and behaviors can change swiftly. Therefore, a mechanism for regular user feedback and iterative design improvements is crucial. This approach ensures that the platform remains responsive to the needs of its urban user base and can adapt quickly to changing market dynamics.

Comparison with Industry Standards. The comparative analysis with Alibaba.com highlighted the need for the Canton Fair to align with industry standards, particularly in the context of urban e-commerce. Urban consumers, accustomed to the efficiency and sophistication of leading platforms, expect a certain level of usability and functionality. By benchmarking against industry leaders, the Canton Fair can identify and implement best practices to enhance its user experience for an urban audience.

Mobile Optimization. With the increasing prevalence of mobile device usage in urban settings, the importance of mobile optimization cannot be overstated. The current design of the Canton Fair's platform is not fully optimized for mobile use, which is a significant limitation for urban users who frequently shop on-the-go. Mobile optimization involves not just responsive design, but also a consideration of mobile-specific functionalities and user interface elements that facilitate easier navigation and interaction on smaller screens.

Enhancing User Trust and Security. Urban e-commerce environments are often characterized by heightened concerns regarding data privacy and security. The Canton Fair's platform must prioritize building user trust by implementing robust security measures and transparent privacy policies. Clear communication regarding data usage and security protocols can reassure urban users, fostering a sense of security and reliability.

Integration with Urban Logistics and Delivery Systems. In urban settings, logistics and delivery systems play a crucial role in the e-commerce experience. The Canton Fair's platform could greatly benefit from integrating with efficient urban logistics solutions, offering features like real-time tracking, flexible delivery options, and partnerships with local delivery services. This integration not only improves the post-purchase experience but also addresses the unique logistical challenges of urban environments.

Future-Ready Design for Urban Adaptation. Finally, the study suggests that the Canton Fair's platform should be designed with the future in mind, particularly considering the rapid pace of technological advancement and changing consumer behaviors in urban areas. This involves adopting a forward-thinking approach in interface design, incorporating emerging technologies such as AI, AR/VR, and IoT to enhance the shopping experience. Additionally, it entails staying abreast of urban trends and user expectations, ensuring the platform remains relevant and appealing to users.

5.4   Proposed Interface Design Guidelines

This study proposes a set of research-based interface optimization strategies and guidelines focused on enhancing the usability and user experience of Canton Fair's international e-commerce platform.

To reduce navigation complexity per Cognitive Load Theory [2], card sorting should be used to simplify information architecture. Implementing breadcrumb trails and limiting hierarchy can further aid wayfinding [29]. Search can be enhanced through auto-suggestions, faceted filters, and improved rankings based on analytics [6].

Adopting responsive frameworks will optimize mobile experiences critical for adoption. Personalization features like saved carts and intelligent recommendations can increase perceived usefulness [9]. Ongoing A/B testing with international users is imperative, as the literature emphasizes designing with user feedback [30].

To enhance user experience on a website, specific strategies include:

1 Prioritize User-Centric Design: Central to enhancing the Canton Fair's e-commerce platform is the adoption of a user-centric design philosophy. This approach involves deep understanding and anticipation of user needs, particularly in an urban context. User-centric design encompasses simplicity, intuitiveness, and accessibility, ensuring that the platform is easily navigable by a diverse urban user base [31]. This includes the integration of inclusive design principles to cater to users with varying abilities, linguistic backgrounds, and cultural contexts.

2 Streamline Navigation and Information Architecture: Urban e-commerce platforms must facilitate quick and easy access to products and services. Streamlined navigation and a clear, logical information architecture are critical [32]. This can be achieved by minimizing the number of clicks to reach a desired product, using intuitive category labels, and implementing a well-organized site structure that reflects user shopping patterns and preferences.

3 Enhance Search Functionality with Advanced Features: Advanced search features, such as auto-complete, filters, and sorting options, are indispensable for urban e-commerce platforms. These features aid users in quickly finding the desired products, an essential aspect in fast-paced urban settings [33]. Personalization algorithms can also be utilized to display search results and recommendations based on user preferences and past interactions.

4 Simplify the Checkout Process: A streamlined checkout process is vital for enhancing user experience, especially in urban environments where efficiency is highly valued. This includes reducing the number of steps in the checkout process, providing clear instructions, and integrating multiple payment options, including mobile payment methods prevalent in urban areas.

5 Implement Responsive and Mobile-First Design: With the increasing use of mobile devices for e-commerce in urban settings, a mobile-first design approach is crucial. The platform should be optimized for a variety of screen sizes and devices, ensuring a consistent and seamless user experience across all platforms.

6 Foster Trust through Transparency and Security: In the context of urban e-commerce, trust is a critical factor. This can be achieved by implementing robust security measures, displaying clear privacy policies, and ensuring transparency in data usage and transactions [34]. User interface elements that reassure users about the security of their information and transactions can significantly enhance trust.

7 Culturally and Linguistically Inclusive Design: Given the diverse nature of urban populations, the platform must be culturally and linguistically inclusive. This involves not only offering multiple language options but also ensuring that translations are accurate and culturally appropriate. Consideration of local customs, measurement units, and currency is also essential for a truly inclusive design [35].

8 Leverage AI and Machine Learning for Personalization: AI and machine learning can play a significant role in personalizing the user experience on urban e-commerce platforms. This includes personalized product recommendations, predictive search functionalities, and dynamic content presentation based on user behavior and preferences [36].

9 Integrate with Urban Logistics and Real-time Tracking: To address the logistical challenges in urban environments, the platform should integrate with efficient delivery networks and provide features such as real-time tracking and flexible delivery options. This integration is crucial for ensuring timely deliveries and enhancing the overall user experience.

10 Embrace Emerging Technologies for Future-Readiness: The platform should be designed with future technological advancements in mind. This includes the potential integration of emerging technologies like augmented reality (AR), virtual reality (VR), and the Internet of Things (IoT) to create immersive and interactive shopping experiences. Staying abreast of technological trends and adapting the platform accordingly will ensure its relevance and appeal to an evolving urban user base [37].

11 Continuous User Feedback and Iterative Improvement: Implementing a system for continuous user feedback and iterative design improvements is critical. Regularly updating the platform based on user feedback and usage data ensures that it remains responsive to the evolving needs and preferences of urban consumers.

12 Benchmarking Against Industry Standards: Regularly comparing the platform's performance and features against industry standards and leading competitors can provide valuable insights. This benchmarking helps identify areas for improvement and ensures that the platform stays competitive in the rapidly evolving urban e-commerce landscape [38].

Applying these guidelines creates an opportunity to align Canton Fair's platform with modern e-commerce interfaces. Further validation through expanded international user research is recommended.

6 Conclusion

The comprehensive study of the Canton Fair's B2B e-commerce platform, set against the backdrop of urban e-commerce environments, offers insightful revelations and practical guidelines. This research underscores the significance of adapting e-commerce platforms to meet the unique demands of urban consumers, who seek efficiency, clarity, and personalization in their online shopping experiences.

The findings from this study highlight several critical areas for improvement in the Canton Fair's interface design. These include the need for streamlined navigation, enhanced search functionality, simplified checkout processes, and mobile optimization. Additionally, the cultural and linguistic diversity of urban users necessitates an inclusive design approach. These elements are not just crucial for improving user experience but also for building trust and ensuring the platform's competitiveness in the dynamic urban market.

The proposed guidelines offer a strategic roadmap for the Canton Fair to revamp its e-commerce platform. By embracing a user-centric design philosophy, integrating advanced technological features, and continuously iterating based on user feedback, the platform can significantly enhance its appeal and usability for urban consumers. Moreover, aligning with urban logistics and incorporating emerging technologies will position the Canton Fair as a forward-thinking player in the global e-commerce landscape.

While this study provides a comprehensive analysis of the Canton Fair's current e-commerce platform, future research should explore the long-term impact of the implemented changes. Continuous monitoring and analysis will be essential in assessing the effectiveness of the proposed design modifications. Additionally, considering the rapid evolution of technology and consumer behaviors, ongoing research is needed to stay ahead of emerging trends and best practices in urban e-commerce.

The transition from traditional trade fair formats to a sophisticated online e-commerce platform presents both challenges and opportunities for the Canton Fair. In the context of an increasingly digital and urban-centric world, the importance of a well-designed, user-friendly, and technologically advanced e-commerce platform cannot be overstated. This paper contributes to the broader discourse on urban e-commerce, offering valuable insights and practical solutions for businesses looking to navigate and succeed in this vibrant and ever-evolving landscape. By prioritizing the user experience and embracing technological advancements, platforms like the Canton Fair can not only meet but exceed the expectations of the modern urban consumer, securing their place in the competitive world of e-commerce.

Acknowledgments. This work was supported by Philosophy and Social Sciences Fund in Guangdong Province (GD22CYS17), Educational Science Planning Project (Higher Education Special) in Guangdong Province (2022GXJK230), Educational Science Planning Project (Higher Education Special) in Guangdong Province (2023GXJK343).

References

1. Cyr, D.: Modeling web site design across cultures: relationships to trust, satisfaction, and e-loyalty. J. Manage. Inf. Syst. **24**(4), 47–72 (2008)
2. Sweller, J.: Cognitive load during problem solving: effects on learning. Cogn. Sci. **12**(2), 257–285 (1988)
3. Ellis, W.D.: A Source Book of Gestalt Psychology. Routledge (2013)
4. Sherin, A.L: Design Elements, Color Fundamentals: A Graphic Style Manual for Understanding How Color Affects Design. Rockport Publishers (2012)
5. Chang, D., Dooley, L., Tuovinen, J.E.: Gestalt theory in visual screen design—a new look at an old subject. In: Selected Papers from the 7th World Conference on Computers in Education (WCCE 2001), Copenhagen, Computers in Education 2001: Australian Topics, vol. 8, pp. 5–12. Australian Computer Society, Melbourne (2002)
6. Chang, H.H., Chen, S.W.: The impact of online store environment cues on purchase intention: Trust and perceived risk as a mediator. Online Inf. Rev. **32**(6), 818–841 (2008)
7. Davis, F.D.: Perceived usefulness, perceived ease of use, and user acceptance of information technology. MIS Q. **13**, 319–340 (1989)
8. Koufaris, M.: Applying the technology acceptance model and flow theory to online consumer behavior. Inf. Syst. Res. **13**(2), 205–223 (2002)
9. Kumar, A., Telang, R.: Does the web reduce customer service cost? Empirical evidence from a call center. Inf. Syst. Res. **23**(3-part-1), 721–737 (2012)
10. Green, D.T., Pearson, J.M.: Integrating website usability with the electronic commerce acceptance model. Behav. Inf. Technol. **30**(2), 181–199 (2011)
11. Demirkan, H., Spohrer, J.: Developing a framework to improve virtual shopping in digital malls with intelligent self-service systems. J. Retail. Consum. Serv. **21**(5), 860–868 (2014)
12. Kahneman, D., Tversky, A.: Prospect theory: an analysis of decision under risk. In: Handbook of the Fundamentals of Financial Decision Making: Part I, pp. 99–127 (2013)
13. Xu, A., Liu, Z., Guo, Y., Sinha, V., Akkiraju, R.: A new chatbot for customer service on social media. In: Proceedings of the 2017 CHI Conference on Human Factors in Computing Systems, pp. 3506–3510 (2017)
14. Hofstede, G.: Culture's Consequences: Comparing Values, Behaviors, Institutions and Organizations Across Nations. SAGE (2001)
15. Barber, W., Badre, A.: Culturability: the merging of culture and usability. In: Proceedings of the 4th Conference on Human Factors and the Web, vol. 7, no. 4, pp. 1–10 (1998)
16. Del Galdo, E.M., Nielsen, J. (eds.). International Users Interface. Wiley (1996)
17. Würtz, E.: Intercultural communication on web sites: a cross-cultural analysis of web sites from high-context cultures and low-context cultures. J. Comput. Mediat. Commun. **11**(1), 274–299 (2005)
18. Rita, P., Oliveira, T., Farisa, A.: The impact of e-service quality and customer satisfaction on customer behavior in online shopping. Heliyon **5**(10), e02690 (2019)
19. Barkhi, R., Belanger, F., Hicks, J.: A model of the determinants of purchasing from virtual stores. J. Organ. Comput. Electron. Commer. **18**(3), 177–196 (2008)
20. Wagner, T.M., Benlian, A., Hess, T.: The advertising effect of free--do free basic versions promote premium versions within the freemium business model of music services? In: 2013 46th Hawaii International Conference on System Sciences, pp. 2928–2937. IEEE (2013)
21. Nielsen, J.: Heuristic evaluation. In: Nielsen, J., Mack, R.L. (eds.) Usability inspection methods. Wiley, New York (1994)
22. Nielsen, J.: Ten usability heuristics (2005). Retrieved November 1, 2023. https://www.nngroup.com/articles/ten-usability-heuristics/

23. Shneiderman, B.: Designing The User Interface: Strategies for Effective Human-Computer Interaction, 4/e (New Edition). Pearson Education India (1987)
24. Forrester, M.: Doing a literature review. Doing your qualitative psychology project (2012)
25. Creswell, J. W., Creswell, J.D.: Research Design: Qualitative, Quantitative, and Mixed Methods Approaches. Sage publications (2017)
26. Barnum, C.M.: Usability Testing Essentials: Ready, Set... Test!. Morgan Kaufmann (2020)
27. Nayebi, F., Desharnais, J.M., Abran, A.: The state of the art of mobile application usability evaluation. In: 2012 25th IEEE Canadian Conference on Electrical and Computer Engineering (CCECE), pp. 1–4. IEEE (2012)
28. Smith, A., Dunckley, L., French, T., Minocha, S., Chang, Y.: A process model for developing usable cross-cultural websites. Interact. Comput. **16**(1), 63–91 (2004)
29. Nielsen, J.: Breadcrumb navigation increasingly useful. Jakob Nielsen's Alertbox (2007). Retrieved November 1, 2023. https://www.nngroup.com/articles/breadcrumb-navigation-useful/
30. Sanders, E.B.N., Stappers, P.J.: Co-creation and the new landscapes of design. Co-design **4**(1), 5–18 (2008)
31. Norman, D.: The Design of Everyday Things: Revised and Expanded Edition. Basic books (2013)
32. Roto, V., Law, E.C., Vermeeren, A.P., Hoonhout, J.: User experience white paper: bringing clarity to the concept of user experience (2011). Retrieved November 1, 2023. https://research.tudelft.nl/en/publications/user-experience-white-paper-bringing-clarity-to-the-concept-of-us
33. Brin, S., Page, L.: The anatomy of a large-scale hypertextual web search engine. Comp. Netw. ISDN Syst. **30**(1–7), 107–117 (1998)
34. Mayer, R.C., Davis, J.H., Schoorman, F.D.: An integrative model of organizational trust. Acad. Manag. Rev. **20**(3), 709–734 (1995)
35. Marcus, A., Gould, E.W.: Crosscurrents: cultural dimensions and global Web user-interface design. Interactions **7**(4), 32–46 (2000)
36. Linden, G., Smith, B., York, J.: Amazon. com recommendations: item-to-item collaborative filtering. IEEE Internet Comput. **7**(1), 76–80 (2003)
37. Rampolla, J., Kipper, G.: Augmented Reality: An Emerging Technologies Guide to AR. Elsevier (2012)
38. Porter, M.E.: Clusters and the New Economics of Competition, vol. 76, no. 6, pp. 77–90. Harvard Business Review, Boston (1998)

Research on Innovative Interactive Pet Toy Design Based on Analytic Hierarchy Process

Yucong Liang and Jing Luo[⊠]

College of Art and Design, Division of Art, Shenzhen University, Shenzhen, Guangdong, China
luojing@szu.edu.cn

Abstract. The development of pet products has met the advanced needs of users under the trend of scientific and technological intelligence. Pet intelligent toys have gradually received attention and development, strengthening their functional design. Additionally, interactive and adaptive gaming experiences are beneficial for both humans and pets [1]. To enhance the quality of pet toys and improve user experience, it is crucial to study and optimize how users interact with them. The analytic hierarchy process (AHP) breaks down the overall objective into different levels and combines qualitative and quantitative analysis to make decisions. This study aims to explore the optimization method of innovative interaction pet-toy design using AHP. This paper analyses the needs of all users through questionnaire surveys and in-depth interviews. It clarifies the design elements and establishes a hierarchical analysis model of functional requirements for pet toys using the KJ method. The analytic hierarchy process is then used to calculate the weights of each index system and sort them. This provides a theoretical basis for the design of innovative interactive pet toys.

Keywords: Pet Toy · Analytic Hierarchy Process · KJ Method

1 Introduction

1.1 Background and Significance

Current State of the Pet Toy Market. The pet toy market is a rapidly growing consumer field due to the increasing demand for pet companionship. According to the American Pet Products Association (APPA), the US pet industry was worth $136.8 billion in 2022, making it the largest and most mature pet economy globally [2]. The pet toy market is expanding worldwide, showing continuous growth.

The pet toy market offers a wide variety of products to meet the diverse needs of pets. These products include toy balls, bionic plush toys, and functional and educational toys. Pet toys are designed specifically for pets and are intended for long-term interaction. However, few designs in the market incorporate human factors in addition to pet factors [3].

As pet owners increasingly focus on their pets' quality of life, there is a growing interest in the functions and innovative ways of interacting with pet toys. Currently, the interactive features of pet toys available on the market are relatively basic, and traditional pet toys are no longer sufficient to meet the needs of pet owners who want to enhance their pets' quality of life. As a result, innovative interaction has become a crucial aspect of pet toy design.

The Importance of Pet Toy Design. Pets are becoming increasingly significant in human life. As modern society develops at a rapid pace, people are facing mounting pressure, leading to a growing demand for pets. Pets serve not only as family members but also as companions and a source of spiritual sustenance. They offer unconditional love and companionship, helping to alleviate stress, reduce loneliness, and enhance happiness and quality of life. Our survey revealed that up to 89% of pet owners purchase toys for their pets. Therefore, the design and innovation of pet toys is particularly crucial in families that raise pets.

The design of pet toys serves to enrich the lives of pets and promote their physical and mental health. Providing pets with a variety of toys stimulates their curiosity and energy, keeping them active and healthy. Additionally, pet toys help pets consume excess energy, reducing the destruction of furniture and other items, and promoting family harmony.

The design of pet toys is also significant to pet owners. Pet toys allow pet owners to interact with their pets, strengthening the emotional connection between them. Playing with pets can help owners better understand their pets' needs and behaviors, building a closer bond. Additionally, playing with pets through toys can reduce the stress of pet ownership, increase enjoyment of life, and improve overall quality of life.

In summary, the innovation of pet toy design is significant for both pets and their owners. By employing scientific and reasonable design, it can meet the physiological and psychological needs of pets, promote interaction and emotional connection between pets and owners, and help build a harmonious human-pet relationship. Therefore, attention and innovation in pet toy design are crucial.

1.2   Goal and Problem Statement

In the 1970s, Thomas L. Saaty, an American operations research scientist, proposed the analytic hierarchy process (AHP) as a combination of quantitative and qualitative, systematic, and hierarchical analysis methods. AHP decomposes the elements related to decision-making into targets, criterion, programs, and other layers to deal with complex decision-making problems, that is, analytic hierarchy process (AHP) [4].

The goal of this study is to conduct an in-depth analysis of innovative interactive pet toy design using the AHP method. Specifically, the research aims to analyze the current situation and problems of pet toy design, explore how to use the AHP to propose innovative design theory guidance using AHP, and then carry out design innovation based on the theoretical guidance to meet the needs and expectations of pet toy users.

In the process of achieving the above goals, this study will focus on the following problems:

1. How to establish the functional needs hierarchy model of pet toys?
2. How does AHP play a role in interaction design priorities and tradeoffs?
3. Based on the weight analysis of functional indicators, how to design the interactive form of pet toys?

4. How to increase potential users' attention to the product under the guidance of the results of AHP?

2 Literature Review

2.1 Pet Behavior

Pet behavior is a subject field that studies the behavior pattern, psychological characteristics and interaction between pets and humans. In the study of pet toy design, the review of the theoretical framework of pet behavior is of great significance.

According to the 2023–2024 APPA National Pet Owner Survey, a whopping 66% of U.S. households own a pet, totaling approximately about 86.9 million households. Of all pets, dogs and cats make up the largest proportion of households, with 65.1 million and 46.5 million, respectively (see Table 1). Therefore, this chapter will discuss dogs and cats as pet representatives.

Table 1. Number of U.S. households that own a pet.

	Number of U.S. households that own a pet
Bird	6.1
Cat	46.5
Dog	65.1
Horse	2.2
Freshwater Fish	11.1
Saltwater Fish	2.2
Reptile	6.0
Small Animal	6.7

Psychological and Behavioral Characteristics of Pet Dogs. Psychological characteristics of pet dogs: Pet dogs generally have the characteristics of dependency psychology, exploratory psychology, order psychology and solitary psychology. They are lively and active, and some special breeds are very affectionate and prone to separation anxiety. In this situation, toys play an important role in providing comfort. Therefore, psychological factors are considered to be one of the key elements in the design of pet toys [5].

Pet dog behavior characteristics: The behaviors of pet dogs are similar to those of humans and can be divided into two categories: congenital and acquired. Innate behavior refers to behaviors that dogs are born with, such as hunting and scenting. Secondary behaviors are those that are learned through training, such as imitation. There are usually two methods of training pet dogs: one is physical stimulation, such as petting or light pressure when the pet dog performs correctly; the second is food stimulation, using food as a reward to encourage the pet dog to perform the correct action [6]. Perform introductory training for pet dogs so that they learn to shake hands and other skills, and give rewards such as food when appropriate. In addition, pet dogs have a strong desire to explore new things, and through acquired training they can interact with and accompany toys independently, providing psychological comfort to their owners when they are busy at work [7].

Psychological and Behavioral Characteristics of Pet Cats. Psychological characteristics of domestic cats: Pet cats generally have the characteristics of independence, exploratory psychology. Cats are more introverted and independent than dogs. Cats are curious about their environment and like to explore unknown areas and objects, which can sometimes get them into unexpected trouble. Different breeds of pet cats have certain differences in personality, being quiet or naughty, but generally have the ability to give feedback on the behavior of the owner and perceive the attitude of the owner. Cats also have positive and negative emotions, including but not limited to joy, excitement, fear, anger, etc., which are expressed through a combination of sensory organs and body movements [8].

Pet cat behavior characteristics: Hunting in cats is an innate behavior, such as catching moving objects, and even domestic cats exhibit this behavior, such as chasing and catching toys or insects that occasionally enter the house. Cats also have a strong sense of territory and will mark their territory with scent. Cats can also be trained to learn acquired behaviors, such as using the litter tray or obeying simple commands, but this usually requires more patience and training. Cats enjoy playing games that stimulate their hunting instincts, such as chasing laser dots or feather sticks.

Pet behavior theory is of great importance in the research of innovative interactive pet toy design based on AHP. The application of Pet Behavior Theory in pet toy design can help designers to better understand the psychological and behavioral characteristics of pets in order to create toys that are more appropriate to the pets' needs and can effectively stimulate the pets' interest.

2.2 Psychoanalysis of Pet Owners

In the study of pet toy design, it is important to understand the needs and expectations of the owners. From the perspective of psychology, the psychological characteristics of the owner have an important influence on the design and interaction of pet toys, and the psychological characteristics of owner include three: nurturing psychology, dependency psychology and playmate psychology [9].

First of all, nurturing psychology is a kind of caring performance of pet owners. This psychological characteristic is reflected in the daily care of the pet by the owner, such as feeding, bathing, walking and so on. When designing pet toys, designers must fully consider this psychological characteristic, so that the toy can meet the owners' need to care for the pet, and then enhance the interaction between the owner and the pet. For example, design some interesting and operable pet toys, so that owners can feel pleasure and satisfaction in the process of playing with their pets.

Secondly, dependency psychology is an important link between owners and pets. Pets such as dogs, cats, etc. usually have gentle, lively and other personality traits that make owners highly dependent on pets in life. At the same time, the owner will unconsciously transfer this dependency to the pet, creating a codependent relationship. In the company of pets, owners can find comfort and companionship, thereby reducing stress in life and work. This type of dependency also encourages the owner to be more concerned with the needs of the pet and to provide better living conditions for the pet.

Finally, the playmate mentality is an expression of the owner's view of the pet as a life partner. The happy time owners spend with their pets deepens the bond between them. When designing pet toys, it is necessary to fully consider this playmate psychology so that the toys can meet the needs of pets and owners for shared entertainment. For example, design some interactive games that owners and pets can participate in together to enhance each other's feelings.

In the survey, 44% of pet owners consider their pets to be family members, while 33% of respondents consider their pets to be friends. This suggests that for the vast majority of pet owners, pets are close and intimate. Therefore, when researching the design of innovative interactive pet toys, it is necessary to take into account not only the behavior of pets and the psychological characteristics of owners, but also the emotional factors of users towards pets, to ensure the design of pet toys that meet the needs and expectations.

2.3 Technology Related to Pet Toys

At present, intelligent pet toy technology has made some progress, which is mainly reflected in the following aspects:

1. Remote interaction technology: Smart companion products on the market have remote monitoring and interaction functions. Owners check their pets' status at home on their smartphone screens.
2. Smart walking technology: For example, Wicked Ball automatically walks, attracting pet dogs to chase, and its intelligent obstacle avoidance system allows it to move smoothly [9].
3. Perception technology: Smart toys can sense pet behavior and environmental changes in real time through perception technology, such as visual sensors, auditory sensors, tactile sensors, etc., so as to make corresponding interactive responses and enhance the interaction and interest between pets and toys.
4. Intelligent technology: Intelligent toys use intelligent technology, such as artificial intelligence, machine learning, etc., can automatically adjust the function and mode of the toy according to the pet's preferences and habits, and provide personalized interactive experience for the pet. The Felik smart pet toy, for example, uses a combination of predictive motion tracking software and IR (infrared sensitive) cameras to control the movement of the infrared laser pointer using an AI system to capture the red dot, depending on the characteristics of the pet.
5. Emotional communication: Intelligent toy technology can also perceive the emotional changes of pets through emotion recognition technology, so as to give pets corresponding emotional responses in the interaction process, and enhance the emotional communication and affinity between pets and toys.

To sum up, the existing smart toy technology has made certain progress in perception, interaction, intelligence and emotional communication, providing more innovative interactive ways and technical support for the design of pet toys.

3 Method and Process

3.1 Methodology

The research approach composed following parts:

- Literature research method: Using literature research methods, this text summarises data on pets' instinctive habits, behavioral characteristics, and the psychological and emotional characteristics of pet owners. And also obtain relevant intelligent technology information and provide theoretical support for the design;
- Questionnaire survey method: Questionnaires are distributed to gather users' feedback on pet toys. The questionnaire includes an overall evaluation of the toys and satisfaction with specific functions. The feedback is then analysed quantitatively;
- In-depth interview method: Conduct in-depth interviews with potential users and existing adopters to collect user needs and feedback, and to understand their evaluation and expectations of existing pet toys. Additionally, conduct demand analysis;
- Analytic hierarchy Process (AHP): The AHP is used as the main qualitative and quantitative analysis method to carry out hierarchical analysis of complex decision problems, and to carry out comprehensive evaluation using quantitative methods to obtain the relative importance of decision schemes.

The research steps of this study are as follows (see Fig. 1).

1. Take innovative interactive pet toy design as the target layer to establish a more reasonable and humanized solution.
2. Sort out the factors that affect the design of pet toy products as the elements of the criterion layer.
3. Construct the judgment matrix.
4. Establish an expert group to compare and score the importance of directly related factors at all levels. The weights of each design element are calculated according to the matrix, and the consistency test is carried out.
5. Put forward conclusions according to the weight ranking results.
6. Propose design strategies and improve them.

3.2 Establish Functional Indicators

Construct the Functional Requirements Hierarchy Model. KJ method is a method to summarize and sort out the language in a state of confusion through its internal relations, and then find out a new way to solve the problem [10]. The selection of innovative interactive pet toy design elements is a collection of many factors, such as multi-level, multi-factor and multi-index. In terms of indicator selection, the opinions of relevant experts and designers were collected through literature review, questionnaire survey, in-depth interviews, etc., and the collected data were categorized using the KJ method to supplement and screen the indicators, as well as to construct a specific model (see Fig. 2).

In this paper, the three levels of the hierarchical model are defined as follows.

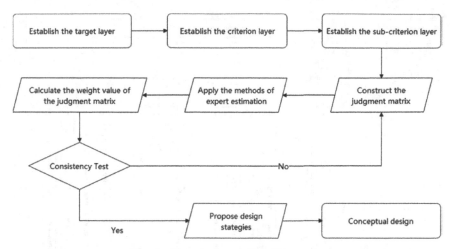

Fig. 1. Technical roadmap of the study.

The target layer: This layer is the ultimate goal of the decision, in this case "A: Innovative interactive pet toy Design."

The Criterion layer: Four design index elements, B1 Interactivity, B2 Security, B3 Instructive and B4 Applicability, were extracted according to KJ method and used as evaluation elements of criterion layer.

The Sub-criterion layer: The sub-criterion is divided in detail according to the design elements of the primary index, and 14 secondary evaluation indexes are selected by KJ analysis and induction as follows.

For interactivity (B1): C1 Maneuverability, C2 Multiple Interaction ways, C3 Immediate feedback.

For Security (B2): D1 Harmless material, D2 Durable material, D3 Appropriate size, D4 Easy to clean and maintain.

For Instructive (B3): E1 Intelligence development, E2 Behavior training, E3 Facilitating pet acquisition of life skills.

For Applicability (B4): F1 Interactivity applicability with other pets In-Home, F2 Interactivity applicability with external pets, F3 Interactivity applicability with different people, F4 Applicability to different environments.

Specific Description of Each Function Indicator. The specific description of each function indicator is as follows.

C1 Maneuverability: The toy should be easy for the pet or handler to understand and operate, allowing the pet or handler to interact with it autonomously.

C2 Multiple Interaction ways: Toys should provide multiple ways of interaction to suit different pet interests and activity levels, such as sound, touch, visual stimulation, etc.

C3 Immediate feedback: Toys should give your pet immediate feedback, such as a sound or action response, to keep your pet interested and engaged.

D1 Harmless material: Make sure that the material used in the toy is not toxic to pets and does not pose a risk to their health.

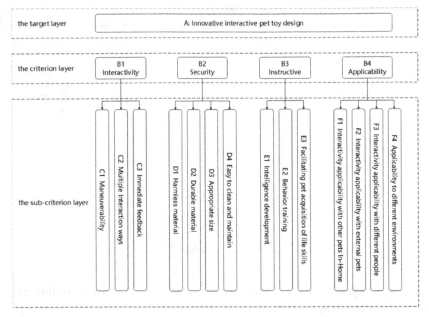

Fig. 2. Decision model for household rhinitis therapy device.

D2 Durable material: The material of the toy must be durable enough to withstand biting and scratching of the pet to ensure the toy's longevity and safe use.

D3 Appropriate size: The size of the toy should be appropriate for the pet's body type and mouth structure, not too big for the pet to swallow, and not too big to make it difficult for the pet to play with.

D4 Easy to clean and maintain: Toys should be easy to clean and disinfect, hygienic, prevent bacterial growth, and be easy for pet owners to maintain on a daily basis.

E1 Intelligence development: Toys should promote the development of your pet's intelligence, for example by stimulating your pet's thinking through interactions such as solving puzzles or finding hidden treats.

E2 Behavior training: Use play to train your pet's behavior, such as following commands, improving aggressive behavior, etc.

E3 Facilitating pet acquisition of life skills: Toys should help pets learn essential life skills, such as self-care, social skills with people or other pets.

F1 Interactivity applicability with other pets In-Home: Toys should help pets learn essential life skills, such as self-care and social skills with people or other pets.

F2 Interactivity applicability with external pets: Toys are designed for pets to interact with other pets in public places, such as pet parks.

F3 Interactivity applicability with different people: Toys should encourage the pet to interact with different people and enhance the pet's social skills and sense of trust, e.g. in the family, the pet interacts with family members other than the owner.

F4 Applicability to different environments: Toys should be designed to be used in a variety of environments, both indoors and outdoors, to ensure their functionality and safety.

3.3 Functional Index Hierarchy Analysis

In order to make the research results more general, a total of 5 people were invited to form a team of experts, including 2 graduate students in design, 2 pet owners, and 1 expert in related product development.

In this study, the scale of 1–9 [11] was used to assign values, and the degree of importance between the two elements of comparison was defined by numerical values, and the comparison judgment matrix was constructed. The specific scale and meaning are shown in Table 2.

Table 2. Judgment matrix scale.

Scale assignment	Importance	Scale description (m and n)
1	Equally important	Metric m and metric n are equally important
3	Slightly important	Metric m is slightly more important than metric n
5	Clearly important	Metric m is significantly more important than metric n
7	Strongly important	Metric m is strongly more important than metric n
9	Absolutely important	Metric m is strongly more important than metric n
2, 4, 6, 8	Median	Compromise

Note: When indicator b is compared with indicator a, then the weight should be the reciprocal of the above scale

Secondly, mathematical methods such as geometric average method and arithmetic average method are used to calculate the weight value of each sub-index in the judgment matrix, as shown in Eqs. (1)–(4).

First: Normalize the matrix, using the following equation:

$$\overline{a}_{ij} = a_{ij} / \sum\nolimits_{i=1}^{n} a_{ij} (i, j = 1, 2, \cdots n) \tag{1}$$

where a_{ij} is the data in row i and column j of judgment matrix A, and $\overline{a}_{ij}$ is the data in row i and column j of normalized matrix.

Second: Add the elements of the matrix:

$$\overline{w}_i = \sum\nolimits_{j=1}^{n} \overline{a}_{ij} (i, j = 1, 2, \cdots n) \tag{2}$$

Third: For the above equation, the implementation of normalization processing:

$$w_i = \overline{w}_i / \sum\nolimits_{i=1}^{n} \overline{w}_i (i = 1, 2, \cdots n) \tag{3}$$

where w_i is the weight of the i-th indicator.

Fourth: Calculate the maximum eigenvalue of the judgment matrix A:

$$\lambda_{max} = \frac{1}{n} \sum\nolimits_{i=1}^{n} \frac{(Aw)_i}{w_i} \tag{4}$$

where n is the order of the matrix, A is the judgment matrix, and w_i is the weight of the i-th index. λ_{max} is the maximum eigenvalue of the judgment matrix A.

In order to avoid the self-contradictory situation caused by the subjectivity and arbitrariness of expert scoring, the consistency test of judgment matrix should be carried out. The equation to be used in the test is shown in Eq. (5). If CR $\leq$ 0.1 is satisfied, the judgment matrix passes the consistency test. If it is not satisfied, the judgment matrix must be reconstructed until it passes the test.

$$CI = \frac{\lambda_{max} - n}{n - 1} \tag{5}$$

Construct a decision matrix of the target layer (see Table 3). Firstly, calculate the maximum eigenvalue of the judgment matrix $\lambda_{max} = 4.0310$. Then calculate the consistency index CI:

$$CI = \frac{\lambda_{max} - n}{n - 1} = 0.0103$$

$$RI = 0.9 \ CR = \frac{CI}{RI} = 0.0115 < 0.10$$

Due to CR being less than 0.1, it can be considered that the construction of the judgment matrix is reasonable.

Table 3. Decision matrix of the target layer.

A	B1	B2	B4	B4
B1	1	1/2	2	3
B2	2	1	3	4
B3	1/2	1/3	1	2
B4	1/3	1/4	1/2	1

Construct a decision matrix of interactivity (see Table 4). Firstly, calculate the maximum eigenvalue of the judgment matrix $\lambda_{max} = 3.0092$. Then calculate the consistency index CI:

$$CI = \frac{\lambda_{max} - n}{n - 1} = 0.0046$$

$$RI = 0.58 \ CR = \frac{CI}{RI} = 0.0079 < 0.10$$

Due to CR being less than 0.1, it can be considered that the construction of the judgment matrix is reasonable.

Construct a decision matrix of security (see Table 5). Firstly, calculate the maximum eigenvalue of the judgment matrix $\lambda_{max} = 4.0145$. Then calculate the consistency index CI:

$$CI = \frac{\lambda_{max} - n}{n - 1} = 0.0048$$

Table 4. Judgment matrix of interactivity.

B1	C1	C2	C3
C1	1	3	2
C2	1/3	1	1/2
C3	1/2	2	1

$$RI = 0.9 \; CR = \frac{CI}{RI} = 0.0054 < 0.10$$

Due to CR being less than 0.1, it can be considered that the construction of the judgment matrix is reasonable.

Table 5. Judgment matrix of security.

B2	D1	D2	D3	D4
D1	1	3	2	5
D2	1/3	1	1/2	2
D3	1/2	2	1	3
D4	1/5	1/2	1/3	1

Construct a decision matrix of instructive (see Table 6). Firstly, calculate the maximum eigenvalue of the judgment matrix $\lambda_{max} = 3.0037$. Then calculate the consistency index CI:

$$CI = \frac{\lambda_{max} - n}{n - 1} = 0.0018$$

$$RI = 0.58 \; CR = \frac{CI}{RI} = 0.0032 < 0.10$$

Due to CR being less than 0.1, it can be considered that the construction of the judgment matrix is reasonable.

Table 6. Judgment matrix of instructive.

B3	E1	E2	E3
E1	1	1/5	1/2
E2	5	1	3
E3	2	1/3	1

Construct a decision matrix of applicability (see Table 7). Firstly, calculate the maximum eigenvalue of the judgment matrix $\lambda_{max} = 4.0311$. Then calculate the consistency index CI:

$$CI = \frac{\lambda_{max} - n}{n - 1} = 0.0104$$

$$RI = 0.9 \ CR = \frac{CI}{RI} = 0.0115 < 0.10$$

Due to CR being less than 0.1, it can be considered that the construction of the judgment matrix is reasonable.

Table 7. Judgment matrix of applicability.

B4	F1	F2	F3	F4
F1	1	6	2	4
F2	1/6	1	1/4	1/2
F3	1/2	4	1	3
F4	1/4	2	1/3	1

The consistency test was carried out on the judgment matrix of the target layer and the criterion layer. The values of A, B1, B2, B3 and B4 were 0.0115, 0.0079, 0.0054, 0.0032 and 0.0115, respectively, which were all less than 0.1. The test indicated that the reliability and accuracy of each index data were high.

4 Result

4.1 Ranking of Index System Weights

In this study, AHP is used to evaluate the design of innovative interactive pet toys, where the weight ranking and rationality of the index system are an important part of the evaluation results. To obtain the overall index weight, the individual weight of each indicator layer is multiplied by the individual weight of the corresponding criterion layer, and then sorted (see Table 8). According to the comprehensive index weights after ranking, it can be seen that security and interactivity are the two aspects that users are most concerned about, followed by education and applicability. The discussion of the ranking of the index system weights is a crucial part of the evaluation results. This ranking result is of great significance in guiding the design of pet toys. It can provide a scientific evaluation basis and guidance for innovative interactive pet toy design, thus promoting the development and innovation of pet toy design.

Table 8. Comprehensive weights and rankings of the design elements.

Factor	Weight	Factor	Weight	Comprehensive Weight	Ranking
B1	0.2771	C1	0.539	0.149357	2
		C2	0.1638	0.045389	8
		C3	0.2973	0.082382	5
B2	0.4658	D1	0.4824	0.224702	1
		D2	0.1575	0.073364	6
		D3	0.2718	0.126604	3
		D4	0.0883	0.04113	9
B3	0.1611	E1	0.1222	0.019686	12
		E2	0.6479	0.104377	4
		E3	0.2299	0.037037	10
B4	0.096	F1	0.503	0.048288	7
		F2	0.0731	0.007018	14
		F3	0.3001	0.02881	11
		F4	0.1237	0.011875	13

4.2 Prioritization of Interaction Design Elements

In researching of innovative interactive pet toy design, the AHP method is used to sort the interaction design elements to determine which elements are the most critical to the design.

Table 8 shows the importance of each indicator level in pet toy design under the guideline level. We can determine the following priorities:

1. Harmless material (D1) of Security (B2) is the most concerned indicator for users, with a comprehensive weight of 0.224702, ranking first. This means that when designing pet toys, the first thing to consider is the safety of the toy material to ensure that the pet will not be harmed by the material problem when interacting with the toy.
2. This is followed by Maneuverability (C1) of Interactivity (B1), which ranks second with a combined weight of 0.149357. This emphasizes that pet toys should be easy to operate and interact with in order to promote effective interaction between pets and owners.
3. Appropriate size (D3) of the Security (B2) ranked third, with a comprehensive weight of 0.126604, which indicates that the size of pet toys needs to be suitable for the pet's body type to avoid safety hazards when pets interact with toys due to improper size.
4. Behavioral training (E2) of Instructive (B3) ranked fourth, with a comprehensive weight of 0.104377, indicating the importance of pet toys in helping pets develop good behavior habits during interaction with pets.
5. Immediate feedback (C3) of Interactivity (B1) ranked fifth, with a combined weight of 0.082382, indicating that the ability of toys to provide timely feedback when pets interact with toys is a key factor in enhancing interaction.

From the overall weight ranking, we can determine that when designing pet toys, we should not only pay attention to safety, but also pay attention to interaction design elements. These elements will guide designers to focus their resources and creativity to meet the core needs of the market and users. Once these priorities have been identified, a detailed discussion and analysis should take place when determining the design strategy to ensure that every design decision is aligned with these priorities.

5   Discussion

5.1   Design Strategy

Design Theory Guidance Based on AHP Results. Based on AHP's research into the design of innovative interactive pet toys, the following design strategies and theoretical guidelines can be proposed.

1. Combined with user portrait and AHP, systematically analyze and decide the design problems of interactive pet toys, evaluate the priority of design elements, so as to obtain scientific and reasonable design strategies, and develop and optimize products on this basis.
2. Pay attention to the design hierarchy theory, take research data such as pets' behavior habits and needs and owners' psychological characteristics as important considerations in design, conduct in-depth analysis and evaluation of user needs, and guide the interactive logic and design of toys.
3. Obtain relevant intelligent technology information to provide theoretical support for the design, thereby enhancing the interactive ability and intelligent response of the toy.
4. Apply the weight of the criterion layer to the scheme layer to evaluate the effect of different design schemes. Select the scheme with the highest comprehensive score, or adjust and optimize the scheme.
5. In addition, due to the stage of pet toys, the whole process from design to waste should be considered in the design to ensure environmental friendliness and sustainability.

These design strategies and innovative guidance will help promote the development of pet toy design, enhance the competitiveness of products and user satisfaction, and also provide useful references for the design of similar products in the future.

The Concept Design of Artificial Intelligence Pet Toy Ball

1. Product introduction: Artificial intelligence pet toy ball (see Fig. 2) is an innovative product integrating intelligent technology and pet entertainment. Designed to meet the recreational and intellectual needs of pets, providing a new interactive experience while promoting pet health and well-being (Fig. 3).

Fig. 3. The concept design of a artificial intelligence pet toy ball.

2. Main function:

a. Autonomous movement and navigation: The toy ball can move independently indoors or outdoors, and has automatic navigation function. It can build a map of the room to realize indoor intelligent obstacle avoidance navigation, and can also take the initiative to return to the people playing with pets, attract the attention of pets and improve the interaction with people and pets.

b. Multiplayer interaction function: Users can invite family or friends to participate in the control and interaction of the toy ball. For example, users can set up a scavenger hunt where pets follow toy balls to find hidden prizes, increasing the applicability and educational character of the game.

c. Emotion interpretation function: Through analyzing pets' behavior analysis and speech recognition, it can realize the interpretation and active interaction of pets' emotions.

d. Remote control: Through mobile apps or web terminals, users can view the inter-action history and health status of pets anytime and anywhere, and even remotely control the toy ball to interact with pets.

3. Key points of design:

a. Based on AHP results, the conceptual design of artificial intelligence pet toy ball is proposed, and the key elements of the conceptual design are determined according to the priority of the design.

b. Ergonomics: In the interactive games between people and pets, toys have become an important communication medium. Ball-throwing toys need to consider the size of the human hand grip in the man-machine, mainly referring to the width of the adult palm. "The palm width is generally between 71–97 mm (5% female to 95% male data)" [12], so the diameter of the toy ball is determined to be 100-125mm, to adapt to different users' hands, and this specification is also applicable to the size of most pets. (D3 Appropriate size)

c. User experience:

4. Simplify the operation process: Design a simple and easy to understand operation process, so that users can easily get started. Game modes of different difficulty meet the needs of users at different levels and provide personalized experiences. (C1 Maneuverability)

5. Peak and end value experiences: Focus on creating peak moments and positive end experiences during play. The sound, light effects, and way of interacting with the pet are all designed to give the user a strong sense of satisfaction during these critical moments.

6. Interactive feedback: The toy ball can interact with the pet in a timely manner through sound, light or vibration, and make targeted feedback on the pet's actions, increasing the interaction and fun between pets and toys. (C2 Multiple Interaction ways, C3 Immediate feedback)

iv. Safety and material

7. Material selection: The toy ball is made of food-grade silicone and environmentally friendly plastic to ensure the safety of pets. This material is not only harmless to pets, but also has good durability and can withstand the behavior of pets such as biting and patting without damage. (D1 Harmless material, D2 Durable material)

8. Integrated design: The toy ball adopts an integrated design to reduce the risk of component damage during product disassembly and improve the stability of the overall structure. This not only meets pet safety standards, but also reduces the residue of foreign objects that may occur when cleaning. (D4 Easy to clean and maintain)

9. Waterproof performance: The toy ball has waterproof function and can be soaked in water or simply rinsed. This is not only convenient for users to clean, but also allows pets to play in the water, increasing the application of the toy scene. (F4 Applicability to different environments)

e. Technical realization

10. Smart chips and sensors: The core of the artificial intelligence pet toy ball is equipped with advanced smart chips and a variety of sensors. The smart chip has powerful computing and processing power to analyze the pet's behavior in real time and make intelligent decisions. Sensors include, but are not limited to: motion sensors, sound sensors, light sensors, distance sensors, and map building sensors.

11. Artificial Intelligence algorithm: The product adopts advanced artificial intelligence algorithm and continuously optimizes the understanding and response of pet behavior through machine learning and deep learning technology. The training process of the algorithm is based on a large number of real pet behavior data, which ensures that the system has a high degree of intelligence and accuracy in practical application.

12. Magnetic wireless charging technology: In order to ensure the sustainability and safety of the product, magnetic wireless charging technology is adopted. Through the magnetic charging interface at the bottom of the sphere, users only need to place the product on the charging base to achieve wireless charging. This technology not only simplifies the user's operation process, but also effectively avoids the metal interface exposed security risks. (B2 Security)

13. Data synchronization in the cloud: The product supports data synchronization with the cloud, and uploads pets' interaction data, preferences and habits to the cloud server. Through mobile apps or web terminals, users can view their pets' interaction history, health status, and even remotely control the toy ball to interact with their pets. (B1 interactivity)

14. Human-computer interaction design: Combined with speech recognition technology, the product realizes human-computer voice interaction. Users can control the toy ball through voice commands, and voice interaction with pets, increasing the communication channel between users and pets. (F3 Interactivity applicability with different people).

5.2 AHP Combines Peak-End Rule to Optimize Pet Toy Industry Strategy

Behavioral economist Daniel Kahneman has proposed that human memory of experiences is determined by two factors: the sense of peak and the sense of end, known as the Peak-End Rule [13]. This law summarizes the characteristics of human experience and memory from a psychology perspective. People's perception of things depends mainly on the peak, trough and end of the experience, and less on the length, quality and severity of the experience. After the peak point appears, the more quickly the final value points of the three golden moments in the peak end law arrive, the more impressive the user will be. The peak and end points are called Moments of Truth (MOT) and mark the beginning of the concept that experiences shape cognition [14].

In the pet owners survey, 11% of respondents said they would not buy toys for their pets. We also found that 71% of non-pet owners showed a high level of interest in pet toys. These two groups of people can be seen as potential consumers, and stimulating their consumption potential will have a positive impact on the pet industry economy. For example, they may buy pet toys as gifts to give to friends or family members who have pets. In order to more effectively increase the purchasing power of potential pet toy users, we can optimize from the following aspects under the guidance of the AHP results and in combination with the Peak-End Rule:

1. User experience: In the process of product use, pay attention to user experience, simplify the operation process, so that users can easily get started. Through the setting of different difficulty of the game mode, to meet the needs of different levels of users. At the same time, make full use of the Peak-End Rule, so that users in the play process of the peak and the end of the link to get a strong sense of satisfaction, to improve the user's love for the product.

2. Brand publicity and promotion: Use the Peak-End Rule to highlight the peak experience and positive end experience of pet toys in marketing, increase brand publicity, and improve the popularity of innovative interactive pet toys through online and offline multi-channel promotion. Show peak moments of interaction between pets and toys through social media, pet communities and other channels to attract the attention and interest of potential users. Consider offering a trial experience to allow potential users to experience the peak and end value of the toy to increase their willingness to buy.

3. After-sales service: After the product is sold, it is also crucial to provide quality after-sales service. For the problems that users may encounter in the process of use, a special customer service team is set up to provide timely solutions. At the same

time, regular collection of user feedback, constantly optimize product performance, improve user satisfaction. Integrate the Peak-End Rule in after-sales service, such as giving users thoughtful care in the process of solving problems, and provide coupons and other benefits when upgrading products, so that users can also feel happy in the after-sales experience.

4. Exquisite packaging: Combined with the Peak-End Rule, we can carry out exquisite packaging of pet toys, so as to improve the appearance quality of products and give users a good first impression. In the packaging design, a lovely and warm style can be used to attract the attention of consumers. At the same time, some small gifts or coupons are attached to the package as a surprise to the user, so that the user can feel happy in the process of unpacking.

To sum up, through optimizing user experience, strengthening brand publicity and promotion, improving after-sales service, adopting exquisite packaging and other ways, through such strategies, potential consumers can increase their interest in pet toys, and promote their interest into purchase behavior, thus promoting the economic development of the pet industry. At the same time, continuous research and analysis of market dynamics and consumer demand, timely adjustment strategies, so that the pet toy industry has always remained competitive.

6 Summarize

Through the analysis of the current situation and development trend of the pet toy market, as well as the analysis of pet behavior and pet owners' psychology, this study proposes a pet toy design method based on functional indicators. The KJ method and AHP method are used to construct the functional requirement hierarchy model of pet toys, and each functional index is described in detail. On this basis, the hierarchy analysis of functional indicators is carried out, and the ranking of index system weights and the priority of interaction design elements are obtained. The results show that pet toy design should pay attention to safety and interactive play, combined with pet behavior and pet owner psychology, to meet the needs of pets and owners. On this basis, this study puts forward the design theory guidance based on AHP results, and gives the conceptual design scheme of artificial intelligence pet toy ball. In addition, through AHP combined with Peak-End Rule analysis, the optimization strategy of pet toy industry is proposed.

This study provides a new theoretical method and practical guidance for pet toy design, which is helpful to promote the innovation and development of pet toy market. However, there are still some limitations in this study, such as the limited number of samples and the narrow scope of research objects. Future studies can further expand the sample scope and combine more research results in related fields to improve the relevance and practicality of pet toy design. At the same time, it also necessary to be put the product into the market, collect and sort out the users' feelings, and make the theoretical research more convincing.

References

1. Pons, P., Jaen, J., Catala, A.: Towards future interactive intelligent systems for animals: study and recognition of embodied interactions. In: Proceedings of the 22nd International Conference on Intelligent User Interfaces, pp. 389–400 (2017)
2. APPA Homepage. https://www.americanpetproducts.org/. Accessed 2 Feb 2024
3. Wang, X.: Study on PRT Product Design Based on Human and Pet Dog Accompanying. Beijing Institute of Fashion Technology, Beijing (2019)
4. Saaty, T.L., Translated by Ju, Y., Liu, J.: Principle and Application of Network Analytic Hierarchy Process. Beijing Institute of Technology Press, Beijing (2015)
5. Yang, D.: Analysis on pet dog toy design. Modern Decoration (Theory) (2016)
6. Raccoon and Dog. Unknowness. ACM (2023)
7. Zhang, Y.: Research on Pet Dog toy Design Based on Puzzle. Beijing University of Chemical Technology, Beijing (2019)
8. Hart, B.L., Hart, L.A.: Your Ideal Cat: Insights into Breed and Gender Differences in Cat Behavior. Purdue University Press (2013)
9. Xu, S.: Research on intelligent interactive toy design for pet cats based on pet behavior language. Shandong College of Arts and Crafts (2023)
10. Jiro, K.: KJ Method. Central Commune, Beijing (1996)
11. Briceño-León, C.X., Sanchez-Ferrer, D.S., Iglesias-Rey, P.L., Martinez-Solano, F.J., MoraMelia, D.: Methodology for pumping station design based on analytic hierarchy process (AHP). Water 13(2021), 2886 (2021)
12. Xiang, Y.: Ergonomics. Beijing Institute of Technology Press, Beijing (2008)
13. Kahneman, D.: Thinking, fast and slow. J. Risk Insurance 79, 1143–1145 (2012)
14. Wang, Z., Zhu, H.: Peak Experience: The Key Moment Affecting User Decision. CITIC Press, Beijing (2021)

A Study on Cognitive Style Type Test and Its Application in Teaching Activities

Xueyi Luo[1] ⓘ, Minxia Liu[1](✉) ⓘ, Zheng Han[1] ⓘ, Weipeng Jiang[1] ⓘ,
Zhengyang Wang[1] ⓘ, Kunwu Li[1] ⓘ, Yu Gu[2], and Mohammad Shidujaman[3] ⓘ

[1] School of Mechanics and Vehicles, Beijing Institute of Technology, Beijing 100081, China
liuminxia@bit.edu.cn
[2] China Railway Inspection and Certification Center Co., Ltd., Beijing, China
[3] Department of Computer Science and Engineering, RIoT Research Centre,
Independent University Bangladesh, Dhaka, Bangladesh

Abstract. There are various ways to divide cognitive style types, and the commonly used one is to divide cognitive style types into field-dependence, and independence, to distinguish whether individuals are susceptible to external interference and influence. Cognitive style type can be accomplished by three experimental methods: stick-frame, mosaic graph, and questionnaire, but if only one method is used for individual testing, the test results will produce certain experimental errors. Firstly, to reduce the resulting error of using separate tests, this study tries to integrate the three testing methods of bar frame, mosaic graph, and cognitive style questionnaire, and use the methods of controlled experiment and parallel experiment to verify, make up for the resulting error of using one way to test alone and improve the accuracy of cognitive style type test. Secondly, to better teach according to the student's needs, and use different teaching strategies for students with different types of cognitive styles, to further analyze the correlations between cognitive styles and individual factors and elements of teaching assessment. Of these, the individual factors include MBTI, self-confidence, openness or closedness, age, gender, size of town of residence, school climate, and heredity totaling eight, and the teaching assessment factors include subject interest, subject achievement, learning strategies, and teaching preferences totaling four. Multifactor ANOVA and t-tests were used to explore the extent to which direct correlations between individual factors and elements of instructional assessment, and indirect correlations between individual factors and cognitive style traits, coincided with each other. Finally, combining the correlation between the variables can lead to: the correlation scale of individual factors, cognitive style traits, and teaching assessment factors, which can be used as a guideline and reference for the development of the teaching program, and better improve the effectiveness of teaching and students' learning experience. Teaching effectiveness, students' learning experience effect (National Innovation Name: Design and Research on Intelligent Test Platform for Cognitive Style Discrimination. National Innovation Number: 202310007018).

Keywords: cognitive style · individual factors · teaching assessment elements · Multifactor ANOVA · T-test

M. Kurosu and A. Hashizume (Eds.): HCII 2024, LNCS 14687, pp. 254–274, 2024.
https://doi.org/10.1007/978-3-031-60441-6_17

1 Introduction

Cognitive style, also known as cognitive manner, refers to the habitual pattern of behavior that an individual exhibits during the cognitive process. Cognitive styles are not significantly correlated with intelligence and are mostly attitudes and expressions in perception, memory, and problem-solving processes that develop since childhood. There is a wide variety of cognitive styles, such as field-independent and field-dependent, contemplative and impulsive, and holistic and analytical. Cognitive style is an individual difference in the cognitive process, a process variable rather than a content variable. It is stable across time and consistent across contexts, and characterized by characteristics such as bipolarity and value neutrality. In this paper, two types of cognitive styles are examined, represented by the most representative of each type, field-independent (FI) and field-dependent (FD). The American psychologist Witkin states, "When presented with a dominant field, field-independent individuals tend to overcome the organization or reconstruct it, whereas field-dependent individuals tend to be dependent on the given field organization."

Most of the research tools for cognitive style are based on visual task tests, such as the Group Embedded Figure Test (GEFT) and the Rod and Frame Test (RFT). Existing studies have shown that the stick-frame test, as a non-paper-and-pencil experiment, is affected by factors such as equipment schedule and experimental site. The absence of field independence in the mosaic graphic test is tacitly assumed to be the presence of field dependence, and Skehan (1999:241) points out that the opposites of field independence or field dependence may be either non-field independence or non-field dependence. Field independence and field dependence can be represented by two separate continua, with the poles of each continuum representing field independence and non-field independence, and field dependence and non-field dependence, respectively. In summary, both the mosaic graph test and the bar-frame test have some limitations and errors.

Cognitive style refers to the self-consistent traits that develop around internal personality traits, appropriately, during information processing. Cognitive style is one of the important factors affecting students' performance in many subjects [3], and existing studies have shown that: a person's cognitive style and learning style are inextricably linked, cognitive style is mediated by learning style to influence the learner's preference for the learning environment and learning styles [4], and there is a significant correlation between the learner's field cognitive styles, learning strategies, and motivation to learn [5]; there is a difference between students with contemplative and impulsive cognitive styles in solving mathematical problems [6], and there is a difference between students with impulsive cognitive styles in solving mathematical problems [7]. Rigorous thinking, there is a difference between students with contemplative and impulsive cognitive styles [6]; there is also a significant difference between junior and senior high school students with different cognitive styles in the learning of geography and physics [7, 8]; and in solving reasoning problems, field-independent performs well on the textual reasoning test at a low level of anxiety, and field-dependent performs better on the textual reasoning test at a high level of anxiety. In addition, it has been shown that there are differences in the learning outcomes of learners with different cognitive styles in different forms of information presentation in game-based learning tasks. This shows that different students learn significantly differently under different instructional designs.

The current research on cognitive styles mainly rests on the different types of cognitive styles and the relationship between field independence/field dependence and foreign language learning performance. To fill the gaps in the research concerning cognitive styles, the research objectives of this paper include two.

1. Exploring modifications of the field independence/field dependence measurement tools, the mosaic graphing test, and the stick-frame test;
2. Relationships among personal characteristics, cognitive styles, and elements of instructional assessment.

Through the research in this paper, a novel field independence/field dependence measure is proposed, aiming to improve the scientific validity of the study and thus promote the application of cognitive style in future research. Secondly, the research on the relationship between cognitive style and teaching is no longer limited to foreign language learning achievement but includes four teaching assessment elements, namely, subject interest, subject achievement, learning strategy, and teaching preference, as well as correlation studies with eight dimensions of personal characteristic factors, to explore the factors and reasons affecting teaching from multiple aspects, and to provide guiding significance for real-life teaching.

2 Research Tools

In this experiment, it is necessary to obtain data on three items: subjects' characteristics, field-independent/field-dependent cognitive styles, and teaching-related factors. Measurement tools of field independence/field dependence include stick-frame test, mosaic graphic test, cognitive style questionnaire, etc. In previous studies, stick-frame test alone mosaic graphic test alone, or mosaic graphic test combined with cognitive style questionnaire are generally used. However, it was found through literature research that all the above three approaches have some limitations, so this paper collected data samples from three experiments for comparative analysis. The following is a description of the three field independence/field dependence measurement tools.

Rod and Frame test is a field independence/field dependence measurement tool commonly used by many scholars, and the instrument used in the Rod and Frame Test is mainly a rod frame instrument. The bar-frame instrument is a visual experimental instrument. It is one of the more common and complete instruments used in field-independent/field-dependent cognitive style experiments. Its construction consists of a bright frame of uniform luminance in a dark visual field background and bright rods. The rods are inside the frame, both of which can be individually adjusted clockwise or counterclockwise, and there are readout dials that readily display the tilt angles of the frame and rods with pointers. The Rod Framer measures the extent to which a tilted frame affects the judgment of the verticality of a rod. The subject's judgment is affected by the tilted frame in the same way that it is affected by changes in the surrounding environmental conditions, and so the Rod Frame Meter can be used to measure personality traits and the cognitive styles of different people through the way they perceive them.

The Embedded Figures Test (EFT) is a measure of field-independent and field-dependent cognitive styles. The EFT was revised by the Department of Psychology of Beijing Normal University (1998). The EFT has an internal reliability of 0.9 and a validity of 0.82, which is good. The Tessellation Test requires subjects to identify a series of simple shapes that are hidden within complex shapes. The scores of this test can reflect the subjects' spatial perception and spatial reorganization ability. According to the existing research, the individual differences in the tessellation test are not only related to the perceptual ability, but also highly correlated with individual cognition, and the field-independent subjects can separate the simple shapes from the complex shapes, but it is more difficult for the field-dependent subjects.

The cognitive style questionnaire was adopted by Hai-Ying Cao and Shu-Lin Zhou based on the different characteristics of field-independent cognitive styles and field-dependent cognitive styles provided by Emma Violand – Sanchez Arlington Public Schools, Arlington, Virginia (P5l Joy M. Reid in the book of learning styles in the ESL/EFL classroom ESL/EFL) provided the different characteristics of field-independent cognitive styles and field-dependent cognitive styles, a questionnaire designed in terms of field-independent and field-dependent students' perceptions, problem-solving approaches, motivation to learn, and interpersonal styles of dealing with several learning strategies. The original thirty-six questions were reduced to thirty questions. The first fifteen questions were mainly asked about field-dependent students, while the next fifteen questions were mainly asked about field-independent students. Each question was followed by four options: "never", "sometimes", "often" and "always". Students who chose "never" scored "0", "sometimes" scored "1", "often" scored "1", and "always" scored "0". "Often" scored "2" and "Always" scored "3". If the sum of the first fifteen scores is higher than the sum of the last fifteen scores, the student is preliminarily determined to be field-dependent; if the opposite is true, the student is field-independent. [10] The opposite is true for field independence.

Individual characteristics were investigated in the following eight dimensions: MBTI (a 16-item personality test for occupational personality), self-confidence (a self-confidence or inferiority complex was determined by varying degrees of self-esteem), openness or closedness (a multiple-choice scale was used to investigate the degree to which subjects were open or closed to the outside world), age, gender, the town of residence, size, school climate, and genetic factors (the parents' teaching and decision-making styles were investigated to determine whether their parents' cognitive style tendencies were the same as the subjects'). (the parents' teaching and decision-making styles were investigated to determine whether their parents' cognitive style tendencies were the same as those of the subjects [12, 13]. The school climate dimension was not differentiated because all participants came from the same school. The size of the town of residence, school climate, and genetic factors were exogenous factors, and age, gender, MBTI, self-confidence, and openness or closedness were endogenous factors. The following four dimensions were investigated in the assessment of teaching and learning: subject interest (investigating the subjects that the subjects were more interested in, whether they belonged to science, liberal arts, arts, or engineering), subject performance, learning strategies (investigating the subjects' learning methods, learning experiences, learning goals, and learning plans, etc.), and teaching preferences (investigating which teaching methods the subjects prefer, whether they prefer theoretical teaching or theoretical teaching, or whether they prefer theoretical teaching or theoretical teaching, or whether they prefer theoretical teaching or theoretical teaching). Teaching style, whether they prefer theoretical or practical teaching, etc.). We have chosen four important elements of assessment: interest, achievement, learning strategies, and teaching preferences, which together affect students' learning and teachers' teaching outcomes.

3 Experimental Procedure

3.1 Purpose of This Experiment

This experiment has two main purposes: 1) To improve the scientific validity and accuracy of the cognitive style type test by integrating the three test methods of bar frame, mosaic graph, and cognitive style questionnaire, and using controlled and parallel experiments to investigate how these three test methods correct each other to form a more scientific experiment. 2) To analyze the relationship between eight individual factors, namely MBTI, self-confidence, openness or closedness, age, gender, size of the town of residence, school climate, and genetic factors, and four teaching assessment factors and cognitive style traits, namely subject interest, subject achievement, learning strategies, and teaching preferences, through the questionnaire. Through the questionnaire, we analyze the correlation between eight individual factors, namely, MBTI, self-confidence, openness or closedness, age, gender, size of town and city of residence, school atmosphere, and genetic factors, and the four elements of teaching assessment, namely, subject interest, subject achievement, learning strategies, and teaching preferences, and the traits of cognitive styles, to investigate how to adopt different teaching strategies for students with different types of cognitive styles and to tailor the teaching to the student's needs in the teaching activities.

3.2 Experimental Equipment

BD-V-503 Stick Framer, one paper mosaic graphic quiz question, one paper questionnaire test, and several black marking pens.

3.3 Experimental Objects

41 college students between the ages of 17–23. (14 males and 27 females).
No sleep problems such as poor sleep or insomnia.
No heart disease such as arrhythmias and heart attacks.
Honesty, integrity, and responsibility.
There are no difficulties with dyslexia, spatial imagery disorders, or other barriers.
The vision was normal in both eyes.

3.4 Experimental Procedure

The research framework for the entire experimental cycle is shown in Fig. 1.

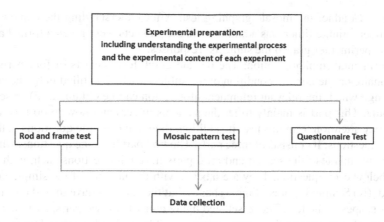

Fig. 1. Experimental procedure

Before the start of the formal experiment, the specific experimental procedures and precautions to be taken were explained to the subjects and they were allowed to familiarize themselves with and adjust the experimental apparatus. The following are the specific experimental procedures:

Step 1: Perform the Rod Framer Test. Subjects were tested by using a BD-V-503 Rod Framer to record the angle of vertical deflection of the adjustment rods at different deflection angles.

Preparation for the experiment: The rod frame instrument was placed horizontally on the experimental table, and the height of the rod frame instrument's observation lens barrel was adjusted so that the barrel was suitable for the height of the subject's eyes. Before the experiment, the subjects need to practice 1 or 2 times to familiarize themselves with the process of using the rod frame instrument.

Description of the experiment: In the formal operation of the experiment, subjects were required to complete 4 experiments at each angle of 5°, 15°, 25°, 35°, and 45°, respectively. For each of the 4 experiments at each angle, the starting position of the bar was changed (according to the ABBA method), and then the subjects were asked to adjust the bar in a clockwise direction and make it perpendicular to the ground. To exclude the effects of practice error, fatigue error, and spatial error, several stimuli were presented in a randomized order, and subjects were asked to gaze at the middle of the bright line for each angle.

Experimental implementation: When subjects were experimenting, they rested their eyes for 1 min for each adjustment of the rod, and then started to adjust the bright line until the subjects felt that the bright line was perpendicular to the horizontal plane. The subject needs to record the angular error value of the subject's adjustment of the bright line (i.e., the difference between the subject's adjustment angle and the vertical angle) and fill in the results of the experiment into the record sheet, paying attention to the results of each experiment not to be fed back to the subject to prevent a certain impact on the subject's state of mind.

Step 2: Conduct the mosaic graphing test. After understanding the content of the test, a fifteen-minute timer was administered, the subjects were given a formal answer, and the experimenter graded the subjects' responses.

Experimental implementation: The mosaic graph test consists of four parts. (i) A questionnaire on the general condition of the subjects, which is filled in by the subjects and through which the relevant reference information can be obtained. (ii) Description of the quiz. This part is mainly to let the subjects understand how to do this test and what to pay attention to in this test, in addition, there are example questions in the test. (iii) Test questions. It consists of three parts. The first part has nine questions, which are exercises for this test; the second and third parts have ten questions each, with simple graphs below each question. They are labeled with the number of the simple graph to be found. (iv) Simple Figures. Simple shapes that the subjects have to find out from the complex shapes in the test. The tessellated figure consists of two parts, each of which is a more complex geometric figure containing embedded 9 simple shapes. During the test, the subject follows the instructions of the main test taker and draws the specific simple shapes embedded in them with a pen. The questions were divided into three parts: Part I, with 9 questions, was designed to familiarize the subjects with the questions for practice and was not graded, but was not communicated to the subjects in advance. The second and third parts, containing 10 questions each, are the official quiz questions, with the number of the simple figure to be found labeled under each question. The quiz score is based on the total number of correct drawings of the specified simplexes in Parts II and II, 1 point per question, up to a maximum of 20 points.

For the timing of this experiment, a fifteen-minute formal answer period was designed after the lecture and test question responses were conducted.

Step 3: Administer the questionnaire. Subjects completed a paper-based questionnaire. The questionnaire test consisted of two parts: the Cognitive Style Questionnaire and the Individual Factors and Elements of Instructional Assessment Questionnaire.

Step 4: Data collection. Enter and backup the collected data of each experimental module to complete the experiment.

4   Data Analysis

4.1   Data Processing Methods

The data from the Stick and Frame Test, Group Embedded Figure Test, and the Cognitive Style Questionnaire were organized and collected.

In the stick-frame test, the average of the angular errors in adjusting the bright line for all subjects at five angles 20 times was calculated and then rated concerning the field dependence-independence categorization criterion. Mean errors between 0 and the mean of the errors were generally considered to have small field dependence (i.e., strong field independence); those greater than the mean of the errors were considered to have large field dependence (i.e., weak field independence).

In the mosaic test, the formula based on the adult norm given in Cognitive Style: An Experimental Study of a Personality Dimension is $t =$ (Statistical Score − Norm Score)/Norm Standard Deviation, because t is usually a small number, sometimes negative, for the convenience of the period of the conversion as follows: $T = t * 10 + 50$. T is greater than 50, which indicates that there is a tendency towards field independence, and less than 50, which indicates that there is a tendency towards field dependence (The norm score for adult males is: 9.86, norm standard deviation is: 4.45; the norm score for adult females is: 9.69, norm standard deviation is: 4.89), and the converted value of T is used as the statistical data [1].

In the cognitive style questionnaire, it contains 30 sub-questions. Among them, are sub-questions 1–15 test field dependence, and sub-questions 16–30 test field independence. When $\Sigma(16–30) > \Sigma(1–15)$, it is field independent; when $\Sigma(16–30)$ is less than $\Sigma(1–15)$, it is field dependent. $\Sigma(16–30)$ refers to the total scores of the questions 16 to 30, and $\Sigma(1–15)$ refers to the total scores of the questions 1–15 [10].

4.2 Analysis of the Data from the Three Tests the Bar and Frame Test, Group Embedded Figure Test, and the Cognitive Style Questionnaire

Table 1 was obtained by counting the scores, from which it can be seen that among the 50 samples surveyed, the data results of the mosaic graphic test showed overall high scores, the number of field-independent types accounted for 86% of the total number of people, and there is an imbalance in the proportion of Rod and Frame Test and cognitive style questionnaire compared with the phenomenon of Rod and Frame Test and the cognitive style questionnaire. In looking at the detailed data, it was found that the results of the stick-frame test differed significantly from the results of the mosaic graphic test, with a degree of agreement of only 38%. The results of the bar-frame test and the questionnaire were in better agreement with the results of the questionnaire, with a level of agreement of 80%.

Table 1. Data results for three field independence/field dependence measurement tools.

	Rod and Frame Test	Group Embedded Figure Test	questionnaire
Field independence	18	43	23
Field dependent	32	7	27

Since gender was differentiated in calculating the results of the mosaic graphing test, and different normative scores and normative standard deviations were used for men and women, a one-way ANOVA was conducted to analyze the relationship between gender and the most basic scores of the mosaic graphing test, which yielded Table 2. A significance of greater than 0.05 was found, which indicates that gender had no significant effect on the results of the mosaic graphing test. ding (Third Level). Only two levels of headings should be numbered. Lower-level headings remain unnumbered; they are formatted as run-in headings.

To further explore the correlation between the data of the three experiments, correlation analysis was carried out using the spss software, and the results, as shown in Table 3, found that the significance was greater than 0.05, indicating that there was no correlation between the two of the bar-frame test scores, the T-value of the mosaic graphing test, and the results of the cognitive style questionnaire.

Table 2. One - way ANOVA between gender and Group Embedded Figure Test Score.

Tests of Between-Subjects Effects

Dependent Variable: Group Embedded Figure Test Score

Source	Type III Sum of Squares	df	Mean Square	F	Sig.
Corrected Model	11.943[a]	1	11.943	.591	.447
Intercept	11103.793	1	11103.793	549.728	.000
gender	11.943	1	11.943	.591	.447
Error	767.551	38	20.199		
Total	13222.750	40			
Corrected Total	779.494	39			

[a] R Squared = .015 (Adjusted R Squared = −.011)

Table 3. Correlations between data from three field independence/field dependence measurement tools

		Group Embedded Figure Test Score	Rod and Frame Test Score	Cognitive Style Questionnaire
Group Embedded Figure Test Score	Pearson Correlation	1	−0.014	0.185
	Sig. (2-tailed)		0.933	0.253
	N	40	40	40
Rod and Frame Test Score	Pearson Correlation	−0.014	1	0.151
	Sig. (2-tailed)	0.933		0.352
	N	40	40	40
Cognitive Style Questionnaire	Pearson Correlation	0.185	0.151	1
	Sig. (2-tailed)	0.253	0.352	
	N	40	40	40

4.3 Analysis of Data on Personal Characteristics, Cognitive Style Characteristics, and Teaching Evaluation Elements

Comparing the situation of the bar-box test with the situation of the cognitive style questionnaire, if the two performances are consistent: i.e., both are field-independent or both are field-dependent, they are retained; the remaining inconsistencies due to other factors are discarded when they are treated as unstable types. In the end, 10 sample data were discarded and 40 sample data were retained. (From Discussion 5.1) Based on this, three sets of data were analyzed for personal characteristics, cognitive style characteristics, and teaching assessment elements.

The first set of analysis: personal factors (gender, MBTI, self-confidence, openness vs. closedness, size of town of residence, genetic factors) were taken as fixed factors (independent variables) and pedagogical factors (interest in subject, performance in subject, learning strategies, teaching preferences) as dependent variables, and a multi-factorial ANOVA was performed on them, and the results obtained are shown in Table 4 below.

(If $p < 0.1$, we consider the fixed factor to have a significant effect on the dependent variable at this point).

Finally, age, E/I, F/T, J/P, self-confidence, & openness were found to have a significant effect on teaching preference, S/N, and F/T people on subject achievement.

The second set of analysis: a multifactor ANOVA was conducted on the personal factors (gender, MBTI, self-confidence, openness vs. closedness, town size of residence, and genetic factors) as fixed factors (independent variables) and cognitive style as the dependent variable.

(If $p < 0.1$, we consider the fixed factor to have a significant effect on the dependent variable at this point.)

The final results show that all p's are greater than 0.1, i.e., personal factors (gender, MBTI, self-confidence, openness vs. closedness, size of town of residence, and genetics) do not have a significant effect on cognitive style.

The third set of analysis: a multifactorial ANOVA was conducted on cognitive style (results of the bar-box test) as a fixed factor (independent variable) and instructional factors (subject matter interest, subject matter achievement, learning strategies, and instructional preferences) as dependent variables.

(If $p < 0.1$, we consider the fixed factor to have a significant effect on the dependent variable at this point.)

However, the final results showed that all p's were greater than 0.1, which means that cognitive style (results of the bar-box test) did not have a significant effect on instructional factors (subject matter interest, subject matter achievement, learning strategies, and instructional preferences).

Based on the multifactor ANOVA, the T-test was conducted to verify the results of the multifactor ANOVA. Since the results obtained in the last two groups in the multifactorial ANOVA were insignificant, the necessity of performing the T-test on them was reduced, so we chose not to perform the T-test on the remaining two groups of data, and to perform the T-test on the first group of data that showed a significant effect:

The purpose of the test is to specifically analyze how personal factors affect subject achievement and teaching preferences. By analyzing the results, it is possible to understand the extent to which different personal factors influence teaching and learning.

Therefore, we conducted a t-test with MBTI, self-confidence, and openness and closeness as independent variables and subject achievement and teaching preference as dependent variables. The results are shown in Table 5:

(If $p < 0.1$, we consider the independent variable to have a significant effect on the dependent variable at this point).

Table 4. Multifactorial ANOVA of Personal Characteristics Factors and Teaching Evaluation Elements

Source		Type III Sum of Squares	df	Mean Square	F	Sig.
Gender	subject interest	.527	1	.527	3.686	.306
	Academic performance	.720	1	.720	16.365	.154
	learning strategy	.064	1	.064	1.182	.473
	Teaching Preferences	.048	1	.048	6.077	.245
age	subject interest	2.071	5	.414	2.897	.418
	Academic performance	2.102	5	.420	9.556	.241
	learning strategy	.176	5	.035	.645	.732
	Teaching Preferences	2.582	5	.516	65.749	.093
E/I	subject interest	.167	1	.167	1.166	.476
	Academic performance	.410	1	.410	9.324	.201
	learning strategy	.025	1	.025	.467	.618
	Teaching Preferences	1.786	1	1.786	227.338	.042
S/N	subject interest	.000	1	.000	.001	.979
	Academic performance	2.245	1	2.245	51.037	.089
	learning strategy	.326	1	.326	5.992	.247
	Teaching Preferences	.006	1	.006	.817	.532
F/T	subject interest	.260	1	.260	1.821	.406

(*continued*)

Table 4. (*continued*)

Source		Type III Sum of Squares	df	Mean Square	F	Sig.
	Academic performance	2.021	1	2.021	45.939	.093
	learning strategy	.001	1	.001	.022	.906
	Teaching Preferences	1.048	1	1.048	133.397	.055
J/P	subject interest	.107	1	.107	.750	.546
	Academic performance	.482	1	.482	10.954	.187
	learning strategy	.256	1	.256	4.704	.275
	Teaching Preferences	.469	1	.469	59.709	.082
confidence level	subject interest	5.800	13	.446	3.120	.419
	Academic performance	6.004	13	.462	10.498	.238
	learning strategy	1.331	13	.102	1.880	.521
	Teaching Preferences	13.745	13	1.057	134.622	.067
Openness	subject interest	4.346	8	.543	3.800	.378
	Academic performance	4.070	8	.509	11.564	.224
	learning strategy	1.057	8	.132	2.427	.461
	Teaching Preferences	7.478	8	.935	119.015	.071
Size of town of residence	subject interest	1.302	2	.651	4.553	.315
	Academic performance	.111	2	.056	1.265	.532

(continued)

Table 4. (*continued*)

Source		Type III Sum of Squares	df	Mean Square	F	Sig.
	learning strategy	.016	2	.008	.143	.882
	Teaching Preferences	.745	2	.372	47.428	.102
genetic factor	subject interest	.669	2	.334	2.338	.420
	Academic performance	1.912	2	.956	21.733	.150
	learning strategy	.016	2	.008	.150	.877
	Teaching Preferences	.613	2	.306	39.007	.112

Table 5. t-test of personal characteristics factors with teaching preference and subject achievement

implicit variable	independent variable	F	Sig	t	df	Sig. (2-tailed)
Teaching Preferences	E/I	.810	.374	.762	39	.451
Academic performance	S/N	7.236	.010	1.007	39	.320
Academic performance	F/T	.869	.357	−.902	39	.373
Teaching Preferences	F/T	3.358	.075	−1.289	39	.205
Teaching Preferences	J/P	.288	.595	−1.607	39	.116
Teaching Preferences	Openness	.187	.668	−.488	39	.628

Finally, through the experimental results, we found that S/N has a significant effect on subject grades and F/T has a significant effect on subject preferences.

5 Discussion

5.1 Comparative Analysis of Three Field Independence/Field Dependence Measurement Tools in This Experiment

It can be seen through the analysis. The results of the mosaic graph test are far from the former two and are significantly higher, indicating that the mosaic graph test has some limitations and errors as a cognitive style measurement tool in this experiment. In Mengju Lu's "On the Limitations of the Field Independence/Field Dependence Measurement Tool Mosaic Graphics", it is mentioned that there are three flaws in the use of mosaic graphics as a field independence/field dependence cognitive style measurement tool. Next, we try to provide solutions to these three flaws by discussing the results of data analysis in this experiment.

The first flaw refers to the fact that whether mosaic graphing is a test of cognitive style, a test of cognitive ability, or something else is still widely debated. Cronbach (1990); cited in (Griffiths and Sheen 1992:147) argues that tessellations are a test of mind rather than a test of cognitive style; other researchers have argued that tessellations should be used in the visuospatial domain, with Vernon pointing out that tessellation scores correlate strongly with scores on other visuospatial tests, etc. In the experiments of this paper, the subjects are all from the same Chinese university, and the students enrolled in this university have excellent grades. As geometry is part of the math test, Chinese students get a lot of training in geometry from childhood, and the correlation is strong, and the overall scores are high, resulting in the mosaic graph test essentially becoming a learning test and losing the ability to measure field independence/field dependence. Second, Chinese education focuses much on test scores, and our students were already among the best of their Chinese peers, winning many exams and placing more emphasis on test scores, leading to the fact that in the experiment, the tessellated graph test was also viewed as a test of competence, resulting in the subjects working harder and more carefully to complete it. Therefore, the mosaic graphing test in this study is good evidence that the mosaic graphing test is in some cases an intelligence test, not a cognitive style test, and therefore the selection of the mosaic graphing test as a cognitive style test should be carefully considered in the context of the experiment when choosing a field-independent/field-dependent measurement tool [11].

The second flaw refers to the lack of an independent field-dependence measurement tool. This division is based on the conceptualization of field-independent/field-dependent cognitive styles as a continuum, with field independence at one end of the continuum and field dependence at the other. Field independence and field dependence are opposites that complement each other, and Skehan (1999:241) points out that the opposites of field independence or field dependence can be non-field independent or non-field dependent. Field independence and field dependence can be represented by two separate continua, with the poles of each continuum representing field independence and non-field independence, field dependence, and non-field dependence, respectively [11]. Cao, H. Y., and Zhou, S. L. (2004). A questionnaire was used to measure field independence/field dependence cognitive style instead of a mosaic graph to overcome the inadequacy of the mosaic graph as a field independence/field dependence measurement tool. In the data analysis, we found that the results of the bar-frame test and the results of the cognitive style questionnaire have a high degree of conformity, and to a certain extent, they can mutually verify their feasibility, while in the linear regression analysis, we found that the results of the bar-frame test cognitive style questionnaire and the T-value of the mosaic graphic test do not have any significant correlation, so it can be concluded that the mosaic graphic test is invalidated as a field-independence/field-dependence measurement tool in this experiment. The results of the stick-frame test were compared with those of the cognitive style questionnaire, and if the two performances were consistent, i.e., both were field independent or both were field dependent, they were retained; the remaining inconsistencies due to other factors were treated as unstable and discarded. In the end, 40 of the 50 samples were retained and 10 were discarded, with the number of samples discarded accounting for 20% of the total.

The third flaw refers to the fact that on mosaic graphing tests, the division between field independence and field dependence is based primarily on the level of scores, and people either fall into the field-independent or field-dependent category. A person may have two or more cognitive styles at the same time, but in a certain scenario, they will only exhibit one style that matches the occasion. To solve this problem, Yuncai Dai (2002) proposed to categorize people into four types of cognitive styles according to field-independent/field-dependent within a two-dimensional framework: i.e., strongly field-independent, and strongly field-dependent; weakly field-independent, and strongly field-dependent; weakly field-independent and weakly field-dependent; strongly field-independent and weakly field-dependent11. In this regard, the questions in our cognitive style questionnaire were designed as follows: questions 1–15 test field dependence, and questions 16–30 test field independence. High scores on questions 1–15 can be regarded as strong field dependence and vice versa; high scores on questions 16–30 can be regarded as strong field independence and vice versa. However, in the existing experiments, the Cognitive Style Questionnaire is often implemented in conjunction with the Group Embedded Figure Test and has not been used independently as a field independence/field dependence measurement tool. Regarding the use of the Cognitive Style Questionnaire as an independent measurement tool, it is necessary to analyze and prove it with more sample data.

5.2 Discuss the Correlations Between Personal Characteristics, Cognitive Style Characteristics, and Elements of Instructional Assessment

Analysis of Results of Multifactor ANOVA. By analyzing the results of the data through multifactor ANOVA, we found that there is a significant effect of age, E/I, F/T, J/P, self-confidence, & openness on teaching preference, S/N, and F/T people on subject achievement. To summarize the following discussion.

- *Age on Teaching Preferences*

In the sample of this experiment, the age of the subjects spanned from 17–23 years old, being in their youth and the middle of their college education, so in this experiment, the age difference also represents the length of time in college education, and therefore different grades in college may have a different focus on teaching preferences. In the detailed data, we found that younger students preferred to study together, while older students preferred to study alone. Perhaps this is because as students move into higher grades, they are typically exposed to deeper and more complex subject matter and need more focused, private study spaces to take in new knowledge.

- **E/I People's Preference for Teaching in MBTI**

E and I in MBTI stand for Extroversion and Introversion. These two types of people have significant differences in their teaching preferences. It is easier to understand that Extroverts (E) usually prefer more interactive teaching methods such as group discussions or hands-on activities. They enjoy interacting and collaborating with others and get energized by it. For Extroverts, interaction and discussion in the classroom stimulate learning and enhance memory and understanding. Introverts (I) prefer independent learning and deep thinking. They usually dislike too many distractions and noise and prefer to explore knowledge and problems alone. For introverts, solitude and quiet environments help them to focus, think deeply, and acquire knowledge better.

- **S/N Person-to-Discipline Scores on the MBTI**

The S (Sensing) and N (intuition) dimensions of the MBTI, which represent the two cognitive styles of real sense and intuition, have a significant effect on subject performance.

1. Realistic (S) people are more inclined to focus on and take in concrete things, and they tend to have a good memory for details and facts. In terms of subject matter, solid-sense (S) students may be better at subjects that require memorization and comprehension, such as geography and history, which require a great deal of detail and factual knowledge.
2. Intuitive (N) types are more concerned with abstractions and they are better at understanding and thinking about concepts and theories. In terms of subjects, intuitive students may be better at subjects that require logical reasoning and abstract thinking, such as math and physics, which require logical reasoning and conceptual understanding.

In addition, if students' S and N values are relatively balanced, the differences between subject grades will be less pronounced and the bias will not be as severe. This suggests that personality type preference is one of the important factors leading to subject bias. Therefore, understanding students' MBTI types can help teachers better guide students to choose suitable subjects and career paths. For practical students, teachers can encourage them to choose more subjects that require memorization and understanding; while for intuitive students, teachers can encourage them to choose more subjects that require logical reasoning and abstract thinking.

- **Preferences of J/P People for Teaching in MBTI**

The J (Judging) and P (Perceiving) dimensions of the MBTI, which represent judgmental and perceptual preferences, respectively, have a significant impact on teaching preferences. This influence is mainly in the areas of students' learning styles, learning goals, and expectations of the teaching environment.

1. Judgmental (J) students tend to learn in an organized and planned way. They like to set clear goals and plans before learning and follow them step by step. Judgmental (J) students tend to focus more on the practicality of learning, and they want to obtain practical results through learning. As a result, they may have a preference for teaching styles that are goal-oriented and well-organized.

2. Perceptual (P) students prefer flexible and free learning styles. They enjoy exploring and experimenting with new areas of learning and do not like to be constrained by fixed programs and goals. Perceptual (P) students tend to pay more attention to the process and experience of learning, and they believe that learning is a process of continuous exploration and discovery. Therefore, they may prefer teaching styles that provide opportunities for exploration and discovery when choosing teaching styles.

3. *Confidence Level in Teaching Preferences*

Self-confidence is an individual's perception of his or her abilities and values, and its impact on teaching preferences should not be overlooked. Students with high self-confidence tend to be more willing to actively participate in classroom activities and express themselves, whereas students with low self-confidence may be more inclined to passively accept knowledge and be reluctant to express themselves in classroom communication.

1. Confidence level affects students' preference for teaching methods. Students with high self-confidence prefer challenging teaching methods, such as group discussions and case studies, and they are willing to learn in cooperation and improve their cognitive level through discussions and exchanges. On the contrary, low self-confidence students may prefer traditional teaching methods, such as lecture-based teaching, because then they can absorb knowledge more safely without fear of being challenged or exposing their deficiencies.

2. Confidence level also affects students' choice of learning content. Students with high self-confidence are more willing to try new areas of learning and take on challenges, whereas students with low self-confidence may be more inclined to choose areas that they are familiar with or can easily master to maintain their sense of security.

3. Self-confidence also affects students' expectations of teachers. High-confidence students prefer teachers to guide them to think independently and develop their critical thinking, while low-confidence students may prefer teachers to give them clear guidance and feedback to help them better master their knowledge.

4. *Openness to Teaching Preferences*

Openness and closedness are individual attitudes toward the world and are important factors that influence teaching preferences. Open-minded individuals tend to accept new things and ideas and like to explore the unknown, while closed-minded individuals prefer to maintain the status quo and avoid trying the unknown.

1. Openness Students prefer creative and exploratory teaching methods. They are eager to learn new knowledge and ideas in the classroom and are willing to participate in

discussions and reflections in pursuit of deeper understanding and cognition. Open-minded students prefer teachers to guide them in independent learning and inquiry, encouraging them to challenge traditional thinking and discover new possibilities.
2. Closed-minded students prefer traditional and conservative teaching methods. They are more concerned with security and stability and do not like to take risks and try the unknown. In the classroom, they may be more willing to accept the knowledge imparted by the teacher than to actively participate in discussions and thinking. Closeted students prefer teachers to give clear learning objectives and guidance to help them gain a solid grasp of knowledge.

Results of T-test Analysis and Discussion.   The results of the multifactor ANOVA and t-test were combined for theoretical analysis and interpretation.

- *Theoretical Level Analysis*

1. Different Assumptions About Data Distribution:

Multifactor ANOVA usually assumes that the observed variable (dependent variable) is continuously and normally distributed. ANOVA is also relatively more lenient for small samples and less dependent on normality.

The t-test also has certain requirements for the normality of the data, especially if the sample is small. If the normality of the data is not satisfied, the results of the t-test may be unreliable.

1. Assumptions of Independence and Chi-square:

The t-test has more explicit requirements for independence and variance chi-square of the data. Independence means that the samples should be independent of each other, and chi-square requires that the variances of the data in different groups are equal.

Multifactor ANOVA is more lenient concerning these two assumptions, especially with larger sample sizes.

2. Sensitivity Differences:

Multifactor ANOVA is suitable for considering the effects of multiple factors on the dependent variable at the same time and is, therefore, more suitable for analyzing situations where multiple factors interact.

T-tests are mainly used to compare whether the means of two groups are significantly different, and may not be as flexible as multifactor ANOVA for simple comparisons.

- *Explanation:*

1. When the dependent variable was subject performance, there was a significant effect of S/N and F/T under a multifactor ANOVA, but only S/N was significant under a t-test. s/N (feeling and intuition) in the MBTI is more likely to influence a person's subject performance relative to f/T (feeling and thinking), which is related to the way an individual processes the subject content.

Sensory (S) individuals are usually more focused on concrete, practical information and tend to focus on details and actual experiences. In subject learning, they may be more likely to understand and grasp practical facts and concrete knowledge and adapt to traditional teaching methods and assessments. This makes them more consistent performers in subject examinations.

In contrast, F/T factors may appear less significant in subject performance. Subject performance of affective (F) and thinking (T) individuals may be more influenced by their interest in subject content, motivation, and learning strategies. F/T focuses on values and decision-making styles, which may be reflected more in subject choices and subjective evaluations of subject content than in direct determinations of knowledge acquisition.

Thus, the reason that the F/T factor appears to be less significant in subject achievement relative to S/N may be because subject achievement is more dependent on the understanding and mastery of practical knowledge, which is more influenced by sensory (S) and intuitive (N). At the same time, F/T may manifest itself more as an effect of subject choice and subject interest, which has less impact on specific subject achievement.

1. When the dependent variable was teaching preference, there was a significant effect of age, E/I, F/T, J/P, and openness under a multifactor ANOVA, while only F/T was significant under a t-test.

Emotions and thinking styles play an important role in teaching and learning. Emotional (F) individuals may focus more on interpersonal relationships and emotional experiences, tend to create a warm, supportive learning atmosphere, and pay more attention to students' emotional needs. Whereas thinking (T) individuals may place more emphasis on the systematic and objective nature of knowledge, pay more attention to logical analysis and rational thinking, and may place more importance on the structure and principles of subject knowledge.

In contrast, factors such as S/N, E/I, and openness to closure may have relatively little influence on teaching preferences. Sensing (S) and intuitive (N) individuals may not have clear preference in teaching preferences because teaching methods and environments may not be as significant to them as emotions and thinking styles. Similarly, extroverted (E) and introverted (I) individuals may be influenced in their teaching preferences by other factors, such as content and teaching methods, rather than just their social preferences. Openness and closeness also did not have a very significant effect on teaching preferences possibly because the methods emphasized in teaching are not directly related to openness and closeness of personality.

Therefore, affect and thinking styles may be more significant for individuals' teaching preferences because they are directly related to individuals' affective attitudes and thinking styles in teaching scenarios. In contrast, factors such as S/N, E/I, and openness-closeness may have relatively less influence on teaching preferences.

6   Conclusion

By comparing and analyzing the results of the data measured by the three field independence/field dependence measurement tools, namely, the Stick Frame Test, Group Embedded Figure Test, and the Cognitive Style Questionnaire, we can get that Group Embedded Figure Test fails to work as a field independence/field dependence measurement tool when the subjects have a higher level of education and better grades, while the Stick Frame Test and the Cognitive Style Questionnaire can be calibrated with each other to a certain degree, and the field independence/field dependence results can be more accurate by eliminating the data that do not match the measurement results. Data that do not match the measurement results to get sample data with more accurate field independence/field dependence results. However, the Cognitive Style Questionnaire is questionable as a stand-alone field independence/field dependence measurement tool, and more experiments are needed to analyze and investigate.

Through the data processing and analysis of personal characteristics multidimensionality, field independence/field dependence, and teaching methodology, it can be concluded that there is no significant effect between field independence/field dependence and teaching methodology, and the personal characteristics discussed in this paper do not have a significant effect on field independence/field dependence, but there is a significant effect of age, MBTI, self-confidence, and openness on teaching preference, where S/N (feeling and intuition) in MBTI has a significant effect on S/N (feeling and intuition) and F/T (feeling and thinking) in MBTI have a significant effect on academic performance, and F/T (feeling and thinking) has a significant effect on teaching preference, so educational practitioners should consider measuring the status of S/N (feeling and intuition) and F/T (feeling and thinking) of individual students, and try to tailor teaching to students' learning needs in combination with other aspects.

References

1. Fan, X., Guo, X.: Current status of research on second language cognitive style and implications for research on preschoolers' Chinese cognition. Lang. Translation **112**(04), 61–65 (2012)
2. Baidu Encyclopedia. Cognitive style [EB/OL], 7 March 2023. https://baike.baidu.com/item/CognitiveStyle/4298628
3. Murphy, H.I., Casey, B., Day, D.A., et al.: Scores on the group embedded figures test by undergraduates in information management. Percept. Mot. Skills **84**(3), 1135–1138 (1997)
4. Jiang, Y.: Impact of cognitive style on learning and its application. Jiangsu Educ. **96**, 52–54 (2017)
5. Wu, Y.: A study on the relationship between college students' learning strategies and field cognitive styles, learning styles, learning motivation, and academic achievement. Shaanxi Normal University, Xi'an (2004)
6. Fitriyani, H., Khasanah, U.: Student's rigorous mathematical thinking based on cognitive style. J. Phys. Conf. Ser. **943**, 012055 (2017)
7. Wei, Y.: Research on Differentiated Teaching of Middle School Physics Based on Field Cognitive Approach. Shanghai Normal University, Shanghai (2019)
8. Zhao, L.: Research on the Influence of Cognitive Style Differences on the Acquisition of Geography Core Literacy Among High School Students. Hunan Normal University, Changsha (2019)
9. Xie, S., Zhang, H.: Cognitive Styles: An Experimental Study of Personality Dimensions. Beijing Normal University Press, Beijing (1988)
10. Cao, H.-Y., Zhou, S.: A study on the efficiency of cognitive style and English learning performance. Jiangsu Foreign Lang. Teach. Res. **01**, 24–29 (2004)
11. Lu, M.: On the limitations of the field independence/field dependence measurement tool mosaic graph. Soc. Sci. **S2**, 333–334 (2006)

12. Firoz, M., Islam, M.M., Shidujaman, M., et al.: University student's mental stress detection using machine learning. In: Seventh International Conference on Mechatronics and Intelligent Robotics (ICMIR 2023), SPIE 2023, vol. 12779, pp. 757–767 (2023)
13. Song, X., Liu, M., Gong, L., et al.: A review of human-computer interface evaluation research based on evaluation process elements. In: International Conference on Human-Computer Interaction, pp. 262–289. Springer, Cham (2023)

Bridging Perspectives: Unveiling Racial Dynamics in Remote Pair Programming Communication

Shandler A. Mason$^{(\boxtimes)}$, Sanket Nain , and Sandeep Kaur Kuttal

North Carolina State University, Raleigh, NC 27606, USA
{samason4,snain,skuttal}@ncsu.edu

Abstract. Remote pair programming is a collaborative method in software development, yet a research gap exists concerning how race influences communication within these interactions. Our study is dedicated to unveiling communication dynamics between pairs, with a specific focus on Black developers, as their representation diminishes in the university-to-industry pipeline, where White developers constitute the majority. We recruited 24 US-based developers, both Black and White, forming 12 pairs. These pairs were equally distributed among same- and mixed-race compositions, between men and women. Employing the think-aloud method, each pair engaged in collaborative programming tasks, followed by independent retrospective interviews. Our results revealed that while mixed-race pairs were actively engaged in the task, they displayed the lowest frequency of happiness facial expressions, highlighting the intricate racial dynamics in communication. Our overarching goal is to gain insights into how communication is influenced by the perceived racial background of partners. This exploration is imperative for shaping the development of inclusive and empathetic collaborative software tools.

Keywords: Pair Programming · Race · Developers · Communication

1 Introduction

Effective collaboration is crucial for software development teams to produce high-quality products. A well-established, agile approach to collaboration is pair programming, where two developers work together to solve programming challenges. One developer assumes the role of the driver by typing code while the other takes on the role of the navigator by contributing ideas [83]. However, fostering seamless collaboration in pair programming poses greater challenges when the software team comprises individuals from diverse backgrounds [44].

Our study is dedicated to unveiling communication dynamics between pairs, with a specific focus on Black developers, as their representation diminishes in the university (20%) to industry (6%) pipeline [64]. In this context, we selected Black and White developers based on a complex history of interracial interactions, in the United States, which has led to differences in collaborative styles

© The Author(s), under exclusive license to Springer Nature Switzerland AG 2024
M. Kurosu and A. Hashizume (Eds.): HCII 2024, LNCS 14687, pp. 275–291, 2024.
https://doi.org/10.1007/978-3-031-60441-6_18

[73]. Beginning with the era of slavery, this intricate history has been marked by a legacy of racial injustices [60]. Today, disparities persist in wealth [1], education [8], and the penal system [32].

Currently, there is a gap in existing research, as no study has investigated how the perceived race of developers influences communication elements such as interruptions, non-verbal cues, and prompts during pair programming.

Pair programming requires collaboration among individuals from diverse backgrounds to solve tasks. The human brain harbors implicit biases which tend to shape stereotypes within the initial moments of meeting an individual [46]. Racial stereotypes may impact communication during collaboration. To investigate how race influences communication in pair programming among both same- and mixed-race pairs, we devised three research questions:

- **RQ1: How do participants' interruption frequencies differ between same- and mixed-race pairs during pair programming?**
- **RQ2: How do the non-verbal cues of participants in same-race pairs differ from those in mixed-race pairs during pair programming?**
- **RQ3: How do same- and mixed-race pairs exhibit different communication prompts during pair programming?**

Our study aimed to address these research questions by employing think-aloud lab studies and retrospective interviews. We created same- and mixed-race, gender-balanced pairs with 24 Black and White professional developers. We observed pairs communication as they utilized the think-aloud method to solve a programming challenge. Afterwards, we retrospectively interviewed participants to gain insight into their feelings and experience with their partner.

2   Background

2.1   Pair Programming

Pair programming is an agile methodology used by both students and professionals [33,76]. Pair programming involves two key roles: the driver and the navigator. The driver is responsible for writing code, managing the keyboard, and task execution, while the navigator focuses on error checking and strategy development [28,54,59]. Pairs can interchange roles throughout the collaborative process [84].

Remote pair programming mirrors the advantages and characteristics of in-person pair programming [35,39,47]. It utilizes software technologies to facilitate collaboration between developers across various geographical locations [81]. Given the global nature of the software development industry and the impact of COVID-19, remote work has become increasingly common in this field [4].

Pair programming offers various benefits, including heightened productivity, code quality, engagement, and communication [11,20,34,55,79]. Additionally, pair programming boosts developers' self-efficacy, fostering resilience in solving coding challenges [7,56,58].

However, pair programming may also present difficulties for partners, such as limiting individual discovery [82], diverting pairs from their goal [51], and causing tension [38] which negatively effects pair efficiency. Other challenges may arise such as the navigator struggling to make significant contributions to the task [61] and partners deviating from their assigned roles [16].

During pair programming communication, both professional and student pairs predominantly dedicate their time to discussing the problem [17] and implementing the code, with the navigator taking an active role in contributing to the discussion [77]. Pairs with mixed personalities exhibit enhanced communication [72], however higher conversational skill levels does not guarantee increased pair productivity [22].

2.2   Racial Dynamics in the United States

Race is a socially constructed label with a diverse range of accepted definitions [27]. Our study characterizes race as a multifaceted concept that includes an individual's personal identity, beliefs, environment, survey responses, and physical attributes [69]. Racial classifications like "Black or African American" and "White" are labels recognized in modern US society [43].

Slavery originated the complex relationship between Black and White individuals, in the US [13]. Legal disparities persisted through discriminatory practices including segregation laws [48] and socioeconomic limitations [12]. Societal inequalities are still prevalent today with lower college graduation rates for Black adults (22.5%) compared to their White (36%) counterparts [2], and a lower loan approval rate for Black borrowers (48%) compared to White borrowers (77%) [80].

Management research pertaining to workplace collaboration amongst diverse groups has found that a negative stereotype of individuals from different racial backgrounds can adversely impact group communication, ultimately limiting productivity [19]. In the workplace, Black individuals may face challenges such as diminished trust [63], stereotype threat [78], and concerns about discrimination [45]. These factors can contribute to heightened anxiety [14] and depression [42], potentially lowering overall workplace performance [30].

2.3   The Tech Industry Pipeline Problem

Complex racial dynamics, in the US, contributes to disparities in education that impact the tech industry. The under-representation of Black developers in the tech industry manifests early in education, spanning from K-12 through college and extending into the industry. Among fourth graders in 2019, Black students encountered an 18–25 point deficit in mathematics scores compared to White students [18]. At the high school level, Black students face less access to advanced STEM courses [8]. This disparity persists into higher education, in 2019, Black individuals earned only 9% of STEM Bachelor's degrees, despite constituting roughly 13% of the US population [18]. Within the tech industry, Black individuals hold just 7% of all computing-related occupations [65], while simultaneously facing wage disparities [25]. Strategies for fostering diversity, equity, and inclusion, at the educational and industrial levels, are essential to addressing the pipeline problem [6,52].

3 Methodology

3.1 Participants

We distributed a study flyer and description crafted without reference to race or gender to recruit participants through snowball sampling and online social media platforms including LinkedIn, Facebook, and Slack.

We employed a systematic screening questionnaire to select 24 developers. Our study participants were professionals or PhD students in a computing-related field, all possessing a minimum of a Bachelor's degree. Our study included participants who self-identified as either man or woman, Black or White, and who were born and spent their formative years in the US. The age range of participants spanned from 18 to over 40 years old. (21/24) held professional experience within the computing sector. Participants self-reported proficiency in programming languages including Java, Python, or C#.

We deliberately created 2 Black-Black, 2 White-White, and 2 Black-White pairs for men and women. We labeled each pair (P#-X#Y#), P# for pair number, X# for gender (M-Man, W-Woman), and Y# for race (B-Black, Wh-White) of the first or second participant.

3.2 Study Design

We used Zoom, a teleconferencing tool [5], to create a controlled study environment. We requested participants to maintain both their video and audio active throughout the study. We guided participants through a series of steps, including completing the consent form, the pre self-efficacy survey, and three instructive video tutorials covering pair programming, test-driven development [9], and think-aloud [53]. Additionally, participants observed a live demonstration of Replit [24], the collaborative development environment we used in our study. Participants were directed to apply these methodologies to both programming tasks.

To enhance pair jelling [50], participants engaged in a 10 min 'Simple Task' focused on checking password validation. For the 'Main Task', participants programmed the basic functionality of a Tic-Tac-Toe game for 40 min. Participants responded to post self-efficacy and pair programming questionnaires. Participants completed individual, semi-structured retrospective interviews held by a racially-matching interviewer to increase comfort levels [10]. We compensated participants with a $30 Amazon gift card in acknowledgment of their completion of our 1.5–2 h study.

3.3   Data Analysis

To address our research questions (RQs), we employed a combination of quantitative and qualitative analyses. For RQ1, we utilized `Pyannote.audio` [15] to examine videos recorded through Zoom's integrated functionalities. This analysis focused on detecting overlapped speech as an indicator of interruptions, with manual verification performed by our researchers. In addressing RQ2, the `Py-Feat` [21] library was employed to evaluate participants' facial expressions. The detector model assessed 6 emotions on a scale of 0 to 1, every 1,000 frames, identifying the dominant emotion for each interval. Our quantitative analysis of RQ1 and RQ2 involved descriptive statistical analysis such as mean and standard deviation.

For our qualitative analysis pertaining to RQ3, we utilized Zoom's integrated functionalities to capture participant utterances. These recordings were transcribed and segmented into individual utterances, with two researchers manually examining inaccuracies in the transcriptions. Each utterance was labeled with the corresponding timestamp, the speaker's label, their self-reported race and gender, and their pair programming role. Table 3 specifies the code set we used to code utterances. For RQ1, RQ2, and RQ3, we implemented thematic analysis to categorize and iteratively open-code developers' retrospective interview responses, aiming to identify relevant patterns [70]. We used the Jaccard measure to assess inter-rater reliability [41]. First, 20% of the transcripts were coded independently by two researchers, who reached agreement on 85% of the coded data. Then, for independent coding, the two researchers divided the remaining transcripts.

3.4   Limitations

We acknowledge that our study is subject to various limitations. The sample size, consisting of 8 same-race and 4 mixed-race pairs, may be considered small for making broad assumptions or performing quantitative comparisons. However, our study marks the initial stride into understanding race's possible influence on communication among professional developers during pair programming. Additionally, our focus was constrained to men and women, based on participants' self-reported gender, limiting the diversity of gender representation. Recruitment challenges, particularly in reaching individuals from marginalized groups such as Black men, Black women, and White women, extended the study duration to 6 months. It is important to emphasize that race is not the only factor contributing to our results, as other factors, including skill level, unique personalities, and awareness of diversity may have played a role. The programming task in our study, implementing a Tic-Tac-Toe game, is simple in comparison to the complexity of real-world programming tasks.

4   Results

4.1   RQ1: How Do Participants' Interruption Frequencies Differ Between Same- and Mixed-Race Pairs During Pair Programming?

An interruption is when one person begins to speak while another person's turn is ongoing [3]. Interruptions are associated with collaborative dominance [85], conversational attentiveness [57], and engagement during the task [74]. Our quantitative analysis compared interruptions overtime (refer to Fig. 1) and interruption frequencies, using descriptive statistical analyses (refer to Table 1), across three groups (4 - same-race (BB), 4 - same-race (WhWh), and 4 - mixed-race (BWh) pairs).

Mixed-race (BWh) pairs interrupted one another more frequently than same-race (BB) and (WhWh) pairs. Mixed-race (BWh) pairs encountered the most interruptions on average, but the total frequency for each pair was dispersed (Mean = 12.5; SD = 9.95), refer to Table 1. Mixed-race (BWh) pairs generally interrupted each other during the beginning (0–500 s) and middle (1000–1500 s) of the task, refer to green in Fig. 1. (4/8) participants in mixed-race (BWh) pairs reported feeling interrupted by their partners, which had a negative impact on their workflow. P12-W1B1 discussed the pairs frequent interruptions, *"[I felt interrupted] probably every 5 min. It felt kind of frequent and interruptions [were] not just me saying stuff, but [when I was] thinking about things."* This could indicate that mixed-race (BWh) pairs were engaged and wanted to be involved in task decisions [74].

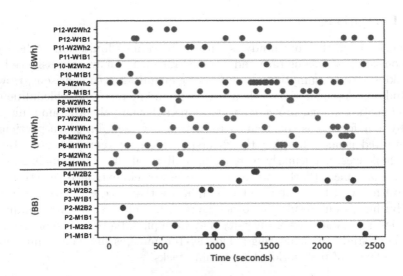

Fig. 1. Participants interruptions overtime (blue) same-race (BB) vs. (red) same-race (WhWh) vs. (green) mixed-race (BWh) pairs (Color figure online)

Same-race (BB) pairs exhibited the lowest frequency of interruptions between partners and the standard deviation suggests that the frequencies were relatively consistent across the pairs (Mean = 5.75; SD = 3.86), refer to Table 1. Same-race (BB) pairs typically interrupted each other during the middle (1000–1500 s) and end (2000-2500 s) of the task, refer to blue in Fig. 1. (6/8) same-race (BB) pair participants reported not experiencing interruptions from their partners. When asked about his perception of interruptions, P2-M1B1 stated, *"No, [I did not feel interrupted by my partner]. He was confident, which I have no problem with. If you feel like you could tackle the answer I don't have a personal problem with it."* This suggests that one partner in same-race (BB) pairs was not as attentive during the tasks [57].

In mixed-race (BWh) pairs, the driver interrupted more frequently, while in same-race (BB) and (WhWh) pairs, the navigator initiated more interruptions. In (3/4) mixed-race (BWh) pairs, the driver exhibited more interruptions, whereas in (5/8) same-race (BB) and (WhWh) pairs, the navigator had a higher frequency of interruptions. P4-W2B2 (the navigator in a same-race (BB) pair) validated the observed pattern, *"The interruptions [didn't work within the partnership] and I'm saying that as somebody that did most of the interruptions. I wish there was an easier way to do that. I feel like she was walking through the process out loud and then I would be like, 'Oh, I have an idea.' I don't think that worked very well."* The observed pattern in same-race (BB) and (WhWh) pairs aligns with a previous pair programming study, suggesting that the navigator typically initiates more interruptions [50], indicating a conversational dominance in this role.

Table 1. Mean and standard deviation (SD) of interruption frequencies for same-race (BB) vs. same-race (WhWh) vs. mixed-race (BWh) pairs

	Same-Race (BB)	Same-Race (WhWh)	Mixed-Race (BWh)
Mean	5.75	10.25	12.5
SD	3.86	5.85	9.95

4.2 RQ2: How Do the Non-verbal Cues of Participants in Same-Race Pairs Differ from Those in Mixed-Race Pairs During Pair Programming?

Facial expressions are a kind of non-verbal communication that can be used to relay a message or portray a feeling [31]. We quantitatively analyzed **anger, disgust, fear, happy, sad,** and **surprise** as the six standard displays of emotions [29] for each group (4 - same-race (BB), 4 - same-race (WhWh), and 4 - mixed-race (BWh) pairs).

Same-race (BB) pairs displayed the highest average frequency of anger, while same-race (WhWh) pairs displayed the lowest. Anger manifests through distinct facial cues, including furrowed eyebrows, raised upper

Table 2. Mean and standard deviation (SD) of facial expression (anger, disgust, fear, happy, sad, surprise) frequencies for same-race (BB) vs. same-race (WhWh) vs. mixed-race (BWh) pairs

		Anger	Disgust	Fear	Happy	Sad	Surprise
Same-Race (BB)	Mean	12	1.1	2.25	11.5	6.6	8.4
	SD	13.2	1.7	3.6	13.8	8.5	12.5
Same-Race (WhWh)	Mean	3.6	0.4	1.5	11.8	20.4	8.6
	SD	5.3	0.7	1.3	10.4	13.8	9.5
Mixed-Race (BWh)	Mean	7.9	1.8	1.1	8.5	17.1	5.3
	SD	8.9	2.6	1.1	9.7	16	8.6

eyelids, lifted lower eyelids and tightened lips [71]. This emotional response typically arises when an individual encounters obstacles or frustrations in achieving a desired goal [62]. Same-race (BB) pairs displayed the highest frequency of anger (Mean = 12), while same-race (WhWh) pairs demonstrated about one-third of that frequency (Mean = 3.6), refer to Table 2 and Fig. 2. The data for same-race (BB) pairs was disperse (SD = 13.2), which is attributed to same-race (BB) men pair participants being labeled with almost triple the frequency of anger (Mean = 17.8), then same-race (BB) women pair participants (Mean = 6.3). This discrepancy between Black men and women may stem from stereotypes perpetuated by AI and machine learning models when analyzing the faces of Black men, suggesting that they are more likely to be perceived as 'angry' [49].

In (3/4) same-race (BB) pairs, the navigator exhibited more anger than the driver which may be attributed to frustration or confusion. P1-M2B2 (the navigator in a same-race (BB) pair) articulated a challenge the pair faced with the programming syntax, *"The thing that didn't quite work well was when we were trying to figure out how to put in the nested for loop...it kind of put a damper on the time constraint."* The heightened expression of anger may be attributed to model stereotyping or pairs encountering programming obstacles while completing the tasks, emphasizing the intricacies involved in understanding pair programming communication.

Mixed-race (BWh) pairs displayed the lowest frequency of happy, while same-race (BB) and (WhWh) pairs illustrated the highest frequency. Happiness facial cues include tightened eyes, raised cheeks, and diagonally lifted lip corners [66]. This expression is observed when individuals experience success or receive praise [62]. Mixed-race (BWh) pairs displayed the lowest frequency of happy (Mean = 8.5), whereas both same-race (BB) pairs (Mean = 11.5) and same-race (WhWh) pairs (Mean = 11.8) demonstrated a nearly equal, higher frequency (refer to Table 2 and Fig. 2). P12-W1B1 delved into possible reasons behind the lack of happiness facial expressions in mixed-race (BWh) pairs, *"I did not like it [pair programming]. It just irritated me.*

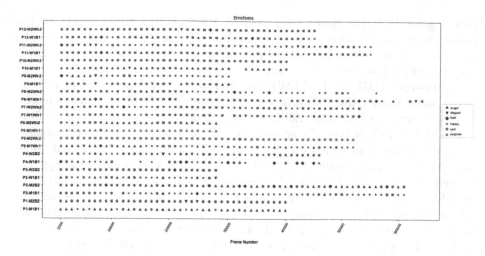

Fig. 2. Participants facial expressions overtime (every 1,000 frames) for same-race (BB) vs. same-race (WhWh) vs. mixed-race (BWh) pairs

[I decided] I'm not trying to hurt her feelings. So I'm just gonna let this happen." Mixed-race (BWh) pairs possibly felt hesitant or uneasy about expressing themselves during the task.

In (5/8) same-race (BB) and (WhWh) pairs the driver exhibited a greater number of **happy** compared to the navigator. P6-M2Wh2 (the driver in a same-race (WhWh) pair) attributed his happiness to his proficiency with the programming language, *"I code daily. So I decided to be the driver. I guess it's primarily to avoid the syntax hurdles and to be able to focus more on the problem rather than battling the code writing itself."* Same-race (BB) and (WhWh) pairs likely experienced higher comfort levels while collaborating, with the driver displaying happiness expressions in an authoritative leadership role, while the navigator assumed a laid-back approach.

Same-race (BB) pairs exhibited the lowest frequency of sad, while same-race (WhWh) pairs exhibited the highest. Sadness is expressed on the face through down-turned eyes and drooping lip corners [66]. Sadness occurs when an individual experiences lack of an anticipated outcome [62]. Same-race (BB) pair participants exhibited the lowest frequency of **sad** (Mean = 6.6), refer to Table 2 and Fig. 2. P1-M2B2 (P1 was a same-race (BB) pair) shed light on the cause of a lower frequency of **sad**, *"I think we collaborated very well. He was very easy to talk to, very easy to work with."* This could indicate that same-race (BB) pairs favored pair programming.

Conversely, same-race (WhWh) pairs exhibited the highest frequency of **sad** (Mean = 20.4), refer to Table 2 and Fig. 2. In (3/4) same-race (WhWh) pairs the driver had more **sad** expressions than the navigator. The same-race (WhWh) women pair participants had roughly double the frequency of **sad** (Mean = 28) compared to same-race (WhWh) men pair participants (Mean = 12.8). This suggest a gender-related effect in our results. P8-W1Wh1 offered insight to the factor contributing to her sadness, *"I don't think I performed well during pair programming, so I don't know that I [would] do it again."* The elevated sadness may indicate a lower self-efficacy while pair programming.

Same-race (BB) and (WhWh) pairs had the highest number of surprise facial expressions compared to mixed-race (BWh) pairs. Surprise is visually conveyed through raised eyebrows, open eyes, and horizontal forehead wrinkles [66]. It typically arises from abrupt activity, unexpected satisfaction, or heightened awareness [62]. Same-race (BB) pairs (Mean = 8.4) and same-race (WhWh) pairs (Mean = 8.6) exhibited the highest frequency of `surprise`, whereas mixed-race (BWh) pairs showed the lowest frequency (Mean = 5.3), refer to Table 2 and Fig. 2. P12-W1B1, from a mixed-race (BWh) pair, shared insight into her reasoning for restricting communication during the tasks, *"If I was more comfortable with her I probably would have said [more] because we all have one goal to try to get this stuff done. I feel like when working with [other] Black students they don't see me [a certain] way and so I feel more okay to [say], hey, can we do this? Let's try this."* Mixed-race (BWh) pairs possibly experienced lower comfort levels, with their partners, resulting in less expressiveness during the programming tasks.

Table 3. Total frequency of communication prompts for same-race (BB) vs. same-race (WhWh) vs. mixed-race (BWh) pairs

Communication Prompts	Definitions	Same-Race (BB)	Same-Race (WhWh)	Mixed-Race (BWh)
"I" Success Statement	Attributing successes to themselves	2	0	1
"I" Mistake Statement	Taking ownership for their mistakes	7	6	5
"We" Success Statement	Attributing successes to the pair	4	1	5
"We" Mistake Statement	Attributing mistakes to the pair	4	1	3
Apology	A regretful acknowledgment of failure	20	30	22

4.3   RQ3: How Do Same- and Mixed-Race Pairs Exhibit Different Communication Prompts During Pair Programming?

Communication prompts are used to build better connections and enhance interpersonal ties [36]. Conversational agents' ability to comprehend dialogue can be improved by understanding communication prompts [68]. Table 3 is the code set we used to label utterances, which was adapted from Robe et al. [67].

Same-race (WhWh) pairs apologized more frequently (30 instances) than same-race (BB) pairs (20 instances) and mixed-race (BWh) pairs (22 instances), refer to Table 3. Apologies serve as a strategic way to rebuild trust [26]

and repair relationships [23] during conflict. Same-race (WhWh) pairs accepted responsibility for mistakes and apologized for failures, but did not credit themselves or the pair with success, refer to Table 3. For example, P6-M1Wh1 apologized to P6-M2Wh2 for his Java knowledge gap, *"Are we checking the third [character] there? I'm sorry. My Java is rusty."* Apologies were potentially used by same-race (WhWh) pairs to build trust during collaboration.

Mixed-race (BWh) and same-race (BB) pairs attributed their success and failure to the group, while same-race (WhWh) pairs did not acknowledge their progress as a collective. "We" statements, are associated with enhanced problem-solving [75]. "We" statements were prevalent among mixed-race (BWh) pairs (5 success; 3 mistake) and same-race (BB) pairs (4 success; 4 mistake), in contrast to same-race (WhWh) pairs (1 success; 1 mistake), refer in Table 3. P10-M1B1, from a mixed-race (BWh) pair, emphasized effective collaboration as a key factor contributing to completing the task, *"What worked well was that we had decent synergy. We sort of found out what we were both good at. I know that I'm good at developing a plan before we go ahead and try to execute versus P10-M2Wh2 was very great hopping into the code."* Mixed-race (BWh) and same-race (BB) pairs possibly encountered heightened problem-solving during the programming tasks.

5   Discussion

We embark on the first step to bridge perspectives between Black and White developers within both same- and mixed-race pairs, aiming for an understanding of how race may influence communication in the context of pair programming. Mixed-race (BWh) pairs displayed a higher frequency of interruptions (RQ1), the lowest average of **happy** facial expressions, and were the least expressive in conveying **surprise** (RQ2). Additionally, they attributed both success and failure to the pair (RQ3). In the context of same-race (BB) pairs, they exhibited the lowest rate of interruptions (RQ1), demonstrated **happy**, had the lowest average of **sad**, and expressed **surprise** (RQ2). They attributed both success and failure to the pair (RQ3). In the context of same-race (WhWh) pairs, there was a prevalence of both **happy** and **sad**, along with a high occurrence of **surprise** (RQ2). They did not attribute success or failure to the pair, and had the highest frequency of apologies (RQ3). P3-W1B1 emphasized the critical role of facial expressions and its impact on pair programming interactions, *"If [my partner is] frowning, I'm gonna get a little bit smaller and not talk as much. If [they are] receiving and smiling I [feel like] they're actually listening to what I'm saying and they care. I think that can also play an effect into how I navigate and lead, just based off of how [my partner] is feeling in that moment which can affect my coding output."* Recognizing the importance of facial expressions during collaboration extends to the broader context of communication as a fundamental component within global software development teams. Communication plays a critical role in facilitating the efficient development of software products [37].

Moreover, implicit bias may impact communication during collaboration. When sharing her workplace experiences while collaborating with individuals from different racial groups, P3-W1B1 stated, *"[It's] a little bit more difficult, because you have to feel around the vibe of the person a little bit more. You have to toggle certain things on and off whether that be slang, or how you talk, or just little inserts. So I do think if I was doing the same program with a White guy I may have not joked as much. I would have tried to refrain from maybe even thinking aloud [to] keep it more concise."*

Our study results underscore the potential benefits of developing an empathetic facilitator agent designed to promote inclusive collaboration within both same- and mixed-race pairs. Facilitator agents are software systems crafted to aid users in identifying and resolving challenges [40]. Detectable elements such as interruptions, facial expressions, and communication prompts can be monitored by facilitator agents. By tracking these aspects, the agent has the potential to offer encouraging feedback to individuals during collaboration, thereby enhancing the overall experience and facilitating cohesive collaboration. This implication aligns with our goal of bridging perspectives between two developers to foster greater synergy.

6   Conclusion

Our study marks an initial approach, in Human-Computer Interaction (HCI) and Software Engineering (SE), to delving into communication between same- and mixed-race pairs of developers engaged in remote pair programming. We employed a blend of quantitative and qualitative methods, to identify key findings:

- **RQ1 (Interruptions):** Mixed-race (BWh) pairs exhibited the highest frequency of interruptions, while same-race (BB) pairs demonstrated the lowest.
- **RQ2 (Non-verbal Cues):** Mixed-race (BWh) pairs demonstrated reduced happiness, in contrast to same-race (BB) and (WhWh) pairs who showcased peak happiness and surprise.
- **RQ3 (Communication Prompts):** Mixed-race (BWh) and same-race (BB) pairs credited success to their collaboration.

Our findings highlight potential complexities of racial dynamics in pair programming communication. To address communication challenges, we aim to contribute to the creation of inclusive facilitator agents to enrich technology and collaboration.

Acknowledgements. This material is based upon work supported by the Air Force Office of Scientific Research under award number FA9550-21-1-0108 and National Science Foundation under award numbers IIS-2313890 and CCF-2006977. Any opinions, findings, and conclusions or recommendations expressed in this material are those of the authors and do not necessarily reflect the view of the NSF and AFOSR. Finally, we would like to thank Raphael Phillips for his assistance in labeling the data.

References

1. https://ips-dc.org/wp-content/uploads/2019/01/IPS_RWD-Report_FINAL-1. 15.19.pdf
2. https://www.census.gov/content/dam/Census/library/publications/2016/demo/ p20-578.pdf
3. Adamczyk, P.D., Bailey, B.P.: If not now, when? The effects of interruption at different moments within task execution. In: Proceedings of the SIGCHI Conference on Human Factors in Computing Systems, pp. 271–278 (2004)
4. Ågren, P., Knoph, E., Berntsson Svensson, R.: Agile software development one year into the COVID-19 pandemic. Empir. Softw. Eng. **27**(6), 121 (2022)
5. Archibald, M.M., Ambagtsheer, R.C., Casey, M.G., Lawless, M.: Using zoom videoconferencing for qualitative data collection: perceptions and experiences of researchers and participants. Int J Qual Methods **18**, 1609406919874596 (2019)
6. Asare, J.G.: Google's 2019 diversity report reveals more progress must be made, April 2019. https://www.forbes.com/sites/janicegassam/2019/04/07/googles-2019-diversity-report-reveals-more-progress-must-be-made/?sh=77eb81a03bef
7. Bandura, A.: Social Foundations of Thought and Action: A Social Cognitive Theory. Prentice-Hall Series in Social Learning Theory. Prentice-Hall, Upper Saddle River (1986). https://books.google.com/books?id=HJhqAAAAMAAJ
8. Barton, P.E.: Parsing the achievement gap: Baselines for tracking progress. Policy Information Report (2003)
9. Beck, K.: Test Driven Development: By Example. Addison-Wesley Professional, Boston (2022)
10. Bergen, N., Labonté, R.: "Everything is perfect, and we have no problems": detecting and limiting social desirability bias in qualitative research. Qual. Health Res. **30**(5), 783–792 (2020)
11. Bipp, T., Lepper, A., Schmedding, D.: Pair programming in software development teams - an empirical study of its benefits. Inf. Softw. Technol. **50**(3), 231–240 (2008). https://doi.org/10.1016/j.infsof.2007.05.006
12. Boccard, N., Zenou, Y., et al.: Racial discrimination and redlining in cities. Technical report, Université catholique de Louvain, Center for Operations, Research & Econometrics (1999)
13. Bogen, D.S.: From racial discrimination to separate but equal: the common law impact of the thirteenth amendment. Ohio Northern Univ. Law Rev. **38**(1), 3 (2023)
14. Bosson, J.K., Haymovitz, E.L., Pinel, E.C.: When saying and doing diverge: the effects of stereotype threat on self-reported versus non-verbal anxiety. J. Exp. Soc. Psychol. **40**(2), 247–255 (2004)
15. Bredin, H., et al.: Pyannote. audio: neural building blocks for speaker diarization. In: ICASSP 2020-2020 IEEE International Conference on Acoustics, Speech and Signal Processing (ICASSP), pp. 7124–7128. IEEE (2020)
16. Bryant, S.: Double trouble: mixing qualitative and quantitative methods in the study of extreme programmers. In: 2004 IEEE Symposium on Visual Languages-Human Centric Computing, pp. 55–61. IEEE (2004)
17. Bryant, S., Romero, P., du Boulay, B.: The collaborative nature of pair programming. In: Abrahamsson, P., Marchesi, M., Succi, G. (eds.) XP 2006. LNCS, vol. 4044, pp. 53–64. Springer, Heidelberg (2006)
18. Burke, A., Okrent, A., Hale, K., Gough, N.: The state of us science & engineering 2022. National Science Board Science & Engineering Indicators. nsb-2022-1. National Science Foundation (2022)

19. Campion, M.A., Papper, E.M., Medsker, G.J.: Relations between work team characteristics and effectiveness: a replication and extension. Pers. Psychol. **49**(2), 429–452 (1996)
20. Celepkolu, M., Boyer, K.E.: Thematic analysis of students' reflections on pair programming in cs1. In: Proceedings of the 49th ACM Technical Symposium on Computer Science Education. SIGCSE '18, pp. 771-776. Association for Computing Machinery, New York, NY, USA (2018). https://doi.org/10.1145/3159450.3159516
21. Cheong, J.H., Jolly, E., Xie, T., Byrne, S., Kenney, M., Chang, L.J.: Py-feat: Python facial expression analysis toolbox. Affect. Sci. 1–16 (2023)
22. Choi, S.: "Better communication leads to a higher output?" An analysis of pair communication on pair programming productivity. IEEE Trans. Prof. Commun. **64**(4), 338–353 (2021)
23. Coombs, W.T., Holladay, S.J.: Comparing apology to equivalent crisis response strategies: clarifying apology's role and value in crisis communication. Publ. Relat. Rev. **34**(3), 252–257 (2008)
24. Cooper, S., Clinkscale, B., Williams, B., Lewis, M.: Exploring the impact of exposing CS majors to programming concepts using ide programming vs. non-ide programming in the classroom. In: Proceedings of the 51st ACM Technical Symposium on Computer Science Education, pp. 1422–1422 (2020)
25. Dake, A.: 2020 state of salaries report: salary benchmarks and talent preferences, September 2022. https://hired.com/blog/highlights/2020-state-of-salaries-report/
26. De Greiff, P.: The role of apologies in national reconciliation processes: on making trustworthy institutions trusted. In: The Age of Apology: Facing Up to the Past, pp. 120–134 (2008)
27. Delgado, R., Stefancic, J.: Critical Race Theory: An Introduction, vol. 87. NyU Press, New York (2023)
28. Dybå, T., Arisholm, E., Sjøberg, D., Hannay, J., Shull, F.: Are two heads better than one? On the effectiveness of pair programming. Software. IEEE **24**, 12 – 15 (2007). https://doi.org/10.1109/MS.2007.158
29. Ekman, P., Sorenson, E.R., Friesen, W.V.: Pan-cultural elements in facial displays of emotion. Science **164**(3875), 86–88 (1969)
30. Feagin, J.R., McKinney, K.D.: The Many Costs of Racism. Rowman & Littlefield Publishers, Lanham (2005)
31. Gallaher, P.E.: Individual differences in nonverbal behavior: dimensions of style. J. Pers. Soc. Psychol. **63**(1), 133 (1992)
32. Gramlich, J.: The gap between the number of blacks and whites in prison is shrinking, April 2019. https://www.pewresearch.org/short-reads/2019/04/30/shrinking-gap-between-number-of-blacks-and-whites-in-prison/
33. Gregory, P., Lassenius, C., Wang, X., Kruchten, P.: XP 2021. LNBIP, vol. 426. Springer, Cham (2021). https://doi.org/10.1007/978-3-030-88583-0
34. Han, K.W., Lee, E., Lee, Y.: The impact of a peer-learning agent based on pair programming in a programming course. IEEE Trans. Educ. **53**, 318 – 327 (2010). https://doi.org/10.1109/TE.2009.2019121
35. Hanks, B.: Student performance in CS1 with distributed pair programming. ACM SIGCSE Bull. **37**(3), 316–320 (2005)
36. Hartley, P.: Interpersonal Communication. Routledge (2002)
37. Herbsleb, J.D., Mockus, A.: An empirical study of speed and communication in globally distributed software development. IEEE Trans. Softw. Eng. **29**(6), 481–494 (2003)
38. Howard, E.V.: Attitudes on using pair-programming. J. Educ. Technol. Syst. **35**(1), 89–103 (2006)

39. Hughes, J., Walshe, A., Law, B., Murphy, B.: Remote pair programming. In: 12th International Conference on Computer Supported Education, pp. 476–483. SciTePress (2020)
40. Ikeda, Y., Shiramatsu, S.: Generating questions asked by facilitator agents using preceding context in web-based discussion. In: 2017 IEEE International Conference on Agents (ICA), pp. 127–132. IEEE (2017)
41. Jaccard, P.: Etude de la distribution florale dans une portion des alpes et du jura. Bull. de la Societe Vaudoise des Sci. Naturelles **37**, 547–579 (1901) .https://doi.org/10.5169/seals-266450
42. Jackson, P.B., Thoits, P.A., Taylor, H.F.: Composition of the workplace and psychological well-being: the effects of tokenism on America's black elite. Soc. Forces **74**(2), 543–557 (1995)
43. Jensen, E.: Measuring racial and ethnic diversity for the 2020 census, June 2022. https://www.census.gov/newsroom/blogs/random-samplings/2021/08/measuring-racial-ethnic-diversity-2020-census.html
44. Joshi, A., Roh, H.: The role of context in work team diversity research: a meta-analytic review. Acad. Manag. J. **52**(3), 599–627 (2009)
45. Kaiser, C.R., Miller, C.T.: Stop complaining! the social costs of making attributions to discrimination. Pers. Soc. Psychol. Bull. **27**(2), 254–263 (2001)
46. Kaplan, S.: Scientists show how we start stereotyping the moment we see a face, May 2016. https://www.washingtonpost.com/news/speaking-of-science/wp/2016/05/02/scientists-show-how-we-start-stereotyping-the-moment-we-see-a-face/
47. Kaur Kuttal, S., Gerstner, K., Bejarano, A.: Remote pair programming in online CS education: investigating through a gender lens. In: 2019 IEEE Symposium on Visual Languages and Human-Centric Computing (VL/HCC), pp. 75–85 (2019)
48. King, R.S.: Jim crow is alive and well in the 21st century: felony disenfranchisement and the continuing struggle to silence the African-American voice. Souls **8**(2), 7–21 (2006)
49. Kyriakou, K., Kleanthous, S., Otterbacher, J., Papadopoulos, G.A.: Emotion-based stereotypes in image analysis services. In: Adjunct Publication of the 28th ACM Conference on User Modeling, Adaptation and Personalization, pp. 252–259 (2020)
50. L. Jones, D., D. Fleming, S.: What use is a backseat driver? A qualitative investigation of pair programming, pp. 103–110, September 2013
51. Lemov, D.: Teach Like a Champion: 49 Techniques that Put Students on the Path to College (K-12). Wiley, Hoboken (2010)
52. Lev-Ram, M.: Apple commits more than $50 million to diversity efforts. Fortune (2015)
53. Lewis, C.H.: Using the "thinking aloud" method in cognitive interface design. RC 9265, IBM (1982)
54. Mcdowell, C., Werner, L., Bullock, H., Fernald, J.: The impact of pair programming on student performance, perception and persistence, pp. 602– 607 (2003). https://doi.org/10.1109/ICSE.2003.1201243
55. Mcdowell, C., Werner, L., Bullock, H., Fernald, J.: The effects of pair-programming on performance in an introductory programming course, vol. 34, pp. 38–42 (2002). https://doi.org/10.1145/563340.563353
56. Mcdowell, C., Werner, L., Bullock, H., Fernald, J.: Pair programming improves student retention, confidence, and program quality. Commun. ACM **49**, 90–95 (2006). https://doi.org/10.1145/1145293
57. Murata, K.: Intrusive or co-operative? A cross-cultural study of interruption. J. Pragmat. **21**(4), 385–400 (1994)

58. Nosek, J.: The case for collaborative programming. Commun. ACM **41** (1998). https://doi.org/10.1145/272287.272333
59. Oviatt, S., Cohen, P.: Perceptual user interfaces: multimodal interfaces that process what comes naturally. Commun. ACM **43**(3), 45–53 (2000). https://doi.org/10.1145/330534.330538
60. Pinel, E.C.: Stigma consciousness: the psychological legacy of social stereotypes. J. Pers. Soc. Psychol. **76**(1), 114 (1999)
61. Plonka, L., Sharp, H., Van Der Linden, J.: Disengagement in pair programming: does it matter? In: 2012 34th International Conference on Software Engineering (ICSE), pp. 496–506. IEEE (2012)
62. Plutchik, R.: The Emotions. University Press of America (1991)
63. Purdie-Vaughns, V., Steele, C.M., Davies, P.G., Ditlmann, R., Crosby, J.R.: Social identity contingencies: how diversity cues signal threat or safety for African Americans in mainstream institutions. J. Pers. Soc. Psychol. **94**(4), 615 (2008)
64. Rankin, J.L.: Learning to code isn't enough, April 2023. https://www.technologyreview.com/2023/04/20/1071291/learn-to-code-legacy-new-projects-education/amp/
65. Riccucci, N.M.: Managing Diversity in Public Sector Workforces. Routledge, London (2021)
66. Rinn, W.E.: The neuropsychology of facial expression: a review of the neurological and psychological mechanisms for producing facial expressions. Psychol. Bull. **95**(1), 52 (1984)
67. Robe, P., Kuttal, S.K.: Designing pairbuddy - a conversational agent for pair programming. ACM Trans. Comput.-Hum. Interact. **29**(4) (2022). https://doi.org/10.1145/3498326
68. Rodríguez, F.J., Price, K.M., Boyer, K.E.: Exploring the pair programming process: characteristics of effective collaboration. In: Proceedings of the 2017 ACM SIGCSE Technical Symposium on Computer Science Education, pp. 507–512. ACM (2017)
69. Roth, W.D.: The multiple dimensions of race. Ethn. Racial Stud. **39**(8), 1310–1338 (2016)
70. Seaman, C.B.: Qualitative methods in empirical studies of software engineering. IEEE Trans. Softw. Eng. **25**, 557–572 (1999)
71. Sell, A., Cosmides, L., Tooby, J.: The human anger face evolved to enhance cues of strength. Evol. Hum. Behav. **35**(5), 425–429 (2014)
72. Sfetsos, P., Stamelos, I., Angelis, L., Deligiannis, I.: Investigating the impact of personality types on communication and collaboration-viability in pair programming-an empirical study. In: Abrahamsson, P., Marchesi, M., Succi, G. (eds.) XP 2006. LNCS, vol. 4044, pp. 43–52. Springer, Heidelberg (2006). https://doi.org/10.1007/11774129
73. Shelton, J.N.: Interpersonal concerns in social encounters between majority and minority group members. Group Process. Intergroup Relat. **6**(2), 171–185 (2003)
74. Sidner, C.L., Lee, C., Kidd, C.D., Lesh, N., Rich, C.: Explorations in engagement for humans and robots. Artif. Intell. **166**(1–2), 140–164 (2005)
75. Simmons, R.A., Gordon, P.C., Chambless, D.L.: Pronouns in marital interaction: what do "you" and "I" say about marital health? Psychol. Sci. 16(12), 932–936 (2005)
76. Sommerville, I.: Software Engineering, 9th edn. Addison-Wesley, Harlow (2010)
77. Stapel, K., Knauss, E., Schneider, K., Becker, M.: Towards understanding communication structure in pair programming. In: Sillitti, A., Wang, X., Martin, A., Whitworth, E. (eds.) XP 2010. LNBIP, vol. 48, pp. 117–131. Springer, Heidelberg (2010). https://doi.org/10.1007/978-3-642-13054-0

78. Steele, C.M.: A threat in the air: how stereotypes shape intellectual identity and performance. Am. Psychol. **52**(6), 613 (1997)
79. Sun, W., Marakas, G., Aguirre-Urreta, M.: The effectiveness of pair programming: software professionals' perceptions. IEEE Softw. **33**(4), 72–79 (2015)
80. Tolan, C., Ash, A., Marsh, R.: The nation's largest credit union rejected more than half its black conventional mortgage applicants – CNN business, December 2023. https://www.cnn.com/2023/12/14/business/navy-federal-credit-union-black-applicants-invs/index.html
81. Tsompanoudi, D., Satratzemi, M., Xinogalos, S., Karamitopoulos, L.: An empirical study on factors related to distributed pair programming. April 2019. https://www.learntechlib.org/p/208576
82. Voss, J.L., Gonsalves, B.D., Federmeier, K.D., Tranel, D., Cohen, N.J.: Hippocampal brain-network coordination during volitional exploratory behavior enhances learning. Nat. Neurosci. **14**(1), 115–120 (2011)
83. Williams, L., Kessler, R.R., Cunningham, W., Jeffries, R.: Strengthening the case for pair programming. IEEE Softw. **17**(4), 19–25 (2000)
84. Williams, L.A., Kessler, R.R.: All I really need to know about pair programming I learned in kindergarten. Commun. ACM **43**(5), 108–114 (2000). https://doi.org/10.1145/332833.332848
85. Youngquist, J.: The effect of interruptions and dyad gender combination on perceptions of interpersonal dominance. Commun. Stud. **60**(2), 147–163 (2009)

Evolution of the Beautiful Game: Analytics and Virtual Reality

Pranav Parekh[✉] and Richard O. Oyeleke

Stevens Institute of Technology, Hoboken, NJ 07030, USA
{pparekh5,ooyeleke}@stevens.edu

Abstract. Soccer (or Football) has become increasingly technical with the times, with the birth of new formations and new player positions. Technology use could grant teams an edge in reaching their maximum potential. The following research study intends to analyze the evolution of soccer with modern computer science technology like Machine Learning (ML) and Virtual Reality (VR). We establish a use-case to predict the most suitable position of a player concerning his initial skillset. This would allow coaches better to categorize a player through physiology and game awareness. On route to our predictions, we discuss various soccer simulations that players use for training and evaluate each simulation based on interaction fidelity. We develop the first-ever VR simulation that trains defenders with tactical drills focused on making interceptions. We also use different ML models to study the difference in predictions and how appropriate the ML model is for such a problem.

Keywords: Soccer · VR Simulations · Machine Learning · Fidelity

1 Introduction

"Beauty is an option for art...but it is not an option for life. It is a necessary condition for life as we would want to live it." The following quote from [1] elaborates on the essential human need to appreciate beauty. Friedrich Schiller defines beauty as a necessary utopian ideal that translates to a deep desire for harmony and balance in our lives [2]. The game of soccer, also eulogized as football or futbol, and widely renowned as the "The Beautiful Game", instills these ideals into our lives. Virtues within the game include self-control, generosity, a sense of fair play and determination. Every game played or observed is a moment in search of perfection: the perfect pass, the perfect tackle, the perfect goal, the perfect save, the perfect victory, or the perfect display of sportsmanship. Acquiring what you hope for is a moment of pure bliss every soccer fan has felt while playing or watching it [3].

Apart from being beautiful to watch, soccer has been pivotal in producing moments that can inspire us. The 1914 Christmas truce in which soldiers of England and Germany fraternized to play soccer depicted World War I as a tragic and futile conflict [4]. The hate crimes in Merseyside dropped by 16%,

M. Kurosu and A. Hashizume (Eds.): HCII 2024, LNCS 14687, pp. 292–308, 2024.
https://doi.org/10.1007/978-3-031-60441-6_19

and anti-Muslim tweets were reduced by 50%. A survey by [5] showed that the support towards Mo Salah enabled positive feelings towards the broader group of Muslims present there. The stories of numerous soccer players are inspirational since many come from poorer backgrounds, and they challenge these odds after rigorous practice to make it to the top. One such story that stood out for me was that of Lionel Messi. Throughout his career, he faced challenges that tested his determination and belief. Before his career even began, it turned out that Messi would require medical treatment to grow normally due to the deficiency of the growth hormone. Due to this, he was rejected by all the major clubs in Argentina, and at a very young age, he had to leave home to go to Barcelona [6]. Throughout his career, his mentality with the national team was criticized, and some journalists even termed him a "fraud who neglected his international duties". After a career that spanned 16 years, Lionel Messi won the World Cup with Argentina, a trophy that had eluded him in 4 previous world cups. Throughout his journey, he faced numerous heartbreaks with the national team, but the story of his success, in the end, teaches us never to give up on our dream.

Soccer is the most researched sport, with the first research paper published in 1947 [7]. Soccer research includes match analysis, detection of behavioral patterns of players, positional analysis, improvement of physiology for soccer, etc. With the introduction of new technology, there have been enhancements in the sport. The game relies greater on positional play and physique. Special diets and workout schedules have been created for soccer players [8]. Currently, it is common practice in soccer to rely on pundits for appropriate game assessment. In recent times, there has been significant interest in analytics to improve the overall quality of the team. In soccer analytics, machine learning (ML) and deep learning (DL) methods have previously been used to assign player ratings and predict match outcomes [9]. For this manuscript, we intend to use machine learning methods to predict player positions based on their attributes.

This brings us to how these attributes are calculated and input within the machine learning models to give us the required label. Virtual Reality (VR) allows for the complete immersion of the user within an interactive and simulated environment. VR has attracted much interest as a training solution since it allows complete and repeatable control over the training drill [10]. A simulation enhances the training experience by providing adaptive difficulty [11], controlling feedback [12], and varying task constraints [13]. We rate the players and their corresponding attributes through different drills simulated on the VR headset. These attributes are input within the machine learning models for analytics. For the real-world transfer of a VR training drill, we require two measures: validity and fidelity. Fidelity is the extent to which a simulation reproduces the behavior of real-world systems [14]. Validity is the degree to which the simulation accurately represents the core features of the task [15]. We study the VR Soccer Simulators and rate them for their ability to collect these attributes according to these two measures.

2   Literature Review

In this section, we shall assess the individualistic physiological and physical requirements for soccer and how a particular player is deemed a good fit within a playing system. We study the use of VR and ML to improve physiology and introduce analytical tools that can be used to analyze a player when he plays within a formation.

2.1   Individualistic Physical and Physiology Attributes During Soccer

It has been studied previously that characteristics like the percentage of body fat, maximal oxygen uptake (VO2 max), strength, repeated sprint ability (RSA), muscle power and endurance greatly influence the position and playing level of a soccer player [16]. During a 90-min game, elite players usually run up to 10 km at an average intensity close to the anaerobic threshold. However, this varies from position to position. Midfielders and fullbacks require high endurance levels to maintain pace at a constant level. On the other hand, goalkeepers usually need to run the least during a game. Apart from endurance, numerous explosive bursts of activity are required, like jumping, tackling, sprinting, passing, shooting, etc. Maximal strength and power are essential for affecting performance during these bursts. Maximal strength is the highest force a neuromuscular system can perform during a voluntary contraction. In contrast, power refers to the ability of the neuromuscular system to produce the greatest possible impulse in a given period [17]. A good level of maximal strength also helps avoid injuries in soccer.

Soccer has traditionally been quick to embrace technology since coaches and teams want to gain a competitive edge over their rivals. Recent research depicts VR technology in sports and physical exercise to improve sports performance and provide enjoyment during exercise [18]. Numerous VR applications are used for endurance training through activities like running [19], rowing [20] and cycling [21]. VR training has also been influential in the development of muscle strength and improvement in balance, especially for older adults [22]. Such exercises can also be extended to soccer to develop calf muscles, thighs and ankle strength.

ML has been influential in sports in analyzing the athlete's attributes microscopically. Regarding physiology, ML is not highly useful in providing environments that can be used for direct development. However, studies show that ML is helpful for injury risk assessment. [23] reviews several studies that are machine learning applications with an emphasis on injury risk in soccer. The paper by [24] used an ML-based approach to predict sprint performance and aerobic features using anthropometric features. On the other hand, a study by [25] performed movement analysis of the players by predicting their turn direction and speed during a game. A Recommender System has also been implemented to recommend the nutrition aspiring soccer players require to improve their strength and stamina [26].

2.2 Tactical Attributes and Playing Within a Formation

The starting formation in soccer refers to how the 10 outfield players are organized on the pitch. They are typically defined by 3 or 4 numbers specifying the number of players in each pitch segment. For example, the 4-4-2 formation comprises 4 defenders, 4 midfielders and 2 attackers [27]. Formations may also change during the game, depending on the number and quality of the substitution and the game's flow. Formations also determine the offensive or defensive mindset of the team. For example, a formation like 5-3-1 employs 5 defenders, making it a defensive formation. Table 1 discusses a few formations that managers have used tactically.

To prepare for modern football, coaches and players must develop tactical creativity and in-game decision-making [28]. Visual Exploratory Abilities (VEA) is the in-game skill required to make accurate judgments and react effectively to unfolding events [29]. Researchers have pondered the need for technologies to investigate player movements and their VEA in open-play situations [30]. The study by [29] developed a VR simulation that improved player passing decisions and reaction to pressure from rivals. They created various in-game passing situations from coaching manuals as practice drills.

Executive Functions (EFs) refer to the cognitive abilities of the players to make appropriate situational decisions. Training these EFs causes an increase in Soccer IQ, thereby establishing better chemistry within a certain formation as a whole [31]. The Bundesliga club TSG 1899 Hoffenheim uses the Helix technology to train and analyze the EFs of first-league soccer players. The Helix application provides two game modes, one for the coach and one for the players. The coach selects the game settings before starting the game. The players need to make decisions and play according to the settings done by the coach. The issue with the application is that the coach presets the configurations of a particular gameplay which could be more interactive and adaptable. To improve upon this, CortexVR provides a VR simulation of adaptable soccer gameplays. Apart from this, they offer more choices of game modes and settings, further enhancing the players' executive functions [32].

Machine Learning is commonly used due to its predictive capabilities for predicting match outcomes and league winners [33]. However, ML research is now being done to understand tactical orientations within a game better [34]. [35] used reinforcement learning to analyze game situations and player positions with a higher potential for successful attacks. [36] provided a measure for the efficiency of different tactical patterns while scoring a goal. Using the heatmaps of the pass locations as features, they reduced the problem to a classification task with labels denoting 'goal' or 'not a goal'. ML can also establish player rankings within a game, giving the coach an idea of where the team as a whole could be lacking [37]. Now that we have reviewed how each field performs in soccer, we intend to use them to enhance the soccer experience and make better decisions.

Table 1. Summary of suggested ML models pertaining to each case study

Formation Name	Type	Strength	Weakness	History
2-3-5 or the 'the pyramid'	highly attacking	Very attack-oriented; possible to score a lot of goals	Horrible defensive setup; cannot be used currently	The first formation, which was used in Britain after the codification of the game
The W-M or 3223	Attacking but central	It serves as a good balance between attack and defense since players are evenly distributed on both ends of the pitch	Fairly central; does not use the width of the pitch effectively	Developed by Arsenal manager Herbert Chapman after the introduction of the offside rule
The 4-2-4	Attacking	Can be successful if they have high work rate midfielders	Can easily be overrun in the midfield due to fewer players	Began initially in Brazil and Hungary. Pep Guardiola's Barcelona in 2009/10 was highly successful with this formation
The 4-4-2	Slightly Defensive	Highly simple and very effective if each player understands his role	Can suffer from a lack of passing options during attacking transitions	Viktor Maslov first developed it. It was very successful for the AC Milan team during 1980's and 1990's
The 4-3-3	Balanced	Used to control the game well, with a lot of passing options to wingers as well as the midfielders	Midfielders need to be very disciplined and wingers need to track back to help their fullbacks while defending	Johan Cruyff brought considerable success to both Ajax and Barcelona by using this formation
The 4-2-3-1	Slightly attacking variation of 4-3-3	More flexibility in attack than 4-3-3	Less stability in the midfield compared to 4-3-3 and is more vulnerable from wider areas	Introduced during the 2000's and was prominent among several teams
The 3-4-3	Highly Attacking	Allows you to dominate possession well, along with sufficient attacking options up field	Defenders can get over-run and pulled out of position easily	It is a modern football formation and was used by Pep Guardiola quite successfully at Bayern Munich
The 5-3-2 or Back 3 Defensive formation	Highly Defensive	Solidarity at the defense and can launch devastating counterattacks through efficient fullbacks	Difficult to create chances and highly dependent on the fullbacks	Used efficiently by Antonio Conte at Chelsea. They had a great defensive backline and played beautifully on the counter through Fabregas

3   Attribute Calculation Through Simulations

Step 1 of this Soccer analytics study calculates the attributes we want to feed into our ML model. The attributes that we want to rate are:

- Attacking Attributes: Dribbling, Shooting, Pace, Heading
- Midfielder Attributes: Long Passing, Short Passing, Vision
- Defending Attributes: Defending
- Physiological Attributes: Stamina

  Before we proceed further, we discuss a few considerations:

- Each player is scored based on the attributes calculated from the VR simulations described.
- We are concerned with how each simulation performs and propose physical methods to evaluate the fidelity of the simulation.
- We want to look at soccer from a strategic point of view. Therefore, each attribute score calculated is focused on the intuitive ability of the player. This approach is considered because the user is wearing a bulky headset within the simulation. Therefore, performing at the same pace as the game could damage the headset and the player.
- For measuring pace and stamina, we use non-simulation physical methods that do not require the user to wear their headset.

3.1   The Used VR Simulations

Currently, numerous VR soccer training simulations are available in the market. They consist of different modules and focus on distinct areas of soccer. We have developed one such module that focuses on defending and gives us the corresponding score. This has been done since there are no available simulations that allow defensive tactical training for soccer. The other simulations that we have used are Rezill, Incisive Clean Sheet, and Be Your Best. Each of the simulations and modules is discussed in this section:

- **Rezill:** Despite being the most popular game in the world, we do not have a complete soccer simulation in VR. This is mainly due to tracking limitations and a lack of space to replicate the continuous movements in soccer. Rezill remedies that to a certain extent by provision of realism that has not been achieved before. However, Rezill focuses on improving attacking attributes like Shooting, Dribbling and Heading. We consider heading in an attacking sense since the scoring module includes heading into the goal. They consist of several shooting modules that test how accurate and powerful the user's shots are toward the goal. The dribbling module consists of restricted movement around practice cones since it is not safe to replicate actual dribbles within a VR simulation.

  Leg tracking is a significant requirement for Rezill, which also takes a bit of getting used to. They have an endless mode where we can dribble, shoot and pass freely. They have multiple finishing challenges from different positions and targets, timed at 30, 60 and 90 s intervals. The simulation is heavily based on physics and actual kicking power comes into play. Short direction is affected by where and how we hit the ball. The evaluation section discusses the interaction fidelity and other simulation metrics for the simulation.

- **Incisive Clean Sheet:** CleanSheet is a revolutionary VR goalkeeping technology designed for goalkeepers to make critical margin gains in their performance by improving their positioning and perceptions. Initial positioning is improved by testing the goalkeeper's stance based on where the shot is coming from. The standard drill is to have shots struck at them at different paces and targets so that they can perceive the incoming strike and react accordingly. They offer two packages, one for professional purposes and the other for recreational. The professional package provides profiling for a particular user with stats accumulated for some time so that improvements can be recorded. The attributes of kicks and wall placement can also be done manually, allowing the user to practice against a particular type of free kick or penalty. The features that we collect from the simulation are GK Positioning and GK Diving.

- **Be Your Best:** This simulation has been created to replicate game scenarios often encountered during professional matches. We can play through professional game scenarios from the player's perspective at any particular position. At a point in the game, we get the ball and test our awareness. With the ball in our possession, the players must scan for movements frequently and pick up moments to make the right pass. The simulation gives us personal stat tracking, position-specific training and improved vision and decision-making. Scanning is an essential soccer skill, especially for good chemistry within the team. A critical scan refers to looking at the next pass while receiving the ball. This particular simulation is used to score the vision attribute.

- **Personal Module:** This personal module has been created by us for scoring the defending attribute. We use the Football Game Engine Asset to provide us with the fields and player animations required for this module's functioning. The Asset gives us multiple game objects for the general functioning of the game placed within the "PersistentGameObject". For example, the "MatchManager" controls the match while the "TimeManager" controls time within the game. The Asset provides us with game functions using different tactics objects. For example, the Defend Tactics object consists of functions like the name, push-back ratio, tight press frequency, and so on.

We establish statistical defending within the game by setting up Player Support Spots. The support spots are points on the pitch where players query to find the point that allows the controlling player to pass to him. During an attack, players will find the points on the pitch that are safe for the controlling player to pass to. We used this idea in the Asset to create a scenario for the defending players. During a defensive strategy, players try to find points on the pitch where the attackers could play the ball, to perform an interception. For setting up the player spots, the algorithm is as follows:

- Step 1: Create a player support spot prefab by creating a cube, removing the box collider and adding a support spot of the controlling entity.
- Step 2: We need multiple support spots for the game to work. We create another empty game object called "PlayerSupportSpots", and add all underlying spots as child nodes within this object.
- Duplicate the player support spots and place them around the pitch. In this scenario, the ball will move from one spot to another, and the controller entity (defender) needs to intercept the ball.

The functioning of the game in a 2D manner on Unity is shown in Fig. 1.

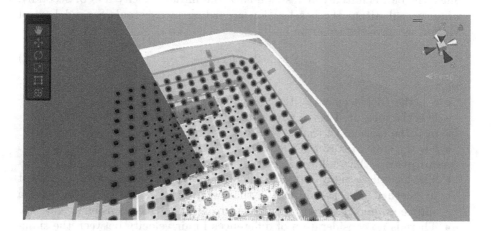

Fig. 1. Personal module support spots

3.2 Simulation Evaluation Using Interaction Fidelity

In the introduction, we have defined validity and fidelity and discussed its importance in evaluating simulations. Concerning soccer, just one study has proposed a method for testing the validity of a certain soccer-specific VR simulator [10]. They test the construct validity through division into three categories of soccer players according to their skill level, i.e., novice, academy and professional players. They used the Rezill simulation in which they were asked to perform 4 soccer drills based on passing accuracy, reaction time, composure and adaptability. Results showed that the VR platform could differentiate the participants based on their skill level, somewhat supporting the concept of construct validity.

On the other hand, the paper by [38] divides fidelity into two types: interaction fidelity and display fidelity. Offering high levels of fidelity increases realism, wherein a simulation with high-display, high-interaction fidelity is similar to the real world. Larger displays, higher resolutions and faster refresh rates have increased display fidelity. We are concerned with interaction fidelity in our scenario since we want to replicate the displacement caused by a specific force on the ball from the real world onto the simulation. We propose an experiment for the calculation of the same.

- **Aim:** To propose using physics to quantify the interaction fidelity for soccer simulations.
- **Requirements:** Force sensors, a soccer ball, an open field, a football simulator like Rezill, a stopwatch, a soccer player.
- **Formulation:** We use the following formula -

$$S = u * t + 1/2 * a * t^2 \tag{1}$$

Since the ball is initially at rest, we have the initial velocity u = 0. Secondly, when we substitute the acceleration according to Newton's Second Law of Motion we have the equation -

$$S = 1/2 * (F/m) * t^2 \tag{2}$$

where,
  - S is the Displacement of the Soccer ball
  - F is the measured Force with which the ball is struck
  - m is the mass of the ball
  - t is the time of travel of the ball
- **Assumptions:** The following are the assumptions for the experiment
  - The formula is used for calculating a simple ground pass from one point to another. The assumption is that whatever calculation is done for a simple ground pass can be extended to all other mechanisms in soccer.
  - There is no consideration of differences in air velocity between the simulation and open field
  - We do not require the whole formula in the experiment. It is important to note that according to Eq. 2 *Displacement is directly proportional to the Force*
  - We measure displacement in terms of the unit foot of the player involved. Since we have the same player for both scenarios, no inaccuracy is caused.
- **Methodology:** The methodology for the experiment is as follows
  - The player is asked to pass the ball within the VR simulation (Rezill). We note down the force applied to the ball via the force sensor, say F.
  - He/she is asked to walk towards the ball in a per-foot manner. We note down the displacement in terms of his/her foot.
  - The player is asked to pass the ball in the open field. We note down the force applied to the ball again.
  - If the force recorded is approximately near that of the simulator (F' $\cong$ F), we again note down the displacement in terms of his/her foot.
  - If not, the player is asked to re-kick the ball with an approximate force closer in value to that of the simulator. Making the force equal in both scenarios, we note the difference in displacement in both cases.
- **Conclusion:** We can study the results and conclude that a smaller difference between the two displacement values proves that the simulation has high interactive fidelity, making it more similar to a real game scenario.

3.3   Calculation of Physiological Attributes

The two main physiological attributes we are concerned with calculating are Pace and Stamina. Power and endurance are concealed skills that every soccer player must develop. These are the tools that enable the player to put up consistent performances game after game. VR headsets are usually bulky and can restrict movement, making the accurate calculation of these two attributes difficult. Therefore, we resort to physical means for their calculation.

- **Pace**: For Pace, we use the simple physical formula of Speed = Distance/ Time. A player is asked to run for a fixed distance of 100 m. The player's time is recorded, giving us both variables within the formula. As discussed in the related works section, we consider pace as bursts of power generated within the athlete. In athletic terms, we want to record the player's sprinting speed which is an essential attribute for wingers and fullbacks. We are not concerned with how long the player maintains his pace; that falls under the second physiological attribute.
- **stamina**: For this attribute, we are concerned with the question, "How long can the player keep up his pace?". We have calculated the sprint speed s in the previous segment. We now measure the distance the player maintains with their high speed. We use the same formula for time; Time = Distance/Speed. We redo the drill by decreasing the pace and calculating the time taken by the player in this scenario. We calculate the stamina attribute based on his endurance while maintaining constant speed in both cases.

3.4   Attribute Score Conversion

We use distinct conversion methods for VR simulator attributes and physiological attributes.

- **VR Simulator Attributes:** Each Virtual Reality simulator has a distinct scoring system. We require a common denominator of each simulator score to feed a generalized score into the learning model. Since most of the attributes within the Fifa dataset are scored out of 130, we perform conversions of a particular simulator score x using the formula:

$$x' = x * (130/T) \tag{3}$$

where,
- x' is the converted output score
- x is the input score within the simulator
- 130 is the maximum score from the Fifa Dataset
- T is the maximum score that can be acquired in the simulator

- **Physiological Attributes:** Physiological attributes are indirect skills that determine the player's position. Therefore, we use them as categorical variables within the dataset, where each label covers a range of values as measured above. Since the Fifa Dataset consists of Pace attribute scores out of 130, we use the following conversion chart to convert it to scores out of 10:

- 121 to 130: 10
- 111 to 120: 9
- 101 to 110: 8
- 91 to 100: 7
- 81 to 90: 6
- 71 to 80: 5
- 61 to 70: 4

No Fifa players have a pace lower than 60; therefore, we do not require labels under 4.

4   Role of the Machine Learning Models

Now that we have the collected attributes from the simulations, we predict the best probable position of the player using ML models. We implement many models since we want the most accurate output possible. The models include:

- Linear classifiers: Logistic Regression and SVM
- Non-linear classifiers like the Multilayer Perceptron (MLP)
- Probabilistic Models: Gaussian Naive Bayes and Multinomial Naive Bayes
- Ensemble Methods: XGBoost and AdaBoost

4.1   The Dataset

Before we discuss the model outputs, we must establish the dataset collected and used by us. We collect data from the Fifa Mobile Game World Cup 2022 event. They have several attributes for each player; however, we are concerned with the attributes that are scored by the simulations mentioned above. Therefore, we train the model on the attributes mentioned above, making them essential for deriving the output label. The dataset consists of 12 features, one output and 314 data points. We drop the player's name from our dataset since it is an unimportant parameter that does not affect the label output. The important parameters include the nine attributes collected by VR simulations (mentioned above) and the two physiological attributes (pace and stamina) The scoring conversions for both attributes have been discussed in the "Attribute Calculation" section. We have six output labels that the model can classify the features into:

- 0 - Striker (ST), Centre forward (CF)
- 1 - Central Midfielder (CM), Central Defensive Midfielder (CDM)
- 2 - Centre Back (CB)
- 3 - Goalkeeper (GK)
- 4 - Winger (RW or LW depending on preferred foot)
- 5 - Fullback (RB or LB depending on preferred foot)
- 6 - Wide Midfielder (RM or LM depending on preferred foot)

4.2   Model Description

We implement and evaluate a wide range of models since we want a clear distinction as to which model is effective for the created dataset. We do so using the scikit-learn Python library that provides us with modules and functions used for creating and evaluating each model. We select models having contrasting features to study how efficient they are for the unbalanced dataset.

The linear classifiers used are logistic regression and Support Vector Machines (SVM). Logistic regression is a probabilistic model that models the probability that a given input belongs to a particular class. It uses a linear decision boundary [39]. On the other hand, the SVM is deterministic by nature, creating a hyperplane that best separates the two sets of data. It is primarily used for linear decision boundaries, but using kernel functions, it can be extended to creating non-linear decision boundaries [40]. Since the dataset is of multiple classes, we can use two strategies for their classification:

- One-versus-one (OVO): A separate classifier is trained on a pair of classes. Therefore, computing for the seven classes in the dataset would require 21 independent linear classifiers. It is appropriate for a smaller dataset since it is computationally expensive [41].
- One-versus-rest (OVR): A separate classifier is trained for each class against all the other classes. For seven classes, we would require 7 independent classifiers. Each classifier gives a confidence score; the class with the highest confidence score is chosen for the final prediction [42].

The MLP is a feedforward neural network used for non-linear classifications. They consist of three layers of interconnected nodes: the input layer, the hidden layer, and the output layer. Each node in one layer is interconnected to the other layer. Information flows forward layer by layer to calculate loss, then backpropagates to optimize the resulting loss. They are computationally expensive as compared to linear classifiers [43].

Naive Bayes is a probabilistic algorithm that works on Bayes' theorem in probability. It works on the "naive" assumption that all features are independent [44]. It uses Bayes' theorem to predict the likelihood of the output labels for a given set of features. Multinomial Naive Bayes (MNB) is suitable for discrete data, while Gaussian Naive Bayes is well suited for continuous data (GNB). Intuitively, GNB should perform better than MNB since our dataset is of discrete nature.

Ensemble models combine multiple weak learners to create a powerful classifying model. The Extreme Gradient Boost (XGBoost) and Adaptive Boosting algorithm (AdaBoost) are examples of such ensemble methods. The XGBoost builds an ensemble of decision trees sequentially, with each new tree correcting the errors of the previous ones. The XGBoost has efficient parallel processing, making it scalable and faster than other boosting implementations [45]. On the other hand, the AdaBoost assigns weights to data points and trains the weak learners accordingly. The decision trees are the baseline algorithm for this model as well. They are computationally efficient but are highly vulnerable to overfitting and outliers. We shall study how each model has performed in the Results section [46].

5   Results and Conclusions

In this section, we would like to evaluate the results from our testing pipeline. We highlight how the different models have performed based on a given input data point. We then evaluate the different outputs acquired along the testing pipeline.

5.1   Model Evaluation

Table 2. Model Evaluation

Model	Max. F1	Corr. Label	Min. F1	Corr. Label	Accuracy
LR OVR	0.98	2	0.15	6	0.80
LR OVO	0.98	2	0.53	6	0.83
SVM OVR	1.00	2	0.53	6	0.83
SVM OVO	1.00	2	0.53	6	0.83
MLP	1.00	2	0.14	4	0.80
' GNB	0.98	2	0.35	6	0.76
MNB	1.00	2	0.47	6	0.82
XGBoost	0.98	2	0.38	6	0.78
AdaBoost	0.93	3	0.00	4,6	0.63

For model evaluation, we generate the classification report for each model we use on the test dataset. The classification report consists of the precision, recall, f1-score and accuracy. Precision indicates how often the ML model is correct when indicating a target class, while recall denotes whether the model finds all objects of the target class. The harmonic mean of both values gives us the f1-score, the collective evaluation measure when considering both quantities. The accuracy tells us how the model works overall and does not consider just the target class. We shall be consider both these entities when deciding which model to use for the problem statement.

Table 2 displays the maximum and minimum F1 scores for a given model and the corresponding target labels. The accuracy is independent of the target label and is a singular value for each model. The following conclusions are drawn from the following table:

- The SVM model would be considered the best choice since it has the highest accuracy.

- Target labels 4 and 6 have been the most difficult to classify since all models have the lowest F1-score for these labels. However, SVM performs better than the other models in detecting the labels.
- The ensemble method, AdaBoost works poorly for such a limited dataset since it becomes highly prone to overfitting.

5.2 The Testing Pipeline

To test the efficiency of the experiment, we invited a Stevens Graduate soccer player to play the required drills on the different simulations; his current position in the team was unknown. We also perform the physiological tests required to attain the stamina and pace attributes. As discussed in the Methodology section, we convert all the scores from the simulations and tests. The following were the scores and converted scores for the corresponding attributes. Note that the converted scores are rounded to the nearest integer and included in Table 3.

Table 3. Testing Pipeline

Attribute	Simulation Used	Actual Score	Converted Score
Dribbling	Rezzil	62/100	81
Shooting	Rezzil	31/100	41
Long Passing	Rezzil	64/100	83
Short Passing	Rezzil	67/100	87
Vision	Be Your Best	45/100	59
Defending	Personal module	65/100	84
Heading	Rezzil	51/100	66
GK Diving	Incisive Clean Sheet	0	0
GK Positioning	Incisive Clean Sheet	0	0
Stamina	None	7/10	7
Pace	None	8/10	8

For this example, we know that the player is an outfield player (not a goalkeeper). Therefore, we need not use the Incisive Clean Sheet simulation for calculating his actual score, since we consider it zero. We do not use any VR simulation for Stamina and Pace since they are calculated using endurance tests. As seen in Table 3, We have the converted scores that we can input within our SVM model for predicting the player's position. Using our SVM, we get the output target label "5" which is the Fullback position. When asked about the experience and corresponding output, it was revealed that he was a left-back within the 4-3-3 structure of the team. Therefore, this system was successful in predicting this particular test case.

6   Drawbacks and Future Scope

The major drawback of using such a system comes with the health issues of a VR simulation. Excessive VR can affect our eyes and lead to eye damage over time. It is possible to feel dizziness and uneven body movements within the headset. Playing soccer within a simulation while wearing the headset can also hurt our neck and posture. The headset's weight was a major drawback when we set up the experiment with our soccer player. We performed one drill per day so that he would be unfazed by the simulations and could perform to his best. Although the weight was a drawback, all simulations were on the same headset, nullifying the effect on the received output. VR simulations can also prove to be quite addictive, especially since there are specific targets to achieve within the training drills. The developed system should be considered an accessory to complement the beautiful sport meant to be played in the open.

The following system is fairly theoretical since it has been experimented on a single player. We need to expand this among a larger group of soccer players to increase trust in the experiment. Apart from this, we would also need to consult coaches on how such a system could be applied alongside their tactics. We would need insight from coaches on how they can use this to determine the position of a player that they are not familiar with. We could also expand the module we created using Unity and develop a user game from its current prototype. The finished version could be sold in VR Asset stores to users who want to improve their defending skills. Improvement in all three aspects is essential for using this method in practical playing and coaching settings.

References

1. Danto, A.C.: The abuse of beauty. Daedalus **131**(4), 35–56 (2002)
2. Schiller, F.: Kallias or concerning beauty: letters to Gottfried Körner (1793). In: Classic and Romantic German Aesthetics, pp. 145–83 (2003)
3. Winston, J.: "An option for art but not an option for life": beauty as an educational imperative. J. Aesthetic Educ. **42**(3), 71–87 (2008)
4. Bajekal, N.: Silent night: the story of the World War I Christmas truce of 1914. Time Mag. (2014)
5. Marble, W., Mousa, S., Siegel, A.A.: Can exposure to celebrities reduce prejudice? The effect of Mohamed Salah on islamophobic behaviors and attitudes. Am. Polit. Sci. Rev. **115**(4), 1111–1128 (2021)
6. Trejo, S.M.F., Williams, J.: 'One hell of a player' the social construction of the early career of Lionel Messi: towards a sociological analysis. Soccer Soc. **21**(3), 356–370 (2020)
7. Kirkendall, D.T.: Evolution of soccer as a research topic. Prog. Cardiovasc. Dis. **63**(6), 723–729 (2020)
8. Clark, K.: Nutritional guidance to soccer players for training and competition. J. Sports Sci. **12**(sup1), S43–S50 (1994)
9. Kumar, G.: Machine learning for soccer analytics. University of Leuven (2013)
10. Wood, G., Wright, D.J., Harris, D., Pal, A., Franklin, Z.C., Vine, S.J.: Testing the construct validity of a soccer-specific virtual reality simulator using novice, academy, and professional soccer players. Virtual Reality **25**, 43–51 (2021)

11. Gray, R.: Transfer of training from virtual to real baseball batting. Frontiers Psychol. (2017). 2183
12. Sigrist, R., Rauter, G., Marchal-Crespo, L., Riener, R., Wolf, P.: Sonification and haptic feedback in addition to visual feedback enhances complex motor task learning. Exp. Brain Res. **233**, 909–925 (2015)
13. Lammfromm, R., Gopher, D.: Transfer of skill from a virtualreality trainer to real juggling. In: BIO Web of Conferences, vol. 1, p. 00054. EDP Sciences (2011)
14. Burdea, G.C., Coiffet, P.: Virtual Reality Technology. Wiley (2003)
15. Gray, R.: Virtual environments and their role in developing perceptual-cognitive skills in sports. In: Anticipation and Decision Making in Sport, pp. 342–358. Routledge (2019)
16. Slimani, M., Nikolaidis, P.T.: Anthropometric and physiological characteristics of male Soccer players according to their competitive level, playing position and age group: a systematic review. J. Sports Med. Phys. Fitness **59**(1), 141–163 (2017)
17. Stølen, T., Chamari, K., Castagna, C., Wisløff, U.: Physiology of soccer: an update. Sports Med. **35**, 501–536 (2005)
18. Neumann, D.L.: On the use of virtual reality in sport and exercise: applications and research findings. Int. J. Comput. Res. **23**(3), 273 (2016)
19. Yoo, S., Kay, J.: VRun: running-in-place virtual reality exergame. In: Proceedings of the 28th Australian Conference on Computer-Human Interaction, pp. 562–566, November 2016
20. Shoib, N.A., Sunar, M.S., Nor, N.N.M., Azman, A., Jamaludin, M.N., Latip, H.F.M.: Rowing simulation using rower machine in virtual reality. In: 2020 6th International Conference on Interactive Digital Media (ICIDM), pp. 1–6. IEEE, December 2020
21. Song, C.G., Kim, J.Y., Kim, N.G.: A new postural balance control system for rehabilitation training based on virtual cycling. IEEE Trans. Inf Technol. Biomed. **8**(2), 200–207 (2004)
22. Sadeghi, H., et al.: Effects of 8 weeks of balance training, virtual reality training, and combined exercise on lower limb muscle strength, balance, and functional mobility among older men: a randomized controlled trial. Sports Health **13**(6), 606–612 (2021)
23. Nassis, G., Stylianides, G., Verhagen, E., Brito, J., Figueiredo, P., Krustrup, P.: A review of machine learning applications in soccer with an emphasis on injury risk. Biol. Sport **40**(1), 233–239 (2023)
24. Bongiovanni, T., et al.: Importance of anthropometric features to predict physical performance in elite youth soccer: a machine learning approach. Res. Sports Med. **29**(3), 213–224 (2021)
25. Zago, M., Sforza, C., Dolci, C., Tarabini, M., Galli, M.: Use of machine learning and wearable sensors to predict energetics and kinematics of cutting maneuvers. Sensors **19**(14), 3094 (2019)
26. Banerjee, A., Nigar, N.: Nourishment recommendation framework for children using machine learning and matching algorithm. In: 2019 International Conference on Computer Communication and Informatics (ICCCI), pp. 1–6. IEEE, January 2019
27. Mesoudi, A.: Cultural evolution of football tactics: strategic social learning in managers' choice of formation. Evol. Hum. Sci. **2**, e25 (2020)
28. Bjurwill, C.: Read and react: the football formula. Percept. Mot. Skills **76**(3 suppl), 1383–1386 (1993)

29. Rojas Ferrer, C.D., Shishido, H., Kitahara, I., Kameda, Y.: Read-the-game: system for skill-based visual exploratory activity assessment with a full body virtual reality soccer simulation. PLoS ONE **15**(3), e0230042 (2020)
30. McGuckian, T.B., Cole, M.H., Pepping, G.J.: A systematic review of the technology-based assessment of visual perception and exploration behaviour in association football. J. Sports Sci. **36**(8), 861–880 (2018)
31. Ingle, S.: Are We a step closer to being able to measure football IQ? (2016). https://www.theguardian.com/football/blog/2016/dec/04/barcelona-andres-iniesta-scope-embrace-brain-game-real-madrid
32. Krupitzer, C., et al.: CortexVR: immersive analysis and training of cognitive executive functions of soccer players using virtual reality and machine learning. Front. Psychol. **13**, 754732 (2022)
33. Bilek, G., Ulas, E.: Predicting match outcome according to the quality of opponent in the English premier league using situational variables and team performance indicators. Int. J. Perform. Anal. Sport **19**(6), 930–941 (2019)
34. Rico-González, M., Pino-Ortega, J., Méndez, A., Clemente, F., Baca, A.: Machine learning application in soccer: a systematic review. Biol. Sport **40**(1), 249–263 (2023)
35. Dick, U., Brefeld, U.: Learning to rate player positioning in soccer. Big Data **7**(1), 71–82 (2019)
36. Brooks, J., Kerr, M., Guttag, J.: Using machine learning to draw inferences from pass location data in soccer. Stat. Anal. Data Min. ASA Data Sci. J. **9**(5), 338–349 (2016)
37. Pappalardo, L., Cintia, P., Ferragina, P., Massucco, E., Pedreschi, D., Giannotti, F.: PlayeRank: data-driven performance evaluation and player ranking in soccer via a machine learning approach. ACM Trans. Intell. Syst. Technol. (TIST) **10**(5), 1–27 (2019)
38. McMahan, R.P., Bowman, D.A., Zielinski, D.J., Brady, R.B.: Evaluating display fidelity and interaction fidelity in a virtual reality game. IEEE Trans. Vis. Comput. Graph. **18**(4), 626–633 (2012)
39. DeMaris, A.: A tutorial in logistic regression. J. Marriage Fam., 956–968 (1195)
40. Patle, A., Chouhan, D.S.: SVM kernel functions for classification. In: 2013 International Conference on Advances in Technology and Engineering (ICATE), pp. 1–9. IEEE, January 2013
41. Liu, Y., Bi, J.W., Fan, Z.P.: A method for multi-class sentiment classification based on an improved one-vs-one (OVO) strategy and the support vector machine (SVM) algorithm. Inf. Sci. **394**, 38–52 (2017)
42. Rifkin, R., Klautau, A.: In defense of one-vs-all classification. J. Mach. Learn. Res. **5**, 101–141 (2004)
43. Noriega, L.: Multilayer perceptron tutorial. School of Computing, Staffordshire University **4**(5), 444 (2005)
44. Rish, I.: An empirical study of the Naive Bayes classifier. In: IJCAI 2001 Workshop on Empirical Methods in Artificial Intelligence, vol. 3, no. 22, pp. 41–46 (2001)
45. Ramraj, S., Uzir, N., Sunil, R., Banerjee, S.: Experimenting XGBoost algorithm for prediction and classification of different datasets. Int. J. Control Theory Appl. **9**(40), 651–662 (2016)
46. Schapire, R.E.: Explaining AdaBoost. In: Schölkopf, B., Luo, Z., Vovk, V. (eds.) Empirical Inference, pp. 37–52. Springer, Heidelberg (2013). https://doi.org/10.1007/978-3-642-41136-6_5

User-Centered Interface Improvements: An Example for Dormitory Administrators

Mengshi Yang⬤, Zhiwen Deng⬤, Yixin Zhang⬤, Mingyu Li⬤, Yudi Cao⬤, and Hongtao Zhou(✉)⬤

Shanghai International College of Design and Innovation, Tongji University, Shanghai, China
2333774@tongji.edu.cn, lifeisfurniture@gmail.com

Abstract. This academic paper delves into enhancing the work experience of dormitory administrators in China, utilizing human-centered design principles. It adopts a comprehensive user involvement approach, incorporating methods like in-depth interviews, detailed observations, and thorough user profiling. These techniques are instrumental in developing a preliminary prototype of an application. The key aim of this prototype is to tackle prevalent challenges in the field, such as complex information management and the issue of low job recognition among administrators. This initiative represents a significant step towards improving administrative processes and acknowledges the critical role of dormitory administrators in educational institutions. The paper provides an in-depth analysis of using the Analytic Hierarchy Process (AHP) for evaluating the usability and decision-making effectiveness of interfaces. This process, which includes the participation of a focus group, is pivotal for conducting comparative importance analysis. By applying AHP, the study facilitates a meticulous reorganization and optimization of interface elements. This optimization is guided by the calculated weights assigned to different elements, with a clear objective to enhance both visibility and usability. The approach demonstrates a structured method to quantify subjective user preferences, thus allowing for a more targeted and user-friendly design. Significant improvements in user satisfaction are observed through System Usability Scale (SUS) questionnaires, indicating the effectiveness of the iterative design process. The study exemplifies the application of human-centered design principles in improving work experience, emphasizing their potential in various fields.

Keywords: Human-Centered Design · Interface Optimization · Dormitory Administration

1 Introduction

In China, managing university dormitories is a significant responsibility for dormitory administrators, as most undergraduate and graduate students reside in these facilities. This role requires exceptional organizational skills and patience, given the complexity and demands of managing a large student population. Administrators often face challenges such as heavy workloads, managing strained interactions with students, and coping with high levels of stress. These factors can greatly impact their job satisfaction and overall efficiency. Additionally, these administrators must navigate a range of duties, from ensuring the safety and well-being of residents to addressing maintenance issues and enforcing dormitory rules, all of which add layers of complexity to their role. This challenging environment underscores the importance of effective support systems and tools to assist dormitory administrators in their multifaceted roles.

To further enhance the work experience of dormitory administrators, this study embraces human-centered design, prioritizing the needs and preferences of these administrators. This design philosophy involves a deep dive into understanding their unique challenges and requirements through rigorous scientific investigations. At the heart of human-centered design is the emphasis on human needs and behaviors, ensuring that the solutions developed are not only practical but also resonate with the administrators' work-related experiences. By focusing on these aspects, the study aims to create an application that is not only functional but also intuitive and user-friendly, thereby improving the overall efficiency and job satisfaction of dormitory administrators. This approach signifies a shift from traditional design methodologies, highlighting the importance of empathy and user engagement in creating effective and sustainable solutions in administrative contexts. Our design process and principles basically follow the standard interactive HCD process shown in the ISO Standard Ergonomics of human-system interaction [1].

In recent times, there has been an increase in the development and research of university dormitory information systems. However, the focus of these systems, as noted in several studies [2–4], has predominantly been on student users, with relatively less emphasis on dormitory administrators. Only a handful of these studies [3, 5] consider the needs of administrators as part of their user base.

Moreover, an analysis of data from CNKI reveals that a significant portion (64.09%) of articles related to Dormitory Management Systems falls within the realm of computer software and application, which is the largest category in this field (see Fig. 1).

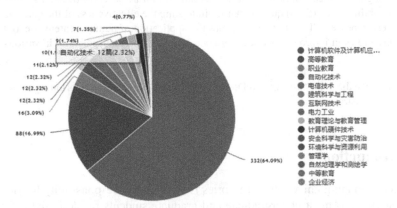

Fig. 1. Dormitory Management System Related Papers Subject Distribution.

Interestingly, none of these studies focus explicitly on design aspects. Additionally, the management systems discussed in these articles [6] are typically structured hierarchically, focusing on functionality rather than user-centric design. This highlights a gap in the current literature, suggesting a need for more research and development in systems that are specifically tailored to the needs of dormitory administrators, with a focus on design and user experience.

2 Method

2.1 Preliminary Prototyping

In this study, we adopted an intensive user involvement design methodology. This approach included several rounds of comprehensive interviews and extensive daily observations. The design team engaged in detailed user profiling, storyboarding, brainstorming, and other creative processes to develop a preliminary prototype of an application (see Fig. 2).

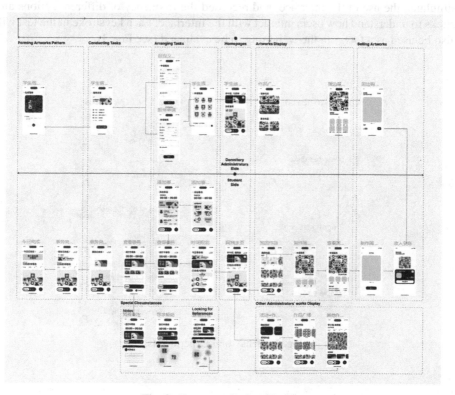

Fig. 2. Prototype Before Testing.

This prototype incorporates commonly used features that have been validated and selected by users. Its primary function is to facilitate the reception of tasks from the school and students, as well as to document each step in standardized operational procedures. Upon completion of a task type, dormitory administrators accumulate a pattern, serving as a record of their consistent hard work. This system offers positive feedback and a sense of achievement derived from their job, acknowledging their dedication and effort.

We keep track of even the simplest of tasks by providing an organized visualization of each task that a dormitory administrator needs to perform, and translating their completed work into beautiful patterns in the app.

Designers takes the prototype for user testing and invites them to experience the process of working with the app and fill out the System Usability Scale (SUS) questionnaire. The data obtained by SUS will be used in the later stages of the design evaluation.

2.2 Weighting

Behavioral experiments were conducted to gain a deeper understanding of how users interact with the interface. Designers imagined themselves as dormitory administrators, simulated the use of the interface, and recorded the frequency of different actions and clicks to understand how users interact with the interface. Each keystroke in the test will also be used as a factor in the weighting to be evaluated (see Fig. 3).

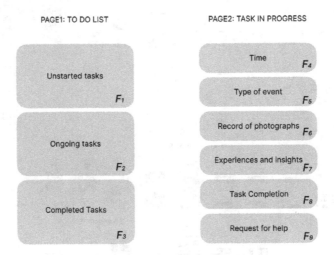

Fig. 3. Behavioral Experiments.

For interfaces with poor ease of use or controversial decision-making, we used the Analytic Hierarchy Process (AHP) to measure the importance of different elements in the prototype interface. Three designers, two users and two design experts formed a focus group to compare the importance of all elements two by two, taking the average of AHP questionnaire results as the data source for weight calculation and constructing a judgment matrix. Subsequently, the geometric mean algorithm is introduced to solve the weight of each requirement, the operation process is as follows, and the results are shown in Tables 1 and 2.

$$
B = \left(b_{ij}\right)_{n \times n} = \begin{bmatrix} b_{11} & b_{12} & \dots & b_{1n} \\ b_{21} & b_{22} & \dots & b_{2n} \\ \vdots & \vdots & \ddots & \vdots \\ b_{n1} & b_{n2} & \dots & b_{nn} \end{bmatrix} \tag{1}
$$

b_{ij} represents the value of the comparison of the relative importance between indicator A_i and indicator A_j. When comparing two indicators, the value is positive and the value on the diagonal is 1, and the anti-symmetry is satisfied, the numerical relationship between the symmetric elements of the matrix is inverse, and the matrix B is a positive inverse matrix, $b_{ij} > 0, b_{ii} = 1, b_{ij} = \frac{1}{b_{ji}}, (i, j = 1, 2, \cdots, n)$ Normalize the values of each column in the correlation judgment matrix B to get $C = (C_{ij})_{n \times m}$

$$
c_{ij} = \frac{b_{ij}}{\sum\limits_{i=1}^{n} b_{ij}} (i, j = 1, 2, \cdots, n) \tag{2}
$$

Summing the matrix C by rows:

$$
d_i = \sum_{j=1}^{n} c_{ij} (i, j = 1, 2, \cdots, n) \tag{3}
$$

Normalize the vector $D = (d_1, d_2, \ldots, d_n)$ to get the resultant weight $\omega_i (i = 1, 2, \cdots, n)$.

$$
\omega_i = \frac{d_i}{\sum\limits_{i=1}^{n} d_i} (i = 1, 2, \cdots, n); \quad \sum_{i=1}^{n} \omega_i = 1 \tag{4}
$$

Table 1. Indicator Judgment Matrix and Weight of Page 1.

	F_1	F_2	F_3	Weight ω
F_1	1	1/5	3	0.188 4
F_2	5	1	7	0.730 6
F_3	1/3	1/7	1	0.080 9

Table 2. Indicator Judgment Matrix and Weight of Page 2

	F_4	F_5	F_6	F_7	F_8	F_9	Weight ω
F_4	1	1/3	2	5	3	4	0.222 5
F_5	3	1	4	7	5	5	0.441 0
F_6	1/2	1/4	1	4	2	3	0.144 1
F_7	1/5	1/7	1/4	1	1/3	1/2	0.039 5
F_8	1/3	1/5	1/2	3	1	2	0.091 7
F_9	1/4	1/5	1/3	2	1/2	1	0.061 1

In the consistency test session, the maximum feature λmax and the consistency ratio CR are calculated with the following process and the results are shown in Table 3.

$$\lambda_{\max} = \frac{1}{n} \sum_{i=1}^{n} \frac{(AW)_i}{\omega_i} (i = 1, 2, \cdots, n), (AW)i \text{ is the } i \text{ component of the vector } AW.$$

The consistency indicator is then calculated: $CI = \frac{\lambda_{\max} - n}{n - 1}$.

When $CR = \frac{CI}{RI} < 0.1$, We can determine that the matrix passes the consistency test and the calculated weights turn out to be valid.

Table 3. Consistency check.

Maximum eigenvalue λ_{max}	λ_{max1}	λ_{max2}
Numerical	3.064 9	6.180 4
Consistency ratio CR	CR_1	CR_2
Numerical	0.055 9	0.029 0

From the calculation results, the resulting consistency ratios are all less than 0.1, which indicates that the matrices are consistent and the calculated weighting results are valid. Figure 4 shows the result of the calculated weights, and this information can help designers clarify which buttons and interfaces are more important and design better-using prototypes.

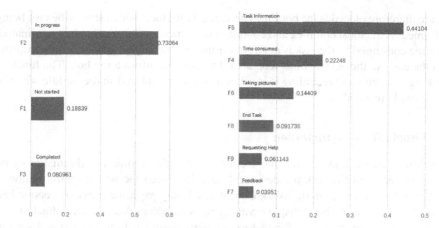

Fig. 4. Result of Weights.

3 Design Optimization

3.1 Page Layout Optimization

After obtaining the weights of each interface element through AHP calculations, the designer used this as a basis to reorganize the positions and sizes of all information displays and buttons. Figure 5 shows a before and after comparison of the two interfaces.

Fig. 5. Comparison of Pages Before and After Optimization.

On the first page, the ongoing tasks have the highest weight and are the most important, so they take up the largest area and are placed at the top where they are more easily seen. Completed tasks do not need to be displayed while other tasks are being performed and are therefore placed at the bottom. The second interface, which shows the task being performed, is the most complex and contains six influences that need to be coordinated. The time consumed by the task is not as important as one might think in communicating with the user, so the designer has relegated it to the task information box. The function of taking a picture and recording it is often used, so it is placed in the middle where it can be easily reached.

3.2 Visual Effects Optimization

In addition, taking into account the feedback from the dormitory administrators on the visualization of the app, the designers have improved the way the information is displayed. For example, on the Work Completed Today page, the previous version had an overly complex graphical display with aggressive colors that attracted much of the user's attention but made it difficult to read critical information. We iterated several versions of the visual scheme for this main visual, and the process is shown in Fig. 6.

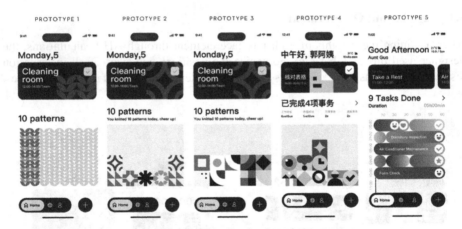

Fig. 6. Visualization Iteration.

With each new visual effect proposed, the designer seeks the user's input until a mutually satisfactory page design is optimized. The optimized interface design is shown in Fig. 7.

FOR STUDENTS

FOR EMPLOYEES

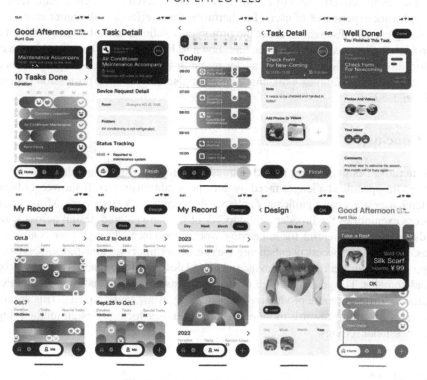

Fig. 7. Optimized Interface Design.

4 Results

We took the optimized prototype back to the users for testing and filled out the SUS questionnaire for the optimized design, a comparison of the SUS results for the two versions of the prototype is shown in Table 4.

Table 4. SUS Scoring Comparison.

SUS Test 1		SUS Test 2	
User 1	82.5	User 1	87.5
User 2	82.5	User 2	90
User 3	75	User 3	85
User 4	85	User 4	87.5
User 5	72.5	User 5	82.5
Average Score	79.5	Average Score	86.5

The data comparison between the pre- and post-implementation questionnaires reveals a notable increase in user satisfaction with the application. This improvement underscores the effectiveness of a human-centered research approach in enhancing the life and work experiences of users. Furthermore, for interfaces with higher complexity, involving users in discussions about the prototype solution can lead to more refined and user-friendly designs. This approach has shown to be particularly beneficial in the case of dormitory administrators, where a user-research-based information management app not only mitigates complex work challenges but also bolsters their professional identity and satisfaction.

5   Conclusion

This iterative design process, rooted in human-centered design principles, is tailored to address the specific challenges faced by dormitory administrators. It showcases how an in-depth user study can significantly enhance their daily work experience. Moreover, this process exemplifies the broader applicability of human-centered design across various fields, offering a blueprint for improving work experiences through user-centric solutions. This study's success in enhancing the role of dormitory administrators serves as an inspiration for further research into user-centered design solutions across diverse professional domains. The goal is to fulfill the unmet needs of professionals in different fields, ultimately fostering more productive and satisfying work environments. This approach advocates for a shift towards more empathetic and user-focused design methodologies in professional settings.

References

1. International Organization for Standardization: Ergonomics of human-system interaction. (ISO Standard No. 9241-210:2019) (2019). https://www.iso.org/standard/77520.html
2. Tang, R., Tang, Q.: Design of informationization management system for higher education dormitory. Electron. Technol. Softw. Eng. **04**, 258–262 (2023)
3. Liu, H., Qian, H., Bi, X.: Design and implementation of dormitory management system in higher education. J. Tonghua Normal Coll. **42**(10), 89–93 (2021)

4. Tu, H.: Database design for MySQL-based dormitory management system. Comput. Program. Skills Maintenance **12**, 104–106 (2021)
5. Sun, F., Li, K., Liu, N.: Design and realization of student dormitory management system. Jiangsu Sci. Technol. Inf. **38**(29), 40–42+75 (2021)
6. Shu, P., Chen, J.: Design and implementation of dormitory management system in digital campus construction. J. Wuhan Eng. Univ. **4**, 108–111 (2008)

Analysis and Research on the Influencing Factors of Kinesthetic Orientation

Lingling Zhang[1] , Minxia Liu[1](✉) , Kai Li[1] , Sitao Wang[1] ,
Zhongxing Luo[1] , Dandan Xie[1] , Yu Gu[2], and Mohammad Shidujaman[3]

[1] School of Mechanics and Vehicles, Beijing Institute of Technology, Beijing 100081, China
562155691@qq.com
[2] China Railway Inspection and Certification, Beijing, China
[3] Department of Computer Science and Engineering, Independent University,
Dhaka, Bangladesh

Abstract. Kinesthetic orientation refers to the human body's perception of the position and direction of its own body parts relative to space. It is realized through the information provided by the human body's motion sensory organs to perceive its position and direction in space and the relative position between body parts, so it has a very important role. Firstly, this paper analyzes the right and left hands to get the conclusion that the dominant hand is stronger than the weak hand, and then eight factors affecting the orientation of kinaesthesia are selected and analyzed and studied, including age, gender, arm pressure, heart rate, ambient chromatic aberration, ambient music, muscle memory, and body posture. Through the multiple regression analysis, correlation coefficient test, and gray correlation analysis of the above factors, it is concluded that muscle memory is a relatively important influencing factor, and based on this, relevant theoretical suggestions are put forward. Then this paper introduces the concept of kinesthetic orientation muscle memory index λ to measure the level of muscle memory ability in the kinesthetic orientation test, which will be defined as $1 - \frac{\Delta\theta}{0.4\theta}$ (where $\Delta\theta$ represents the error of the rotation angle, θ represents the target angle). Next, based on the definition of the kinesthetic orientation muscle memory index to further carry out research on the kinesthetic orientation muscle memory, the kinesthetic orientation muscle memory forgetting law to explore and study, and get the results of the time as the We obtained the kinesthetic orientation muscle memory forgetting law curve under different training conditions with time as the horizontal coordinate and the kinesthetic orientation muscle memory index as the vertical coordinate, and found the law of the fastest decline point of muscle memory, which can be used as a guide and reference to guide the patients to recover their kinesthetic awareness quickly or the athletes to improve their kinesthetic orientation perception.

Keywords: kinesthetic orientation · muscle memory · kinesthetic orientation muscle memory index · kinesthetic orientation muscle memory forgetting law curve (National Innovation Name: Development of Kinesthetic Orientation Testing and Training Instrument · National Innovation Number: S202310007110)

M. Kurosu and A. Hashizume (Eds.): HCII 2024, LNCS 14687, pp. 320–342, 2024.
https://doi.org/10.1007/978-3-031-60441-6_21

1   Introduction

Kinesthetic orientation is one of the many human senses, which refers to the ability of the human body to perceive the position and orientation of its own body parts in relation to space [1]. Nowadays, kinesthetic orientation is widely used in virtual reality, medical rehabilitation, human-computer interaction and sports [2]. Despite the wide range of applications of kinesthetic orientation, as a physiological sense of the human body, kinesthetic orientation is affected by a number of factors such as the human body itself and the environment, which makes it difficult to be accurately measured, studied, and applied in depth. An in-depth study of the influencing factors of kinesthetic orientation is of constructive significance to the development of virtual reality, medical rehabilitation, human-computer interaction and sports in China [3–9].

The team's research expects to experiment and analyze nine factors (left-handedness, right-handedness, age, gender, arm pressure, heart rate, ambient color difference, ambient music, muscle memory, and body posture) that may affect kinesthetic orientation, and explore the degree of their influence, thus giving a theoretical basis for the influence of various factors on kinesthetic orientation, which will make the application of kinesthetic orientation in the fields of virtual reality, medical rehabilitation, human-computer interaction, and sports more persuasive and systematic. This will make the application of kinesthetic orientation in virtual reality, medical rehabilitation, human-computer interaction and sports more convincing and systematic. At the same time, we expect to obtain a muscle memory forgetting curve similar to the Ebbinghaus memory curve, and we propose the hypothesis that the muscle memory forgetting in kinesthetic orientation is similar to the Ebbinghaus memory curve. Therefore, in the next experiments, we draw a muscle memory forgetting curve through the correlation analysis of experimental data, which is used to analyze and understand the effect of muscle memory on kinesthetic orientation. This curve can be used as a guide and reference to instruct patients to quickly recover kinesthetic awareness or athletes to improve kinesthetic orientation perception.

This experiment aims to:

1. study the effects of left-handedness and right-handedness, age, gender, arm pressure, heart rate, environmental color difference, environmental music, muscle memory, and body posture on kinaesthetic orientation, and provide a theoretical basis for the application of kinaesthetic orientation in the fields of virtual reality, medical rehabilitation, human-computer interaction, and sports.
2. To draw muscle memory forgetting curves and investigate the intrinsic mechanism of muscle memory effects on kinesthetic orientation, so as to enhance the persuasiveness and feasibility of muscle memory forgetting in medical rehabilitation and sports in the future.
3. To promote the research in the field of kinesthetic orientation and to provide a theoretical basis for other scholars' research.

The main instrument used in this experiment is the kinesthetic orientation test instrument as shown in Fig. 1.

The Kinesthetic Orientation Test Training Instrument is usually used to evaluate and train the human body's sense of balance and spatial orientation ability, and its operation steps are as follows:

Fig. 1. Kinesthetic Orientation Test Equipment

- Conduct an inspection: Before use, ensure that the kinaesthetic orientation test training device is in good condition, including: detecting whether the rotating bearings are rusty, whether the rotating platform is intact, and whether the dial scale is clear and legible.
- Prepare for the test: record the age, gender and environment of the tester, detect and record the tester's heart rate, the pressure exerted by the tester's arm, and the tester's test position.
- Performed a kinesthetic orientation perception exercise: the tester fixed an angle on the dial and subsequently swung the arm to the pre-fixed angle at least three times or more.
- Performing a kinesthetic perception test: the fixation of the angle is canceled, the tester closes his/her eyes, swings the arm at a certain angle to the previous position, and subsequently opens his/her eyes to check the angle of the arm's position.
- for result recording: the error value between the pre-fixed angle and the experimental angle was read out and recorded.

2   Research Method

2.1   Selection of Indicators

(1) Age. Through research young people usually learn new kinesthetic orientations more easily than older people. This may be due to the fact that younger people's nervous systems are more flexible and have faster reaction times. Younger people's muscles are also more adapted to learning and adapting to new movements quickly. And as people age, they may be more likely to forget previously learned kinesthetic memories. Therefore, we hypothesize that age has an effect on human kinesthetic orientation perception and is one of the necessary indicators for the team to select the study [10–12].

(2) Gender. Gender differences between men and women are mainly caused by changes in hormone levels. Some research suggests that males may perform better on certain muscle memory learning tasks relative to females. However, this does not mean that females cannot successfully learn kinesthetic orientations. Some studies suggest that females may retain kinesthetic orientation memory for longer periods of time relative to males in some situations. We therefore hypothesized that gender may have some effect on human kinesthetic orientation perception and was one of the necessary indicators for the team to select the study [13–15].

(3) Environmental Color Difference. Environmental color difference refers to variations in factors such as light, color, and background in the environment. For kinesthetic orientation perception learning speed, environmental color difference may interfere with the kinesthetic orientation learning process. When the light, color, or background in the environment changes, it may take more time for people to adapt to the new situation, thus slowing down the rate of learning. Changes in the environment may also result in new perceptual inputs that interfere with the retrieval and representation of old kinesthetic sensations. Therefore, we hypothesized that environmental color difference may have an effect on human kinesthetic orientation perception, and is one of the necessary metrics for the team to select for the study [16]. Here, we change the color of the light to change the environmental color difference.

(4) Environmental music. Whether there is music in the environment and whether it is noisy will have an effect on the tester's emotion, too noisy environment will make the tester anxious, too relaxed environment will make the tester unable to concentrate, so this paper assumes that the ambient music will also have an effect on the tester's kinesthetic orientation perception, which is one of the necessary indexes for the team's selection study [17].

(5) Body Posture. Body posture refers to the specific positions that the human body adopts when performing various activities and movements [18]. By reviewing the literature body posture may affect the speed of learning kinesthetic orientation. Proper body posture can help people better understand and master specific movement skills, thus facilitating the perception of kinesthetic orientation. For example, proper posture can help people maintain balance, stability, and proper movement execution, improving learning. Therefore, body posture may have a certain impact on the human body's kinesthetic orientation perception and is one of the necessary indicators for the team to select for the study.

(6) Heart Rate. Heart rate is the number of times the heart beats per minute. Some research suggests that a moderate increase in heart rate may promote cognitive functioning of the brain and the ability to learn. However, too high or too low a heart rate may negatively affect learning. Too high a heart rate may lead to anxiety and inattention, while too low a heart rate may make a person drowsy. In this study, we measured the heart rate using BD-C-2 wireless ECG acquisition and analysis system for ECG signal analysis, which is the process of measuring, processing and interpreting the electrical activity of the human heart [19]. It involves recording the electrocardiogram (ECG) to obtain information about the electrical activity of the heart, and then applying signal processing and analysis techniques to extract useful physiological and pathological information.

The ECG measuring instrument used in the experiment is the BD-C-2 wireless ECG acquisition and analysis system, and the analysis interface is shown in Fig. 2.

(7) Arm Pressure. Shi Yan scholars in the study of quantitative exercise load and elbow joint kinesthetic orientation accuracy pointed out that when the quantitative exercise conformity increase can significantly improve the elbow joint kinesthetic orientation

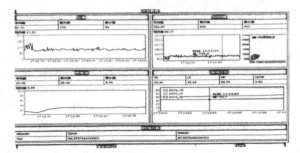

Fig. 2. Electrocardiogram

accuracy [20], so we can get the arm pressure has a certain effect on the perception of kinesthetic orientation, so the arm pressure can be used as one of our indicators.

(8) Muscle Memory. Muscle memory and kinesthetic perception are different concepts, but there is a certain correlation between them, the establishment of muscle memory needs to rely on the feedback and information processing of the kinesthetic perception system. Training muscle memory is mainly through repetitive practice and the establishment of motor patterns, which leads to the formation of stronger connections and coordination between the brain and muscles for specific movements. This training enhances neural circuits and synaptic connections, allowing for more automated and fluid movement execution. As muscle memory becomes more skillful and accurate, the perception of movement details, position and body orientation improves accordingly. By training muscle memory, the position and orientation of body parts can be better perceived and controlled, thus potentially improving the body's kinesthetic perception. Therefore, muscle memory is one of the indicators we selected.

2.2 Methods of Analysis

The team considered the experimental data using two-way ANOVA, multiple regression analysis, gray correlation analysis, and correlation coefficient analysis.

Multiple regression analysis is a statistical method that explores the degree of correlation and influence between multiple independent variables and a dependent variable by modeling the relationship between them [19]. Its core principle is to minimize the squared error of the dependent variable, given multiple independent variables, to obtain estimates of the coefficients of the independent variables, thus modeling the linear relationship between the independent variables and the dependent variable. Its mathematical expression is:

$$Y = \beta_0 + \beta X_1 + \beta_2 X_2 + \ldots + \beta_K X_K + \varepsilon \tag{1}$$

where Y is the dependent variable, X_i is the independent variable, β_i is the coefficient of the independent variable and ε represents the random error term. Through the measured data, the team regarded the kinesthetic orientation value as Y, the related indicators as. X_i, and fitted a multivariate linear curve thus obtaining β_i, i.e.: the weights occupied by the indicators. The use of multiple regression analysis in this experiment aims to find out the main factors affecting muscle memory, ignoring the secondary factors, to carry out a deeper investigation, and to get some meaningful conclusions.

Simply put, the coefficients in front of each independent variable represent the degree of importance.

Gray correlation analysis is a method used to study the degree of correlation between factors, which is especially suitable for the case of small or incomplete sample data [20]. Its core principle is based on the gray system theory, through the original data sequence for gray processing, to get the gray series, and then through the calculation of the degree of correlation between different factors, to determine the degree of influence of each factor on the object of study, and finally according to the correlation ranking results of the results of the analysis and interpretation of the results, to find out the key factors of influence, and to provide a reference basis for decision-making. The degree of correlation between the factors is transformed into a correlation index, which reflects the similarity and correlation of the factors in the process of change. The correlation weight coefficient, which usually takes the value range of [0, 1], is calculated by the following formula:

$$r_{(i,j)} = (\min |X_{(i)} - X_{(j)}| + \rho * \max |X_{(i)} - X_{(j)}| / |X_{(i)} - X_{(j)}| + \rho * \max |X_{(i)} - X_{(j)}|)$$

(2)

where, $r_{(i,j)}$ denotes the correlation between the ith factor and the jth factor, $X_{(i)}$ and $X_{(j)}$ denotes the observed value of the ith factor and the jth factor respectively, and ρ is the correlation weight coefficient. In this experiment gray correlation analysis is mainly used to explore the similarity and correlation between the factors, so as to get a more accurate judgment to find the most important influencing factors and draw more accurate conclusions.

Simply put, the larger r, the more important it is.

Pearson correlation coefficient analysis is a method used to study the strength and direction of the linear relationship between two variables and is usually used to measure the degree of association between two continuous variables. It measures the degree of linear correlation between two variables and takes values in the range of $[-1, 1]$. The Pearson's correlation coefficient is calculated using the following formula:

$$r = \Sigma[(X_i - X_{mean}) * (Y_i - Y_{mean})] / [(n - 1) * S_X S_Y]$$

(3)

where r is the Pearson correlation coefficient, X_i and Y_i denote the score of the ith individual on each of the two variables, X_{mean} Y_{mean} and are the mean values of each of the two variables, n is the sample size, and S_X and S_Y are the standard deviations of each of the two variables. The closer the absolute value of the Pearson correlation coefficient is to 1, the stronger the linear relationship between the two variables. When r is positive, it means that the two variables are positively correlated; when r is negative, it means that the two variables are negatively correlated. In this experiment, Pearson correlation coefficient analysis is mainly used for the test of correlation factors, to further prove the validity of correlation factors, the validity of the experiment, and to verify whether there is a strong linear relationship.

Simply put, the larger the value of r, the stronger the correlation.

Spearman's correlation coefficient analysis is a method used to study the non-linear relationship between two variables and is usually used to measure the degree of association between two serial variables. It is calculated by converting the scores of the variables into ranks and then calculating the sum of squares of the rank differences. The formula for Spearman's correlation coefficient is given below:

$$\rho = 1 - [6\Sigma d^2 / n(n^2 - 1)] \tag{4}$$

where ρ is the Spearman correlation coefficient, n is the sample size, and d is the difference between the two variables in rank. The Spearman correlation coefficient takes the range of $[-1, 1]$, and the closer its absolute value is to 1, the stronger the correlation between the two variables. When ρ is positive, it indicates that the two variables are positively correlated; when ρ is negative, it indicates that the two variables are negatively correlated. In this experiment Spearman correlation coefficient analysis is also mainly used for the test of correlation factors, and Pearson correlation coefficient conclusions are compared to increase the accuracy of the results.

Simply put, the larger the value of ρ, the stronger the correlation.

3 Experimental Design

3.1 Purpose of Experiment

In order to investigate what factors are related to kinesthetic orientation, we looked for the following factors including left-handedness and right-handedness, age, gender, arm pressure, heart rate, ambient color difference, ambient music, muscle memory, and the effect of body posture on kinesthetic orientation, and based on which we want to investigate the forgetting law of muscle memory and explore the forgetting curve of muscle.

3.2 Experimental Equipment

Kinesthetic orientation tester (used to quantify kinesthesia), BD-C-2 wireless electrocardiogram acquisition and analysis system (used to collect electrocardiograms), dumbbells (to put pressure on the arms), jump rope (used to change the tester's heart rate in time), warm and cold light source regulator (used to change the color difference of the light source environment), and audio equipment (used to change the music played in the environment).

3.3 Experimental Subjects

- 50 students from Beijing University of Technology (Recruited 19 girls and 31 boys due to school reasons)
- Experimenters are responsible and able to follow the arrangement
- The experimenters are in good spirits, no fatigue or insomnia, etc.
- The experimenters have no color blindness and other diseases
- The experimenter is able to get 7–8 h of sleep before the experiment.
- The experimenter can have certain ability of kinesthetic perception.

3.4   Experimental Process

(1) Overall Experimental Flow Fhart. Figure 3 shows the overall flow chart of our experiment, and the following is based on the flow chart to start the experiment.

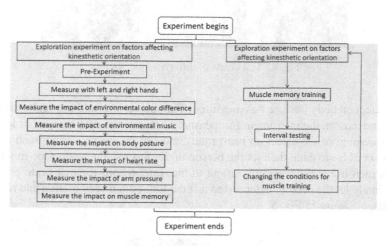

Fig. 3. Overall experiment flowchart

(2) Experiment to Explore the Factors Influencing Kinesthetic Orientation.

- Pre-experiment is needed before the official start: Check and debug the equipment including, BD-C-2 wireless electrocardiographic acquisition and analysis system and the kinesthetic orientation test instrument, prepare all the equipment as well as determine the experimental place and position of the person under test and the placement of the test instrument.
- Measurement of the effects on the right and left hands: At the beginning of the formal measurement: the tester came to measure the left and right hands of the tested person with the kinesthetic test instrument at 30°, 45°, 60° and 75° respectively, and recorded the measured data.
- Measurement of the effect of environmental color difference: Testers in ordinary indoor lighting conditions for measurement, here by considering the choice of measurement angle of 50° (subsequent measurement process angle remains unchanged). Record the data; then the operator changed to warm light for measurement, record the data; then changed to cold light for measurement record the data; and finally closed all light sources to create a dark environment for measurement, record the data (Fig. 4).
- Measurement of the effect of ambient music: The tester played gentle music (here the gentle music was chosen to be the piano piece kiss the rain) and let the subject listen for one minute before starting the test and recording the data; the tester took measurements in rocky manic music (here the manic music was chosen to be Rolling in the deep) and recorded the data.

Fig. 4. Test charts of different light sources

- The effect on body posture was measured: The subject was told to stand up and place the hand axis on the instrument for measurement, and the data were recorded
- Measurement of the effect on heart rate: First use the electrocardiograph to test to get a set of basic data, then let the person under test use the jump rope to jump 100 times then use the electrocardiograph to measure, record the heart rate of the test, and finally let the person under test to test the kinaesthetic orientation and record the results, as shown in Fig. 5.

Fig. 5. Experimental cardiac test chart

- Measurement of the effect of arm pressure: let the person under test lift dumbbells 2.5 kg5 times, measurements, record data; rest 1 min, lift 5 kg5 times to measure, record data rest 1 min, as shown in Fig. 6.

Fig. 6. Arm pressure test chart

- Measurement of the effect on muscle memory: According to the kinesthetic orientation test instrument, assist the tested person to find 50° of sensation collision five times, the feeling of collision we use here to indicate muscle memory, and then measure and record the data; rest for 30 s, followed by collision 10 times to measure and record the data; rest for 30 s, followed by collision 15 times to measure and record the data.

Finally, we can get the data table (take No. 1 person as an example) as follows (Tables 1 and 2):

Table 1. Table of left and right hand test results

Left hand	Result	Right	Result
Left 30°	28.3	Right 30°	14.8
Left 45°	43.3	Right 45°	34
Left 60°	54.4	Right 60°	48.2
Left 75°	64	Right 75°	59.3

Table 2. Factors analysis table

Experimenter	Kinesthetic orientation value	age	gender	color	music	position	heart rate	Arm pressure	muscle memory
0.956	47.8	19	1	ordinary	No	sit	Reference	0	0
0.946	47.3	19	1	warm	No	sit	Reference	0	0
0.788	39.4	19	1	cold	No	sit	Reference	0	0
0.926	46.3	19	1	dark	No	sit	Reference	0	0
0.826	41.3	19	1	ordinary	Gentle	sit	Reference	0	0
0.922	53.9	19	1	ordinary	Manic	sit	Reference	0	0
0.956	47.8	19	1	ordinary	No	stand	Reference	0	0
0.962	43.9	19	1	ordinary	No	sit	Increase	0	0
0.944	52.8	19	1	ordinary	No	sit	Reference	2.5	0
0.734	63.3	19	1	ordinary	No	sit	Reference	5	0
0.98	51	19	1	ordinary	No	sit	Reference	0	5
0.958	52.1	19	1	ordinary	No	sit	Reference	0	10
0.914	54.3	19	1	ordinary	No	sit	Reference	0	15

(3) Muscle Memory Forgetting Curve Exploration Experiment. We chose 10 subjects out of 50 as our subjects for the second round of the experiment, and our experimental procedure was as follows:

- muscle memory training:

Let the test persons perform five strokes of muscle memory collision training and start the test on the sixth stroke.

- Interval testing:

Have the test person perform the test at one-minute intervals to find where 50° is until ten minutes.

- Changing the conditions of muscle memory training:

We changed the conditions of the muscle memory training to performing ten and fifteen strokes of muscle memory collision training and starting the interval test.

4 Data Analysis

4.1 Data Analysis of the Experiment on the Effect of Factors in the Kinesthetic Orientation Test

(1) Two-factor Analysis of Variance (ANOVA). In this paper, in order to investigate the relationship between the left and right hands, a two-factor ANOVA was conducted to analyze the results of the left and right hands with movements of 30°, 45°, 60°, and 75° as shown in the table below (Tables 4 and 5).

Table 3. ANOVA table for 30° of motion

Sources of Differences	SS	df	MS	F	P-value	F crit
Different testers	4075.7381	49	83.17832857	2.068584531	0.006137149	1.60728946
Left Hand and Right Hand	723.0721	1	723.0721	17.98227719	9.84422E-05	4.03839263
Error	1970.3029	49	40.21026327			
Total	6769.1131	99				

The relationship of the factors was analyzed based on the data between Table 3 and Table 6 and a two-factor ANOVA. Regardless of the angle, differences between observers do lead to significant differences in measurements, and there is a strong relationship between the test of kinesthetic orientation and the measurer. For differences in the hand of the measurer's measurements, a greater correlation between differences in hand selection and kinesthetic orientation was seen at low angles, with an alternating state of correlation and non-correlation later in the analysis, but with an increasing tendency for the two to be uncorrelated. Overall, the relationship between kinesthetic orientation and hand selection of the measurers varied with angle, first correlated, then uncorrelated, with a general trend toward uncorrelatedness.

Table 4. ANOVA table for 45° of motion

Sources of Differences	SS	df	MS	F	P-value	F crit
Different testers	7555.3229	49	154.1902633	6.707744988	2.62696E-10	1.607289463
Left Hand and Right Hand	47.1969	1	47.1969	2.053208567	0.15823546	4.038392634
Error	1126.3581	49	22.9869			
Total	8728.8779	99				

Table 5. ANOVA table for 60° of motion

Sources of Differences	SS	df	MS	F	P-value	F crit
Different testers	10924.4676	49	222.9483184	13.32089047	2.98529E-16	1.607289463
Left Hand and Right Hand	129.0496	1	129.0496	7.710556415	0.007755593	4.038392634
Error	820.1004	49	16.73674286			
Total	11873.6176	99				

Table 6. ANOVA table for 75° of motion

Sources of Differences	SS	df	MS	F	P-value	F crit
Different testers	11657.99	49	237.9181633	4.447895783	3.12871E-07	1.60728
Left Hand and Right Hand	18.1476	1	18.1476	0.339270581	0.562921384	4.03839
Error	2621.0124	49	53.49004898			
Total	14297.15	99				

Multiple Regression Analysis. In this paper, we looked for the remaining eight indicators except the right and left hands: age, gender, arm pressure, heart rate, environmental color difference, environmental music, muscle memory, and body posture, in order to explore what factors are related to the kinesthetic orientation, we used multiple regression analysis for each indicator, and we got the results in the following table (Table 8).

Table 7. Sample independence table

Models	R	R square	R square after adjustment	Errors in standard estimates	Durbin-Watson
1	0.324a	0.105	0.052	0.08737	1.508

Table 8. Description of symbols

symbol	implication
y	grade
x1	age
x2	gender
x3	environment color difference
x4	environment music
x5	body posture
x6	heart rate
x7	arm pressure
x8	muscle memory

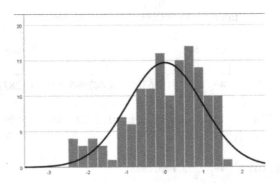

Fig. 7. Comparison of normal distribution of residuals

According to the data in Table 7 and the characteristics of sample independence in multiple regression analysis, the R-square of this experiment is 0.105, which can better reflect that the degree of explanation of the factors in the kinesthetic orientation test of this experiment is in line with the standard. According to the Durbin-Watson number of 1.508 obtained from the experiment, it is close to the standard of independence of

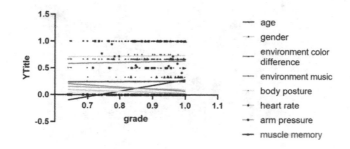

$$y = 0.858 + 0.0039x_1 + 0.0035x_2 + 0.0103x_3$$
$$-0.0167x_4 + 0.0264x_5 - 0.0210x_6 + 0.0012x_7 + 0.0855x_8$$

Fig. 8. Multivariate regression analysis

experimental data, so it can be considered that the various samples in this experiment are close to being independent of each other.

In the covariance statistics of the factors of this experiment, it is obvious to find that the VIF of each factor is less than 5, which meets the standard of like mutual non-interference between the indicators of independent variables, so it can be considered that the factors of this experiment are like mutual non-interference with each other. According to the comparison between the histogram of residuals and the regression line in Fig. 7, we think that the distribution of the data is approximately in line with the normal distribution. According to the distribution plot of the multivariate distribution in Fig. 8 and the function introduced by the data obtained from this experiment, the relationship between the kinesthetic orientation test and the factors can be determined, in which muscle memory accounts for a large proportion and is the main factor in the kinesthetic orientation test.

(3) Correlation Coefficient Analysis. According to the calculated correlation coefficient, the strength and direction of the correlation between two variables can be determined. If the correlation coefficient is close to 1, it means that the positive correlation between the two variables is strong; if the correlation coefficient is close to -1, it means that the negative correlation between the two variables is strong; and if the correlation coefficient is close to 0, it means that the correlation between the two variables is weak (Figs. 9 and 10).

Comparing the heat map of Pearson and Spearman's slow correlation coefficient analysis, among the various factors affecting the internal and external environment of the human body, the positive correlation between gender and age is the strongest among the correlations. Secondly, there is also some positive correlation between gender and muscle memory. The positive correlation between the other factors is weaker. In response to the negative correlations between the factors, there was a strong negative correlation between muscle memory and ambient music, followed by a negative correlation between muscle memory and arm stress. The negative correlations of the other factors can be disregarded.

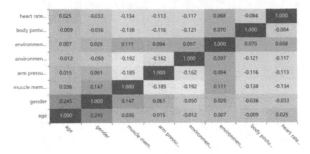

Fig. 9. Heat map of Pearson's correlation coefficient

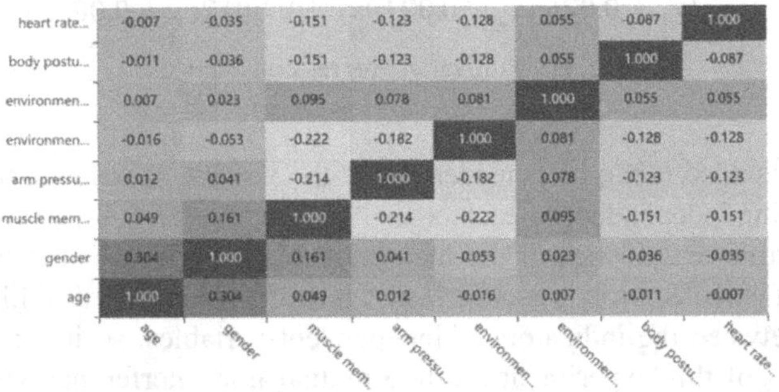

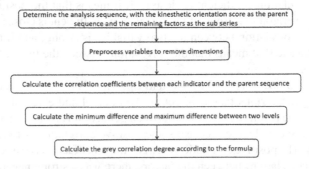

Fig. 10. Heat map of Spearman's correlation coefficient

(4) Gray Correlation Analysis. Gray correlation analysis is mainly used to judge the connection through the similarity of the fit of the graphic curve of the sequence set, when the curve fit is closer to indicate a higher degree of similarity, when the curve fit is worse to indicate a lower degree of similarity, here we will be our eight indicators with our kinesthetic orientation to start the study of the fit between the relationship, the specific process is as follows (Fig. 11):

Determine the analysis sequence, with the kinesthetic orientation score as the parent sequence and the remaining factors as the sub series

Preprocess variables to remove dimensions

Calculate the correlation coefficients between each indicator and the parent sequence

Calculate the minimum difference and maximum difference between two levels

Calculate the grey correlation degree according to the formula

Fig. 11. Gray correlation analysis flow chart

We define our parent series as the testee's kinesthetic orientation test score counted as y. The remaining eight factors: age, gender, ambient color difference, ambient music, body posture, heart rate, arm pressure, and muscle memory are denoted respectively as X1, X2, X3, X4, X5, X6, X7, X8, So the parent sequence and the subseries can be represented as follows:

$$y = (y(1), y(2), y(3) \cdots y(n))$$

$$x_1 = (x_1(1), x_1(2), x_1(3) \cdots x_1(n)) \tag{5}$$

$$\vdots$$

$$x_8 = (x_8(1), x_8(2), x_8(3) \cdots x_8(n))$$

The data is then preprocessed to perform the elimination of the magnitude, using Eq:

$$x\prime = \frac{x - x_{min}}{x_{max} - x_{min}} \tag{6}$$

Take the results of Experimenter 1 as an example in the following table (Table 9).

Table 9. Experimenter 1 elimination scale

Kinesthetic orientation value	age	gender	environmental color	environmental music	body position	heart rate	Arm pressure	muscle memory
0.956	0	1	0.66666666	0	0	0	0	0
0.946	0	1	1	0	0	0	0	0
0.788	0	1	0.33333333	0	0	0	0	0
0.926	0	1	0	0	0	0	0	0
0.826	0	1	0.66666666	0.5	0	0	0	0
0.922	0	1	0.66666666	1	0	0	0	0
0.956	0	1	0.66666666	0	1	0	0	0
0.962	0	1	0.66666666	0	0	0.853982	0	0
0.944	0	1	0.66666666	0	0	0	0.5	0
0.734	0	1	0.66666666	0	0	0	1	0
0.98	0	1	0.66666666	0	0	0	0	0.33333333
0.958	0	1	0.66666666	0	0	0	0	0.66666666
0.914	0	1	0.66666666	0	0	0	0	1

We let each indicator be processed by dividing it by the mean of that broad category, and then calculate the bipolar minimum difference a and the bipolar maximum difference b, with the following formulas

$$a = \min\{\max|y(k) - x_i(k)|\} \tag{7}$$

$$b = \max\{\max|y(k) - x_i(k)|\} \tag{8}$$

Next, the gray correlation coefficient was found according to the formula:

$$g(y(k), x_i(k)) = \frac{a + \gamma b}{|y(k) - x_i(k)| + \gamma b} \tag{9}$$

Finally, the average correlation of each sub-series is derived as the gray correlation, and the results are presented in the following table (Table 10):

Table 10. Gray correlation analysis table

age	gender	environment color	Environmental music	body position	heart rate	Arm pressure	muscle memory
0.5124	0.3216	0.4576	0.4398	0.6265	0.5946	0.6123	0.8765

4.2 Experimental Data Analysis for Muscle Memory Forgetting Curve Exploration

We took the average value of the data for ten testers (with 50° as the standard) and organized the data table for five, ten and fifteen times of testing as follows (Table 11):

Table 11. Forgetting curve data sheet

Number	0	1	2	3	4	5	6	7	8	9	10
5times	49.2	43.8	39.7	38.3	38.9	35.6	38.1	37.5	33.8	30.16	35.6
10times	50.4	49.8	47.8	48.7	46.6	42.3	40.1	41.3	38.4	39.3	37.6
15times	50.2	45.8	46.8	47.3	44.5	43.5	41.2	42.3	42.1	39.4	40.3

For ease of analysis we propose the muscle forgetting index λ, defined as:

$$\lambda = 1 - \frac{\Delta\theta}{0.4\theta} \tag{11}$$

(Where $\Delta\theta$ represents the rotation angle error and θ represents the target angle)

Therefore, the relationship between muscle forgetting index and time can be obtained as shown in Figs. 12, 13 and 14:

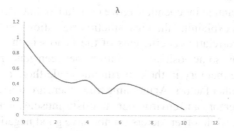

Fig. 12. Relationship of muscle forgetting index for 5 training sessions

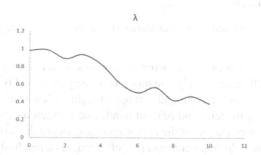

Fig. 13. Relationship of muscle forgetting index for 10 training sessions

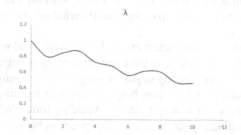

Fig. 14. Relationship of muscle forgetting index for 15 training sessions

4.3 Conclusion of the Experiment on the Effects of Factors in the Kinesthetic Orientation Test

1. The data from the test were analyzed using two-way ANOVA for the difference between the right and left hand of the human body. We concluded that "the presence of the left and right hand at small angles has an effect on the kinesthetic orientation test, and the effect is weaker at large angles".

2. Among the factors that may affect the internal and external environments of the human body and lead to changes in the results of the experiments, the experiments were conducted to analyze age, gender, ambient color difference, ambient music, body posture, heart rate, arm pressure, and muscle memory. Using multiple regression analysis, we initially concluded that muscle memory was the main factor affecting the kinaesthetic orientation score, and after analyzing the confidence level and the

characteristics of sample independence, we concluded that muscle memory was part of the main factors explaining the kinaesthetic orientation test.

3. We analyzed the correlation coefficients of the factors in the experiment, and concluded that "there are some positive correlations between gender and age, and between gender and muscle memory in the experiment, while there are no positive correlations between the other factors. At the same time, there are some negative correlations between muscle memory and environmental music, muscle memory and arm pressure in this experiment, while other factors do not have good negative correlations".

4. Gray correlation analysis for the experimental data, we get the same conclusion as linear regression analysis, our muscle memory has the greatest influence on our kinesthetic orientation.

Through that experiment we synthesize the analysis we can get the following conclusion:

- The vast majority of people have stronger kinesthetic orientation perception in the right hand at small angles, and locate more accurately and quickly. Scientifically, the vast majority of people have the advantage of right or left hand, that is: there is a clear habit of using the left hand or right hand. The formation of this dominant hand is related to the lateralization of the cerebral cortex, where the left brain controls the right hand and the right brain controls the left hand. As a result of the long-term use of the dominant part, the corresponding muscle movement patterns and memories are more fully trained and developed. This means that if you need to train coordination, you need to strengthen the training intensity of the non-dominant part; if you need to master the perception of a certain part for a short period of time, training the dominant hand part will be better.

- There are also differences in muscle memory between men and women. Experimental data show that men's kinesthetic orientation perception is better than women's, so women tend to need more training in performing accurate orientation perception.

- In a quiet and familiar environment helps to improve learning and concentration when performing muscle memory training. Avoiding loud background sounds and distractions and creating a quiet space familiar space can help individuals better focus on the training task for better training results. Stress during training may then have an effect on muscle memory. Experiments have shown that the right amount of stress is more conducive to muscle training to achieve faster muscle memory, while too much stress can lead to inefficient training.

- A moderate increase in heart rate may help to promote the body's adaptive ability and muscle training effect and correct posture can help muscles participate in exercise more effectively and help form correct muscle memory. In contrast, incorrect posture is detrimental to the formation of muscle memory.

- Research that addresses these factors can provide important relevance to the fields of rehabilitation medicine, athletic training, and human-computer interaction, and we offer several suggestions.

- Utilizing the advantages of the dominant part: the dominant limb may have an effect on kinesthetic orientation, and the dominant limb is more likely to form muscle memory. Understanding the impact of its strengths on kinesthetic orientation can help to design more effective rehabilitation programs and can help to individualize and tailor rehabilitation therapy.

- Be aware of age and gender differences: the body's ability to perceive kinesthetic orientation may change with age. At the same time, gender may also have an effect on kinesthetic orientation. In general, with age, the ability to perceive kinesthetic orientation may decline. This is due to the deterioration of the function of sensory neurons and sensory organs in the elderly. In geriatric rehabilitation, specific training programs and technical support for age-related problems in kinesthetic orientation perception can be designed to improve patients' daily functioning and quality of life. At the same time there may be differences in kinesthetic orientation perception between males and females. Women often need to design longer cycle programs to improve kinesthetic perception.
- Pay attention to the regulation of arm pressure and heart rate: arm pressure and heart rate may have an effect on kinesthetic orientation, especially under high pressure or high heart rate, the human body's ability to perceive kinesthetic orientation may be affected, resulting in poorer training results. Excessive stress should be avoided, but appropriate stress may enhance kinesthetic orientation perception and motor control training. The study of these factors can help to understand the balance and spatial localization ability of the human body under stress and provide a reference basis for related fields.
- Pay attention to environmental color differences and body posture changes: environmental color differences and body posture may also have an effect on kinesthetic orientation, familiar environment and correct training posture can help to enhance the effect of kinesthetic perception training, so it is important to design more suitable for the individual's specific environment and standardize the training posture in order to achieve the effect of rehabilitation training or to improve the ability to perceive.

4.4 Muscle Memory Forgetting Curve Exploration Experimental Conclusion

We draw the forgetting curves of the three training methods with the increase of time as shown in Fig. 15, where $\lambda 1$, $\lambda 2$ and $\lambda 3$ represent different training times 5 times, 10 times and 15 times respectively. By analyzing we can get the following conclusions:

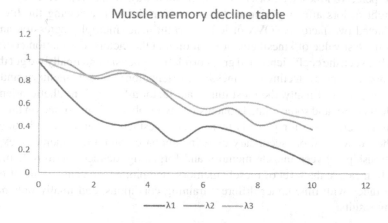

Fig. 15. Muscle memory index decline chart

1. We can see from the muscle memory decline graph that the value of the muscle memory index is decreasing with the increase of time, indicating that the muscle memory is decreasing with time.
2. We can see that with the increase of time, the decline rate of muscle memory is different for different number of training times, and it is obvious from the graph that the decline trend of blue > the decline trend of orange > the decline trend of yellow, which indicates that the decline trend of training five times > the decline trend of training ten times > the decline trend of training fifteen times, and therefore it can be concluded that the higher the number of training times, the slower the decline trend.
3. We can find that the transient memory just after training has a very big influence by observing the initial value (when the horizontal coordinate time is 0), the initial value is higher under each number of training times, and with the increase of the number of training times, the transient memory is also stronger, and the accuracy is also higher.
4. We can get a point of the fastest decline under each training number (the red point in the figure), which is recorded as the fastest decline point of muscle memory, and the fastest decline point varies with different training numbers, and the time of the fastest decline point is gradually moving backward with the number of training numbers increasing. We can also be inspired by the fastest descending point: in the process of kinesthetic treatment for patients or kinesthetic exercise for athletes, we should pay attention to the fastest descending point when the initial training value is certain, and we just conduct one training, muscle memory will certainly decline gradually, but rehabilitation training and athletes need to be repeatedly trained, so we must pay attention to training before the arrival of the fastest descending point in the process of repeated training. The conclusion is instructive in that we must train before the point of maximal decline so that we can achieve the goal of the training more effectively.

5   Conclusion

Kinesthetic orientation refers to the human body's ability to perceive and recognize its own posture and movement state. This experiment can radiate the human body's ability to perceive kinesthetic orientation in a small way. In this article, first of all, we found eight factors affecting kinesthetic orientation through reviewing the literature, we conducted two-factor ANOVA of left and right hand, multiple regression analysis between the test value of kinesthetic orientation and the factors, correlation coefficient analysis between the coefficients, and grey correlation analysis, and finally we got that the most important factor affecting the kinesthetic orientation is muscle memory, and some related conclusions. Finally, the most important factor affecting kinesthetic orientation is muscle memory and some related conclusions were obtained, and based on this, some suggestions were made for patients to recover kinesthetic awareness and athletes to train. Then we carried out secondary experiments based on muscle memory, explored the relationship between muscle memory and forgetting, defined the muscle memory index λ to measure the level of muscle memory, and plotted the change rule of muscle memory index with time under different training conditions, and finally obtained the following results:

1. There is a certain relationship between left and right hand, age, gender, environmental color difference, environmental music, body posture, heart rate, arm pressure, muscle memory and kinesthetic orientation perception ability, in which the influence of muscle memory is relatively significant, while the dominant hand in a small angle of the manual perception of orientation ability is obviously stronger, but with the increase of the angle of the dominance of the gradual decline. There is also a certain correlation between the various indicators, and based on the analysis results we proposed training and rehabilitation recommendations.

2. We plotted the muscle forgetting curves under different initial training conditions, and obtained the conclusion that muscle memory declines gradually with time and some correlations, and defined a new concept of "the fastest declining point of muscle memory", based on which we also put forward medical and training rehabilitation recommendations, which is of guiding significance.

Limitations and Future Work. There are some limitations in this paper due to the conditions, as the experimenters were recruited from the campus, the age variation is not very big for 18–24 years old college students, the sample size in this aspect of the age is a little bit insufficient. At the same time, the male to female ratio in the University of Technology is high, and the sample size of male students is much larger than the sample size of female students, so there is a certain error in terms of gender. At the same time, this paper only puts forward some basic concepts and conclusions in the study of muscle memory amnesia curve, gives some suggestions and does not go deeper to put forward quantitative methods, the follow-up still needs to be further explored under the condition of expanding the sample capacity.

References

1. Liu, Y.: Design of human-computer interaction system based on virtual reality and its application in the dissemination of study lodge culture. In: 2023 4th International Conference on Intelligent Design (ICID), pp. 251–256. IEEE (2023)
2. Zhang, Q.L.: Research on fall risk assessment of the elderly based on postural control ability. Soochow University (2017). https://doi.org/10.27351/d.cnki.gszhu.2017.000085
3. Song, X., Liu, M., Gong, L., et al.: A review of human-computer interface evaluation research based on evaluation process elements. In: Kurosu, M., Hashizume, A. (eds.) HCII 2023. LNCS, vol. 14011, pp. 262–289. Springer, Cham (2023). https://doi.org/10.1007/978-3-031-35596-7_17
4. Yan, Z.: An experimental study on the effects of visual and kinesthetic representations on learning effects at different stages of aerobics motor skill formation. Ningbo University (2015)
5. Wang, J.: A review of research on kinesthesia in the field of sports. Contemp. Sports Sci. Technol. **5**(04), 250+252 (2015). https://doi.org/10.16655/j.cnki.2095-2813.2015.04.001
6. Chen, G.D.: Vocal training based on human muscle memory to neural conditioning. Huang Zhong (China. J. Wuhan Conservatory Music) (02), 179–184 (2013)
7. Wang, B., Gao, Z., Shidujaman, M.: Meaningful place: a phenomenological approach to the design of spatial experience in open-world games. Games Cult. 15554120231171290 (2023)
8. Shan, L., Liu, Y., Zhang, X., et al.: Bioinspired kinesthetic system for human-machine interaction. Nano Energy **88**, 106283 (2021)

9. Zhang, Y., Cao, Y., Liu, Y., et al.: Intelligent human-computer interaction interface: a bibliometric analysis of 2010–2022. In: Duffy, V.G. (ed.) HCII 2023. LNCS, vol. 14029, pp. 590–604. Springer, Cham (2023). https://doi.org/10.1007/978-3-031-35748-0_40

10. Huang, A.-Q., Ruan, L., Wang, F.-Q.: An experimental study of wrist kinesthetic orientation discrimination in ice hockey players. Ice Snow Sports (01), 23–25 (2008)

11. Liu, M., Song, X., Shidujaman, M.: A study of driver fatigue states in multiple scenarios based on the fatigue and sleepiness indicator. In: Kurosu, M., et al. (eds.) HCII 2022. LNCS, pp. 581–596. Springer, Cham (2022). https://doi.org/10.1007/978-3-031-17615-9_41

12. Yu, J., Liang, C.: On kinesthesia. In: Professional Committee of Exercise Psychology of the Chinese Society of Sport Science, Professional Committee of Sport Psychology of the Chinese Psychological Association. Proceedings of the 8th National Sport Psychology Conference. College of Sports Science, Shenyang Normal University; College of Sports and Human Body Science, Beijing Sport University (2006)

13. Jiang, J.: A comparative study of perceptual abilities of athletes in cyclic and non-cyclic sports. Northeast Normal University (2006)

14. Hou, Y., Wang, K.: On the application of "kinesthetic orientation" in the formation of gymnastic skills. J. Jilin Inst. Phys. Educ. **S1**, 115–116 (2005)

15. Li, X., Zhao, X., Huang, Q.: Research on the effect of trial movement on the performance of motor skill practice. Modern Skill Dev. (01), 14–15 (2001)

16. Yan, S.: Accuracy of elbow joint kinesthetic orientation at different time intervals after quantitative exercise loading. J. Psychol. (01), 84–89 (1999)

17. Bai, L., Chen, Q.: Muscle memory. J. Northwest Normal Univ. (Nat. Sci. Ed.) (01), 61–63 (1993). https://doi.org/10.16783/j.cnki.nwnuz.1993.01.012

18. Xu, S.: Relationship between kinesthetic perceptibility of upper extremity joints and physical training. J. Psychol. (01), 94–102 (1964)

19. Hess, R., Zaal, P.: Visual perception in manual control. In: AIAA Modeling and Simulation Technology Conference (2012)

20. Cardullo, F., Stanco, A., Hosman, R.: Somatosensory systems: physiology and modeling. In: AIAA Modeling and Simulation Technology Conference (2012)

Abstraction Level: Evidence from an Event-Related Potential Study

Yu Zhang, Jinchun Wu, and Chengqi Xue[✉]

School of Mechanical Engineering, Southeast University, Nanjing 211189, China
ipd_xcq@seu.edu.cn

Abstract. Icons, essential for Human-Computer Interaction (HCI), significantly influence interface interaction efficiency. The representation and recognition of icons are crucial, and concise, accurate design enhances usability. Excessively abstract icons may hinder recognition, increasing learning costs and cognitive difficulty. This study explores the impact of abstraction levels on recognition efficiency and usability in two types of product icons (practical and hedonic). Reaction time, recognition accuracy, and ERP data were measured for high, medium and low abstraction levels. Results indicate that, for practical products, medium-abstraction icons had better matching, while high-abstraction icons showed better matching in hedonic products.

Keywords: Icon design · Icon abstraction level · Practical products · Hedonic products · ERP

1 Introduction

The study of icon usability and characteristics is a significant topic in the field of HCI. Traditional icon design methods employed by designers, such as holistic abstraction and metaphorical abstraction, are based on design principles and personal experience, rather than a standardized approach to icon design. In the context of smart home interfaces, where product icons are prevalent, the design process involves an evolution from the actual product form to a more abstract representation, a process known as abstraction. If an icon design is overly abstract, it can increase the cognitive complexity for users; conversely, if the icon is too concrete and includes many feature elements, it can clutter the interface and obstruct the transmission of the icon's semantic meaning. Therefore, examining the impact of product icon abstraction on cognitive efficiency is crucial for enhancing the efficiency of icon design and guiding the design of product icons. Common sense suggests that higher levels of icon abstraction make the icons more challenging to recognize and require more cognitive attention resources. However, whether this rule applies uniformly across different types of products needs to be empirically validated.

M. Kurosu and A. Hashizume (Eds.): HCII 2024, LNCS 14687, pp. 343–362, 2024.
https://doi.org/10.1007/978-3-031-60441-6_22

2 Product Type Categorization

Through literature research, it has been found that the main bases for product classification include familiarity, product functionality and economic aspects [1]. Studies have used familiarity as a basis for product classification to explore the impact of product familiarity on brand recognition. This was investigated through a cognitive experiment on the match between 40 home appliance products and brands (20 of which were common brands in the market, and the other 20 were artificially created brands that had never been sold in the market). This study aimed to determine how product familiarity affects users' brand recognition. The results revealed that participants showed a higher acceptance for products and brands with high familiarity and low conflict [2]. Although classifying products based on familiarity aligns with common sense, the variability in individual users' familiarity with products makes it difficult to apply the findings universally. Therefore, this approach was not adopted for product classification in this paper.

On the other hand, classification from the perspective of product functional value has been considered. Holbrook and Hirschman, among others, describe hedonic consumption as a form of consumption that transcends emotional experience, involving continuous satisfaction and pleasure. This implies that consumers purchase hedonic products for their emotional value rather than practical utility. Practical products focus more on tangible returns during consumption, i.e., the practical functionality of the product [3]. For example, when purchasing a washing machine, consumers are more concerned about whether it can clean clothes effectively and whether it has complete washing functions, focusing on its practical functionality. In contrast, gaming consoles are different. Regardless of the type, users pay more attention to the pleasure and excitement brought by the game content, thus classifying them as hedonic products. Literature research indicates that practical and hedonic are commonly used product classifications. Compared to other methods, the classification into practical and hedonic products has a closer relationship with design and offers more topics for discussion. Therefore, this study classifies products into practical and hedonic for researching the impact of icon abstractness on cognitive recognition efficiency.

Relevant research on these two types of product classification mainly stems from the different purchasing desires they evoke in consumers [4]. Dewi and Ang's study indicates that practical products have strong functionality, and consumer behavior towards these products is primarily driven by cognition with a clear goal orientation [5]. Consumption of this type rarely brings sensory pleasure or guilt to the user [6]. Hedonic products, on the other hand, bring physiological and psychological satisfaction to users in the form of fun and pleasure, but may also trigger guilt in consumers before, during or after consumption [7]. Holbrook and Hirschman propose the concept of "experiential" consumption for hedonic products from the cognitive-affective dimension of information [3]. When assessing the hedonic attributes of a product, emotion plays a crucial role, involving basic human motivations like satisfaction, pleasure, and enjoyment, which are inherent in the product's attributes [8]. Practical products, in contrast, are considered from a rational perspective and are usually task-related. For instance, when purchasing practical products, consumers typically consider using the product to complete a task rather than for emotional consumption, so evaluations of practical products often focus on their functional attributes and usage efficiency.

2.1 Characteristics of Practical Products

In this study, products were categorized based on their practical and hedonic attributes. The practical attribute of a product refers to its primary function, with consumers focusing more on its practical value rather than emotional value [9]. For example, a washing machine provides the function of washing clothes, and consumers primarily consider its effectiveness in cleaning clothes when making a purchase. Overall, practical products are characterized by the following features:

1. Simplistic and Uniform Design: Extensive research and comparisons have shown that practical products often have a more uniform and simplistic design. For instance, laptops (see Fig. 1) generally have a regular rectangular shape, with little variation across different brands.
2. Prominent Functional Attributes: Practical products need to offer practical value, thus highlighting functional elements. For example, the drum of a washing machine and the keyboard of a laptop are their main visual elements, both representing functional attributes.
3. High Familiarity with Users: These products are often used frequently in daily life, making them highly familiar to users. As such, they do not require much attention or learning effort to be perceived and have high transferability in terms of learning.

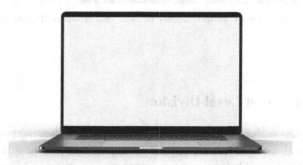

Fig. 1. Example of a practical product (using a laptop as an example).

2.2 Characteristics of Hedonic Products

Unlike practical products, the hedonic attributes of a product primarily refer to the emotional and physical pleasure and satisfaction that users derive from such products. When purchasing hedonic products, consumers focus more on the emotional value they provide. Hedonic products are characterized by the following features [10]:

1. Basic Functionality: As a product, achieving a certain functional task is a fundamental characteristic. On this basis, if it can offer additional emotional value to the user, it qualifies as a hedonic product.
2. Diverse and Unique Forms: Hedonic products often adopt a variety of designs to attract consumers' attention and meet different aesthetic needs. For instance, humidifiers, as found through research, have at least five different forms.
3. Higher Learning Cost: Compared to practical products, the variety in design of hedonic products means that consumers need to spend more time to use them, and the transferability of learning is relatively lower.
4. Metaphorical Design: To satisfy consumers' emotional needs, hedonic products often use metaphorical design approaches. For example, the humidifier in the first image of Fig. 2 is designed in the shape of a ghost, while the humidifier in the third image adopts a spacecraft design for its exterior.

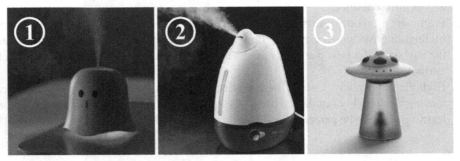

Fig. 2. Schematic diagram of various forms of hedonic products (taking humidifiers as an example).

3 Icon Abstraction Level Division

Abstractness refers to the degree of abstraction of an icon, indicating how much an icon deviates from real-world objects. The level of an icon's abstractness is a key factor in its recognizability [11]. Abstraction often appears as an antonym to concreteness. For example, Fig. 3 shows designs with varying levels of abstraction. Taking the computer monitor icon as an example, a concrete icon contains more features of the object, closely resembling the actual item. As the level of abstraction increases, fewer internal features are retained in the icon, often just keeping outlines or area lines [12]. In icon research, abstract and concrete icons are frequently contrasted against each other to compare their perceptual characteristics, user recognition and search performance to select the optimal design.

Fig. 3. Computer display icons with different levels of abstraction (increasing abstraction from left to right).

3.1 Icon Abstraction Level Control Method

To ensure a consistent degree of abstraction across all generated icons at various nodes, this study utilized Adobe Illustrator 2021 software and its Blend Tool to quantitatively set the process of icon abstractness changes. The specific implementation method for icon abstractness is as follows: First, based on the product's actual image, a corresponding wireframe diagram (i.e., the starting point of icon abstraction) is drawn. Next, the external geometric outline that represents the overall shape characteristics of the icon is selected as the endpoint of the icon's abstraction process. The abstraction step from the starting point to the endpoint is set to N, where a larger step value indicates a slower change process, and a smaller step value indicates a faster change process. The specific process is detailed in Fig. 4 (using a power bank as an example).

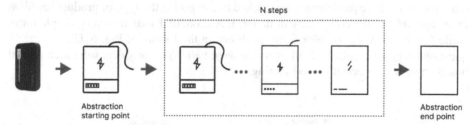

Fig. 4. Schematic diagram of the specific implementation process of icon abstraction level control method.

Assuming a step value of N = 10, the effects of icon generation can be seen in Fig. 5. Taking the example of a socket from practical products and a humidifier from hedonic

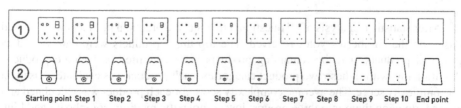

Fig. 5. The sequence of continuous changes of icons (1 is a practical product, 2 is a hedonic product).

products, a continuous sequence of their abstract icons was created using the tool, with abstraction levels of the icons increasing progressively from left to right.

3.2 Icon Abstraction Level Selection

Previous studies on icon abstractness have typically categorized icons into just two types: concrete and abstract. However, this paper, referencing other scholars' research on icon complexity based on the number of graphic features and elements an icon contains, classifies icon complexity into three levels: low, medium and high [13]. In conjunction with Adobe Illustrator 2021's Blend Tool, the abstractness of icons was quantitatively controlled at three levels: low, medium and high. These levels of abstractness, as validated by design experts, correspond to 20%, 50% and 80% abstraction, respectively. In the software-generated continuous abstract icon sequence, these correspond to the 2nd, 5th and 8th steps, respectively.

4 Material and Methods

4.1 Material

In this experiment, all products selected for testing were based in the field of Internet of Things (IoT) applications, with a total of 60 products chosen. Considering the impact of product complexity on the experimental results, a survey was conducted using Wenjuanxing (https://www.wjx.cn). Each product was scored using the Likert five-point scale method, where participants were asked to categorize the type of product based on its image and rate the complexity of its form. A score of 1 indicates very simple form, while 5 indicates very complex form, as shown in the format of Fig. 6. Ultimately, 30 questionnaires were collected, all of which were valid. The products were then ranked based on their categorization and scoring.

Fig. 6. Example of a product classification and complexity questionnaire.

After statistical analysis of all questionnaire data, the practical products were ranked based on the number of votes received. The top thirty products were categorized as practical products, and the remaining products were classified as hedonic products. Additionally, within these two product categories, each product was evaluated based on its complexity score. The average complexity score for each product was calculated and ranked, dividing them into three groups: low complexity, medium complexity and high complexity, with ten products in each group. This ensured that the complexity levels of products within both categories were approximately equivalent.

4.2 Stimuli

After the selection and categorization of products, a further step was to vectorize the chosen product images. This was accomplished using Adobe Illustrator 2021, where the Pen Tool was utilized to create vector graphics of each product. Following this uniform procedure for all products resulted in wireframe diagrams of each. Subsequently, each product wireframe diagram was subjected to an abstraction process. The starting point of abstraction was the product's original wireframe diagram, while the end point was its basic geometric outline. The abstraction process was set to a 10-step sequence, and the 2nd, 5th and 8th step graphics in this sequence were selected as the experimental stimulus icons. To ensure the icons' aesthetics and recognizability, minor adjustments were made. The resulting stimulus icons are as shown in Table 1.

Table 1. Examples of stimulus icons (using power banks and humidifiers as examples).

	Practical products (power bank)	Hedonic products (humidifiers)
Low abstraction		
Medium abstraction		
High abstraction		

4.3 Icon Recognition Experiment

Design. This experiment employed a dual-stimulus presentation approach to observe the behavioral responses and cognitive brain signals of participants when stimuli were presented. The experimental paradigm used was the classic S1-S2 format, where Stimulus 1 is presented first, followed by Stimulus 2. There were two levels of experimental factors: product type (practical and hedonic products) and icon abstraction degree (low, medium, and high abstraction). Thus, the experiment had a 2 (product type) x 3 (abstraction level) = 6 levels design. The detection items were icons, with a total of 60 products, each having three levels of abstract icons, resulting in 180 standard trials. To prevent learning effects in participants, an additional 20% of distractor trials were added, meaning each participant needed to complete 245 trials. The experiment was divided into three sessions with two breaks in between, taking approximately 25 min in total.

Procedure. The experimental procedure began by displaying a 500 ms fixation cross (" +") at the center of the screen to balance the visual field. This was followed by the presentation of Stimulus S1 (product name) at the screen center for 1000 ms, for participants to memorize. Then, a 500 ms fixation cross was displayed again at the screen center to balance the participants' vision. Subsequently, Stimulus S2 (test icon, including both matching and non-matching cases with S1) was presented at the screen center. Participants were required to determine whether the icon matched the previously presented product name, pressing the 'q' key for a match and the 'p' key for a non-match. Finally, a blank screen appeared for 1000 ms to complete one trial, as illustrated in Fig. 7. The experiment comprised 225 trials in total, with 80% (180 trials) being standard trials and the remaining 20% (45 trials) being distractor trials.

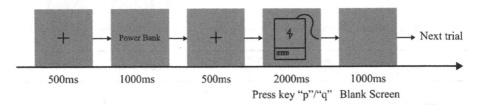

Fig. 7. ERP experimental process.

Participant. The participants of this experiment were undergraduate and graduate students from Southeast University, totaling 22 individuals. The group was evenly divided by gender, with 11 males and 11 females, ranging in age from 19 to 25 years ($M = 23$, $SD = 1.79$). The participants were equally divided between those with and without a design background to mitigate the impact of educational background on the experimental results. All participants were free of color blindness or color weakness, were right-handed, and had no known brain abnormalities or psychiatric disorders.

Apparatus and Environment. The experiment was conducted in the Human Factors Engineering Laboratory at Southeast University. The experimental program was set up using E-prime 2.0 software. The display used was a 27-inch monitor with a resolution of 1920*1080, and the brightness of the monitor was set to 92 cd/m2. The equipment utilized in this study was the 64-channel EEG system from Brain Products, USA. Additionally, a computer equipped with E-prime 2.0 was required for the experiment. Essential items such as EEG paste and syringe needles were prepared in advance. Participants were asked to wash and dry their hair before the experiment. An EEG cap was fitted on each participant, and electrode paste was applied.

ERP Data Recording. During the experiment, reaction time and accuracy data were collected using E-prime 2.0, while participants' Event-Related Potentials (ERP) data were recorded using the Vision Recorder software (see Fig. 8), which was later used for data analysis. Behavioral data were analyzed using SPSS 20 software through a two-way repeated measures ANOVA to observe differences and perform statistical analysis. EEG data were analyzed using the EEG Lab tool in Matlab. This involved initial filtering to remove artifacts such as eye movements and blinks, followed by segmenting and averaging the continuous EEG data to obtain the final EEG waveform data. This process allowed observation of peak changes at different levels and times, facilitating analysis of the variations caused by each independent variable.

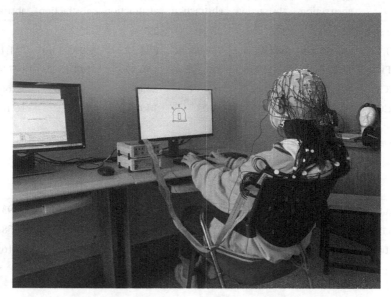

Fig. 8. Data collection scenario during the experiment.

5 Results

5.1 Behavioral Data Analysis

Based on the experimental records, a repeated measures ANOVA was conducted on all participants' reaction times and accuracy rates. The data statistical analysis was carried out using IBM SPSS 20. The results can be found in Tables 2, 3, 4 and Figs. 9, 10.

Table 2 shows the descriptive statistics of the experimental data. It indicates significant differences in reaction times and accuracy rates between different levels of abstraction within both practical and hedonic products. Moreover, it is observed that as the level of abstraction increases, reaction times also increase, while accuracy rates decrease.

Reaction Time. A repeated measures ANOVA was conducted on the reaction time data (see Table 3). The analysis revealed a significant main effect for product type (F (1, 21) = 5.007, p = 0.036 < 0.05, η^2 = 0.193) and a significant main effect for the level of icon abstraction (F (2,42) = 26.463, p < 0.001, η^2 = 0.558). However, there was no significant interaction effect between product type and icon abstraction level (F (2,42) = 0.336, p = 0.696 > 0.05, η^2 = 0.016).

Table 2. Descriptive statistics of behavioral data.

	Practical products			Hedonic products		
	Low abstraction	Medium abstraction	High abstraction	Low abstraction	Medium abstraction	High abstraction
Sample size	22	22	22	22	22	22
M (RT)	663.36 ms	682.45 ms	727.94 ms	694.32 ms	699.33 ms	751.14 ms
SD (RT)	139.51	130.23	143.97	146.42	144.15	147.86
M (ACC)	82.62%	75.29%	46.73%	84.69%	71.99%	52.66%
SD (ACC)	16.72	16.92	21.03	14.45	17.65	16.10

Table 3. Significance effect analysis of reaction time.

	F	p	η^2
Product type	$F(1,21) = 5.007$	0.036*	0.193
Abstraction	$F(2,42) = 26.463$	< 0.001**	0.558
Product type $\times$ Abstraction	$F(2,42) = 0.336$	0.696	0.016

Note: * indicates significance at $0.01 < p < 0.05$; ** indicates $p < 0.01$

In practical products, icons with high levels of abstraction had the longest reaction times (M = 727.94 ms, SD = 143.97), followed by those with medium abstraction (M = 682.45 ms, SD = 130.23), while icons with low abstraction had the shortest reaction times (M = 663.36 ms, SD = 139.51). The difference in reaction time between low and medium abstraction icons was about 19.09 ms, and between medium and high abstraction icons was 45.49 ms. This indicates that for practical product icons, as the level of abstraction increases, the recognition speed becomes slower. The shift from low to medium abstraction is more easily accepted by participants, whereas the shift from medium to high abstraction slows down the recognition speed by almost double compared to the shift from low to medium.

A similar pattern was observed in hedonic products, where icons with high levels of abstraction had the longest reaction times (M = 751.14 ms, SD = 147.86), followed by those with medium (M = 699.33 ms, SD = 144.15) and low abstraction (M = 694.32 ms, SD = 146.42). The difference in reaction time between low and medium abstraction icons was 5.01 ms, while the difference between medium and high abstraction icons was 51.81 ms. This indicates that for hedonic product icons, as the level of abstraction increases, the icon recognition speed decreases. The change in abstraction from medium to high has a greater impact on participants' recognition efficiency compared to the change from low to medium abstraction.

Comparing the reaction times for icons of practical and hedonic products reveals that in low abstraction icons, the recognition reaction time for hedonic products (M = 694.32 ms, SD = 146.42) is greater than that for practical products (M = 663.36 ms, SD = 139.51), with a difference of 30.96 ms. In medium abstraction icons, the

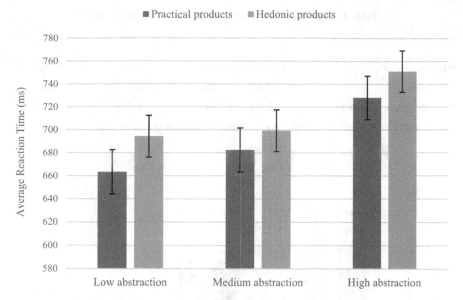

Fig. 9. Reaction time bar chart.

recognition reaction time for hedonic product icons (M = 699.33 ms, SD = 144.15) is 16.88 ms longer than that for practical product icons (M = 682.45 ms, SD = 139.51). Furthermore, in high abstraction icons, the reaction time for hedonic product icons (M = 751.14 ms, SD = 147.86) is 23.2 ms longer than for practical product icons (M = 727.94 ms, SD = 143.97). Thus, regardless of the level of abstraction, the reaction time for hedonic product icons is consistently longer than for practical product icons. This can be attributed to human long-term memory; in daily life, practical products generally have a uniform shape and a simple design, whereas hedonic products have diverse and variable forms, making them more difficult to recognize.

Response Accuracy Rate. A two-way repeated measures ANOVA was conducted on the participants' response accuracy data (see Table 4). There was no significant effect between product types (F $(1, 21)$ = 0.000, p = 0.989 > 0.05, η^2 = 0.000), indicating the absence of a main effect and suggesting that the accuracy rate differences between the two product categories were not substantial. A significant effect was observed between levels of abstraction (F $(2, 42)$ = 31.501, p < 0.001, η^2 = 0.600), indicating a main effect where the level of abstraction significantly impacts accuracy rates. The interaction between product type and level of abstraction showed no significant difference (F $(2, 42)$ = 0.254, p = 0.765 > 0.05, η^2 = 0.012), suggesting that the relationship between participants' response accuracy and the interaction of product type with icon abstraction level is relatively weak.

From the average accuracy rates, it is observed that in practical products, the response accuracy decreases with increasing icon abstraction. The order is as follows: low abstraction icons have the highest accuracy (M = 82.62%, SD = 16.72), followed by medium abstraction icons (M = 75.29%, SD = 16.92), and high abstraction icons have the lowest

Table 4. Significant effect analysis of response accuracy rate.

	F	p	η^2
Product type	$F(1,21) = 0.000$	0.989	0.000
Abstraction	$F(2,42) = 31.501$	$< 0.001**$	0.600
Product type × Abstraction	$F(2,42) = 0.254$	0.765	0.012

Note: * indicates significance at $0.01 < p < 0.05$; ** indicates $p < 0.01$

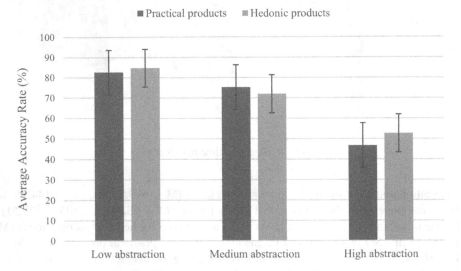

Fig. 10. Response accuracy rate bar chart.

accuracy (M = 46.73%, SD = 21.03). The accuracy difference between low and medium abstraction icons is about 7.33%, which is not significant. However, the difference in accuracy between medium and high abstraction icons is 28.56%, approximately four times that of the former. This indicates that in practical products, the higher the level of abstraction, the more difficult it is for participants to recognize the icons, resulting in lower accuracy rates.

In hedonic products, the same trend is observed: as the level of abstraction of the icons increases, the response accuracy gradually declines. The order is low abstraction icons (M = 84.69%, SD = 14.45), followed by medium abstraction icons (M = 71.99%, SD = 17.65), and finally, high abstraction icons have the lowest accuracy (M = 52.66%, SD = 16.10). The difference in accuracy between low and medium abstraction icons is 12.7%, while the difference between medium and high abstraction icons is 19.66%, slightly greater than the former.

Comparing the icons of practical and hedonic products, in the case of low abstraction icons, the response accuracy of hedonic product icons is slightly higher than that of practical products, but the difference is marginal. In medium abstraction icons, the response accuracy of practical product icons is higher than that of hedonic product icons.

For high abstraction icons, the response accuracy of hedonic product icons is higher than that of practical products. This suggests that practical products have a higher cognitive efficiency and icon usability at medium abstraction levels, while compared to practical products, hedonic products have higher cognitive efficiency with high abstraction icons.

ERP Data Analysis. The collected EEG data were first preprocessed using the EEGLab toolbox in Matlab 2013. Initially, the raw data were segmented to extract the effective wavebands from 200 ms before to 800 ms after stimulus presentation. The data were then filtered to remove frequencies below 0.1Hz and above 30Hz, as shown in Fig. 11. Using TP9 and TP10 electrodes as reference, the data from each participant were categorized and averaged, resulting in the final ERP data.

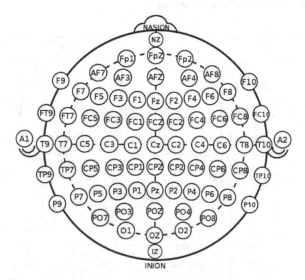

Fig. 11. Diagram illustrating the distribution of electrodes on the human brain.

Based on the waveform (see Fig. 12) and topographic maps (see Table 5), it is evident that peak values vary under different product types and abstraction conditions, with three distinct components being P2, N400, and LPP. Figure 12 shows clear differences in the P2 component, which occurs at 200 ms post-stimulus presentation, between practical and hedonic products. Icons of varying abstraction levels all triggered the N400 component, with the N400 peak being largest for low-abstraction practical product icons and significantly more negative than that for low-abstraction hedonic product icons. There are noticeable differences in peak values at 600 ms across different levels, with the LPP being largest for low-abstraction hedonic product icons, followed by low-abstraction practical product icons.

According to the waveform graph at the Fz electrode (see Fig. 13), it is observed that icons with high abstraction elicited the largest N400 amplitude, followed by medium abstraction, and the lowest amplitude was caused by low abstraction icons. This suggests that high abstraction icons create difficulty in understanding for participants, leading to a sense of mismatch. Among high abstraction icons, the N400 amplitude generated by practical product icons was greater than that of hedonic product icons, consistent with the behavioral data results. This indicates that high abstraction in practical products leads to a significant sense of mismatch. When medium abstraction icons were presented, the N400 amplitude induced by hedonic product icons was significantly higher than that of practical product icons. Similarly, at low abstraction levels, the N400 amplitude caused by hedonic product icons was higher than that caused by practical product icons. This indicates that under medium abstraction conditions, practical product icons are easier to recognize and understand compared to hedonic product icons. This result aligns with the behavioral findings, suggesting that practical products are more easily recognized and understood at medium abstraction, while hedonic products have higher icon recognition efficiency under high abstraction conditions.

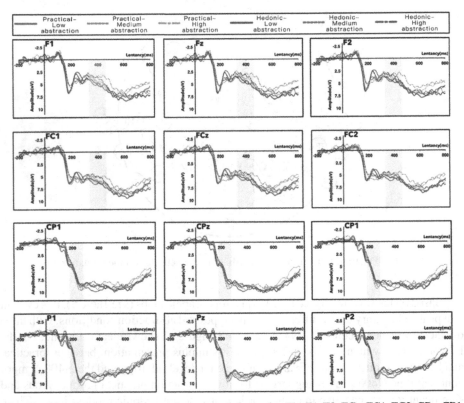

Fig. 12. Waveform graphs from twelve selected electrodes (Fz, F1, F2, FCz, FC1, FC2, CPz, CP1, CP2, Pz, P1, P2) at different levels (low abstraction practical icons, medium abstraction practical icons, high abstraction practical icons, low abstraction hedonic icons, medium abstraction hedonic icons, and high abstraction hedonic icons).

LPP, also generated due to semantic processing mismatches, typically appears between 600-800 ms post-stimulus presentation. The waveform graphs from the Fz electrode site (see Fig. 13) exhibit clear differences in LPP across different levels. In practical products, the LPP amplitude for medium and high abstraction icons is notably higher than under other conditions, with the high abstraction icons producing a greater amplitude than the medium abstraction icons. This indicates that high abstraction icons in practical products lead to a more intense semantic mismatch, consistent with behavioral data results. The graph shows that the LPP amplitude induced by high abstraction hedonic product icons is roughly similar to that caused by medium abstraction practical product icons, almost overlapping around 600 ms. This suggests that the sense of semantic mismatch caused by high abstraction hedonic product icons and medium abstraction practical product icons is similar. The smallest amplitude is observed with low abstraction icons, where the amplitude induced by practical product icons is greater than that caused by hedonic product icons.

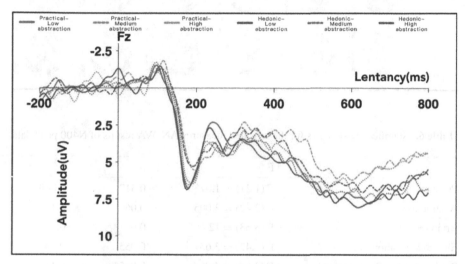

Fig. 13. Waveform graphs at different levels at the Fz electrode.

N400. According to the topographic maps in Table 5, the amplitude size and regions vary across different brain areas. Therefore, the peak data between 350-450 ms for each participant were extracted for analysis. A repeated measures ANOVA was conducted comparing 2 product types (practical vs. hedonic) × 3 levels of abstraction (low, medium, high) × 4 brain regions (frontal, frontocentral, centroparietal, parietal) (corresponding to electrodes F, FC, CP and P) × 3 electrode positions (left, center, right). The results are shown in Table 6.

A two-way repeated measures ANOVA conducted on data from 350 ms to 450 ms revealed no significant effect between product types (practical × hedonic) on the average ERP peak values (F (1, 21) = 1.075, p = 0.312 > 0.05, η^2 = 0.049), nor was there a significant effect between levels of abstraction (low × medium × high) and N400 peak averages (F (2, 42) = 3.005, p = 0.06 > 0.05, η^2 = 0.125). However, there was a significant effect among different brain regions (F (3, 63) = 12.686, p = 0.001 < 0.05, η^2 = 0.377), with the N400 amplitudes generated in the parietal and centroparietal regions being greater than those generated in the frontal and frontocentral regions (CP > P, p

Table 5. Topographic maps under different level conditions for P2 (180-220 ms), N400 (350-450 ms), and LPP (600-800 ms).

	Practical products			Hedonic products		
	Low abstraction	Medium ab-straction	High abstraction	Low abstraction	Medium ab-straction	High abstraction
P2						
N40 0						
LPP						

Table 6. Significance statistics for the repeated measures ANOVA results of N400 peak data.

	F	p	η^2
Product type	F (1,21) = 1.075	0.312	0.049
Abstraction	F (2,42) = 3.005	0.060	0.125
Brain region	F (3,63) = 12.686	0.001**	0.377
Electrode position	F (2,42) = 3.651	0.055	0.148
Product type × Brain region	F (3,63) = 4.068	0.045*	0.162
Abstraction × Brain region	F (6,126) = 3.880	0.020*	0.156
Product type × Abstraction × Brain region	F (6,126) = 0.612	0.585	0.028

Note: * indicates significance at $0.01 < p < 0.05$; ** indicates $p < 0.01$

= 1 > 0.05, CP > F, CP > FC, p < 0.001). No significant effect was observed among the left, center, and right electrode positions (F(2, 42) = 3.651, p = 0.055 > 0.05, $\eta^2 = 0.148$). There was a significant interaction effect between product type and brain regions (F (3, 63) = 3.068, p = 0.045 < 0.05, $\eta^2 = 0.162$), indicating that different product types lead to varying N400 amplitudes across brain regions. In the parietal region, the N400 amplitude produced by practical products was significantly greater than that produced by hedonic products (MD$_{P-H}$ = 0.755, SD = 0.355, p = 0.046 < 0.05, subscript refers to P(Practical)-H(Hedonic)). Within practical products, significant differences were observed across brain regions (F < FC < CP, p < 0.001, F < P, p = 0.019 < 0.05). A significant interaction effect existed between abstraction levels and brain regions (F (6, 126) = 3.880, p = 0.02 < 0.05, η^2 = 0.156), where different levels of abstraction caused variations in N400 amplitudes across different brain areas. At the frontal and frontocentral regions, the N400 amplitude produced by low abstraction icons was greater than that produced by high abstraction icons (Frontal: MD = 1.582, SD = 0.46, p = 0.007 < 0.05; Frontocentral: MD = 1.140, SD = 0.427, p = 0.043 < 0.05). Significant differences were found between the frontal and frontocentral regions and the centroparietal region under low and medium abstraction conditions (F < FC < CP, p = 0.001 < 0.05, p = 0.019 < 0.05), while significant differences were present among all brain regions under high abstraction conditions (F < FC < P < CP, p < 0.001, p = 0.009 < 0.05). No significant interaction effects were found between product types, levels of abstraction and brain regions (F (6, 126) = 0.612, p = 0.585 > 0.05, η^2 = 0.028).

LPP. The LPP component, also known as the P600 component, is a differential wave that appears around 600 ms after the presentation of a target stimulus. Analysis of peak data across different level factors can yield relevant conclusions. Using IBM SPSS 20, a two-way repeated measures ANOVA was conducted on the average peak values between 600-800 ms for 2 product types (practical vs. hedonic) × 3 levels of abstraction (low, medium, high) × 4 brain regions (frontal, frontocentral, centroparietal, parietal) (corresponding to electrodes F, FC, CP and P) × 3 electrode positions (left, center, right). The results are shown in Table 7.

Table 7. Significance statistics for the repeated measures ANOVA results of LPP peak data.

	F	p	η^2
Product type	F (1,21) = 3.325	0.082	0.137
Abstraction	F (2,42) = 2.936	0.064	0.123
Brain region	F (3,63) = 2.825	0.104	0.119
Electrode position	F (2,42) = 4.326	0.040*	0.171
Product type × Brain region	F (3,63) = 6.679	0.007**	0.241
Abstraction × Brain region	F (6,126) = 6.849	0.002**	0.246
Product type × Abstraction × Brain region	F (6,126) = 1.903	0.155	0.083
Product type × Abstraction × Brain region	F (4,84) = 0.305	0.730	0.014

Note: * indicates significance at 0.01 < p < 0.05; ** indicates p < 0.01

The statistical results revealed no significant differences between product types (F (1, 21) = 3.325, p = 0.082 > 0.05, η^2 = 0.137) or within levels of abstraction (F (2, 42) = 2.936, p = 0.064 > 0.05, η^2 = 0.123). However, significant differences were observed among different brain regions (frontal, frontocentral, centroparietal and parietal) (F (3, 63) = 2.825, p = 0.104 > 0.05, η^2 = 0.119) and electrode positions (left, center, right) (F (2, 42) = 4.326, p = 0.04 < 0.05, η^2 = 0.171). The midline LPP amplitude was greater than that of the sides (MD$_{M-L}$ = 0.051, SD$_{M-L}$ = 0.114, p$_{M,L}$ = 1.00 > 0.05,

$MD_{M-R} = 0.489$, $SD_{M,L} = 0.170$, $p_{M,R} = 0.028 < 0.05$, subscript refers to L(Low), M(Middle), H(High)). No significant difference in LPP amplitude was found between the left and right sides ($MD_{L-R} = 0.438$, $SD_{L,R} = 0.241$, $p_{L,R} = 0.251 > 0.05$). There was a significant interaction effect between product types and brain regions ($F (3, 63) = 6.679$, $p = 0.007 < 0.05$, $\eta^2 = 0.241$), indicating that different product types elicit LPP in different brain areas. In practical and hedonic products, significant differences were observed in LPP amplitude between the centroparietal and parietal regions (Practical: $MD_{CP-P} = 1.834$, $SD = 0.417$, $p = 0.002 < 0.05$; Hedonic: $MD_{CP-P} = 2.105$, $SD = 0.439$, $p < 0.001$), whereas no significant difference existed between the frontal and frontocentral regions (Practical: $MD_{FC-F} = 0.736$, $SD = 0.296$, $p = 0.127 > 0.05$; Hedonic: $MD_{FC-F} = 0.348$, $SD = 0.234$, $p = 0.907 > 0.05$). At the frontal region, the LPP amplitude induced by hedonic products was significantly greater than that produced by practical products ($MD_{H-P} = 1.367$, $SD = 0.446$, $p = 0.006 < 0.05$, subscript refers to P(Practical)-H(Hedonic)), with no significant amplitude differences induced by different product types in other brain regions (Frontocentral: $MD_{H-P} = 0.979$, $SD = 0.484$, $p = 0.056 > 0.05$; Centroparietal: $MD_{H-P} = 0.539$, $SD = 0.474$, $p = 0.268 > 0.05$; Parietal: $MD_{H-P} = 0.268$, $SD = 0.442$, $p = 0.55 > 0.05$). A significant interaction effect was also observed between levels of abstraction and brain regions ($F (6, 126) = 6.849$, $p = 0.002 < 0.05$, $\eta^2 = 0.246$), with significant differences between the centroparietal and parietal regions across different levels of abstraction (Low abstraction: $MD_{CP-P} = 2.112$, $SD = 0.453$, $p < 0.001$; Medium abstraction: $MD_{CP-P} = 2.034$, $SD = 0.433$, $p < 0.001$; High abstraction: $MD_{CP-P} = 1.761$, $SD = 0.403$, $p = 0.002 < 0.05$). At the frontal and frontocentral regions, the LPP amplitude induced by low abstraction icons was significantly greater than that produced by high abstraction icons (Frontal: $MD_{L-H} = 1.539$, $SD = 0.427$, $p = 0.005 < 0.05$; Frontocentral: $MD_{L-H} = 1.286$, $SD = 0.391$, $p = 0.011$). No significant interaction effects were found between product types, levels of abstraction and brain regions ($F (6, 126) = 1.903$, $p = 0.155 > 0.05$, $\eta^2 = 0.083$), nor between product types, levels of abstraction and electrode positions ($F (4, 84) = 0.305$, $p = 0.730 > 0.05$, $\eta^2 = 0.014$).

6 Discussion

From the analysis of behavioral data and ERP data, the following conclusions can be drawn: with increasing levels of abstraction, participants' reaction time lengthened, and the amplitude of the N400 component increased. Moreover, the reaction time for hedonic products were consistently longer than for practical products. This suggests that participants' long-term memory stores the specific form of products rather than abstract representations. When presented with low-abstraction icons, there is a higher match with the product form stored in the brain, making it easier for participants to recognize and understand. The longer response time for hedonic products is attributed to the variability in their forms in daily life, making it difficult for icons to match prototypes in long-term memory. For example, there are more than ten different designs of humidifiers seen in daily life, making it challenging for participants to match even less abstract icons with the mental prototype, thereby increasing response times.

The accuracy results also revealed cognitive differences between the two types of products and their respective levels of icon abstraction. As the level of abstraction increased, the accuracy of participants' responses decreased, and the difference in accuracy between practical and hedonic products grew larger. With low-abstraction icons, the accuracy of hedonic product icons was slightly higher than that of practical products, both above 80%, with a difference of only 2.07%. The N400 amplitude at this level also showed a slightly greater amplitude for hedonic products compared to practical products. This indicates that participants found low-abstraction product icons easier to perceive and recognize, with no significant cognitive difference between the two types of products at this level of abstraction. However, with medium-abstraction icons, the accuracy rate for practical product icons was higher than for hedonic product icons, with a difference of 3.3%, and both N400 and LPP amplitudes showed significantly larger values for hedonic products. This suggests that under medium abstraction conditions, practical product icons are easier to recognize than hedonic ones. When high-abstraction icons were presented, the response accuracy of hedonic product icons was significantly higher than that of practical products, with a difference of 5.93%, and the N400 amplitude showed that practical products had slightly higher amplitudes. This indicates that compared to practical products, hedonic products with high-abstraction icons have a higher cognitive efficiency.

Therefore, the study suggests the following guidelines for abstract icon design in products: for practical product icons, the level of abstraction should be kept moderate. Too low abstraction can lead to an overload of information elements in the icon, hindering interface information presentation, while too high abstraction impedes icon recognition and understanding. In contrast, icons for hedonic products can be highly abstracted, as these products often have diverse forms in daily life, and there is no fixed prototype in users' long-term memory to match them. Higher abstraction can reduce information load and highlight local features of the icon, making it easier for users to learn and recognize.

7 Conclusion

This study explored the relationship between icon abstractness and product type building on the cognitive characteristics of icons. For practical products, it is appropriate to retain their basic form with a moderate degree of abstraction. In contrast, for hedonic products, it's beneficial to preserve their unique internal features and maintain a higher level of icon abstraction, facilitating easier recognition and understanding by users, and enhancing icon usability.

However, the study also has several limitations. Firstly, it only investigated line icons and did not consider other types of icons. Secondly, the study's scope was limited to household icons, suggesting the potential for future research to extend into the application of icons in other scenarios.

Acknowledgements. The presented study was jointly sponsored by National Key R&D Program of China (Grant No. 2022YFF0607000), and the National Natural Science Foundation of China (Grant No: 72271053 and 71871056).

References

1. Weisstein, F.L., Choi, P., Andersen, P.: The role of external reference price in pay-what-you-want pricing: an empirical investigation across product types. J. Retail. Consum. Serv. **50**, 170–178 (2019)
2. Ma, Q., Wang, M., Da, Q.: The effects of brand familiarity and product category in brand extension: an ERP study. Neurosci. Res. **169**, 48–56 (2021)
3. Holbrook, M.B., Hirschman, E.C.: The experiential aspects of consumption: consumer fantasies, feelings, and fun. J. Cons. Res. **9**(2), 132–140 (1982)
4. Batra, R., Ahtola, O.T.: Measuring the hedonic and utilitarian sources of consumer attitudes. Mark. Lett. **2**(2), 159–170 (1991)
5. Dewi, I.J., Ang, S.H.: Assessing the imagination scale's nomological validity: Effect of hedonic versus utilitarian product types and abstract versus concrete advertising execution. Gadjab Mada Int. J. Bus. **22**(2), 118–136 (2020)
6. Strahilevitz, M., Myers, J.G.: Donations to charity as purchase incentives: how well they work may depend on what you are trying to sell. J. Cons. Res. **24**(4), 434–446 (1998)
7. Chen, Q.Y.: Research on the influence difference of consumers' perception of product attributes on repurchase intention. Master's thesis, Yunnan University of Finance and Economics (2022)
8. Dhar, R., Wertenbroch, K.: Consumer choice between hedonic and utilitarian goods. J. Mark. Res. **37**(1), 60–71 (2000)
9. Che, C., Wu, G.H., Zhang, Z.H.: The impact of social comparison orientation on consumer purchase decisions: from the perspective of emotional-rational decision-making. Chin. J. Manage. Sci., 1–9 (2021)
10. Ji, M.X.: Research on multi-characteristic enterprise product intelligent pricing method. Master's thesis, Yunnan University of Finance and Economics (2022)
11. McDougall, S., de Bruijn, J.P., et al.: Exploring the effects of icon characteristics on user performance: the role of icon concreteness, complexity, and distinctiveness. J. Exper. Psychol. Appl. **6**(4), 291–306 (2000)
12. Yang, T., Liu, B.Y.: Analysis of flat design of smartphone interface icons and user acceptance. J. Liaoning Tech. Univ. (Soc. Sci. Edition) **18**(06), 948–952 (2016)
13. Yang, C., Peng, Y., Zeng, J.: Research on cognition and application of icon complexity based on EEG. CCF Trans. Pervasive Comput. Interact. **3**, 170–185 (2021)

Author Index

© The Editor(s) (if applicable) and The Author(s), under exclusive license
to Springer Nature Switzerland AG 2024
M. Kurosu and A. Hashizume (Eds.): HCII 2024, LNCS 14687, pp. 363–364, 2024.
https://doi.org/10.1007/978-3-031-60441-6

Printed in the United States
by Baker & Taylor Publisher Services

Printed in the United States
by Baker & Taylor Publisher Services